PRESERVING MARITIME AMERICA

A VOLUME IN THE SERIES

Public History in Historical Perspective

EDITED BY

Marla R. Miller

PRESERVING MARITIME AMERICA

A Cultural History of the Nation's Great Maritime Museums

JAMES M. LINDGREN

University of Massachusetts Press
AMHERST AND BOSTON

Printed in the United States of America

ISBN 978-1-62534-463-2 (paper); 462-5 (hardcover)

Designed by Jen Jackowitz
Set in Minion Pro and Australis Pro

Cover photo by Carol M. Highsmith,
Charles W. Morgan whaling ship, Mystic Seaport, c.1980.
Courtesy of Prints & Photographs Division, Library of Congress.

Library of Congress Cataloging-in-Publication Data
Names: Lindgren, James Michael, 1950– author.
Title: Preserving maritime America : a cultural history of the nation's great maritime museums / James M. Lindgren.
Description: Amherst : University of Massachusetts Press, [2019] | Includes bibliographical references and index. | Summary: "The United States has long been dependent on the seas, but Americans know little about their maritime history. While Britain and other countries have established national museums to nurture their seagoing traditions, America has left that responsibility to private institutions. In this first-of-its-kind history, James M. Lindgren focuses on a half-dozen of these great museums, ranging from Salem's East India Marine Society, founded in 1799, to San Francisco's Maritime Museum and New York's South Street Seaport Museum, which were established in recent decades. Begun by activists with unique agendas—whether overseas empire, economic redevelopment, or cultural preservation—these museums have displayed the nation's complex interrelationship with the sea. Yet they all faced chronic shortfalls, as policymakers, corporations, and everyday citizens failed to appreciate the oceans' formative environment. Preserving Maritime America shows how these institutions shifted course to remain solvent and relevant and demonstrates how their stories tell of the nation's rise and decline as a commercial maritime power"
—Provided by publisher.
Identifiers: LCCN 2019019892 | ISBN 9781625344625 (hardcover) | ISBN 9781625344632 (paperback) | ISBN 9781613767078 (ebook) | ISBN 9781613767061 (ebook)
Subjects: LCSH: Maritime museums—United States—History.
Classification: LCC V13.U5 L56 2019 | DDC 387.5074/73—dc23
LC record available at https://lccn.loc.gov/2019019892

British Library Cataloguing-in-Publication Data
A catalog record for this book is available from the British Library.

AS ALWAYS,

For Mary Ann

CONTENTS

ACKNOWLEDGMENTS

The making of *Preserving Maritime America* resembles a long voyage by a steamer trying to reach home port. It began in a maritime history doctoral seminar in 1980 at the College of William and Mary under the legendary William Appleman Williams. At the time, according to the American Historical Association, "maritime history in the United States was close to extinction." Bill wanted to revitalize the field, as did the Council of American Maritime Museums. As I spoke to him about expanding my seminar essay into a publishable work, he cautioned me (as he tapped his Annapolis ring on the desk): "You need less Bill Williams and more Raymond Williams!" That meant less said about foreign policy and more on culture and society as they related to economic change. He was right. As this project simmered on a back burner, the study of maritime history was reviving, but Bill's inspiration can be seen herein.[1]

Preserving Maritime America is part of "Preserving America's Past," my series on the social and cultural meaning of preserved history. Since the 1980s, my writing has benefited from not only the cultural studies of Raymond Williams but also the "thick description" embraced by anthropologist Clifford Geertz, the scrutiny of the "relations of power" suggested by Michel Foucault, and the tried-and-true practice of professional history. This book owes much to colleagues and critics. One piece of advice prolonged the process, all for the better: Questioning my plan to study only the early years of each museum, one critic suggested that I bring each story up-to-date and add a comparative analysis to the conclusion. This revised, more-balanced approach better showed each museum's evolution, especially because some had a difficult coming-of-age.

In so doing, I'm able to speak to a larger audience. Museums are going through a difficult transition with today's changing technology, funding, and turnstile. Knowing that today's scholars are writing fewer institutional histories, in favor of broader cultural studies, I wanted to show how earlier institutions faced comparable problems. I'm also writing for maritime historians who are debating whether to seek a popular or an academic following. And, finally, there are even more readers who focus on cultural preservation. Though I've written about and taught historic preservation for decades, I've shied away from making too many comparisons between building and maritime preservation. I concentrate on the latter, as it considers not only the authenticity, viability, and culture of its principal form, ships, but the expanding definition of "maritime." As a groundbreaking study, *Preserving Maritime America* lays a foundation for diverse readers who want to examine its topics regionally, nationally, or globally.

I want to thank many colleagues. My appreciation goes out to the *New England Quarterly* and especially its former editors William M. Fowler and Lynda Smith Rhoads for their help in introducing two exploratory essays. In 1995, the *NEQ* published "'That Every Mariner May Possess the History of the World': A Cabinet for the East India Marine Society of Salem," and in 1999, "'Let Us Idealize Old Types of Manhood': The New Bedford Whaling Museum, 1903–1941." Both essays have been revised and expanded. Helping with one or both were Elizabeth Blackmar, Paul Burlin, Briton Busch, Warren Cohen, Frank Costigliola, Edward Crapol, Harvey Green, Lisa Norling, Emily Rosenberg, and Robert Rydell. For this book, I'm most indebted to Professors Crapol, Fowler, and Rydell, as well as James Delgado and my peer reviewers. In addition, I'm thankful to New York University Press, its former director, Steve Maikowski, and their help with *Preserving South Street Seaport* (2014), which was condensed and updated for this book. And, finally, I'm grateful to Matt Becker, executive editor at the University of Massachusetts Press, and Marla Miller, editor of its series Public History in Historical Perspective, for their unwavering support.

For assistance with one or more of these six museums, my thanks go out to Justine Ahlstrom, Doug Alves, Peter Aron, Ray Ashley, Kent Barwick, Donald Birkholz, Jeff Bolster, Jonathan Boulware, David Brink, Norman Brouwer, Stephen Canright, J. Revell Carr, James Revell Carr III, Susan

Crane, Michael Creamer, Paul DeOrsay, Charles Deroko, Richard Dorfman, Joe Doyle, Michael Dyer, Richard Everett, Gary Fagin, Elizabeth Fenn, Richard Fewtrell, Daniel Finamore, Glenn Gordinier, Frederic Grant, Scott Harmon, John Hightower, David Hull, Ada Louise Huxtable, Steve Hyman, Jakob Isbrandtsen, Robbyn Jackson, Steven Jaffe, Chris Jannini, Shari Galligan Johnson, Paul Johnston, Steve Kesselman, Stephen Kloepfer, Paul Koistinen, John Kortum, Terese Loeb Kreuzer, Christopher Lowery, George Matteson, John Maounis, Michael Naab, Peter Neill, David Nelson, Paul O'Pecko, Dennis O'Toole, Warren Riess, Robert Rocha, Walter Rybka, Pete Seeger, Whitney North Seymour, Yvonne Simons, Howard Slotnick, Peter and Norma Stanford, Daniel Vickers, Thomas Wilcox, Jeanne Willoz-Egnor, Philip Yenawine, and Sally Yerkovich. I also want to thank the staff at the Peabody Essex Museum, the New Bedford Whaling Museum, the Mystic Seaport Museum, the Mariners' Museum, the San Francisco Maritime National Historical Park, and the South Street Seaport Museum.

My stylistics warrant mention. First, *Preserving Maritime America* uses abbreviations for the many organizations, a list of which is included. Second, I follow the *Chicago Manual of Style* by using the neutral pronoun "it" when referring to ships, unless the traditional "she" appears in quoted matter. Lastly, I've deleted the article "the" before a ship's name, unless using quoted sources; its italicized name identifies it as a material entity.

Working at the State University of New York–Plattsburgh for over thirty years, I've been helped by modest grants from our union-negotiated funds, the College of Arts and Sciences, and the College Foundation's Nina Winkel Fund and John L. Myers Fund, as well as by a small presidential award and sabbaticals every seven years. I am also indebted to our interlibrary loan staff. In the end, my biggest thanks goes to my wife, Mary Ann Weiglhofer, who reviewed the manuscript and endured through my labors. Yet, the project brought tremendous enjoyment; while I spent days in some great archives, she and our two sons—Brian and Charlie—had time to ramble through these fascinating towns.

PRESERVING MARITIME AMERICA

INTRODUCTION

From Cabinets of Curiosities to Remade Waterfronts

Beginning in the late eighteenth and continuing into our twenty-first century, *Preserving Maritime America* delves into the origins and growth of a half dozen of the nation's great maritime museums. While America has relied so much on the high seas, U.S. maritime preservation is, ironically, "a very sparsely documented field." Most popular books resemble the coffee-table types that sea writer William McFee called "the 'yo-heave-ho' school of maritime history." As for scholarly books, "the great majority of academic historians," noted Daniel Vickers in 1993, had paid "maritime subjects little heed." Those who did were "weak on analytic content." But, in the last generation, wide-ranging studies have focused on humankind's interaction with the sea. *Preserving Maritime America* adds a new dimension. Besides its in-depth analysis of the most influential saltwater museums, it sets them within an often contentious political, economic, and cultural history.[1]

After examining the cabinet of curiosities formed by the East India Marine Society (Salem, Massachusetts, est. 1799), I develop the New Bedford Whaling Museum (Massachusetts, 1903), the Mystic Seaport Museum (Connecticut, 1929), the Mariners' Museum (Newport News, Virginia, 1930), the San Francisco Maritime Museum (1951), and the South Street Seaport Museum (New York, 1967). These six institutions best demonstrate the changing scope of U.S. maritime preservation, which focuses on the history, society, culture, and technology associated with commercial and recreational vessels, and their impact on the world scene. They are different from the navy's museums and warships, which attract bigger audiences and donors.

Maritime museums in the United States are an ocean apart from those in Europe. Because the United States lacks a national maritime museum, ship trusts, and government subsidies, its maritime past has been defined by local and regional institutions. What is most revealing about that past is how land and sea have interconnected. Unlike maritime museums in America's heartland, which emphasize ships on rivers and lakes, these coastal museums highlighted a global U.S. influence or even an imperial presence. Yet they also focused on their home communities, often resisting forces that inhibited American overseas activity. As such, global and local concerns mutually defined their perspectives and agendas.

These museums have evolved and now differ considerably. They have retreated in varying degree from their founders' globalism. Like many of the nation's identity-defining institutions, five are still privately run, while a sixth has shifted from private to public. Three offer displays of historical art and cultural artifacts, while three additionally have fleets in the water with remade waterfronts and accompanying educational programs. Reflecting trends that began in the 1970s, two are affiliated with or have become national parks. But, illustrating larger neoliberal patterns, all are changing as they seek a financially supportive constituency, a meaningful interpretive program, and institutional stability.

For many reasons, these brick-and-mortar museums are an important link between an interested, but often unknowledgeable, public and professionally trained historians and curators. Eighty-three percent of Americans have not taken a U.S. history course beyond high school, and only 18 percent of colleges and universities still require a U.S. government or history class. But, as electronic media attract a bigger slice of everyday life and learning, American citizens reportedly trust and respect museum presentations more than what their grandparents, books, or television has to offer. Surprising to many, these museums do have their own message, as readers will discover in the following chapters. They construct a public history by not only packaging or revising what we have learned about people and places but also extracting artifacts and events from a deeper context. Although museums rely on their turnstiles to cover an increasing portion of their expenses, they have long promoted (as do their state charters) popular education, especially of children and young adults. But few of us know what they have been teaching.[2]

In comparison with traditional history museums, maritime museums are unique because their scope, collections, and importance have been largely unrecognized by landlubbers. Though "95 percent of what comes and goes to this country comes and goes by ships," said a U.S. Coast Guard admiral, most Americans have little experience—personally or academically—with the economic, political, and cultural forces that have defined global maritime society. Typically, they think of America's frontier as Frederick Jackson Turner's West, not the ocean's endless horizon. But, as the English sage John Ruskin wrote, "Men who cannot enter into the Mind of the Sea, cannot for the same reason enter into the Mind of Ships."[3]

The origins of both U.S. ship preservation and maritime museums stem from the experiences of the two generations after American independence. In 1799 the East India Marine Society of Salem (EIMS) established a cabinet to display the cultural and marine curiosities that its members were collecting from mostly faraway places. As such, the EIMS cabinet preceded the formation of the national Smithsonian Institution (1846). Moreover, the ship preservation movement was launched nearby after a Boston newspaper reported (erroneously) that the U.S. Navy intended to scrap the famed frigate *Constitution* (1797). Outraged, Oliver Wendell Holmes penned his poem "Old Ironsides" in 1830. That sparked a drive by Yankees promoting patriotism, civic duty, and traditional values. In so doing, the safeguarding of *Constitution* preceded the effort, inspired by similar goals, to save George Washington's Mount Vernon in the 1850s. But ships then receded to the backstage of the preservation movement.[4]

That was the case because ships, whether naval, commercial, or recreational, have mostly served a utilitarian function that was determined by practical needs and changing technology. With the advent of steam power in the early nineteenth century, for example, the dominance of sailing ships, which had ruled the seas for five millennia, began to fade and those vessels were consigned to the breakers or boneyard. Thus, the saving of USS *Constitution* was the exception, not the rule, in ship preservation. In the twentieth century, sporadic attempts were made to save some vessels, as in the case of *Tusitala* (formerly *Inveruglas*, 1883), one of the last full-rigged merchant ships to fly the U.S. flag. Purchased in 1923 by a New York writers club for adventure and then by magnate James A. Farrell, it became their private yacht; it later became a packet ship for Farrell's Argonaut Line and finally in 1939 a training vessel for the U.S. government, which scrapped it in 1948. More typical was *Glory of the Seas* (1869), the last clipper launched by the famed designer-builder Donald McKay of Boston. After sailing between San Francisco, Liverpool, and Sydney, it was idled in 1911. *Glory of the Seas* was ingloriously burned for its metal in Seattle in 1923. An original builder's half model was later displayed at the Mariners' Museum, while Farrell acquired its figurehead for New York's India House, an elite club of business-minded, global expansionists.

In the late 1920s, *Constitution* again became the most noted case of ship preservation. After postwar disarmament, the U.S. Navy faced the doldrums. To boost its stature, it began restoring the vessel, which had been converted into an unsightly floating barracks in the 1880s but partially restored in 1906–7. Secretary of the Navy Charles Francis Adams III marked the centennial of Holmes's drive by recommissioning the frigate; towed from the Atlantic to the Pacific Coast, it visited ninety ports from 1931 to 1934. By then, however, commercial sailing ships had almost disappeared. That sparked the establishment of not only museums in Mystic and Newport News but also the Historic American Merchant Marine Survey (1936–37) of the Works Progress Administration (WPA), which documented the last vessels. In 1941, the scholarly journal *American Neptune* also began publishing. It narrowed the scope of maritime preservation from Salem's broad ethnographic and historical displays by focusing largely on the history of earlier voyagers, their ships, trade, and empires, and the fine arts and models related to those ventures. But ship preservation was neglected: none of the wooden clippers, packets, or Down-Easters was saved for posterity. In 1941, the rescue of *Charles W. Morgan*, America's last wooden whaling bark and now the oldest U.S. commercial vessel afloat, was inspiring but insufficient. By the late 1950s, only a score remained of the globe's large, commercial sailing ships, whether iron- or steel-hulled. A handful of preservationists in Mystic, San Francisco, and New York scrambled to save what they could.

Thus, by the 1980s, fewer than three hundred U.S. ships of historical significance existed; the vast majority were World War II–era vessels. While architectural preservationists were lamenting that they had saved only 10 percent of worthwhile buildings that stood in the 1920s, ship preservationists fared much worse, rescuing "less than one-tenth of 1% of the vessels built in the U.S." Today, of the more than twenty-five-hundred properties listed as National Historic Landmarks (NHLs), less than 5 percent are ships, of which 40 percent originated in the navy or coast guard. Within recent years, NHL-listed ships have even been abandoned, most tragically in San Francisco in 2013 with *Wapama* (1915), America's last steam schooner. Meanwhile, the future of Honolulu's *Falls of Clyde* (1878), the nation's last surviving iron-hulled, four-masted, full-rigged ship, is cloudy. If historians must rely on documents and the public must see real artifacts, we have a disconcerting absence in maritime history, because the preservation of ships, especially ones still in the water, has been much more neglected, difficult, and expensive than structures on land.[5]

Meanwhile, maritime interests have expanded culturally, scientifically, and experientially. After the WPA's Writer's Program of the mid-1930s slighted Jack-tar in the fo'c'sle, the "new social history" of the 1960s and after focused on the lives of seamen and their shore communities, often through the lenses of race, class, and gender. With the "living history" movement, artisans also rallied to connect past and present and thereby better inform society about handwork as modern technology pushed forward. As environmentalism rose in the 1970s, moreover, scholars were introducing ecology into maritime studies, while highlighting the relationship between traditional topics and newer concerns, such as the emergence of steam power and whale depletion. And others, including myself, began looking at the interrelationship between land and sea cultures. Despite this enlarged scope of maritime studies, a preservationist conceded that "few inanimate objects solicit more emotion than ships do." For many, maritime preservation still means saving those vessels and their cultures. As metaphors, ships have represented our core values and aspirations.[6]

Significant generational and professional shifts have accompanied that expanding definition of "maritime preservation." If, as Ralph Waldo Emerson wrote, "an institution is the lengthened shadow of one man," the makers and shapers of these museums became committed to sea culture after an invigorating saltwater experience. But the passing of generations, the increasing importance of raising money, and the changing priorities inherent in the professionalization of the movement brought a shift from their personal interests to a more impersonal, bureaucratic, or academic approach of later administrators, curators, and historians. These six museums were chartered as not-for-profit institutions, but their managers adopted corporate practices; their "bottom-line" concerns, institutional growth, hierarchical management, and professional mindset have become dominant forces. They all are part of a heritage industry whose adroit use of the past has been for both beneficial and less-than-altruistic purposes.[7]

Chapter 1 begins with the formation of the East India Marine Society (EIMS) by an aspiring group of Salem master mariners and supercargoes who had traveled to the Far East. They were trying to capitalize on the nation's neutrality as the French and British battled globally between 1793 and 1815. In so doing, Salem won unprecedented wealth during the French War. Touting their success, those mariners created a museum to show the riches of Asia and the South Seas. Establishing a broad definition of "maritime," they included not only ship models and navigational instruments but also an array of curiosities mostly from the lands bordering the Indian Ocean and running eastward through the South Pacific. Those artifacts encouraged young and old to see Salem's future as a trader in distant markets and a consumer of exotic goods. With the death of those mariners and the eclipse of their shallow port, however, the EIMS transferred its holdings in 1867 to the newly created Peabody Academy of Science, a museum of ethnology that touted Anglo-American superiority but neglected Salem mariners. Beginning in 1905, the Peabody Museum slowly returned to its EIMS roots by displaying and expanding its holdings related to those mariners, their ships, and their interaction with distant peoples. The Peabody was a top-notch maritime museum. But, after its 1990s merger with the Essex Institute and new management, the Peabody Essex Museum (PEM) became a hybrid institution, with the EIMS materials comprising but one small part. Today PEM is a world-class museum of art and culture, rivaling Boston's Museum of Fine Arts. As such, the cabinet created by EIMS traders has become part of its global showplace.

Chapter 2 focuses on the New Bedford Whaling Museum. Founded by the Old Dartmouth Historical Society (ODHS), which had displayed everything from local history to foreign oddities since its founding in 1903, the museum took center stage in 1916 by occupying an impressive new building. Imbued with antimodernism (a longing for a mythical past rooted in a qualified acceptance of the present), its leaders watched New Bedford become the nation's largest textile manufacturer. As a counterpoint, the ODHS mythologized nineteenth-century whaling's once-dominant global role. Pictured as an opportunity for young white, Anglo-Saxon, Protestant men, whaling had actually become a workplace of exploited, dark-skinned foreigners, whose descendants worked in those textile mills. The ODHS brushed their story aside. Beginning in the 1970s, however, shifts in local politics, the regional economy, and professional history prompted the museum to tack. Pushed by local leaders, preservationists, and federal agencies, it gradually emphasized whaling's once-neglected, equatorial whalers. Moreover, as its historic district became a national park, it still homeported New England's largest fishing fleet. Finally, the museum, which once glorified the slaughter of whales, joined environmentalists to boost species conservation. In a still-ongoing transformation, the museum is becoming a community institution to teach a more encompassing local history, including its seafaring industries and cultures.

Chapter 3 introduces the first of three major U.S. ship preservationists, Carl Cutler, and his founding of the Marine Historical Association (MHA) of Mystic, Connecticut, in 1929. Reflecting his era's antimodernism, he was disillusioned by the 1920s retreat from commercial global shipping and the advance of corporate industrialism. Through his museum and writing, he promoted the merchant marine and romanticized an old-time Yankee individualism and community. With the MHA's acquisition of *Charles W. Morgan* and its creation of a waterfront that was christened Mystic Seaport in 1948, Cutler melded maritime and architectural preservation. As his "maritime Williamsburg" was becoming the state's top attraction, however, it fell under a corporate-style administration in the 1950s that alienated Cutler. Those managers, in turn, neglected the fleet and collection. Only in the 1970s did Mystic shift course by emphasizing professional management. After much duress, the redefined museum by the 1990s touted a preservation shipyard, a small craft program, and a raft of educational opportunities. While traditional values and community were celebrated but expanded demographically, Mystic Seaport was calling itself "the Museum of America and the Sea." It is today's standard-bearer.

Chapter 4 shifts to the Mariners' Museum of Newport News, Virginia. Founded in 1930 by megamillionaire Archer Milton Huntington, it was an adjunct of the nation's largest private shipyard, which he inherited in 1927. Shaped and administered by Annapolis graduate and yard president Homer L. Ferguson, the museum worked to make America more ship minded after the yard's business was undermined by post–World War I naval disarmament and the downsizing of the globe's largest commercial fleet. Deploring that retreat from the sea, the museum became a cog in the naval-industrial complex, pushing for ship construction and global expansionism. With Huntington's largesse, Mariners' acquired a world-class collection. Needing a better turnstile, however, it opened an innovative Chesapeake Bay wing in 1987. It was financially disappointing, partly because a competing nautical edutainment complex had opened in Norfolk. As its major endowment was expiring, Mariners' changed course. Thanks to Virginia's congressional delegation, it was designated as America's National Maritime Museum (along with South Street Seaport) and custodian of the remains of the fabled USS *Monitor* (1862), for which government and private benefactors built a museum wing. Both failed, however, to boost its audience or donations. Today, pressed financially, the Mariners' Museum has returned to its roots as an advocate of the global navy and the region's industry.

Chapter 5 introduces the second major ship preservationist, Karl Kortum, and his opening of the San Francisco Maritime Museum in 1951. Captivated since childhood by the sea, he joined the crew of the square-rigged *Kaiulani* in 1941. Outbound from Washington State, he sailed to Australia via Cape Horn and the Cape of Good Hope; along the way, he heard of Cutler saving *Charles W. Morgan*. After serving as an officer aboard army transports in the Pacific theater, he enlisted the help of Scott Newhall, an editor of the *San Francisco Chronicle*, to found a museum devoted to the West Coast's oft-forgotten maritime history. With exhibits in a ship-like building, the museum revived a shabby waterfront, built consensus among quarrelsome workers and shippers, and reminded visitors of trade's importance. Wanting more, Kortum acquired, in 1954, the square-rigged *Balclutha*, which became a centerpiece of Fisherman's Wharf tourism. He then persuaded Sacramento to open a state park with a fleet next to his museum in 1963.

Both became financially tenuous in the 1970s, however, and Representative Phillip Burton placed them under the National Park Service (NPS). But Kortum became distraught as the NPS failed to manage its first-ever fleet and full-spectrum museum. Some improvement came with the creation of the stand-alone San Francisco Maritime National Historical Park (1988), better economic times, and more public scrutiny. Contending now with uncertain federal funding and administration, it is unique among all U.S. maritime museums.

Lastly, chapter 6 presents Peter Stanford, the third major ship preservationist. In 1967, inspired by Kortum's private and public ventures, he founded the private South Street Seaport Museum (SSSM) in New York. The year before, Albany had passed legislation to create a state maritime museum on the East River. Both wanted to spotlight the history of Gotham as the world's largest port. Stanford then acquired a fleet, including the square-rigged *Wavertree.* Maritime preservation was pushed aside, however, as Mayor John Lindsay, along with banker David Rockefeller, designated Stanford's museum as the *un*assisted sponsor of an urban renewal area (the first ever for a U.S. museum). Although New York State canceled its own museum project, Stanford's SSSM displayed the nation's largest historical fleet alongside a still-working Fulton Fish Market. For the U.S. Bicentennial, it was the centerpiece of Op Sail 76 as international ships filled the harbor. But the financially pressed museum was overwhelmed by the district's commercial development. Only in the 1990s did it begin to recover. Yet the 9/11 terrorist attacks, its own mismanagement, and the seven-foot surge of Superstorm Sandy left it at death's door. Today, the downsized museum is alive, thanks to grassroots supporters and City Hall, but it is reballasting its load in a district dominated by commerce.

Throughout, *Preserving Maritime America* examines the nation's rise in the nineteenth century as a commercial maritime power, the twentieth-century decline of its U.S.-flagged fleet, and how museums told the story of Americans' interaction with the sea. In these six chapters and the conclusion, I'll assess the underlying questions shaping the history of maritime preservation. First, how and why were maritime museums formed and influenced by their global and regional contexts? Second, how did each address what its makers and shapers perceived as critical failings in America's society, economy, and sea policy? Third, how did artifacts symbolize abstract notions, such as community, individual, and country, in the context of an era's "cultural politics"? Fourth, how and why did museums evolve into sometimes very different institutions? And, fifth, what do the findings of *Preserving Maritime America* tell us today about these museums (and institutions elsewhere), their changing definition of "maritime," and their interconnections with the ocean's culture, economy, and future?

CHAPTER 1

"THAT EVERY MARINER MAY POSSESS THE HISTORY OF THE WORLD"

A Cabinet for the East India Marine Society of Salem

On October 14, 1825, "a vast concourse of citizens" in Salem, Massachusetts, watched a procession of the East India Marine Society (EIMS, 1799), whose shipmasters had opened rich Asian markets. Dedicating a new building and museum, the cavalcade included President John Quincy Adams, many dignitaries, and one hundred smartly attired EIMS members with dress swords. Joined by the Boston Brigade Band, they received "repeated cheers and greetings" as they passed brightly decorated buildings. A lavish palanquin in which sat a Salemite dressed as "a young Hindoo potentate" was "borne by Salem Negroes" in Indian garb; their "faces glowed in the joyousness of the occasion." Clothed in Chinese gowns, other mariners carried trade goods, weapons, or curiosities for their museum. That night, a banquet at the museum "was served in a style of magnificence heretofore unequalled in this town." Joining Adams were U.S. Supreme Court justice Joseph Story, Salem congressman Benjamin W. Crowninshield, and Boston mayor Josiah Quincy. They shared forty-four toasts, including Adams saluting "The Trade to India–No commercial nation has been great without it, may the experience of ages induce us to cherish this rich source of national wealth."[1]

As the economy shifted, however, the banquet was Salem's last hurrah. Its merchants and masters had won tremendous fortunes during the French War (1793–1815); as Britain warred against Revolutionary and Napoleonic France, Salem took advantage of America's neutral flag, intermittent British cooperation, and Europe's inability to control its colonies. Salem's success led to, said historian James Fichter, "one of the most significant recombinations of wealth" in capitalism's creative destruction. But the glory was short lived: Salem's losses from Thomas Jefferson's embargo in 1807–9 and James Madison's war in 1812–15, together with the return of European rivals to world trade in 1815, undermined its brief dominance and forced its ships into less profitable markets. Outside forces contributed to Salem's decline: its mediocre harbor; Boston's better financial, cultural, and trade opportunities; New York's boom with the Erie Canal and its hold on European and southern commerce; and the higher return on factory investments. Adams, who quit Federalism to join the National Republicans in the 1824 election, was also trying to heal the three-decades-long partisanship that had riven Salem. Making a toast at the banquet, Federalist diehard Timothy Pickering recognized that political harmony was "important to the prosperity of all."[2]

Fostering harmony, the EIMS had developed a cabinet in 1799. As its collection and membership grew, it opened East India Marine Hall in 1825. Melding commerce and culture, it rented the ground floor to the Asiatic Bank and the Oriental Insurance Company, while the society occupied the spacious second floor. There it showed curios from all continents, but most spectacularly from the Orient and the South Seas. Sprinkled in between were ship models, paintings, and display cases of mementos gifted by mariners. It resembled London's East India House, where, said scholar Richard Davis, "the downstairs business rooms envisioned British sovereignty" and the upstairs India Museum (1799) "offered a synecdoche of India as colony."[3]

While the EIMS was spurring mariners to explore, develop trade, and bring wealth home, its museum linked America's rising land and sea empires. Offering a visual medium to those reading about Asia's mysteries, the cabinet encouraged visitors to imagine faraway worlds. Although Cornish traveler James Silk Buckingham suggested in 1841 that it would help break down "prejudices and antipathies" and build "kindly feelings and sympathies" toward foreign peoples, museum artifacts, when removed from their original contexts, became representations or symbols of a strange, sometimes savage, place awaiting Western uplift. But, as the museum rose in popularity, EIMS's membership fell with declining trade. In 1865, it sold the building and its holdings to George Peabody of London, a philanthropist. Adding the anthropological holdings of Salem's Essex Institute, in 1867 he created the Peabody Academy of Science, an ethnological and natural history museum; its "marine objects" were mostly "relegated to the attic." The EIMS survived for another forty years until its last member died.[4]

Later writers have had difficulty making sense of the EIMS. In 1916, one ascribed its museum to the wish of globetrotting mariners to tout their superiority over ordinary coasting captains. Equally dismissive was Peabody's assistant director, Walter Muir Whitehill, who claimed in 1949 that the museum resulted simply from "the human foible of wishing to be admired for irrelevant reasons." As an ethnology and natural history museum, it amassed such an odd mix that it was dismissed as a "Glory Hole" by the naturalist Thomas Barbour. Beginning in 1905, however, the Peabody also displayed a small maritime collection, which took center stage in 1941 with the museum's reorganization. Today, after another shift, the Peabody Essex Museum (PEM) is a hybrid emphasizing global art and culture. The EIMS cabinet once offered a window into the making of empire, consumerism, and identity, but PEM's evolution now shows how the mariner's empire has become an imperial collection.[5]

"A SAILORTOWN FROM STEM TO STERN": SALEM'S MARITIME WORLD

Creating much misunderstanding, twentieth-century observers usually separated the EIMS from its context in the decades after American independence. After the Treaty of Paris (1783) and the opening of Canton (1785) by New York's *Empress of China*, Salem masters pushed their reach beyond the confines that Britain had allowed. Paving the way was Salem's leading merchant, Elias Hasket Derby. In 1785, besides inaugurating the Russian trade, he sent *Grand Turk* around the Cape of Good Hope, becoming the first New England vessel to do so (fig. 1). *Grand Turk* pushed on to Isle de France (Mauritius), Batavia (Jakarta), and Whampoa Reach (Canton). Returning to Salem, its cargo of tea, china, and cloth was sold to the likes of Governor John Hancock. In 1788, Derby first showed the U.S. flag in Calcutta and Bombay, while India was coming under the control of the British East India Company. His ships also opened Siam and Mocha (Arabia). During the French War, when global conflict restricted the trade of French and British merchant fleets but led their navies to capture U.S. ships in the West and East Indies, Salem's barks, brigs, and ships became global tramps. More U.S. trade originated in India than in China.[6]

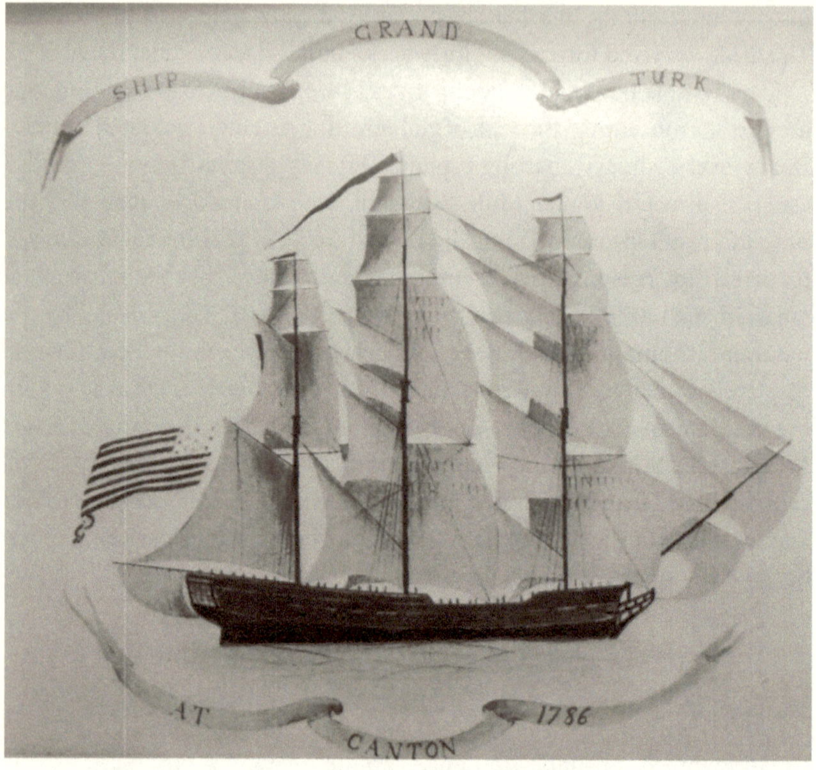

FIGURE 1. Ship *Grand Turk*, in Ralph D. Paine, *The Ships and Sailors of Old Salem* (New York: Outing, 1908), 204–5.

Because the tea market was glutted, the pepper trade was most profitable. After Captain Jonathan Carnes secretly sailed to Sumatra in 1795, and later gave the EIMS its first curios, Salem monopolized the trade until 1799, but it profited over the next half century by reshipping pepper globally. That pulled youth to the sea. As the pioneering maritime historian Samuel Eliot Morison wrote, "A Salem boy in those days was born to the music of windlass chanty and caulker's maul; he drew in a taste for the sea with his mother's milk; wharves and shipyards were his playground; he shipped as a boy on a coaster in his early teens, saw Demerara [British Guiana] and St. Petersburg before he set foot in Boston, and if he had the right stuff in him, commanded an East-Indiaman before he was twenty-five." Nathaniel Silsbee lived that tale, ultimately serving as a U.S. congressman and senator. Knowing that officers could use their "privilege" (carrying personal cargo for profit), he toasted his EIMS colleagues in 1825, "May their success as masters of *good* ships enable them to become owners of *better ones*."[7]

Whether in the British, French, or Dutch empires, Americans practiced "hitchhiking imperialism," whereby they established a trade niche by taking advantage of cracks in the empires of stronger powers. Trade with the Caribbean and South America was still vital for Salem's access to silver, which Asian merchants demanded but upset the specie-starved U.S. economy. In 1800 Salem's fleet included 1,325 vessels, while its Custom House duties soon accounted for up to 15 percent of the national tariff. That commerce led a Salem minister around 1800 to claim: "After a century of comparative quiet, the citizens of the little town were suddenly dispersed to every part of the Oriental world, and to every nook of barbarism which had a market and a shore." The town's few wharves jumped to forty by the 1840s, but they caused the buildup of silt, which thwarted deeper-draft ships by midcentury.[8]

Of all factors, it was Derby's death on September 8, 1799, that most shook the town's trade and pushed the founding of the EIMS. Named "King Derby" by Salem's Nathaniel Hawthorne, he was, said Fichter, "among the wealthiest 1 percent of the wealthiest 1 percent of the population." His death reconfigured what historian Daniel Vickers called Salem's "chains of personal dependency." Rival merchants, including his brother-in-law George Crowninshield Sr., capitalized on his passing. So, too, did captains who sailed under the Derby flag. At a time when a master's rise to merchant depended on skill, luck, and a market, those captains formed the EIMS. Besides Carnes and Silsbee, Derby's nephews, Benjamin and Jacob Crowninshield, joined.[9]

Beginning their discussions in August 1799, over thirty captains established the EIMS in October. To create opportunities and networks for rising men and to share information about distant lands and peoples, they opened their ranks *only* to those Salem captains and supercargoes who had navigated the seas at or beyond the Cape of Good Hope (and later Cape Horn). That excluded not only such wealthy global merchants as William Gray but also most Salem masters. Because the majority of Salem ships traded with the Caribbean, and 222 of their captains had already joined the Salem Marine Society (1766), the EIMS was the most select. The EIMS chose Benjamin Hodges as president and Jacob Crowninshield as treasurer. The Committee of Observation managed its affairs and included founder Benjamin Carpenter. Incorporated in 1801, EIMS had three stated purposes: to encourage navigation, to aid the widows and children of deceased members, and to create a cabinet. That third goal occurred well before the Boston Marine Society formed its own "collection of rare and valuable curiosities" in 1832. The EIMS asked the Reverend Dr. William Bentley, pastor of Salem's East Church (Unitarian), to sketch a plan, and he even gave "his own well-stocked cabinet of specimens and curios." Within a year it had fifty-three members, fifty being past or present captains in the Indies.[10]

The EIMS prospered as Salem's empire expanded. Salem and Boston ships were so prevalent in East Indian ports that Asian merchants regarded the two as powerful countries. But, gaining at the expense of the Europeans, there was "nothing intrinsically American" about their success, noted Fichter, who disputed the claim of U.S. exceptionalism. "No cultural trait, no Protestant ethic distinguished American businessmen from their Dutch or British cousins." With mariners present in all neighborhoods, especially in Bentley's East Parish near the docks, Salem was, said Vickers, "a sailortown from stem to stern." In 1796, it was the second largest town in Massachusetts and sixth largest in the nation with a population of almost 10,000. A French duke called it "one of the handsomest small towns in the United States," and it had the greatest wealth in proportion to its population of any U.S. town. As a result, said a southern journalist in 1826, "You find few gentlemen in Salem, who have not visited almost every part of the world, and who do not possess more general knowledge than those of any other town in the Union."[11]

As Salem accumulated "the largest fortunes ever made by trade in America," it split geographically. Its more prosperous merchant captains moved from the waterfront to (or built residences on) Chestnut, Essex, and Federal Streets, often by builder-craftsman Samuel McIntire, "the architect of Salem." That neighborhood near McIntire's resplendent Hamilton Hall became an elite Federalist enclave. In 1817, Martin Van Buren called Chestnut Street "the most beautiful street I have ever seen." Hawthorne later complained about "the sway of [Salem's] aristocratic class," but its merchants were divided politically. In the early nineteenth century, Democratic-Republicans and Federalists read different newspapers and even staged their own separate Independence Day festivities until 1824.[12]

The EIMS united those factions, as in its yearly parade beginning in 1800. Still, there was dissension. For its annual dinner in 1802, for example, EIMS secretary Nathaniel Bowditch previewed all toasts to cool the tensions created by inviting two extreme Federalists of the Essex Junto, Benjamin Goodhue and Timothy Pickering. Said Bentley, Bowditch "omitted a part of some [toasts] & the whole of others," but those who were censored demanded "a publication of the Toasts for the public judgment." That "ebullition of party spirit" led Bentley to warn that "the Society will undoubtedly be injured." Soon after, the EIMS (like the Boston Marine Society) issued a gag order. It resolved that "politics shall not on any occasion be introduced into the Society." Then, in what one historian called "Salem's bitterest year since the witch trials," Jacob Crowninshield defeated Pickering in the 1802 congressional election.[13]

Tensions abated, temporarily. At a dinner in early 1804, the toasts were "without any offence," while the November banquet was proceeded by a cavalcade with the palanquin, a band, and the Second Corps of Cadets, which was primarily Republican. The 1805 parade was escorted by the Salem Light Infantry, which was Federalist. "Everyone approves of your public festivals," a correspondent said, "for they give consequence to your society; and a generous pleasure to yourselves—a pleasure arising from consciousness of past and a determination of future endeavours." Its dinner in 1806 emphasized unity before an intensifying storm. After a sixteen-gun salute was fired from its nine-foot model of the 342-ton East Indiaman *Friendship* (1797), a member toasted, "*Improvement* 'ahead,' *Harmony* 'on the beam,' and *Party Spirit* 'astern,' *hull-down*." Another toast railed against "the enemies of our country," though Federalists and Republicans had different enemies, "May they be blessed with *Leaky clamps, Choak'd pumps, Sails rent, Grog spent, Wormy bread, Wind ahead, Cloudy noon, At night no moon, Compass lost, Tempest tost, A winter's coast*." But unity was fleeting in the rising partisanship, which was keen in the Federalists' *Gazette* and Democratic-Republicans' *Register*. The *Gazette* called Democratic-Republican head George Crowninshield Sr. "the leader of the Jacobin party," though he was joined by Nathaniel Silsbee and merchant Joseph White. They had taken control of the town in 1805, defeating Federalist Bowditch and William Gray.[14]

The European war shaped those feuds. While Barbary pirates preyed on Salem's Mediterranean trade, the British were capturing more U.S. ships overall. Still, Salem's trade was reaching its zenith, especially in pepper. In 1807, 236 Salem ships entered the port from distant markets. That number and the associated duties were, said local historian George G. Putnam, the greatest of any year. Federalists feared President Jefferson's response to British attacks. But when he declared an embargo on December 29, the town's selectmen split. With the trade stoppage, said a visitor, "the streets near the waterside were almost deserted." While rich merchants made do, the real victims were, Bentley thought, "the young seamen, mates & captains." With "a growing class consciousness" in Salem, some worried about a civil war.[15]

Through a bipartisan governing committee, the EIMS calmed the discontent by holding "A Grand Concert" in January 1809. Designed to encourage "fellow townsmen to acts of charity and benevolence," it raised $564 ($10,932 in 2018 dollars) for poor relief. During the embargo, the EIMS discontinued its parades, perhaps to avoid the 1760s denunciation of merchants "rioting in luxury." Unlike the Boston Marine Society, which canceled its 1808 dinner, the EIMS still held its private banquets. Reflecting Federalist noblesse oblige, a member toasted, "May we always have in mind the objects of the institution, promotion of knowledge and releaf [*sic*] of the distressed." Criticizing the Republicans in 1809, a shipmaster toasted to "American enterprise. May it never be restrained by lawless power or rival jealousy."[16]

Shortly before the inauguration of his friend James Madison, Jefferson ended the embargo on March 7, 1809. Within two months, one hundred ships departed Salem, but Napoleon seized dozens. As tensions also escalated with England, Salem Federalists, including Bowditch, asked Congress to avoid war. Its Republicans were "literally Devils incarnate," said future Salem mayor and U.S. senator Leverett Saltonstall. Madison signed the war declaration on June 18, 1812; Boston Marine Society historian William Avery Baker claimed: "It became the declared policy of maritime Massachusetts to sabotage the war." While some EIMS members became rich privateers, another toasted: "East India Commerce; may it soon resume with safety, its former state of Prosperity." Optimistically, the U.S. government hired Charles Bulfinch, designer of the state capitol, to build a customhouse (1819) opposite Derby Wharf.[17]

"ONE OF THE NOBLEST ROOMS IN NEW ENGLAND": CREATING THE EAST INDIA MUSEUM

Since the EIMS cabinet was a unifying force representing foreign adventure and business success, it was different from earlier natural and history museums. After the Charleston Library Society (South Carolina) created the first cabinet in English America (1773), Charles Willson Peale opened a museum (1786) in Philadelphia. His iconic self-portrait, *The Artist in His Museum* (1822), showed his era's relish for collecting an array of curiosities. In Boston, Daniel Bowen began his Columbian Museum (1795) with wax figures, art, natural history, and curios. Plagued by fires, he rebuilt his structure, once with the help of William Bentley, who quipped that it was "well accommodated with everything but taste." In 1825 Bowen sold his operation, which then became the New-England Museum. James Silk Buckingham visited there and Philadelphia, where Peale's operation had closed and merchant Nathan Dunn had created a new institution focusing on China. Dunn's museum was "equal to many of the best in Europe," he thought, but Boston's was "a place of amusement" that had "to attract the greatest number" of twenty-five-cent-paying customers. It resembled many other U.S. museums "full of worthless and trashy articles."[18]

Buckingham missed the trend-setting American Museum in New York, opened by P. T. Barnum in 1841. Before its building succumbed to fire in 1865, it sold thirty-eight million admission tickets, exhibiting everything from Roman artifacts to a fraudulent Little Woolly Horse. It attracted the likes of not only everyday Americans but Walt Whitman, the Prince of Wales, and Harvard's great naturalist, Louis Agassiz. One of America's most popular attractions, and in an era of notorious con men, the museum was "the largest and most comprehensive [U.S.] establishment of its kind."[19]

Visiting Salem in 1841, Buckingham noted the "imposing appearance" of the East India Marine Hall. Touring it several times, he was "abundantly gratified" by its holdings. Because the EIMS relied on individual donations, those items reflected the interests of members and friends. In almost seven pages of his travelogue, Buckingham praised the display's "excellent order" and his ability to examine "any article at leisure." The museum "cannot fail," he concluded, "to furnish abundant information and amusement to visitors of all classes, from the venerable navigator and hydrographer to the holiday pupil, as there is as much to entertain as to inform."[20]

By 1841 Salem's museum had grown from the small cabinet begun in 1799. Located first at the corner of Essex and Washington Streets in a second-floor room, it moved in 1804 to a hall above the Salem Bank. Also housing EIMS meetings, it was open daily, except Sunday. Recognizing its power to inspire, a mariner toasted at the 1804 banquet: "A Cabinet. That every mariner may possess the history of the world." While the whaling captains of Nantucket were seeking "curiosities and trinkets of native manufacture to bring back to their wondering families," Salem's captains also collected for their cabinet. In 1804, Bentley noted that they "spared no pains to supply & to decorate" the new room. On one chimney they painted the Pilgrim landing of 1620, and on another, the Salem launching of USS *Essex* in 1799, which was partially funded by Salem merchants during the Quasi-War with

France (1798–1800). The room included "many hundred Articles happily displayed." By 1820, however, "happily" was not the case because so many things had been acquired that the collection was in disarray.[21]

Instituting order was Nathaniel Bowditch, who served as EIMS secretary (1802–3), inspector of journals (1804–20), and president (1820–23). As a child, he was dependent on his father's annual $15 pension from the Salem Marine Society. He was forced to leave school at the age of ten, indentured as a bookkeeper, and educated himself, thanks to the local Athenaeum. In 1796, Derby hired him as a supercargo; as such he traveled to Portugal, Java, and Manila on the first American voyage to the Philippines. On board, he taught the crew, including its black cook, to calculate longitude by lunar observation. After joining the EIMS in 1800, he voyaged as master and part owner of the ship *Putnam*. Because Salem vessels lacked expensive marine chronometers, he wrote the *New American Practical Navigator* (1802). Published as an EIMS report, it corrected thousands of errors in European navigation books. As a member toasted in 1804: "The Practical Navigator. Facts first, then theories." It became "the seaman's Bible" and is still in print. Described as "a thinking machine," he imposed a scientific regimen on the society's bid for empire. Later, the museum displayed his desk, spyglass, quadrant, and manuscripts. "No sailor can view this exhibit without emotion," said Morison.[22] (See fig. 2.)

In 1820, Bowditch not only solicited forty new members to boost the aging ranks but hired Dr. Seth Bass as curator. Discarding deteriorated natural specimens and placing artifacts in glazed cases to deter pilfering and handling, he renumbered the holdings and compiled a catalog in 1821. With the collection's 2,269 items, he included a brief description and the donor's name to inform visitors walking the room. Though shells, coins, and medals were separately cataloged, Bass's listing, as well as a sequel, provided valuable information for future students; some "curiously carved" scrimshaw, noted later curator Daniel Finamore, were actually "the oldest known documented examples" in the nation. Former president Madison and the Marquis de Lafayette visited and commended the society's work; Jefferson said the nation was "indebted" to its "public-minded" mariners. Despite the praise, Bass moved sixteen miles south to become the second librarian at the Boston Athenaeum in 1825.[23]

In 1823, Salem had more than 140 ships in foreign trade, with many more delivering their cargoes to New York or Boston and returning empty to

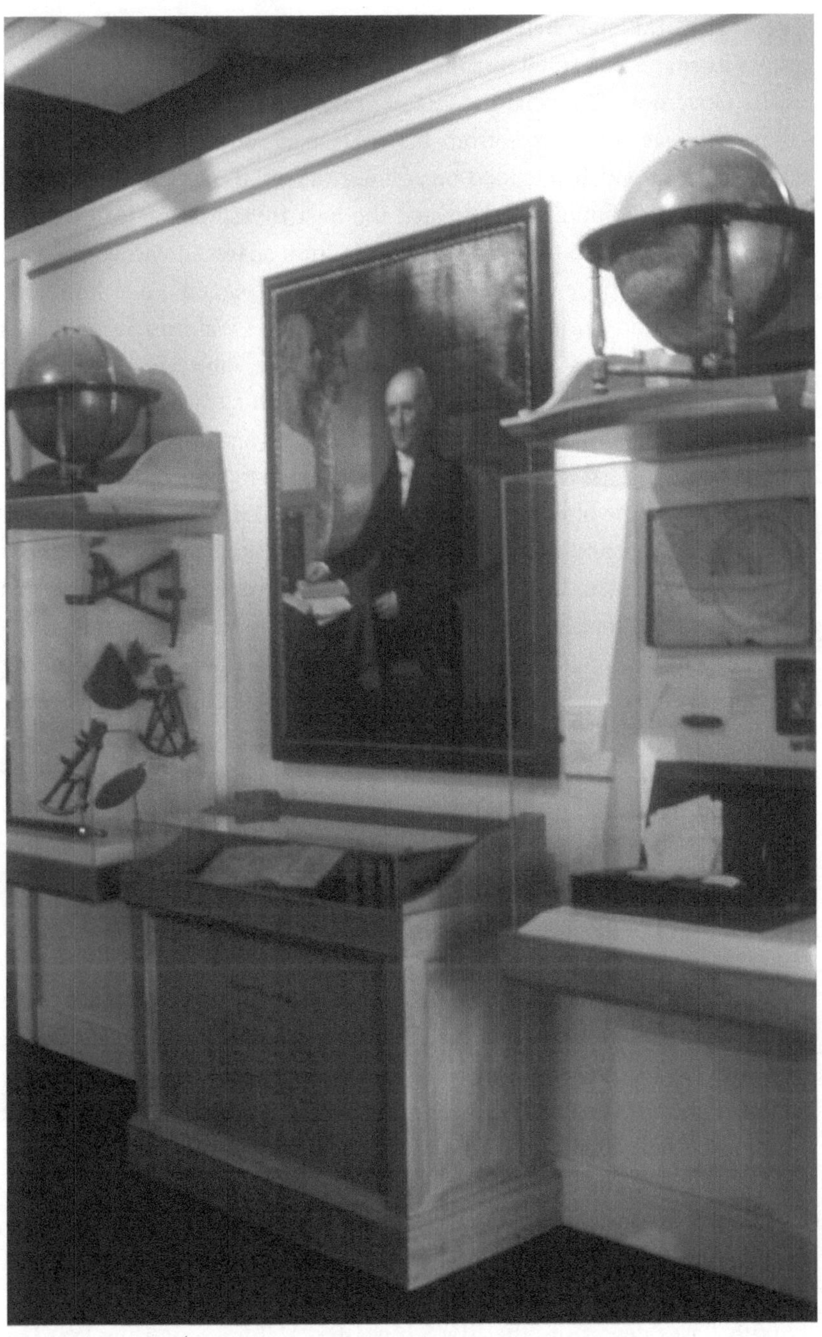

FIGURE 2. Nathaniel Bowditch Exhibit, Peabody Museum. *Photo by author, 1992.*

Salem. The EIMS membership had risen to 230, and its collection had outgrown its space; as a result, Stephen White, a state representative, member of the Governor's Council, and EIMS president, built a more impressive edifice. The site was across from his columned countinghouse on Essex Street, both of which intruded on a fine residential district. To own and manage the new building, he created the East India Marine Hall Corporation, which was capitalized at $15,000 in $100 shares. It earned revenue from two first-floor tenants and the EIMS, which signed a one-hundred-year lease at $200 per annum. Its architect, Thomas Waldron Sumner, was forced by the society's "growing financial prudence," however, to revise his design. Removing a third floor, he clad the two-story facade and gable in granite; its sidewalls were red brick. "East India Marine Hall" was carved into its frieze (fig. 3). With the ground floor rented to White's Asiatic Bank, which pictured the building on its bank notes, and the Oriental Insurance Company, the second-floor EIMS had, said Morison, "one of the noblest rooms in New England." Measuring one hundred feet by forty-five feet, this floor held the cabinets, meetings, and dinners and is occupied to this day.[24]

To reach the exhibits, visitors navigated a dark corridor before ascending the central stairs. The hall's layout is imprecisely documented before an 1867 alteration, but visitors entered an exotic world lit by tall windows and a pair of Venetian glass chandeliers, presented by EIMS president Benjamin Carpenter and still in use. They first glimpsed a pair of seated East Indian mannequins in native costume; an even larger group of Asian figures occupied the room's center. The hall was lined with glass-fronted, mahogany wall cases topped by commemorative ship models, large curios, and spears; the cases held travel accounts, books, and bizarre artifacts. Atop the stairs' door were more models and the palanquin. Four of eight fireplaces were active with fireboards picturing the Pilgrim landing, a village in India, the Cape of Good Hope, and Canton; they were drawn by the era's premiere American maritime artist, Michele Felice Cornè. Brought to Salem by the Derbys, Cornè painted house interiors and ship portraits. Staring down from on high was Elias Hasket Derby, in a portrait by James Frothingham. In between freestanding glass cases at each end was either a life-size Chinese mandarin or a Hawaiian idol. Visitors learned about the artifacts from the catalog or a member, who told stories of his travels.[25]

With Bass's departure, the EIMS hired Dr. Malthus Augustus Ward as curator (or superintendent). With roots in Salem, he presented a letter of introduction from his Bowdoin College associate, Nathaniel Hawthorne,

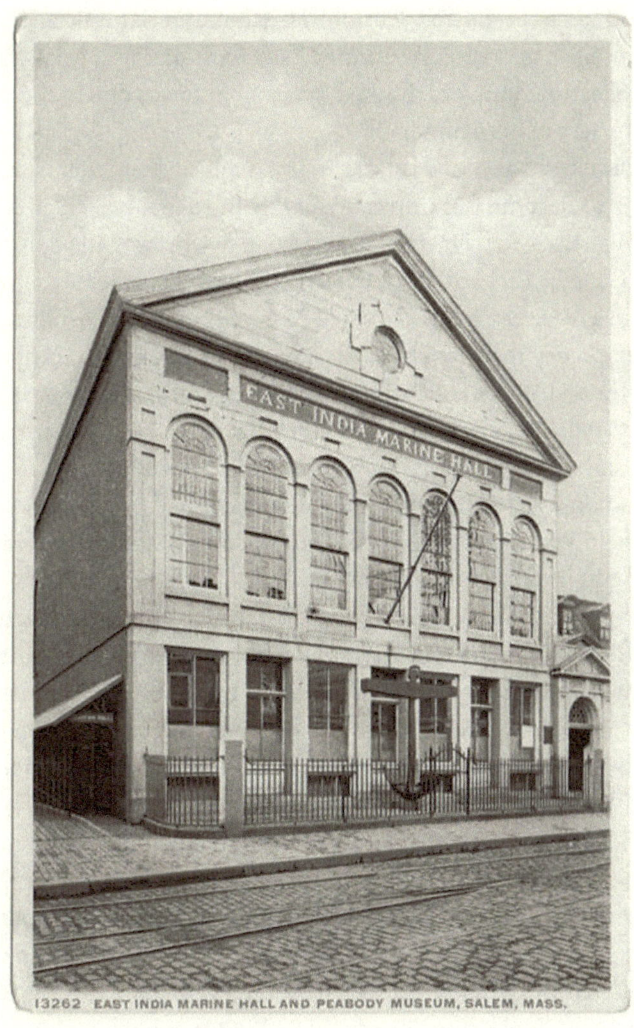

FIGURE 3. East India Marine Hall. Detroit Publishing Co. *Courtesy of the Detroit Publishing Company Collection, Prints & Photographs Division, Library of Congress.*

who little knew his own EIMS father (Nathaniel Hathorne). In command of the brig *Nabby*, Hathorne had died in Surinam of yellow fever in 1808, perhaps a victim of the curse against Judge John Hathorne in 1692. Residing in Salem, Hawthorne visited the museum in 1832 with his friend Franklin Pierce (future U.S. president). Triggering his imagination, the visit led him to satirize the museum in "A Virtuoso's Collection" (1842). Hawthorne was then working at the Boston Custom House measuring salt and coal but called himself "a sort of Port-Admiral." He took similar license in "A Virtuoso's Collection" and was disliked by many in town "due to the rudeness and discourtesy of his manners."[26]

Ward developed a second catalog in 1831, which listed 4,299 items, but he left in 1832 to become the University of Georgia's first professor of natural history. His successor, Dr. Henry Wheatland, who was the son of EIMS member Captain Richard Wheatland, produced a supplement in 1837. Its addition of a mere 434 items mirrored Salem's commercial decline. Reflecting contemporary theories about the steps from "savage" to "civilized," the Harvard-trained Wheatland assembled things by function or type, such as daggers or musical instruments, to allow for technical comparisons. But, said later anthropologist Nicholas Thomas, that scientific method was judgmental and imperial as it denied the individuality of those different people and set them within a Western-defined schema. Wheatland's array lasted until the museum was reordered in 1867.[27]

Ambling about the hall, Hawthorne noticed, he wrote, "the tendency to whimsical combinations and ludicrous analogies, which seemed to influence many of the arrangements of the Museum." While he invented much in "A Virtuoso's Collection," those artifacts told tales of foreign adventure and empire. Said the EIMS, moreover, it assisted "the philosopher" in the study of "the influence of climate, laws, superstition and habit" in shaping society and "the powers and faculties of the human mind." Thus, the collection is best explained within the context of its acquisition and display. For the first generation of members, the highlight was the society's annual banquet, which was replaced after 1825 by meetings, some with dinner. Of all the Chinese porcelain used to serve the banquet's libations, the most ornate was a Lowestoft punch bowl presented by Pinqua, a hong merchant, to the officers aboard Derby's *Grand Turk*. Symbolizing the opening of Asia's market, the bowl, reported the EIMS, had "a correct painting of the Ship, and the date, 'Canton, 1786.'" But a later curator discovered that it depicted a West Indiaman and was copied from a British book.[28]

Those libations were sometimes accompanied by fireworks. After a five-foot, full-rigged USS *Constitution* was gifted in 1813 by its former commander Isaac Hull, the EIMS floated the frigate in a tub and fired a salute from its cannons. But the concussion damaged its rigging, which was repaired, ironically, by British prisoner-of-war sailors held in Salem harbor. A George Ropes watercolor (1814) in the museum depicting Old Ironsides overwhelming HMS *Java* in 1812 was based on that model. The deaf-mute son of an EIMS shipmaster, Ropes had learned his trade under Cornè and produced iconic maritime folk art. Shooting another broadside was the nine-foot model of Captain Israel Williams's *Friendship*. Though the model was built by the ship's carpenter, its brass cannons were cast by a Sumatran metal worker. Various ships were crafted from soup bones, including a five-inch, eighty-gun ship, given by William Bainbridge, who succeeded Hull aboard *Constitution*. First attributed to American prisoners at Dartmoor Prison in County Devon from 1812–15, they were actually built by French prisoners and depicted their own warships.[29]

Around the models and paintings, mariners admired the Chinese goods shaping Salem's consumerism. Generations earlier, most Yankees believed in what historian Vickers called "competence," whereby a family sought only enough wealth and material goods to live on and retire comfortably. As such, Benjamin Franklin had said that it was extravagant to purchase a porcelain tea set. But standards changed with independence and the market revolution. With the booming trade, Bentley exclaimed: "So rapid are our Strides to wealth & Luxury." By the early 1800s an ordinary fifty-piece tea service cost as little as three dollars—or what the EIMS charged for its dinners—because of its lower quality and use as ballast. As Morison suggested, the East India trade had "whetted the appetite of every Massachusetts merchant, and (what was equally important) fixed his good wife's ambition on a chest of Hyson, a China silk gown, and a set of Canton china."[30]

Tantalizing mariners and visitors, the museum displayed Chinese clothing, figures, and curios. Lacquer fans were, for example, "some of the most handsome of all the export wares." One of the museum's most unique Chinese curios was "a superb white nephrite pagoda with carved and gilded bells." Standing 22¾ inches high, it was called "one of the finest examples of pagoda stone carvings of the early nineteenth century." Its distinction qualifies the observation of later museum director, Ernest S. Dodge, that "most of the material . . . from China and other places in the Far East was of souvenir or trade nature." Nathaniel Ingersoll, who joined the EIMS in 1801, gave the pagoda and Mandarin figures, including a 3¾-inch-long "model of the foot of a Chinese lady of fashion." Seeing the practice of foot binding, visitors imagined a freakish East. But, while Cornish visitor Buckingham called it "an absurd and pain-creating custom," he considered it less harmful than the tight corsets worn by Western women.[31]

Though known as liberal minded, Bentley commented on the racial implications of expansionism. Watching the 1801 parade, he objected to a mariner attired "in a Mandarin's dress," thinking that a black servant should have worn the garb of an inferior race. He was referring to the dress of Yanqua, a hong merchant at Canton, which was given by Benjamin Hodges in 1801 and for which Samuel McIntire carved a six-foot figure. Admired for his prowess, Yanqua was, said historian Frederic Grant, "one of the VERY few financially successful hong merchants." Hodges had also given Bentley a "richly ornamented" nodder, a two-foot Mandarin figure whose "head & right hand move but not gracefully." In addition, Captain Wheatland gave 14½-inch-high clay figures depicting a Mandarin's wife, a Chinese laborer packing tea, and a Chinese porter. These many representations familiarized Salem's mariners and consumers with those distant people.[32]

Business deals caused misunderstanding, however. While Pinqua's punch bowl was appreciated, he was nonetheless called untrustworthy because he would "promise everything & perform what he pleases." Consequa, another hong merchant, seemed arbitrary, but he had entered a "legal netherworld" when U.S. merchants refused to pay their debts after the 1807 embargo. To better his commerce, he employed the merchant Eshing, who commissioned a portrait by the Cantonese artist Spoilum that the EIMS displayed. But overall, concluded historian James Gibson, "dishonesty and corruption were standard at Canton, on the part of the lowest coolie and the highest mandarin." Other gifts to the EIMS tell the story of that business, such as "A Chinese Swanpan, or Abacus, used by most Asiatic nations in making Arithmetical calculations," and "A Dotchin or Ballance, for weighing gold in China." While Yankees little used the abacus, despite its superiority to their shorthand, they did not trust the Dotchin, which was used to weigh coins, jewels, and opium and had been standard in Chinese marketplaces for centuries. Instead, as in Sumatra, they used their own scales, which they rigged to cheat the pepper sellers.[33]

The extravagant consumption of hong merchants like Howqua (Wu Ping-chen), whose modest portrait in the EIMS did not suggest that he was "probably the richest man in the world," led some Yankees to worry, as did their forebears who read John Bunyan's cautionary tale of England, *Pilgrim's Progress* (1678), that New England could similarly be corrupted by the materialism of Vanity Fair. At the 1825 banquet, Israel Williams, the society's second vice president, toasted: "China Produce: Once considered nectar for the Gods—may it never make scandal for our Goddesses." Yet he feared that Salem's daily consumption, whether a silk shawl, a lacquered chest, or Nanking porcelain, was already corrupting its society. At that banquet, John White Treadwell, an EIMS officer and cousin of President Stephen White, hoped that while the East was being enriched by trade, the West would be strengthened. He toasted: "The drain of Specie from the West to the East, and its magical effects—which enriches [the Chinese] who spend, in proportion to their prodigality; and those countries [America and Britain] which it exhausts the most, it renders the most inexhaustible." In 1825, most U.S. purchases in Canton were made in silver (72.8 percent), but its use peaked in 1826. Merchants offset silver with opium, which became their single largest medium of exchange.[34]

Salem mariners found their greatest opportunities in India, where the Treaty of Paris had given them the right to trade. Exploiting cracks in the East India Company's monopoly, they procured fine textiles, coffee, and spices in Calcutta, Bombay, and elsewhere. The trade was exemplified by Joseph Peabody's 328-ton *George*, which made twenty-one round-trip voyages between 1815 and 1837. *George* was a training ground for Salem boys, creating thirty-five masters and augmenting EIMS ranks. Those larger ships required greater navigation skills, employed more heterogeneous crews, and demanded more shrewd supercargoes. But because many East Indiamen were too large for Salem's shallow harbor, said Daniel Vickers, "the chance of rising to a position of command was much thinner," making fewer eligible for the EIMS.[35]

The museum exhibited Indian curios, including ones given by their merchants to solicit business. Besides his oil portrait (1803), Nasservanjee, a rich Parsi Bania of Bombay, gifted his "whole dress," to which the EIMS added a carved head and body. His family, the Wadias, became "one of the most influential" in Bombay. Mannequins also depicted Raj Kissen Mitter (1838), who headed a Calcutta trading firm. Using his personal space aboard the 271-ton *Emerald*, Captain James B. Briggs gave the EIMS seven life-sized clay figures from Calcutta in 1823, including a juggler with a cobra, a palanquin-bearer, and a fakir. The museum centered its hall round the seated Raj Kissen Mitter with a half dozen of the lower castes.[36]

Representing India's mystery, opulence, and subjection, the wooden palanquin was memorable. Five captains purchased it in Calcutta for the museum in 1802. Carried on two long poles by four coolies, it measured 15¼ feet long by 2½ feet deep by 3½ feet high; behind two sliding doors was its compartment upholstered in green silk. To divert the sun, a coolie alongside carried a parasol. Though used for centuries, palanquins were adopted by British elite in the late 1700s. Other curios reinforced the sense of the bizarre, including hookahs (hubble-bubbles) for tobacco or opium, some of which were carried in the 1823 EIMS parade and given by Nathaniel Silsbee. Indian musical instruments struck a discordant note. A mariner gave a three-string Bengalese violin, but one Salemite mocked the Indians' "wretched, squeaking music," with singing that "resembled the screams of persons whom I have seen labouring under a severe paroxysm of the cholic!"[37]

Misconceptions abounded, as museumgoers were ill prepared to understand a culture so different from their own. Just as Yankees were horrified by a widow's suttee, they dismissed human hooking, during which hooks were placed under the ribs and the body was suspended with no sign of suffering. Witnessing the practice in Calcutta in 1822, Captain Joseph Webb donated the hooks. It disgusted EIMS president Dudley Pickman, who instead expressed interest in the erotic dancing of Nautch girls. Another captain lambasted India's alleged indolence and licentiousness. Hoping to show India's better side, John White donated Sanskrit copies of the Old and New Testaments, while Stephen White gave "part of the beard of a Brahmin, who was shaved on being converted to Christianity." But "fanciful misinformation about India" was widespread, said later critic Raj Kumar Gupta. That included "a great deal of exaggerations and distortion," as well as "a disposition to select and play up the lurid, the sensational, and the bizarre."[38]

"CURIOUSLY ILLUSTRATING THESE CHILDREN OF NATURE": DEPICTING THE EAST INDIES, SOUTH SEAS, AND MORE

The archipelagos from the Indian Ocean to Polynesia seemed dangerous and primitive. Mariners told their story through curious weapons, cutthroat pirates, and perilous voyages. After curators grouped items by function, visitors could see contrasts between the savage, semicivilized, and more advanced peoples of Asia and the Pacific. Samuel G. Derby gave "an elegant Sword" from Japan with Wootz steel and gold ornaments; nearby cabinets revealed dazzling Malay and Javan krises (asymmetrical daggers), including a poisoned one from Sumatra; more startling were the war clubs, battle axes, spears, and poisoned arrows from the Pacific islands.[39]

But artifacts need explanation. Of the many Maori war implements donated by Captain William P. Richardson was what the catalog called "a wooden instrument, curiously carved, and edged with the teeth of a Shark, from New Zealand, used by the natives . . . to cut up human bodies, both those taken prisoners and those slain in battle."[40] Though modern scholars discount stories of cannibalism, the era's books included them, as in New Caledonia where a victim's organs and genitals were allegedly broiled on coals before being eaten. Ethnologist Augustus Hamilton later ironically called the same wooden instrument "one of the most Beautiful specimens of scarifying-knives" in existence, a blade that mourning widows used, in theory, to mark themselves. Seeing that knife, along with the "embalmed head of a New Zealand Chief" and war clubs "headed with tufts of human hair, from the Marquesas," writer Ann Royall remarked in 1826 that the cabinet's "artificial curiosities mostly consist[ed] of the implements of war used by the rude Islanders of the Indian Ocean and the southern seas."[41]

Some pieces resembled those pictured in Captain James Cook's *A Voyage toward the South Pole* (1777). Their acquisition by the EIMS was perhaps a self-justifying act, as mariners sought out weapons associated with savagery and natives complied. According to later anthropologist Nicholas Thomas, "It is clear from the voyage journals that very little apart from arrows, bows, and clubs was ever offered to the visitors" throughout Melanesia. Yet, appearances could be misleading. Some axes or adzes had handles of shark teeth or bits of shell that showed such "fine and intricate work," especially with primitive tools, that they could only have been used for ceremonial or religious purposes.[42]

Still, museum visitors melded those weapons with stories of piracy (which Yankees differentiated from their own privateering). In search of coffee, for example, the 256-ton *Essex* was lured in 1806 into the Red Sea, where brigands murdered its crew, stole $60,000, burned the ship, and left the headless corpse of EIMS captain Joseph Orne adrift in the flotsam. Mariners told other blood-curdling stories as they escorted museum visitors. Capturing the 366-ton *Friendship* in 1831, pirates in the Strait of Malacca took everything, including $9,000 in opium and $12,000 in specie. Clouding the matter was the weapons trade because, as Java's governor lamented, the Americans were not "scrupulous how they acquire their profits." The museum displayed the matchlock guns of Arab and Malay pirates, as well as their watercraft. A curator later realized, however, that one Marquesan boat was "the only known specimen" of the islands' outrigger canoe.[43]

Trading opium for over a decade was Captain Charles Moses Endicott. Descended from Puritan governor John Endicott, the EIMS president of eighteen years knew that natives were angered by "the frauds and oppressions, the debauchery and violence, *sometimes* perpetrated by American seamen." Yet they were "opium smokers, rendered desperate by their habits." Pirates took his ship, but, aided by raja Po Adam, he regained control. The owners, including Senator Silsbee, demanded action by President Andrew Jackson. During the First Sumatran Expedition (1832), USS *Potomac* bombarded the pirates' town of Aceh, perhaps the nation's first case of East Asian jingoism. The EIMS exhibited Po Adam's sword, but Sumatrans saw him as a quisling. Destabilized by the opium and weapons trade, relations with the natives remained tense. The U.S. Navy retaliated in the Second Sumatran Expedition (1838), but the museum emphasized a civilizing mission by displaying its "New Testament in the Malay Language."[44]

The opium trade was implicit in the cabinet. During the French War, Yankees controlled "almost the entire Levant opium trade to China." While the British East India Company dominated India's opium trade in Canton, Americans "came in a strong second." Besides the hookahs, the cabinet included "two Turkish-pipes for smoking Opium" donated by EIMS president Stephen White. The Chinese emperor deplored the trade and suppressed it in 1820, but smuggling only increased. The English retaliated in the First Opium War (1839–42). Touring the United States, the Cornish traveler Buckingham denounced those British and American traders who, motivated by "the filthy lucre of gain," introduced "the poisonous and demoralizing drug of opium." He noted the absolute hypocrisy of simultaneously bombarding their towns and sending them Bibles, thereby "offering them Christianity with the one hand; and in the other, giving them a choice between being degraded and demoralized by opium, or slaughtered in war." To Buckingham's disappointment, his lectures in Salem in 1838 were only "slightly attended."[45]

Another lucrative trade was the human cargo of slaves, but town boosters denied its existence. Knowing that some of his parishioners were involved, Bentley regretted, "We know men will do anything for money." In 1820, Congress declared the slave trade to be international piracy and subject to the death penalty for Americans. Salem's trade with West Africa, which included more than slaving, was extensive from 1832 to 1864 with some 558 ship arrivals. In return, Yankees sold rum, guns, and tobacco. West African artifacts in the cabinet indirectly evidenced that business. A musical drum of wood, animal skin, and glass from the Congo, which pictured a Portuguese slaver, was presented in 1843 by Captain William T.

Julio, who sailed between Salem and West Africa for the firm Brookhouse & Co. East India Marine Society shipmasters Charles Hoffman and Robert Brookhouse were "the chief beneficiaries" of the slave trade in the Cacheu River (Guinea-Bissau) in the mid-1840s. As late as 1859, the *New York Times* reported, slavers were "fitting-out at Salem."[46]

In the South Seas, Salem masters acquired bêche-de-mer. They contracted with Fijian rulers to collect and cure the edible sea slug, which was sold from Manila to Canton as a delicacy and aphrodisiac. With payment in muskets and cutlasses, the trade intensified intertribal warfare. By 1834, fourteen EIMS masters had been or were monopolizing its trade. Like many of the museum's natural history specimens, however, the shelf life of what it called "Trepany, or Beach le Mar" was short. Its natural supply would be exhausted, as would the sandalwood that Chinese used to make furniture, boxes, and joss sticks. "Every stick of the wood had blood upon it," said a Fiji historian, as chiefs drove their people to collect it, acquired iron for weapons, warred against rivals, and even murdered traders. With the trade at its height between 1810 and 1825, the Sandwich Islands felt its brunt. Living profligately, King Kamehameha II bought George Crowninshield Jr.'s *Cleopatra's Barge* for $90,000 in sandalwood, which was over a million pounds and forcibly carried by his subjects. The hermaphrodite brig (and the first U.S. yacht) was, wrote journalist-historian Ralph Paine, "one of the most remarkable vessels ever launched," as it had Oriental draperies and plate glass mirrors. But the king's drunken captain wrecked it on a reef in 1824. Its luxurious saloon and stateroom were later re-created at the museum.[47]

Exciting stories about cannibals and krises nurtured what Vickers called a "simple instinct for survival" among Salem mariners. In general, U.S. adventurers of the early nineteenth century were, wrote historian Amy Greenberg, more aggressive and combative than their eighteenth-century forebears. In 1834, Richard Henry Dana Jr. witnessed this "overstrained sense of manliness" at sea. At an EIMS banquet, Charles Saunders toasted "the strong limbs, hard faces, and free-born manners of our Sailors," whose traits were definitely "not the product of spinning-jennies." Yet EIMS masters, upon retiring from the sea, often diversified their portfolios by investing in textile mills. Stephen White's former EIMS captain, Nathaniel Griffin, formed a consortium to build the massive Naumkeag Steam Cotton Company, which required filling in part of the harbor.[48]

Inherent in that manhood was an encounter with cultures whose attitudes differed on everything from sex to dress. While Peabody director

Ernest Dodge claimed that Salem sailors pictured Polynesia as "peopled by a beautiful race leading a Utopian life," the era's accounts depicted the islands as more varied. The contrast with New England was stark. In Salem, masters were toasting their women's virtue, while authorities were campaigning against brothels and miscegenation, but captains and crews overseas were experiencing another world. In Canton, the "flower boats" of the Pearl River ran "an aggressive and competitive" prostitution business, but the EIMS's many idyllic paintings of Whampoa Reach omitted the "flower boats," as did the history books. But in the eastern Pacific, EIMS master James Cheever observed in 1830 upon entering an Ecuadorian harbor, "The ladies came on board, a good assortment of sizes, ages, and sexes." In Manila, Bowditch showed interest in mestizo girls, admitting that "a small puff of wind would discover their nakedness," but he chided a Swedish captain for hiring "a miss" to live "in stile."[49]

The South Seas showed more scanty costumes. William Richardson donated a "Girdle, or Sashes, being the entire dress of females at the Fegee Islands." Significant because it was acquired in the first stage of cultural contact, the cabinet included what was later called "the single surviving example of a Marquesan *malo* or loin cloth," which was given by Israel Williams in 1802, as well as many Marquesan necklaces and ornaments (breast, ear, finger, wrist) that bore no relation to anything from Europe. Raising eyebrows were explicit drawings of African women, whose "external sexual organs" (labia), said a later curator, were "characteristic of Hottentots." While a Yankee sailor admitted that the Sandwich Islands offered the opportunity to "mate the copper coulered lasses," a missionary in Tahiti protested in 1832 that there was even "a cry for little girls" from the "officers who come in ships." European American visitors commented about the prevalence of female and male nudity and casual sexual intercourse across Polynesia. Puritanical missionaries imposed vice laws, which the natives and the U.S. Navy challenged in 1826 with limited success.[50]

Sharpening the cultural clash, mariners observed full male nudity, revealing the fine physique and the tattoos that had intrigued European writers since Cook's voyages of the 1770s. Others, including Captain William Bligh on Cook's third (and last) voyage, even commented on male homoerotic acts, though Western taboos discouraged such commentary. Punishable by death in the eighteenth-century English navy, but rarely prosecuted, buggery was reportedly common, yet few records exist. If it happened in a port's Sailortown, on a Polynesian beach, or under the ship's "boom cover," it is difficult to find in the museum's closet. Still, sailors sang songs and wrote ditties about such behavior well into the nineteenth century.[51]

Missionaries fought more than the natives' sexuality. As they converted islanders to Christianity, they forced them to discard the idols that, as in Hawaii, lined the walls of the *heiau* (temple), which were in turn destroyed. In Hawaii, the eighteen-foot statue Kolia Moku (Ku) was to be ceremoniously sacrificed by a native chief who converted to Christianity, but John T. Prince intervened. "As he is actually, the last of the gods on these Islands," Prince declared in 1844, "I deem him worthy of preservation, as curiously illustrating the moral degradation and mechanical skill of these children of nature before Christians had commenced their work among them." Prince thought that Salem's museum was best fit to display it because its curiosities were arranged "so admirably." Before sending it to Salem, the idol was castrated, presumably to accord with Yankee sensibilities. Just as Westerners introduced new ways, so, too, did they bring diseases, such as measles, and Hawaii's population would fall 90 percent by 1893.[52]

As Dodge later wrote, "Little did the captains realize that this fascinating native life, together with its arts and crafts, would collapse like a house of cards under the impact of white traders and missionaries, and their trade goods and new philosophy." But, typical of those who expected Western acculturation, he added, "Usually only the priestly class along with a few old hardshells were normally opposed to the white intrusion." As mariners and missionaries opened distant doors, island rulers played their own hands. They not only capitalized their traditional control over the masses, as in the extraction of sandalwood and bêche-de-mer, but used Western weapons and connections to increase their power. The anthropologist Marshall Sahlins suggested that change in the South Seas was "externally induced yet indigenously orchestrated," but other scholars have countered that Westerners played a larger role than is acknowledged. Mariners helped topple that house of cards by pushing Western ways, exploiting natural resources, and using artifacts to create a mythology.[53]

Science was a handmaiden of imperialism. Since 1799, the EIMS had worked to make voyages more safe, direct, and speedy. A pioneer in its own ranks, the society led in the collection and application of scientific data. Prior to such work, wrote historian Josef Konvitz, "information about the sea was nearly as unsystematically organized and processed in the 1790s as it had been a century before." But, through the likes of the EIMS, "from 1790 until 1850, most of the advances in oceanographic science were no longer achieved by scientists, the vast majority of whom had lost interest in the sea and its problems, but by mariners with scientific training." Besides sharing information on the errors in English and Dutch maps and navigation books, as well as the dangers they experienced sailing, EIMS members began to map faraway shores even before the U.S. government established an Office of Coast Survey (1807).[54]

For each trek, the EIMS gave the master "a blank journal in which he is to insert all things worthy of notice which occur on his voyage, and upon his return to be deposited with the Society." Unlike the published accounts of Cook's three voyages, which focused on the people and their products, the EIMS was concerned particularly with accurate navigational readings and sailing advice. It was mandated "without any excuse whatsoever" that the journal be completed, submitted, and made available to fellow members. A member toasted in 1804, "May each mariner record, so that Enterprise may discover." Yet those logs were for members only. As they scientifically put the globe in order for their trade, the collection of maps and logs became, said geographer Lloyd Brown, "the key to the empire." By 1841, there were 105 bound and indexed logs.[55]

Even after Cook's voyages, the Pacific Ocean was little known. Salem masters successfully pressed President John Quincy Adams to request an expedition to chart these waters. After funding stalled, the EIMS petitioned Congress in 1834; its memorial on behalf of the "Voyage of Discovery and Survey to the South Seas" was called by historian William Stanton "the most eloquent" of the many appeals. In 1836, the Secretary of the Navy instructed Lieutenant Charles Wilkes to acquaint himself with the EIMS materials, which included the most accurate charts of the Dutch East Indies. As his pilot and interpreter for other uncharted islands, Wilkes chose the society's Captain Benjamin Vanderford, who had been shipwrecked in the Fiji Islands in 1817. Besides its wealth of information, the expedition produced the (John) Tyler Doctrine, through which, said historian Edward Crapol, Americans declared their hegemony over the Hawaiian archipelago.[56]

The cabinet also included navigational instruments, natural resources (metals, woods, and plants), and numerous antiquities. Snatched from the Catacombs of Thebes, for example, was the "thumb of a female Mummy" and "a Ring made of blue enamel" found on another finger. More numerous were souvenirs from the East Indies, as when Captain Nathaniel Page gifted a "Statue of Durga . . . beautifully carved in Sienite, from an ancient Temple in the interior of Java." Buckingham was impressed by a "hand broken from a granite statue in the Cave of Elephanta, at Bombay." As fellow explorers, these mariners admired Christopher Columbus; at least two mariners took bricks from "the house in which [he] was born." Like the Bowery museums that claimed to have the club that killed Captain Cook in 1779, the EIMS displayed pieces "of the Rock, on which [he] was killed." It also commissioned a Cornè portrait.[57]

The most popular antiquity was a late medieval Flemish rosary given in 1806 by Elias Hasket Derby Jr. Carved in boxwood, its two-inch-diameter terminal bead opens to reveal 109 intricate figures and heads. Known as Heaven and Hell (or Heaven and the Day of Judgment), the figures represent the blessed in the Northern Hemisphere and cursed in the Southern. Using an accompanying magnifying glass, visitors were told that the twenty-eight full-length figures in the southern half included those in Purgatory. The rosary was attributed to a fourteenth-century monk employing a premodern cartography. By the nineteenth century, however, Western observers regarded the upper hemisphere as their own, whereas the lower (East Asia and the South Seas) was waiting for Western civilization. Buckingham called it "one of the most curious specimens of skill and patience united, that I have ever seen."[58]

Thus, whether it was a Javan kris, a Hawaiian idol, or a medieval rosary, the museum's collection was gathered by individuals to reflect their travel and tell Salemites about distant worlds. Just what those artifacts meant to visitors was often difficult to establish. Perhaps a retired mariner would use pieces to tell a story, recount his adventures, and offer a cautionary note. Yet, when assembled as a whole, those artifacts showed not only the progress made by coastal Massachusetts through foreign trade but also what was regarded as the semicivilized or crude regions that sold their wares, offered their resources, or waited to be lifted from the purgatory of primitivism.

"STOP, TRAVELER! STOP TO MARVEL!": TOURISM, LOCAL IDENTITY, AND COMMERCE

As the museum's collection grew during the 1820s, Salem's economy was being upended. A global depression began in 1819, decreasing by 25 percent the value of Salem's commerce. Meanwhile, competitors in Europe, Boston, and New York were gaining at its expense. Even the Custom House (1819) was "too large," noted Hawthorne, who became surveyor of the Port of Salem and Beverly in 1845. Amid this shakedown, Salemites took more pride in their museum, which expanded in 1825. That pride was boosted in 1826 when the Italian political exile and explorer Giacomo Costantino Beltrami visited. Impressed, he noted in the museum's book, "Stop, Traveler! Stop to marvel!" at "the prodigies of man." The collection was "without question, the first in the world." The first in town, too, according to Leverett Saltonstall, who admitted that Salem was otherwise "*dull, dull, dull.*" Said a writer for New York's *Journal of Commerce* in 1831, it was "the most interesting Museum we have ever entered" as it afforded "a fine illustration of the enterprise, science and taste of the Salem ship masters."[59]

Retired masters used those artifacts as mnemonic props to recount their exploits. Captain George Nichols, for example, had joined the EIMS in 1800 after sailing to Batavia, Manila, and Bombay. Said his granddaughter, Martha, he "cherished a love for the institution throughout his life," which was perhaps augmented by the failure of his merchant firm, Pierce & Nichols, with the 1820s shipping depression. Many a captain joined him "to see if his last contribution from the East had been placed to advantage," recalled Caroline Howard King. So, too, did Harriet Bates remember her cousin, Captain William Rockwell. In his stories of India and China, she said, "he added a fund of lore of a more romantic if less reliable sort, which made him the most entertaining of companions to us children."[60]

Salem's adolescents were captivated by the museum's otherworldliness. Martha Nichols remembered wandering for hours "almost breathlessly around the hall." Caroline King, for another, maintained a "constant presence there" and was drawn to the palanquin's smell "of myrrh and frankincense." She recalled that the museum had a "touch of the dear old Arabian Nights," but having likely read an expurgated version, acknowledged little of those tales' sexual fantasy: "I think I came as near fairy-land as one ever can in this work-a-day world." Crossing the antebellum race barrier, she admitted that the Indian figures "became real friends of mine." In many Salem homes, moreover, there were "quaint tokens of the East." Referring to a string of beads, Harriet Bates imagined "strange Hindoo rites, Nautch dances, and women with dusky throats." Propriety was most challenged, however, by the museum's "dried head of a Feejee islander." A pull curtain offered a glimpse to adults, but curator Henry Wheatland had cleaned off the tattooed skin. Yet as Rear Admiral Sam Morison (USN, ret.) later joked, a "pair of tattooed heads" looked "strangely like certain Maoris whom I encountered" in World War II.[61]

That sense of mystery led to what Wheatland called "excessive handleing by visitors," especially of the fully dressed mandarin, which was later encased in glass. That handling was "a habit to which the [females] are very much addicted." Marianne Silsbee admitted that as a youngster she "gazed with delight and wonder" on "the group of Orientals, life size, with rigidly correct toilettes." The caretaker deemed it inappropriate, however, for young girls to be examining men too closely because he redirected their eyes to what "was most proper to look at"—the scrimshaw. Striking "mortal terror" in those children, that caretaker was Captain Thomas Saul, who had joined the EIMS in 1820 and was its last custodian.[62]

More controversial was the visit of President Andrew Jackson in 1833. He first toured the Charlestown Navy Yard, where a campaign to refit USS *Constitution* had succeeded, but partisanship erupted when its new figurehead—that of Old Hickory—was vandalized. With Vice President Martin Van Buren, he then visited Salem. Though "the great mass of people" were Whigs, the town held a parade. Both Democrats signed the museum register, but a vandal clipped their names. Captain William Story proposed (unsuccessfully) that the EIMS condemn "such a dishonourable act." As Caroline Howard recalled, "The newspapers were filled with vindictive accusations" against the Whigs. The museum showed the register with the caption: "Mutilated by some person or persons unknown." Many decades later the culprit was outed—eleven-year-old Caroline, who admitted being one of those "staunch little Whigs" who "felt that our beloved Museum [was] desecrated by his presence."[63]

The debate over slavery also intensified tensions. African Americans were scattered around town in small colonies, one of which Bentley disparagingly called "Roast Meat hill," as they worked at sea as cooks, stewards, and sometimes sailors; and with industrialization, better transportation, and southern emigration, more were coming to town. In 1827, John B. Russworm visited the museum. Founder of *Freedom's Journal*, the nation's first paper owned and operated by African Americans, he wrote therein that "there [were] but few museums equally valuable" in the land but regretted that the mariner guide snubbed him. As Boston abolitionists mobilized in 1831, tensions flared. In 1833 Captain Joseph Ropes responded by introducing a resolution (successfully) "that people of Colour shall be excluded from visiting the Museum of this Society, during the usual hours of admission, excepting as attendants on visitors." Salem's antiabolitionists rioted in 1835 and 1837 despite the small black population.[64]

Salem's localism was further compromised when the Eastern Railroad routed a Boston train through Salem in 1838. As the museum attracted even more "strangers from all parts of the world," members complained that accommodating over two thousand annual visitors required "too great a sacrifice of time." The EIMS resolved to impose an admission charge of twenty-five cents for visitors not accompanied by a member. Tickets were ordered, but the policy was inexplicably rescinded. Entry remained free for members, who received passes that they gave to interested parties. Then, as a national crisis stirred over slavery's possible expansion into Kansas in 1854, Charlotte Forten, granddaughter of a prominent black Philadelphia sailmaker, arrived to teach at an integrated public school. She was disheartened by Salem's racism after her friend, Caroline Putnam, a "cultured Salem Negro," along with her daughters, were, she wrote, "refused admission to the Museum, after having tickets given them, solely on account of their complexion. Insulting language was used to them" by those "miserable doughfaces who do not deserve the name of men." The museum's racial barrier lasted until 1865.[65]

Over those past three decades, Salem's trade declined further. While many leading families looked to the future by moving to Boston, the seal of the newly incorporated city pictured the past: a Sumatran man, pepper plants, and a bark; it was inscribed, *Divitis Indiae usque ad ultimum Sinum* ("To the Farthest Port of the Rich East"). East India Marine Society membership peaked at 136 in 1843; within a decade, it fell to 111. Showing that decline, the last Custom House entry from Batavia occurred in 1855 and Manila in 1858. Meanwhile, whaling was increasing; sixty-one whalers sailed out of Salem between 1834 and 1868, despite the inability of the city's two refineries to compete with Nantucket or New Bedford. Other ships became tramps, staying out for years to avoid the nation's high tariff.[66]

With Spain's retreat from the Western hemisphere and the Monroe Doctrine's claim of U.S. hegemony, more ships shifted to South America's Atlantic ports. At the 1825 banquet, the society's treasurer and later president, William Fettyplace, toasted: "The Independent Governments of South America. May they, like this distinguished Republic, be ever supported by civil and religious liberty." Yet, Yankee Calvinists distrusted Latin America's Catholics, as depicted in the cabinet's "Medal of the Pope and the Devil." With the Latin American trade, membership fell, as Salem mariners did not pass either cape. Only seventeen joined from 1840 to 1850, and in the next decade, a mere dozen.[67]

By 1864, 334 masters and supercargoes had become members, but only 70 then survived (on average, over sixty years old). Thus, the EIMS sold its building lock, stock, and barrel to George Peabody of London for $140,000.

A native of nearby Danvers and a cousin of shipping magnate Captain Joseph Peabody, he was a banker whose firm was the precursor of J. P. Morgan & Co. Having recently funded new natural history museums at Yale and Harvard Universities, he accepted custody in 1867. Also acquiring the ethnological and natural history holdings of the Essex Institute (1848), he created the Peabody Academy of Science. As EIMS president B. H. Silsbee admitted, "Old ideas, with the rust of age on them, must give way to new ones, fresh with vigor of youth." The EIMS provided relief to its members or families for forty more years.[68]

Frederic Ward Putnam, a former student of Louis Agassiz, became the academy's first director and strove to re-create Agassiz's Museum of Comparative Zoology, which purveyed the later discredited idea of polygenesis. Called the "father of American anthropology," Putnam emptied the museum and rebuilt its interior, thus destroying the original Federal design. Reorienting exhibits to ethnology, his goal (as was typical in the era's natural history museums), said later critic Stephen Weil, was "to locate the place that its Western and predominantly Caucasian visitors occupied in the terrestrial order of things. And that place, beyond any doubt, was at the top of things." In 1873, while West Coast Americans were flocking to the Fiji Cannibal Exhibition or New Yorkers to the Bowery's dime museums, the academy had two departments, Ethnology and Natural History. The large crowds were fascinated by the sight of "savage curiosities," said raconteur George F. Davenport, noting that the Fiji islanders "used to eat each other when opportunity offered and baked missionary was a sort of Thanksgiving delicacy." He wrote of a "dreadful Hindoo idol" from torrid India, the "queer machine for reckoning accounts" (the abacus), and "a skull nicely clean and plugged up to make a drinking cup" from Fiji.[69] (See fig. 4.)

Set in a romanticized but imperial framework, another visitor was enthralled by "the ancient mariner" interpreting the room. "It was as if one had been transported in a moment to far off tropic lands, where palms are waving in air, [and] serpents and strange beasts lurking in jungles." A *Kansas City Times* correspondent crowed that those curiosities "would make [P. T.] Barnum's cheek turn green with envy." During the 1876 depression, almost thirty-seven thousand attended. Most Salem visitors made the pilgrimage, including President Chester Arthur in 1882. While many Americans were questioning the veracity of traveling shows, Salem emphasized its authenticity. "Begun before civilization and [the industrial revolution set off by] Birmingham had reached these far off regions," a guidebook said,

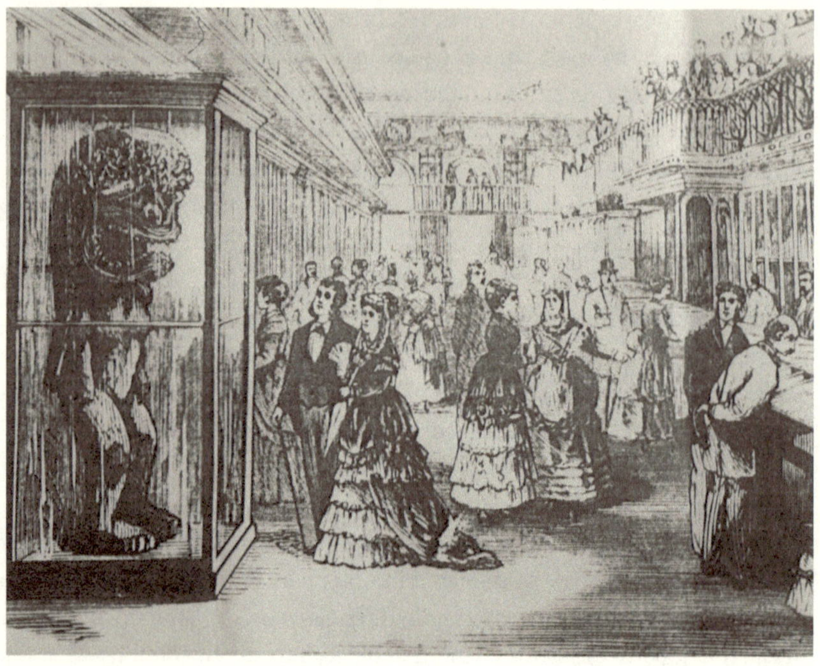

FIGURE 4. Kolia Moku, Peabody Academy of Science, *Frank Leslie's Illustrated Newspaper*, September 4, 1869.

the Polynesian materials were "free from the effect of European contact and their genuineness is assured." With the advance of "civilization," moreover, "the natives who made many of these objects have, as tribes, become extinct." Directing the academy from 1880 to 1916, Edward S. Morse added a trove of Japanese clothing, swords, and tools from before the Meiji Restoration.[70]

While Salem's coasting trade was healthy, its arrivals from distant ports had "entirely ceased" by 1878, but retired captains still entertained visitors "by the hour with tales and reminiscences of those stirring days." Near the Custom House and the wharves, Derby Street conjured "ghostly shadows of stately East Indiamen, Canton tea-ships, and African treasure ships," said a reporter. By the 1890s, however, the neighborhood was packed with foreigners in tenements and factories. As such, Davenport told visitors to walk a half mile to the museum and escape "the bustle of the crowd and the turmoil which marks the daily battle of life." In 1906 the *Boston Globe* reported that the EIMS experienced its own battle as its fifteen survivors were "in a neck-and-neck race with death."[71]

But academy treasurer and trustee John Robinson took action because the displays slighted those mariners, including his deceased father, an EIMS supercargo. In 1889, he began to retrieve marine objects from the building's attic and solicit additions. As China was disintegrating in the mid-1890s and Americans eyed its markets, romanticism was budding. Creating "a memorial of the commercial marine period," he opened the Marine Room in 1905. It uniquely blended ship models, portraits of merchants and masters, and "objects of every sort illustrating the life of a sailor." As such, it was the nation's first gallery to focus solely on men at sea. In 1907 he added a whaling display after receiving items, including scrimshaw, from the 1893 World's Fair that were deemed inferior by Chicago's Field Museum.[72]

In 1915 the academy was renamed the Peabody Museum. In 1918 the Essex Institute gave its shipping-related objects, and Robinson acquired, through the Crowninshield family, the sumptuous furnishings of *Cleopatra's Barge*; its saloon was later replicated. In 1921 he authored an illustrated, two-hundred-page octavo volume on the Marine Room, which revealed that, according to Salem's leading antiquarian George F. Dow, the Peabody Museum had "few competitors on this side of the Atlantic." Robinson and Dow also founded the Marine Research Society, a commercial venture that published twenty-five books over the next twelve years. After Robinson died in 1925 and the room again expanded, it was named after him. By the mid-1920s, Peabody's attendance had reached seventy-thousand annual visitors.[73]

Van Wyck Brooks kindled further interest in the town in *The Flowering of New England, 1815–1865* (1936). Hearing Salem's "ancient skippers" tell stories at "dilapidated wharves," he felt the town's "immemorial air." But Caroline King called those old wharves "a sad and pathetic sight." As Depression-era federal programs recorded the region's history and boosted interest in its past seafarers, William Sumner Appleton Jr. and the Society for the Preservation of New England Antiquities (SPNEA) acquired the home of merchant Richard Derby (1762), which was near the Custom House. In 1936, SPNEA transferred it to the National Park Service (NPS), which in 1937 purchased a former warehouse (1804) and remade it for tourists as the West India Goods Store. The NPS also acquired the Benjamin Hawkes House (1800), whose construction Samuel McIntire had started in 1780 for Elias Hasket Derby. In 1938 Congress designated a small area around Derby Wharf as a national historic site. To supplement those buildings, a federal staffer considered acquiring the century-old whaling bark *Charles W. Morgan*, but he concluded, incorrectly, that the project would have led "visitors to the erroneous conclusion that Salem was a whaling port."[74]

Meanwhile, the Peabody was tacking. In 1936 it hired Walter Muir Whitehill as assistant director, and he proposed mounting exhibits on Nathaniel Bowditch and the EIMS. But, because its natural history collection was so large, yet inferior to that of Harvard or Yale, the museum had no available space. So, over the next six years, it discarded its natural specimens; one electrician even "carried off a ten-foot alligator" to surprise his wife. Spotlighting maritime history, the second-floor hall, which was restored to its presumed 1825 appearances, was rededicated by museum trustee Governor Leverett Saltonstall in 1943. With America's ongoing two-ocean war, maritime history was regaining popularity. The Peabody concluded that the EIMS was its "chief claim to distinction."[75]

The seafaring revival also launched *The American Neptune: A Quarterly Journal of Maritime History* (1941). Inspired by Lincoln Colcord, who had founded the Penobscot (Maine) Marine Museum in 1936, the scholarly journal was guided by Morison and Whitehill and headquartered at the Peabody. Free and open daily, the museum was attracting fifty thousand visitors annually by 1949. As it showed its holdings in a new wing, *Antiques* magazine called it "one of the richest marine collections in the world." By the 1960s, boasted maritime curator Marion Brewington, its library held "the second largest collection of log books in the United States," as well as the "largest collection of business documents relating directly to shipping." With its journal, library, and collections, it inspired Karl Kortum to create the San Francisco Maritime Museum.[76]

But the seafaring revival did not stop the destruction of the city's historic environment. In 1965, Salem proposed a plan for thirty-nine downtown acres. Designed to boost automobile access and commerce, it targeted the museum's Essex Street block by proposing a four-lane highway—right through its Japanese garden! Bringing "national notoriety to Salem," the plan, according to *New York Times* critic Ada Louise Huxtable, was "rape by renewal." Salem did save the Japanese garden (for five decades) and added a pedestrian mall fronting the museum, but it lost "one of the oldest brick town houses in the country"–a prerevolutionary home on Essex Street once owned by an EIMS member–"to make room for a parking lot for exactly 13 cars." By 1973 the city had become "a series of demolition sites." Then, said Huxtable, the much-criticized Salem authorities began "backtracking in a desperate attempt to do it right." Her sensitivity had been heightened because the Peabody was one of her favorite little museums, especially for its "marvelous evocation of the early China trade."[77]

With "fully half" of its exhibits devoted to maritime subjects by the 1960s, the Peabody blossomed under Ernest Dodge, who became director in 1950, edited *American Neptune* for twenty-five years, and wrote prolifically about the mariners and their collecting and encounters. Its display space nearly doubled in 1976 with a forty-five-thousand-square-foot addition, built provocatively in the Brutalist style. The museum was also producing praise-winning displays and catalogs. In 1982, for example, the exhibit *Dogwatch and Liberty Days: Seafaring Life in the Nineteenth Century* challenged the romanticism that pervaded maritime history. Curated by historian Margaret Creighton and accompanied by a book, it traveled to New York and Newport News; the Mariners' Museum called its expanded show "one of [its] most popular exhibits ever." Another wing was added in 1988, tripling its space to accommodate the defunct China Trade Museum of Henry Ashton Crosby Forbes. Peabody's Asian export art is still one of the finest collections in the world.[78]

More powerful currents were pushing the institution's course, however. Disturbing many Salemites, the focus of tourism had been shifting to the witchcraft trials and a ghoulish audience around Halloween. Promising a "new paradigm for Salem," the museum wanted to tell "a different story." Because of a recession, increasing costs, and federal cuts in the 1980s, moreover, museums needed more earned income. Dramatically in 1992, the Peabody Museum and Essex Institute merged; their strengths included the former's artifacts and the latter's twenty-six outstanding historic properties. The merger's outcome was left to newly hired executive director, Dan L. Monroe. "It scared me to death," he said, while imagining "a new museum" with a "new institutional culture, goals, and values." But knowing that its annual attendance of 120,000 represented less than one-fifth of Salem's 650,000 yearly visitors, he announced an expansion for the Peabody Essex Museum (PEM).[79]

After expanding its library, storage, and offices, PEM needed more galleries in order to rotate the permanent collection in six-year cycles. When a Boston investment firm offered "an unprecedented $20 million grant," in 1997 PEM controversially proposed building a waterfront satellite museum in Boston. It was predicted to yield "big audiences and well-heeled donors" there, but the city of Salem, which was struggling economically, called it "a fatal heart transplant." While the *Boston Globe* encouraged PEM to stay in Salem, the *Salem Evening News* editorialized: "We can't imagine Salem without its museum." Salem residents lobbied politicians, whose concessions kept the museum in town.[80]

The Peabody Essex Museum was remade by a spectacular 111,000-square-foot wing designed by architect Moshe Safdie. Meant "to evoke a 'Wow!' response from visitors," it increased gallery space to 250,000 square feet. For the first time, separate permanent galleries showed its strengths in holdings from Africa, Native America, Oceania, and contemporary India. It also added "a museological triumph": the two-story, sixteen-bedroom Yin Yu Tang House, built by a wealthy merchant in southeastern China about 1800. Reported the *Globe*, PEM was proving that it was "no longer all about dusty ship figureheads mounted on the walls." The museum was candid about increasing its gate, but Ada Louise Huxtable was conflicted. Admitting that the older museum was "a special favorite" that she "visited often during childhood," she regretted that its wonderful collections were "bypassed for somewhat pedantic [art] scholarship." Yet she conceded that PEM had "used [Safdie's] architecture to recast a city's image and heritage."[81]

Local observers expressed similar ambivalence. As PEM opened a contemporary art exhibit, for example, it showed "an anatomically correct, nude, plastic family of four" to greet visitors; it also ran "a series of radio ads mock[ing] other museums for being a snooze." The *Globe* asked, "Is this any way to run the country's oldest museum?" Salem's mayor, Stanley J. Usovicz Jr., wondered about the shift. Remembering his youthful days standing by the bust of John Paul Jones and imagining global trade, he looked at that nude family and thought, "The Peabody Museum as I knew it was gone." But, he said, it would help Salem "transition from an industrial to [a] tourism-based economy."[82]

Director Monroe's "new museum" introduced a different business model. Whereas 65 percent of its audience had been tourists and 35 percent metropolitan residents, PEM wanted to reverse that number. Stressing art and culture, not history, it wanted to make the residents of Greater Boston repeat visitors. Becoming one of the more highly regarded art museums in the country, its attendance reached about 270,000 in 2018. The museum also focused on building its treasury. When Monroe arrived in 1992, PEM's endowment stood at $23 million, but it rose to $500 million by 2018; its operating budget similarly rose from $3 million to $33 million. As reported in the *Wall Street Journal*, more than half of its expanded operations would be financed by that larger endowment. Few museums could match that figure.[83]

Billed as "the oldest continuously operating museum in the United States," PEM maintained its membership in the Council of American Maritime Museums, but some asked, Was it still a maritime museum? While the maritime historian Benjamin Labaree applauded a broader interpretation of the word "maritime," he noted: "They've broadened to emphasize only the dimension of art," which was "too narrow." So, too, did historian William Fowler, director of the Massachusetts Historical Society, question the shift. "If they had asked me, I would have said, 'Stick to the sea,'" because the older Peabody "was America's great maritime museum."[84]

Partly filling the void, the National Park Service began to interpret more of the historic waterfront, as in its publication of a guidebook that was richly illustrated, textually informative, and a model of its handbooks. After a $28 million federal investment, it also opened a visitor center across the street from PEM in 1994. To picture an East Indiaman in Salem's days of empire, Congress funded $4.5 million (with another $1.5 in private money) to build the 171-foot *Friendship of Salem* for its empty Derby Wharf. An NPS superintendent in Boston rebutted, however, that the park service "should not be in the shipbuilding business." Salem Maritime National Historic Site included what was called "the last remaining waterfront complex representative of America's early maritime era," but its re-created ship came when San Francisco's real NPS fleet was starved for cash and sinking (see chapter 5). The park's interpretation repeated popular myths but said little about Salem's impact on distant cultures. While picturing Nathaniel Bowditch as a typical commoner who rose through the ranks, for example, it left unmentioned the fact that the rise was made possible by the French War and undone by the hardening racial, ethnic, and class barriers of antebellum America.[85] (See fig. 5.)

To celebrate the EIMS bicentennial in 1999, the Peabody Essex Museum held "a procession of costumed historical characters," a chantey singalong, and an 1825-style banquet. But despite its hefty endowment in 2002, the museum scuttled its six-decades-old *American Neptune*. Still, its maritime holdings were impressive, with a 3,000-strong permanent collection of marine paintings that was "generally regarded as one of the finest in the country." It also periodically staged special maritime shows. But the museum's identity had shifted. While Ernest Dodge admitted that EIMS mariners "were interested only in trade," Monroe insisted that "this was never a museum about international trade."[86] (See fig. 6.)

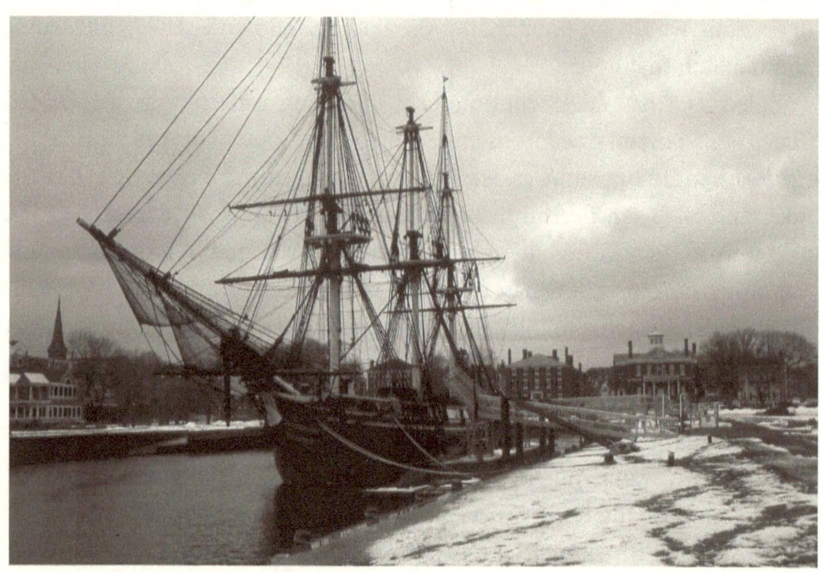

FIGURE 5. Salem Maritime National Historic Site, *Friendship of Salem* (1996) at Derby Wharf. In the background, note the Custom House (with cupola) and the Benjamin W. Crowninshield House (center, 1810–12), which was later owned by Captain Robert Brookhouse. *Photo by author, 2008.*

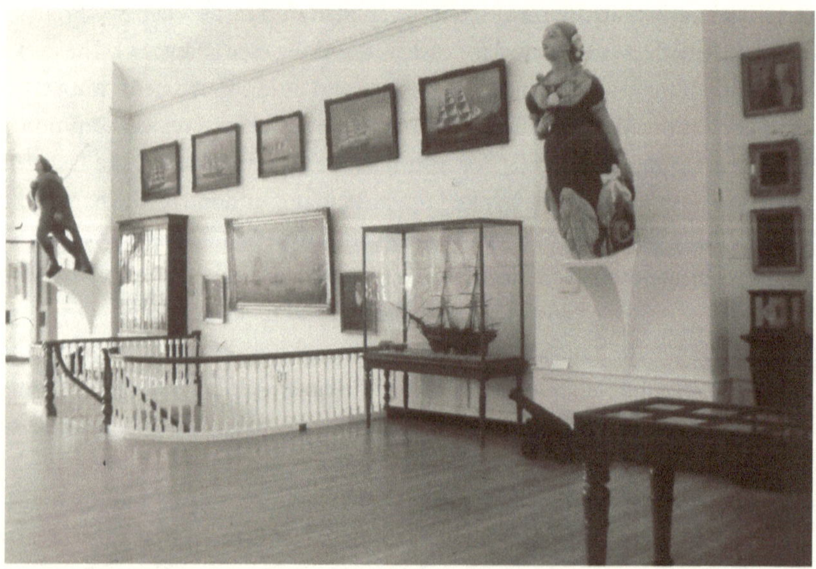

FIGURE 6. East India Marine Room. *Photo by author, 1992.*

CONCLUSION: "AN INTENSELY HYBRID AFFAIR"

Privileging art and culture, PEM is what the *New York Times* called "an intensely hybrid affair." It is the nation's oldest museum, having evolved from a cabinet of curiosities to an institution focusing on natural history and ethnology, then maritime history, and today cultural aesthetics. Each phase has a tale to tell. But for *Preserving Maritime America*, the cabinet sets the story: its mariners and their collections, interactions, and legacy. Their cabinet lives on, but its place in nineteenth- and twentieth-century society is misrepresented or little understood. While it seemed like an odd jumble to some observers, the cabinet was instead a highly personalized, multilayered display; the meaning of an artifact varied from its creator to its donor and to observer as it traveled across time and cultures. To the mariner who donated the curiosity, it told of his adventures and perspective; it encouraged museumgoers to think of distant empires and people.[87]

Individual mariners and patrons donated distinct items, often for reasons unique to themselves, but the museum blended those artifacts, and from that synergy emerged an image that could have been quite different from the intent of the patron-mariner. Yet those curiosities reinforced the fantasies and myths that circulated through Western society about the rich, bizarre, or dangerous cultures in faraway lands. As westerners extended their global authority, those representations justified the imposition of order by allegedly superior people. Imperial powers have commonly used *representations* of foreign cultures not simply as a means for legitimizing and celebrating their control but also as a lens through which the home population can view "the other" as inferior. Stripped of their original context, floating in a vacuum, and lacking ethnographic understanding, those representations, as once displayed in the museum, were rarely sympathetic or realistic. From a nineteenth-century Salem perspective, what most mattered was not the social or cultural meaning of, say, curiosities from China and India but the fact that its mariners had been there, brought them home, and enticed friends and families to imagine their empire.

In the early years of the nineteenth century, the East India Museum played an especially important role in gradually reorienting New England's economy from the confines of British mercantilism to the seemingly unlimited opportunities of global markets. As Salem mariners reached the Orient, they not only brought Yankee ways that altered traditional patterns but also returned with consumer goods and curiosities, wrapped in an aura of enlightenment, empire, and exotica. The artifacts, parades, and rhetoric associated with their museum exaggerated the wealth of the East Indies, romanticized its conquest, and often inaccurately represented its people. Still, the museum was a vital link between the domestic and imperial cultures of New England.

Shifting from its historical and maritime focus, PEM's pursuit of aesthetics and what Huxtable called pedantic art scholarship illustrates more than an attempt to redefine Salem. It is an unvarnished pursuit, almost reflective of King Derby, of bigger markets, returns, and stature. As we'll see in subsequent chapters, museums will periodically recalibrate their focus, shift their direction, and seek a broader audience, but rarely does that involve such a dramatic change. Today, PEM is not strictly a maritime museum, but it does stage intriguing shows with its rich maritime holdings. Initially regretting the shift to art and culture, William Fowler revisited PEM with a group of students in 2016. While the galleries for two visiting art shows "were crowded," he said, East India Hall and the Maritime Gallery "were completely empty." Though lamenting "the eclipse of maritime history at PEM," he noted: "The institution is thriving!" As such, it can only be hoped that another day will bring a brighter light on maritime history, perhaps with the opening of a new forty-thousand-square-foot wing in 2019.[88]

CHAPTER 2

"FROM PURSUIT TO PRESERVATION"

The New Bedford Whaling Museum

Like the East India Marine Society in 1825, the Old Dartmouth Historical Society (ODHS) of New Bedford, Massachusetts, dedicated a new building in a 1916 ceremony. Resembling Salem's Custom House, the Bourne Whaling Museum centered round a half-scale replica of *Lagoda*, the favored bark of Jonathan Bourne Jr., who owned it from 1841 to 1886. It was the largest ship model ever built under a roof. Officiating was William Wallace Crapo, an ODHS founder who underscored one fact: New Bedford had been "the foremost whaling port of the world." At its midcentury zenith, it sent 329 vessels to sea and employed over ten thousand men. Of the "score or more of managing owners," Bourne and his twenty-four ships dominated an "exceptionally prosperous" empire. While millionaires were being disparaged as robber barons during the Progressive Era, Lieutenant Governor Calvin Coolidge commended Bourne's "business sagacity and ability."[1]

Folk scholar Francis Barton Gummere also spoke. Rebutting Herman Melville's picture of whaling as a "disreputable pursuit," he not only praised the "courage, resourcefulness, agility, clear eye, and steady nerve" of whalers but also cursed "the deplorable fad of blackwashing our past and deprecating old types of manhood." He commanded: "Let us rather idealize them." That was the museum's mission. Whaling's legacy, said Crapo, could not be "entrusted to the city government" with its intrigue. Instead, the ODHS museum would recount whaling's "romance and tragedy" and assemble "the most complete and perfect collection of whaling data in the world."

Such inspiration, stated Coolidge, fostered "good citizenship." That became public policy in 1996 when this private museum—the best of its kind worldwide—became the nucleus of the New Bedford Whaling National Historical Park (NBWNHP).[2]

What is most revealing about the museum's development is the complex process of constructing a public history. A few years before that 1916 ceremony, the Old Dartmouth Historical Society (est. 1903) was moribund and split between members who valued colonial history and those who stressed whaling's fame and fortune. Then, Emily Bourne's gift of a building and its ship redefined the ODHS and set her father's reputation. By headlining Bourne, the museum emphasized New Bedford's entrepreneurs and their global reach. Meanwhile, it focused solely on Yankees, though they had been largely absent in whaling's closing decades. Moreover, while emphasizing New Bedford's preindustrial era, the ODHS turned a blind eye to the fact that whaling had been intertwined with factories and imitated their harsh regimen. In so doing, it dodged the controversial forces behind global capitalism that compromised traditionalism's much-prized individualism, including the industry's advancing technology, inequitable wages, and declining investment.

The ODHS's story became the city's official history, but it contrasted with the real New Bedford of 1916—a mill town populated by darker-skinned immigrants living in poverty and a diaspora. Beginning in the 1970s, however, the story slowly shifted with movements promoting civil rights, the new social history, environmentalism, and historic preservation. In the process, the museum was remade for another era, focusing on a community of once-marginalized people, a historic district, and the endangered mammals whose annihilation it once extolled.

"WE LIGHT THE WORLD": NEW BEDFORD AS WHALING'S METROPOLIS

As New Bedford's whaling declined, its advocates were remaking its past. Zephaniah W. Pease, for one, cherished his Yankee roots and headed the museum. A descendant of *Mayflower*'s John Howland, he was the town's most influential newspaper editor from 1894 to 1933. The *Boston Globe* called him "the best informed man on the history and lore of the whaling industry." As whaling waned, he said, local residents felt duty-bound "to rear monuments to the men who brought fame and opulence to the city." Disconcerting to many was the waxing of textile mills and foreign workers, which led to the loss of the city's "pleasant shaded streets, its quiet prosperous homes," and "its old time population of sturdy [Yankee] men and women." One female antiquary rued, "We of an older generation regret this passing."[3]

Called Dartmouth in 1664, the region at the mouth of the Acushnet River on Buzzard's Bay was settled by English dissenters. A century later, Joseph Russell III, the town's founder, convinced Joseph Rotch to move his Nantucket whaling business to the protected, deepwater harbor. After U.S. independence, the newly incorporated town of New Bedford grew at the expense of Nantucket, the world's whaling capital since the 1730s. However, the ravages of periodic war in the four decades after 1775 took their toll on both towns and their fleets. With peace in 1815, global whaling shifted. While Nantucket waned because of harbor silt and England's fleet was not competitive, New Bedford became the world's largest whaling port.[4]

New Bedford's business-minded Quakers included the Rotch, Rodman, Russell, and Howland families. As their square-rigged tonnage equaled Nantucket's in 1823 and almost doubled by 1830, the nature of whaling changed. What began in Nantucket as "family-based operations" evolved into New Bedford's impersonal, joint-stock companies. Yet competition arose. By 1835, nearly thirty U.S. towns were sending out ships, and by 1860 nearly fifty. In 1856, in the Tenth U.S. Customs District, of which New Bedford was the administrative center, there were 418 whaling vessels, including those of neighboring Fairhaven. Whaling became the third largest business in Massachusetts. Between 1850 and 1860, there were over six hundred U.S. whaling vessels scouring the globe; their owners extended hunts from two to four or five years.[5]

New Bedford became whaling's showcase. After the British burned its port in the War of 1812, the town rebuilt. In 1835, Charles Francis Adams, the son and grandson of U.S. presidents, wrote that New Bedford "has lately risen like magic." By 1843, it was the nation's fourth-largest port in tonnage. Melville published *Moby-Dick* in 1851, but his novel became the world's most famous whaling tale only a half century later. He wrote, "Nowhere in all America will you find more patrician-like houses; parks and gardens more opulent." A web of interrelated families controlled the town through whaling, banking, insurance, and marine supply. Beginning mostly as Quakers, those families split to the gain of Unitarians and Congregationalists. As in the case of Charles W. Morgan, the builder and first owner of the eponymous ship, they solidified their standing by capitalizing on European scientific learning.[6]

In 1848, a year after New Bedford incorporated as a city of sixteen thousand, its citizens saw their empire portrayed in a *Grand Panorama of a Whaling Voyage around the World*. The eight-and-one-half-foot-high painting on muslin ran 1,275 feet; its four sections were rolled from cylinder to cylinder in a two-hour showing. Later viewing across the East and Midwest, it was based on sketches by Benjamin Russell, which were translated by painter Caleb Purrington. Melville reportedly saw it in Boston and used it to imagine *Moby-Dick*. "Accurate in its delineations, and beautiful in its execution," opined the *Boston Post* in 1849, it was shown again in New Bedford in 1886 and at Coney Island before being donated to the ODHS, which initially dismissed it as folk art. Also exuding Yankee pride, New Bedford's city hall (1852) displayed its seal with the motto, "*Lucem Diffundo*" (translated locally as "We light the world"). The U.S. whaling flotilla reached its apogee of 736 ships in 1864, but only eighteen towns were left in the business. Three disasters then hit New Bedford: in 1865, at least twenty-five ships were destroyed by Confederate raiders; in 1871, Arctic ice crushed twenty-two, and in 1876, another dozen. The industry's death knell was sounded by competition from rapeseed oil and petroleum, but whale oil was still used for tanning leather and making soap, margarine, and cooking oils. The market for whalebone, which had been used for making stays in corsets, carriage whips, and umbrellas, was undercut by spring steel. Nantucket quit its fishery in 1870.[7]

From 1876 to 1880, New Bedford controlled almost 89 percent of U.S. whaling tonnage, but its capitalists were shifting investments to higher-earning textiles and moving most of their fleets to San Francisco. There, smaller ships and barks, including *Charles W. Morgan* (1841), were profitable as San Francisco became the nation's chief whaling port. By 1890, New Bedford's textile industry was attracting 70 percent of its capital. From 1896 to 1900, its share of whaling tonnage resultantly fell to 18 percent as it relied on old ships and sweated labor. As Norway took over whaling, the U.S. fleet shrank to under one hundred hulls after 1890 and still further by the early 1900s. When the ODHS was founded in 1903, recalled booster Clifford Ashley, "wrinkly-eyed old men paced the wharves gazing seaward, and every day was hushed as a Sabbath morning." All told, 733 whalers had sailed out of New Bedford, of which 30 percent were lost at sea; more than 2,700 vessels had once comprised the entire U.S. whaling fleet.[8]

By then, the remaking of memory had begun. A key figure was New Bedford's most respected citizen, W. W. Crapo. After attending Harvard Law School and establishing a local practice, he rose to the highest circles of the Republican Party. Like antimodernist elites elsewhere, he endorsed the new order while romancing the old. From 1889 to 1918, he served as president of the city's first textile factory, Wamsutta Mills (1846). Founded by retired whaling master Abraham Howland, it was by 1892 "the largest cotton weaving plant in the world." Wamsutta attracted capital retreating from whaling so that, as economist Dan Georgianna concluded, "the same merchant families controlled the finance and commerce of the city." In 1890, the city was third nationally in the number of spindles and fourth in looms. By World War I, it was the largest center of U.S. cotton textile manufacturing. According to Yankee critics, its foreign-born laborers only slowly learned their traditions of self-reliance and self-respect. Challenging the city's laissez-faire capitalism, which rationalized their exploitation, mill hands won the town's sympathy during the strike of 1898. But the mayor recognized the mill owners' power, read the riot act, and the strike failed.[9]

Remaking memories, painters re-created old-time scenes that had vanished, such as William Allen Wall's *Birth of the Whaling Industry* (1853). His painting of the business district, *Old Four Corners* (ca. 1855), became a popular lithograph, *New Bedford Fifty Years Ago*. Near that corner of Union and Water Streets, a later building became home to the ODHS. As Yankees used the Colonial Revival movement to document their founding of and primacy in New England, New Bedford also honored Dartmouth's own founder, Bartholomew Gosnold, who landed on Cuttyhunk Island in 1602, eighteen miles to the south. By the late nineteenth century, however, the sole Cuttyhunk vestige of "the first white settler's house," lamented a reporter, had been abandoned and was "a chicken-roost." In 1902, therefore, Yankees marked the tercentenary of Gosnold's landing with a seventy-foot stone tower, which the ODHS later acquired.[10]

Meanwhile, Crapo stoked Yankees' historical consciousness. Speaking to the Unity Club in 1903, he predicted that the formation of a historical society would cultivate "a greater spirit of loyalty and a greater affection for our homes." Population trends were alarming. In 1890, the city numbered 40,773; it doubled by 1900, but the "old stock [was] seriously diminishing." Those Yankees comprised less than 20 percent. As immigration swelled, the largest group, the equatorial Portuguese, drew the most attention because of their color and culture. By 1912 they included twelve thousand Cape

Verdeans in southeastern Massachusetts who spoke Creole (*Crioulo*), kept to their own ranks, and retained their traditions and Catholicism. Of mixed Portuguese-Negro-Berber stock, they were more darkly complected than Portugal's Azorean immigrants. Arriving on packet ships, the Portuguese crowded into tenements near the mills. Though New Bedford had "welcomed these aliens from every quarter of the world," Crapo rued, "they know and care little about our early history."[11]

Neither did many Yankees, who had ignored their past. Ellis L. Holland, an *Evening Standard* reporter, told the same Unity Club audience that Yankee whalers had been "the pioneer invaders of the frozen mysteries of the polar seas," but, lacking a historical society, the city neglected its "treasury of romance and adventure." Ship's logbooks, for example, were "the living witnesses of those thrilling adventures," but "tons and tons of them" were discarded and recycled "into wrapping paper." He declared: "It is almost criminal that there is in this city no general museum of the whaling industry." A committee formed to organize the ODHS as a charitable and benevolent corporation, whose focus included, besides New Bedford, the towns of Fairhaven, Acushnet, Dartmouth, and Westport. Elected president, Crapo promised that it would preserve "pleasant memories of the generations who have preceded us."[12]

Crapo suggested that donors give once commonplace things because each had "a tale to tell." Shaped by his era's cardinal belief in the forward stride of American civilization, he wanted to show "the progress of the community and demonstrate the advance in social conditions." Ironically, that progress had jeopardized his old-time culture. His interests, too, were primarily material. Like Henry Ford's later dismissal of written history as bunk, he regarded historical commentaries as typically "cold and severe and often times colored and prejudiced," but "the real life of a people" could be felt through artifacts. Still, ODHS secretary Henry B. Worth wanted diaries and letters, but he thought that some townspeople, who were accustomed to books glorifying great men, did not recognize their forebears' importance. Despite the museum's celebratory intentions, he also wondered if donors would fear publicizing "the foibles and family eccentricities." The ODHS inherited the local mantle of cultural guardian after the New Bedford Lyceum Society (est. 1828) began to disband in 1904. Its demise illustrated the era's cultural shifts as newer institutions, like the ODHS, were less bookish and more geared to popular memory and visual impression.[13]

Opening on February 15, 1904, the museum occupied three large rooms in a building owned by the nativist Masons. One room displayed borrowed artifacts, which had won a gold medal at the London Fisheries Exhibition in 1883 and included what the *Providence (RI) Journal* called "the greatest collection of whaling relics in the world." Another room displayed artifacts of the South Seas and Alaska. The ODHS women used the third room for Colonial-era mementos, such as portraits and lace. At a time of vigorous manhood, nationalism, and Pacific empire, the day's guest speaker praised New Bedford's trailblazers and his sea captain father. Once the exhibition closed, the museum opened on Saturdays and reportedly drew "all sorts and conditions of people, young and old, rich and poor," though mill hands worked on Saturdays. The exuberance of children, particularly their urge to throw a harpoon or work the blubber mincer, worried guides to no end. Out-of-towners visited too. Boston's Old South Historical Society made a pilgrimage in 1905. Those patricians, said historian Dona Brown, "felt stifled in their parlors and libraries" and hoped "to experience some of the dangers and difficulties once faced by hardy pioneers."[14]

In 1906, the ODHS moved to a "large, modern, and commodious" structure, which had been a failed bank and was donated by Henry Huttleston Rogers, a Fairhaven philanthropist and associate of John D. Rockefeller. The adjacent Board of Trade had already fled the deteriorating riverfront. On Water Street, the Rogers Building faced Centre Street, which was "strewn with rubbish," lined with "dilapidated buildings," and ended at Central Wharf's rotting whaleships and Cape Verdean packet ships As bad, the polluted Acushnet River generated the most typhoid fever fatalities in the state in 1908.[15]

The number of artifacts in the Rogers Building multiplied, but the town was "curiously deficient in [some unique] trophies of the whaling chase" after a buyer for the Smithsonian Institution had combed the city. The expanded museum showed whaling implements, "ship models, ship stern boards, [and] fiddle heads and flags that once flew from the lofty mastheads of the whalers." In the center was a regulation-size, thirty-foot, cedar whaleboat, which had been stove by a whale. Another room displayed "a fine exhibit of war clubs, battle axes and ceremonial clubs," and later what curators called "Queer Drums" from the South Seas, Africa, and the Caribbean. A voodoo drum had been "taken from the [Haitian] natives to prevent them using it in religious ceremonies, as a human life was sacrificed in connection with the ceremonies." In contrast, the "suitably furnished" colonial room illustrated an ostensibly superior civilization. In deference to city leaders, a textile room highlighted a spinning wheel and hand loom; their earlier Yankee female operators differed noticeably from the Cape Verdean and Azorean mill workers being photographed by the famed Lewis Hine a mile away. The two thousand annual museum visitors imagined the clash between the old and new societies.[16]

"A DEAD WHALE OR A STOVE BOAT!": CHALLENGING WHALING'S DISREPUTE

As the ODHS approached its tenth year, its future was uncertain. Meetings were not held, and its ten-year assembly was postponed. The doldrums resulted from its limited appeal. Ladies, who were the backbone of historical and preservation societies, were interested in domesticity, not harpoons. Gentlemen were deterred by privatism and business. Whaling's unsavory reputation was another issue. When compared with other sailors, whalers had been exploited more and paid less and were more socially unstable. The Reverend Henry Cheever, who sailed on the whaler *Commodore Preble*, claimed in 1849, for example, that its fo'c'sle was "made up to a great degree . . . of the very refuse of humanity."[17]

No better redeemer of whaling could be found than Clifford Warren Ashley. After growing up along the city's wharves, he left to study art with Howard Pyle. Through his connection to the Brandywine School of Illustrators, Ashley received many commissions, including an illustrated article on whaling for *Harper's Magazine*. Signing on as a mechanic in 1904, he spent six weeks aboard *Sunbeam*, which took three whales. Of the thirty-nine men aboard, only eight were Yankees. The darker-skinned majority were "profane, dissolute, and ignorant," but he called them "as courageous and willing a lot as one could desire." His sketches, said later historian Stuart Frank, were "a kind of fanfare for the common foremast hand." Returning to town to paint and write, he helped design the society's exhibits and interpret their history.[18] (See fig. 7.)

So unlike *Sunbeam*'s reality, Ashley's writings romanticized an earlier Anglo-Saxon era, prompting Frank to call them "naive, myopic, [and] ill informed." Ashley's *The Yankee Whaler* (1926) and *Whaleships of New Bedford* (1929) rebutted the likes of Melville, rejected the modern period, and strove to "make a race of heroes live." He declared: "The Yankee whaleman has written for himself a glorious page in American history. His courage and hardihood are so well attested that his reputation should be secure. But

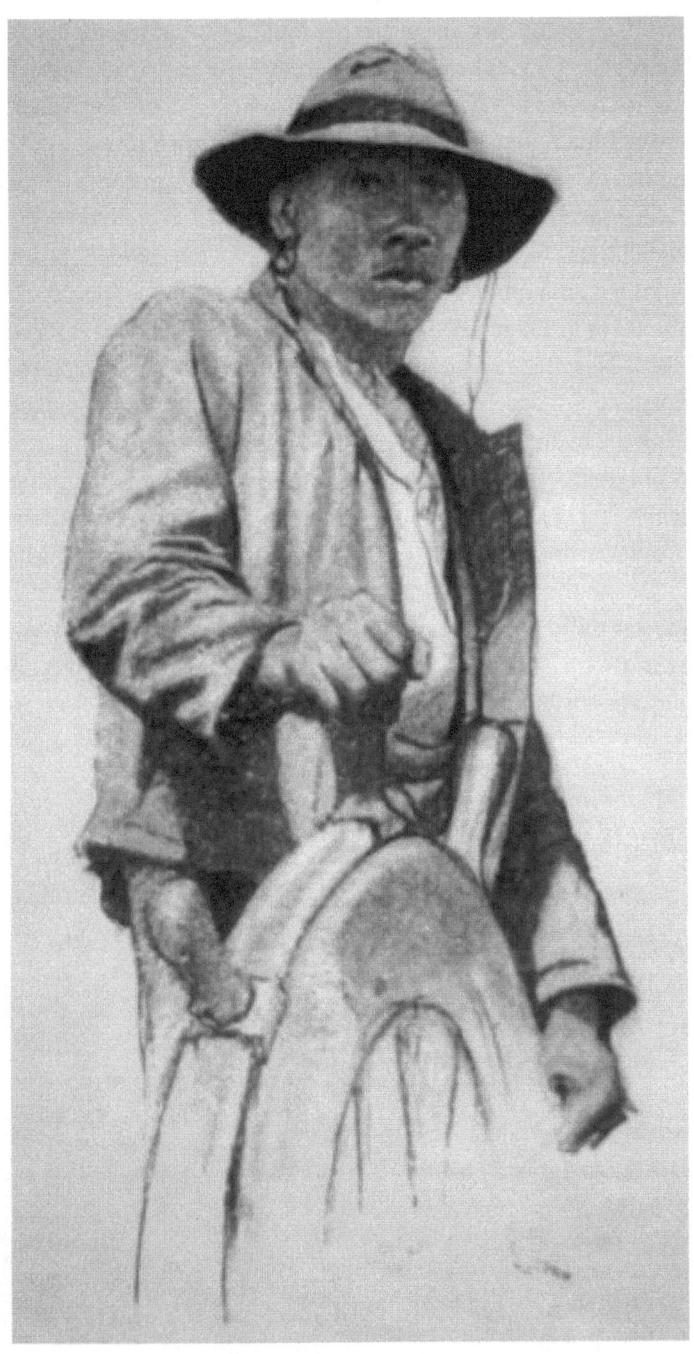

FIGURE 7. *At the Wheel*, Clifford W. Ashley, "The Blubber Hunters," *Harper's New Monthly Magazine*, April 1906, 676.

there has been a tendency among writers of fiction to discredit him. Certain widely circulated books have painted him in false and lurid colors. So long as this was confined to fiction, no great harm was done. But when fiction began to masquerade as fact, and sciolists solemnly borrowed from fiction, labeling their wares 'history,' it was time for some one to come to the rescue of the whaleman's tarnished reputation. I have endeavored to correct some of these fallacies." Central to that redemption, the museum's friends remade the tale of whaling and its crew. They were captivated by the "golden" age from the 1820s to the 1850s. Ashley worked in tandem with Pease, who pictured 1850s New Bedford as "a haunt of perfect peace." They repaired whaling's image to enhance the prestige of local families, foster Yankee pride, and shape the region's identity.[19]

This remaking was spurred by Crapo, who financed the sculpting of *The Whaleman* (fig. 8). Unveiled in 1913 before thousands of spectators, the $25,000, eleven-foot-tall bronze statue of a harpooner in his whaleboat was placed outside the Free Public Library (1837), which had been called "the handsomest building in New England devoted to civic purpose." There, pedestrians were "reminded of the rugged sailors who made New Bedford possible." Nearby buildings buttressed that message. Two blocks toward the

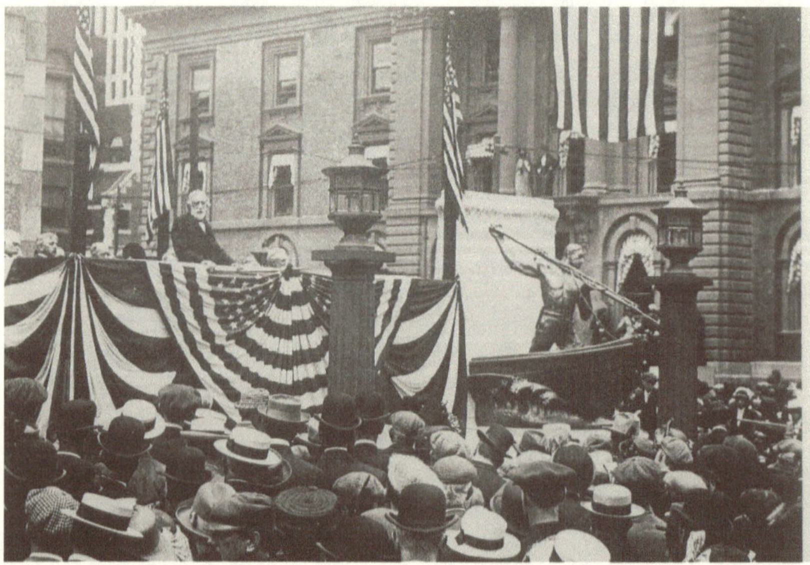

FIGURE 8. Dedication of the Whaleman Statue, 1913. Standing on the stage is W. W. Crapo. *Courtesy Bela Lyon Pratt Archives (no longer available online).*

river, the Custom House (1834–36) was one of the finest Greek Revival edifices designed by Robert Mills, the architect of the Washington Monument. Around the corner were the Mariner's Home (built 1795 and moved 1851) and the Seamen's Bethel (1832). Both were owned by the New Bedford Port Society, founded in 1830 for the moral improvement of seamen. The Bethel was made famous in *Moby-Dick*, which introduced its fictional pastor, Father Mapple.[20]

A student of sculptor Augustus Saint-Gaudens, Bela Lyon Pratt created *The Whaleman*, saying it was "the most interesting thing I have ever tackled." His image of the boatsteerer (harpooner) as a Yankee generated debate. The city's oldest whaling firm had suggested that Pratt "model a native of the Cape Verde Islands." They could be, noted *The Real Story of the Whaler*, as "black as ebony, but hardworking, industrious, and good whalers." Mindful of New England's changing complexion, Samuel Eliot Morison complained, however, that they were "the most numerous alien element in the Old Colony." They also were "ignorant of the hardships and struggles" of Yankee founders, added ODHS committee chair and later mayor Walter H. B. Remington. "The [American] eagle should scream a little," he told the ODHS, "to make an impression on the minds of these foreigners."[21]

With Anglo-Saxonism threatened, race was the issue. Pease's *Mercury* rejected copying *Moby-Dick*'s boatsteerers—the Polynesian Queequeg, the Gay Head Indian Tashtego, or the African Daggoo—because they were not "God-fearing men" or "typical of the glorious host of whalemen who made the fame of New Bedford." Pratt admitted that Crapo wanted to mark "the whaling industry which he had known in his boyhood." Echoing the myth of the self-made Yankee, Crapo praised the golden era's "strong, venturesome, ambitious men" who worked up the ladder from boatsteerer to master, ship owner, and beyond. Criticizing his own overly civilized peers, as was common, he lauded whalers who "had been reared in a school which made them neither narrow-minded nor timid."[22]

Chiseled on the monument's granite wall was Melville's line, "A dead whale or a stove boat!" The *Mercury* recommended that the slogan be "inscribed in the schoolroom and on the wall of the bed chamber of the youth of New Bedford," as it underscored old values allegedly in decline. Just as philosopher William James sought an alternative to war in shaping manhood, whaling was, said one captain, paradoxically, "a field for soldierly courage purged of soldierly brutality." Old Dartmouth Historical Society president Edmund Wood made the same point. A *Mayflower* descendant, he had sailed aboard the whaler *Eliza Adams*. That made him "a truer son of New Bedford," he felt, but whaling had fallen into a "sad decadence" with the "new appliances" of killing used by alien crews.[23]

The ODHS escaped the doldrums by hiring Frank Wood (Edmund's brother) in 1915 as its first full-time curator. Hearing that Emily Bourne wanted to memorialize her father, he appropriated her idea. Since 1905—when the ODHS adopted its seal depicting a stove boat, boatsteerer, and whale—it had spotlighted whaling, and her $150,000 gift set it in the building's new brick. Just where to build the Bourne Whaling Museum was the first question. As the old waterfront decayed, the city's commerce was moving westward, pressuring its once-fine antebellum structures. On Second Street, the Third District Court of Bristol, which was built as a bank by Russell Warren in 1853, abandoned its Greek Revival home in 1914; the mansion of Quaker Benjamin Rodman had been encased by storefronts. On a block to the east on Bethel Street (later, Johnny Cake Hill), the ODHS and Bourne purchased a row of three-story, early nineteenth-century wooden buildings. Part of the Progressive Era's moral cleansing, their demolition displaced boardinghouses, brothels, and saloons. The organization's new headquarters was styled in the Georgian Revival by Boston architect Henry Vaughan (fig. 9). Its octagonal cupola included a sperm whale weathervane. Looking west, it rose above the Bethel; looking east was the waterfront's busy trade in cotton and coal.[24]

The ODHS spent one year and over $20,000 crafting *Lagoda* (fig. 10). A colonnaded gallery wrapped around three sides of the model's fifty-foot-high mainmast. Its name was a misspelling of Russia's Lake Ladoga, but the ship was left as carved because, as different stories go, sailors deemed it unlucky to change the name or the thrifty owner did not want to pay a new registration fee. The model became a stage on which to tell of whaling's adventure. Though Ashley admitted that real whaleships looked worn and ragged after extended cruises, the model was shipshape. The eighty-nine-foot *Lagoda* was built by the last whale craftsmen "down to the most minute details of construction." Yet it deleted the tryworks, whose smoke, sweat, and smell were notorious miles away. Moreover, no photograph or blueprint existed of the original ship. Instead, architect Edgar B. Hammond relied on the Custom House file and the bark *Charles W. Morgan*, which had returned to Fairhaven in 1906. Speculating on the rigging, he conceded, "There is no one left [who] can say you are wrong." Still, as historian George

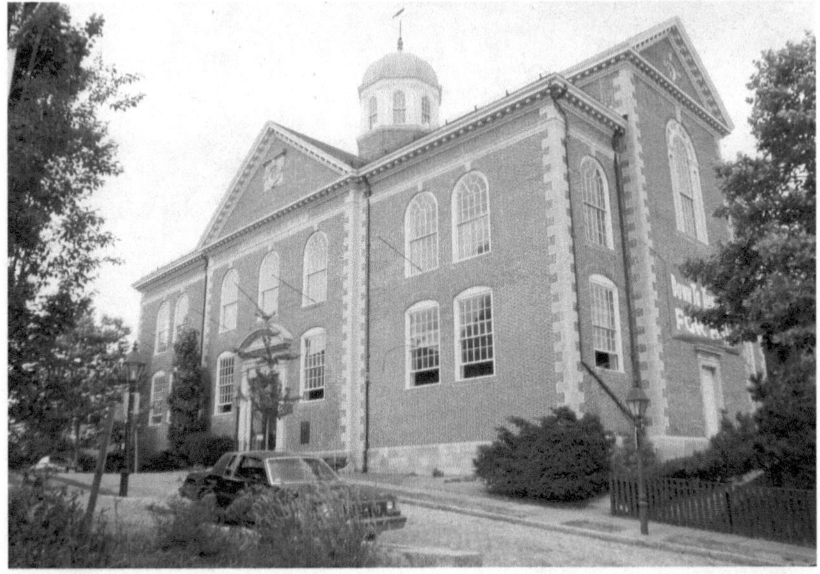

FIGURE 9. ODHS, Bourne Whaling Museum. *Photo by author, 1993.*

Sarton joked, "The half-sized model is . . . ready to sail on a *greasy* voyage, if half-sized seamen could be found to man her."[25]

Nearby stood a bronze tablet and bust of Jonathan Bourne. Its creator, Gutzon Borglum, a prominent New York sculptor who had just accepted a commission for a grandiose neo-Confederate carving in Georgia, attended the dedication with his wife, Mary, a friend of Emily Bourne. The museum stressed Bourne's entrepreneurial record. From 1841 to 1886, *Lagoda* had made twelve voyages with net profits of $651,958.99. Crapo praised his former associate, saying, "We should not forget the men . . . who risked their fortunes in the ventures." The 1916 context was unmistakable, as risky investments and voyages (bank loans to and trade with England and France) were pulling a neutral United States into World War I. Long dedicated to open seas and market expansion, museum leaders used the building's dedication to support those embattled nations. While Crapo criticized the likes of antiwar senator Robert La Follette (R-WI) for allegedly hampering trade and discouraging "the display of the nation's flag on the ocean," Oliver Prescott, a partner in his law firm and later an ODHS officer, lauded French efforts "to preserve the liberties of all the peoples of Europe, yes and of the whole

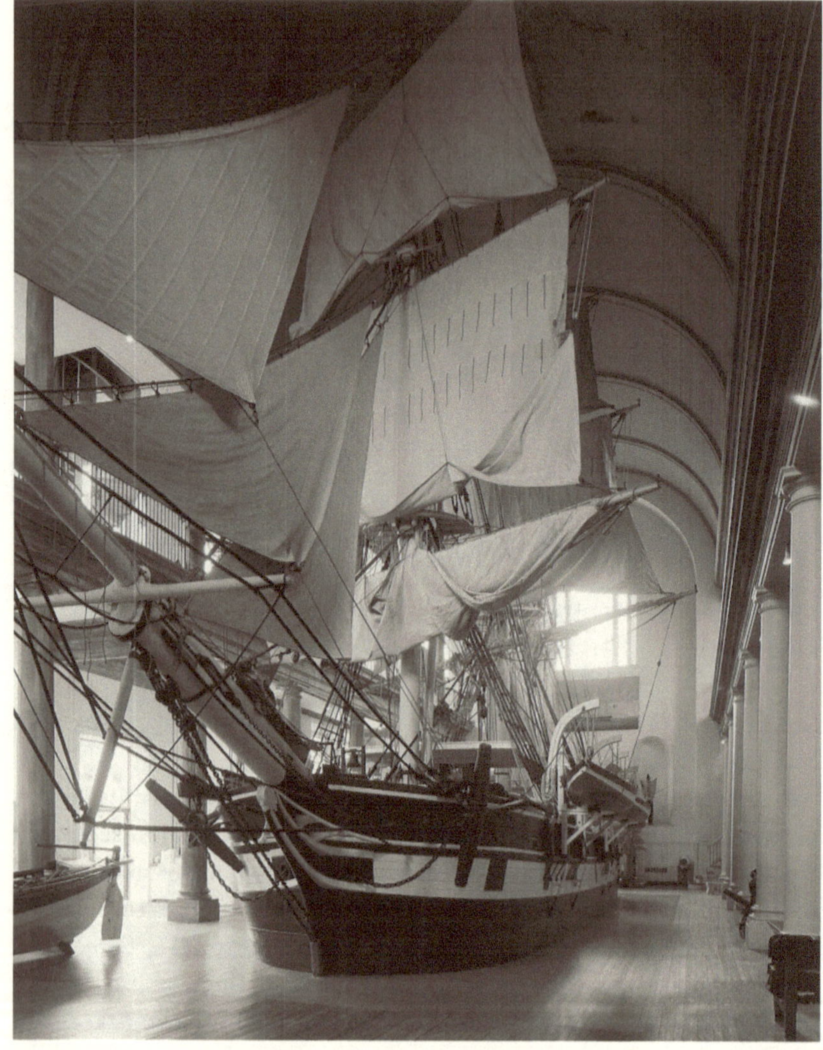

FIGURE 10. *Lagoda. Photographs in the Carol M. Highsmith Archive, Prints and Photographs Division, Library of Congress.*

world." *Lagoda* also became a platform after the war. During the Pilgrim Tercentenary in 1920, a clergyman lambasted Senator Henry Cabot Lodge (R-MA) for blocking President Wilson's League of Nations, for which "the prophets and seers and poets . . . have prayed since the beginning of time."[26]

Typical of antimodernism, the ODHS debated its mix of tradition and progress. Recalling whaling's decline, Edmund Wood claimed that New

Bedford, like Nantucket and Salem, was "drifting into that stagnant life, the chief occupation of which was to recall the glories of the past, and to worship it." He praised the investors who turned from whaling to textiles, which peaked in 1924 with seventy mills and 41,630 workers. Still, Clifford Ashley cursed the toll taken by those factories, whose chimneys "belch forth blackened smoke" and whose "wooden tenement houses" dominated "three quarters of [the city's] outlying settled area." He sneered, "This was called progress." Yet, he saw "real commercial value" in the port's "old charm," and the ODHS capitalized on the postwar commercialization of history. As transportation improved, income increased, and angst intensified, more Yankees of property and standing were nostalgically seeking legendary New England. With tourism heavy in July and August, the *New York Times* advised in 1928: "No one should fail to visit the whaling museum, as it is the only one of its kind in the world."[27]

Having "very little money," the ODHS monetized a remade past. At a Mardi Gras party in 1919, for example, "red and blue electric lights blazed" aboard *Lagoda*, whose ocean-blue-painted perimeter accommodated "dancers on the slippery waters." The 250 partygoers sang chanties, savored punch (during Prohibition), and enjoyed the gallery of Ashley sketches. They boarded *Lagoda* "to see how the inside of a whaler looked." Another program, "An Evening around the Ship," made an era golden. While the nation reverberated with postwar strikes and anxiety in 1919, actors dressed merrily in costumes of 1857 (though it was a depression year) and presented two fanciful skits. The first included *Lagoda*'s departure with tearful goodbyes, while a man was being "shanghaied"; the second idealized a night "with the 'Old Man' pacing the quarter deck, and the sailors doing scrimshaw work and singing chanties." Oddly, it included a sanitized cutting-in of a whale, which in reality was bloody, disgusting, and dangerous as the carcass could burst.[28]

Other occasions followed, as in 1922, when the motion picture *Down to the Sea in Ships* premiered at a local theater. Set in 1850s New Bedford and shot aboard *Morgan* (for deck scenes), the bark *Wanderer* (for sailing), and the schooner *Gaspe* (for the hunt), the silent film depicted the life of Quaker whaling merchants. New Bedford's leading whaling families subsidized the shoot, appeared in the film, and used costumes from their attics. Its actors included Clara Bow (before becoming the "It Girl"). It was shown around the world. Twentieth Century Fox sponsored a "gam" at the museum, drawing four hundred in old-fashioned costumes. More Americans were also reading *Moby-Dick*, which had not been widely circulated until the 1920s. Its film version in 1930 included sound.[29]

"ONE OF THE GREATEST SPORTS KNOWN TO MAN": REPRESENTING WHALERS AND WHALING

With *Lagoda* as a backdrop, museum leaders crafted a mythology that sometimes gave whalers their due but often revised the story through omission or misrepresentation. Old-time whaling was recast as more a test of a man's prowess than a profit-driven industry. Featuring the "golden era" in a 1924 exhibit, curator Arthur C. Watson called it "one of the greatest sports known to man." Its "supreme moment" was harpooning "the monster," though Charles W. Morgan had told a New Bedford assembly in 1830 of the sperm whale's timidity and attempts to avoid humans. Once the iron pierced its skin, the famed Nantucket sleighride began as the whale tried to escape with the whaleboat in tow. A stove boat could mean the crew's death. It ended when "the whale rolled over on his side, dead."[30]

Admiring this man-against-monster combat, Watson deplored the new technology, whose bomb guns "practically butchered" the whale. Cast in brass, the gun shot a projectile that exploded inside the whale. Modern hunters also used shoulder-held guns. Because they were usually shot from the main ship, the Nantucket sleighride became a thing of the past. Inspired by the ODHS, the popular author and illustrator Gordon Grant so detested the new technology that he omitted bomb guns in *Greasy Luck* (1932), whose original sketches he gave to the museum. Reflecting the postwar trauma, he said, "They savour too much of modern methods and wholesale slaughter."[31]

Not only did that hand-thrown iron represent a once vigorous manhood, the scrap whalebone was used to craft scrimshaw. As described in *Moby-Dick*, some whalers had "little boxes of dentistical-looking implements, specially intended for the skrimshandering business. But, in general, they toil with their jackknives alone; and, with that almost omnipotent tool of the sailor, they will turn you out anything you please, in the way of a mariner's fancy." Later unappreciated, scrimshaw was discarded or relegated to dusty shelves, but the Colonial Revival movement roused interest. Over the years, the museum developed the world's largest collection. Ashley called scrimshaw the "one enduring monument" of whaling and "the only important indigenous folk art, except that of the Indians, we have ever had in America." He claimed that it declined when "Yankee sailors gave way to foreigners in the service." Yet, indigenous it was not. Europeans had begun the art, while New Bedford sailors learned from Asians, Polynesians, and Native Americans.[32]

Picturing scrimshaw as an atavism, Pease repeated *Moby-Dick*'s Ishmael that whalers had returned to their folk roots over their "long exile from Christendom and civilization." In Victorian America, they were thus freed from women's domesticity and its restraints on men. Believing, like many, that the wilds of nature reshaped a man, Pease and Ishmael claimed that "your true whale hunter is as much a savage as an Iroquois." But Pease saw differences. While an Iroquoian war club exhibited an aborigine's violence, scrimshaw revealed the Yankee's inner salvation. "Often with skill and imagination," he wrote, "these engravings were wrought with the patience and loving care which the monks of old devoted to the illumination of the missal." For Pease, a Yankee's soul was productive, while the other's was destructive.[33]

The scrimshander's earlier scenes of a ship or whale hunt gave way, as home life became sacred for Victorians, to his "dreams of fair women." The whaler reputedly "lavished his most sentimental regard, and limned his most inspired pictures" on the busk for the corset. Of the museum's many busks, one read:

> This bone once in a sperm whale's jaw did rest,
> Now 'tis intended for a woman's breast.
> This my love I do intend
> For you to wear and not to bend.

Rough-and-tumble whalers could even express submission, as in a three-inch-high creation made from whale teeth. "The Proposal of Marriage" depicted a whaler on bended knee before his betrothed. Ironically, such submission was uncertain once men returned home, because their long absences had left their wives more self-reliant. Interestingly, the women who received these pieces, said historian Lisa Norling, made no mention of them in their writings. The jagging wheel, which was used to cut pastry, most revealed the home's civilizing influence. It was, said Ashley, "the *magnum opus* of every scrimshander." Frank Wood donated his collection of 150 jagging wheels in 1924. The craft included a masculine side. While Pease whimsically wanted Captain Ahab's fictional ivory leg, some scrimshaw became a manly "trophy of the whale-hunt."[34]

The ODHS highlighted Yankees, but the crew had changed between 1825 and 1830. "Provincialism and homogeneity gave way to cosmopolitanism and heterogeneity," the economist Elmo Paul Hohman wrote in his magisterial study, *The American Whaleman* (1928). Gay Head Indians and African Americans had regularly appeared from 1800 to 1820. Because of New Bedford's hospitable reputation and booming economy, it attracted blacks seeking opportunity. By 1843, a few whaling ships included 30–40 percent who were "black" (or had "wooly" hair). One estimate calculated that over three thousand African Americans worked on New Bedford vessels from 1803 to 1860; some experienced "a relative equality." But only 20 percent chose to make a second voyage. Reflecting landed society, racism became more open on the sea after 1830. Wages for African Americans decreased so that, contrary to Samuel Morison's claim that New England "never had a deep-sea proletariat," people of color fell into debt slavery. Charles S. Raleigh added a painting, *A Fighting Sperm Whale* (1879), to the ODHS collection; it depicted a black man aboard a stove boat in the clenches of his prey.[35]

After a Westport monument honored Captain Paul Cuffe (or Cuffee), the museum's guidebook, which Pease produced, devoted two pages to the black Quaker. Born in 1759 on Cuttyhunk to a freed slave from Ghana and a Wampanoag mother, Cuffe began as a whaleman. He then built, operated, and owned seven commercial vessels, which relied on black hands. Becoming the region's most famous and wealthiest African American merchant of the early nineteenth century, he was the first black in Massachusetts to gain civil equality. He also built "the first public school in America" for children of all colors and classes. Yet few other qualified black men experienced similar opportunities, given the era's racism.[36]

By the 1850s, undermanned ships in the Pacific were recruiting dark-skinned Kanakas because they were regarded as loyal and docile. United States–flagged vessels were legally required to carry crews that were two-thirds American, but captains did otherwise. In 1870, Bourne's *Lagoda* signed on twenty-three Kanakas, who, like other men of color, seldom rose above boatsteerer. They arrived in New Bedford where, as a clergyman told the ODHS, Yankees tried to change the "heathen," but "did not meet with very good success." Their presence riled Melville, who wrote that "in New Bedford, actual cannibals stand chatting at street corners; savages outright; many of whom yet carry on their bones holy flesh. It makes a stranger stare." But, future mayor Walter Remington gladly reminded the ODHS that they "did not come to stay."[37]

Shipmasters also viewed the Portuguese (Azoreans and Cape Verdeans) as cheap, manipulable hands. In 1856, the Azoreans were, said a writer, "held in great esteem by ship owners and captains, but [were] often despised by their shipmates in the forecastle." Melville derided the Cape Verdeans. By the 1860s Portuguese made up 20 percent of crews and over 35 percent in the 1880s; by 1900 they, along with blacks, dominated the fo'c'sle. By then, Cape Verdeans and Azoreans also captained over half of New Bedford's fleet.[38]

While remaking the image of whaling, museum leaders celebrated the work and community that existed in earlier Nantucket more than in later New Bedford. In Nantucket, where a communal ethic controlled work and society, men typically went whaling for a few voyages before settling down on land. In a two-tier system, said historian Daniel Vickers, the bottom was composed of "young men disadvantaged by race, origin, or indebtedness," while the top offered upward economic mobility to "a restricted pool of white, locally born, and well connected Nantucket men." The latter group became the basis for the rags-to-riches stories of the island. Yet, with the ascent of New Bedford, a newer model akin to the factory system was developing whereby crews were unrelated, foreign, and exploited. Ashley and others commonly used the experiences of Nantucket to describe New Bedford, while ignoring the latter's oppressive regime and limited economic mobility. But because of that sweated labor, even as late as 1900, "the owners of the fifteen or so barks, brigs, sloops, and schooners that remained in the fleet were earning nearly 70 percent per year on their investment."[39]

The ODHS ignored the perspective of most sailors in its exhibits. Repeating the line of whaling agents, merchants, and masters, it explained that the whaleman's service had been "contractual and voluntarily entered into." In the *American Whaleman*, which the *New York Times* called "a true and human history," Hohman offered a dissenting, but hardly new, perspective. Unlike the museum's happy skit of a man being shanghaied, New England whalemen were usually snared by a "landshark," who worked with "the keepers of grog-shops and brothels." Aboard ship, the situation worsened. An officer's authority, often despotic, was maintained by harsh punishment. So unlike the ODHS idealization, *Lagoda*'s captain in 1862 flogged a black hand (perhaps repeatedly) for refusing duty and then marooned him on a Pacific island. Clifford Ashley rejected charges of brutality.[40]

Living quarters were separated: officers occupied the aftercabin, which resembled a Victorian home; boatsteerers and stewards took the steerage; and the crew occupied the fo'c'sle. *Lagoda*'s half-size fo'c'sle could hardly depict the reality of emetic air, clothes washed in urine, or bugs in food and bedding, nor could it portray its cholera, scurvy, consumption, and dysentery. Such a focus on the ship's environment might prompt museumgoers to think of their contemporary unsafe conditions, including nearby slums and factories. Ashley, who evidently forgot the "wretchedness" of *Sunbeam*'s quarters in 1904, suggested in 1928 that the museum create a fo'c'sle exhibit to counter the disturbing "stories about the treatment of sailors." Instead, the museum depicted *Lagoda*'s fo'c'sle as spick-and-span.[41]

Central to this context was a system of payment called the "lay," which contrasted with payment by Nantucket owners, who took 25 percent of the catch and left the rest to the crew. As whaling competed with petroleum, managers pursued lower costs and higher returns. "A whaleman received no wages," Ashley misleadingly wrote. "His reward for labor directly reflected the quality of his work, since his 'lay' was a proportionate share in the proceeds of the voyage." The differential between captain (at 6.58 percent) and lowest crewman (0.54 percent) was large, and as the years passed, the captain's share increased, while the crew's decreased. The lay was one strand in a web of charges that enmeshed the whaler. Often he ended a long voyage in peonage, owing the slop chest money. Life aboard whaleships, a Cape Verdean later said, was slavery in the 1890s. "How do you think those ship owners built their fine mansions on the hill?" he asked. "We seamen worked and slaved for nothing while the owners got rich."[42]

Exploiting this web was one of New Bedford's most prominent whaling agents and outfitters (and landsharks), a firm headed by Joseph and William R. Wing (est. 1849). By 1870, the Wings controlled the nation's largest whaling fleet, including *Morgan* and, later, *Sunbeam*. Lasting into the twentieth century, the firm was, according to a Mystic Seaport writer, "less interested in the production and sale of the whale products taken by their ships than they were in the profits to be made from the men employed on their ships." While Ashley implausibly concluded that "the prices [of the slop chest] appear to have been fair," an American consul in a faraway port estimated that a whaler earned a mere $54.17 from a four-year voyage.[43]

With the rate of desertion running as high as 50 percent or more, captains coped with inexperienced crews. New Bedford's most famous whaleship, *Charles W. Morgan*, regularly left its home port with a crew of up to forty men, but, as the years passed, it returned with entirely different seafarers. Desertion represented an abandonment of the work ethic, rejection of discipline, and breach of contract. It could only be attributed to, said Ashley the "stupidity or stubbornness" of the sailor. The rebelliousness decreased with the enlistment of more Azoreans, Cape Verdeans, and Kanakas. The ODHS and shipowners alike repeated the rhetoric of factory managers who claimed that workers' resistance to "disciplined labor and longer hours" necessitated a different workforce. Ironically, museum leaders idealized the Yankee era, but they prized the deference of those immigrants.[44]

Though filtered by their authors, logbooks mentioned topics little covered in museum exhibits. One entry, for example, disclosed a surprising fact about a crew member: "Learned today that James Weldon was a woman," but the museum claimed (incorrectly) it was "the only occasion on which a woman, masquerading as a man, ever shipped on a whaler." Other logs suggested that women and boys were used for the crew's pleasure. Said Hohman, "The South Seas became the scene of drunken revels and bestial orgies of the most revolting and degrading character." For instance, the log of the ship *Dauphin* for 1820–23 recorded a witty confession:

And now our decks with girls are filled
Of every sort and kind
And every man picked out a wife
The best that he could find.

After 1840, Hohman concluded, there were only "two or three sober, thrifty, self-respecting men who were happily married" in the average fo'c'sle. The increased presence of Kanakas and Cape Verdeans, he noted, diminished these sexual encounters. The museum represented the era's moral agents, whose influence was marginal, by exhibiting a "Whaleship Library," placed by the American Missionary Society, and a chair that hoisted a captain's wife aboard a ship, which sailors contemptuously called a "Hen Frigate."[45]

The ship's return to homeport was little different. In Nantucket's era, said Hohman, "the clear majority" of men spent their leave in "happy and respectable homes," but New Bedford changed that. At the dedication of *The Whaleman* in 1913, said the Reverend Charles S. Thurber of the Seamen's Bethel (using the *present* tense), once the whaler landed in New Bedford, "all the means for the gratification of his fatal instincts are poured upon him in every form of allurement," whether in bars or brothels. The museum illustrated a watercolor showing *Ark*, a former whaleship that was topped off with a house in the 1820s and converted into a floating brothel. "There were two New Bedfords in this early day," Pease conceded. One was "a fair and dignified village" shaped by Quakerism, the other a "squalid" spectacle with saloons and "houses where female harpies reigned and vice and violence were rampant." Vigilantes took action by torching *Ark*, whose defenders then burned the Elm Street Methodist Church. Vigilantes later torched a second *Ark*. Reformers created the Port Society to provide moral uplift, but bars and brothels proliferated.[46]

Typical for the era's history museums, the ODHS was most interested in finding role models for emulation. Ashley, for one, worshipped earlier captains, saying, "I doubt if ever there will be a braver or a sturdier race of men bred in this world than the officers of that vanished fleet." Establishing discipline, their task was making "whalemen out of the raw youngsters" and protecting them "from themselves." Hohman countered that "many masters and mates were harsh, brutal, profane, ignorant, and tyrannical." Even officers "of good character" were "much given to undue sternness and astounding parsimony on shipboard." But looking at the museum's *Lagoda*, it would have been difficult to imagine such an officer managing a floating factory.[47]

"WHERE WE MAY PONDER UPON THOSE WHO HAD GONE BEFORE": ESTABLISHING MUSEUM GALLERIES AND COLLECTIONS

Just as Thurber fretted about nearby bars and brothels, the ODHS nervously watched its neighborhood change. In 1920, fearing that Johnny Cake Hill (formerly Bethel Street) would "deteriorate into garages" and gas stations, ODHS president Herbert E. Cushman asked for help from Boston textile magnate William Madison Wood (née Silva), the son of an Azorean whaler and a former New Bedford resident. Hoping to clear part of the hill, he wanted to re-create "the different stores or shops representative of the old whaling industry." When added to the Mariner's Home and Bethel, it "would be about as complete and unique as anything in the United States." But Wood declined, as he was building his own historical re-creation at Shawsheen Village. Cushman shrugged, "There are men of vision in this world, but I am afraid that not many of them are living in New Bedford."[48]

The ODHS scaled back its plan. Frank Wood installed a series of displays in the gallery's balcony with designs by Ashley and the help of Edward T. Pierce Jr., grandson of a textile baron. One booth portrayed whaling's business operation. Curator Arthur Watson first described it as "a ship agent's office," but Ashley admitted that those "outfitters were always referred to locally as 'sharks.'" The name shifted to the Whaling Merchant's Counting Room. Extolling Bourne, it exhibited his furnishings "exactly as he left them." Other booths depicted artisans. Critiquing the "soft living" of his "machine-made age," Ashley lamented that "the old handicrafts were forgotten." He arranged a cooper shop, shipsmith shop, sail and riggers' loft, and whaleboat shop. They were the antithesis of the city's massive mills. Expertly crafted, the cooper's handmade casks, said Pease, "never shed a tear." New Bedford once had sixty cooperages. While the Whaleboat Shop showed "the best seaboat evolved by man," the shipsmith had been "as great a hero as the [harpooner] who hurled" his iron.[49]

The guidebook focused on Lewis Temple. Few New Bedford residents knew that the "colored" man who later earned "a pittance" as a barber had been the smith who invented "the Temple iron" in 1848. Ashley called it "the single most important invention in the whole history of whaling." His toggled, barbed harpoon became universal because a wounded whale could escape an older-style harpoon. "If Temple had patented his iron," Pease conjectured, "he might have been a millionaire," but he died poor in 1854 after a prolonged legal struggle to gain his due. Instead of noting Temple's obstacles to securing that patent, Pease called his case "a pathetic example of the queer manner in which the Fates allot their gifts." Yet, the Fates had racially and economically blessed F. Gilbert Hinsdale, who helped assemble the shipsmith shop, gifted his collection, and patented a variation of Temple's iron in 1920. Another black who lived near Temple's shop and worked in the whaling industry was missed by the guidebook, Frederick Douglass.[50]

Through models, the museum showed ships' evolving form and meaning. Debuting a collection, Edward Pierce highlighted thirty-two models donated by the estate of Louis de Coppet of New York in 1931. Though Pierce was a Harvard University graduate and director of his father's textile mill, he deplored the industrial revolution. The decline of sail and the ascent of steam, he said, was "the most tragically dramatic episode in maritime—perhaps in human—history." He suggested that "the Goths and Vandals . . . would admire the work of the machine against Christian or feudal culture, and doubtless their shades look expectantly to Moscow for that new mechanism which shall annihilate the remaining vestiges of humanity."[51]

Pierce's feelings were hardened by a bitter strike in 1928. Just as whaleship owners had earlier quit the city, textile barons were fleeing to the South. Said Pease, New Bedford offered "the unprecedented case of a city that [had] struck twelve twice in succession." The Depression then tested the city's mettle as unemployment skyrocketed. By 1933, museum attendance was down almost 60 percent from 1927. For the remaining visitors, Pease thought, it became "a haven, remote and restful, where we may be diverted and ponder upon those who had gone before, undaunted by adversity." Giving hope in 1932, William Cameron Forbes, a Boston investment banker and ambassador to Japan, told the ODHS that "the possibilities of future trade with the Orient simply stagger the imagination." But the ODHS was facing another crisis as membership declined and it watched the opening of the Nantucket Whaling Museum (1930), fifty miles distant. Better depicting "the golden era," Nantucket cast itself as racially pure, socially peaceful, and historically rooted.[52]

New Bedford countered that it owned "as complete a collection of whaliana as may anywhere be seen." That included a skeleton of a thirty-five-foot humpback, slain by a killer whale in 1933. It was the only specimen east of Detroit, but when mounted from the ceiling, it was strangely altered "to be approximately the correct scale of the *Lagoda*." Besides Wood's collection of lances and harpoons, the room displayed photographs taken by William H. Tripp aboard the schooner *John R. Manta* on the nation's last whaling voyage in 1927. After working as a bank teller, Tripp became the museum's assistant curator in 1930. When *Manta* docked at Merrill's Wharf with three hundred barrels of sperm whale oil, the anachronism was evident: the waterfront storage tanks were full of gasoline and kerosene.[53]

Disturbing trends were apparent. Prices for whalebone had collapsed, while those for oil were wildly inconsistent. Industrial whaling by factory ships prolonged the hunt, as did science, which was "finding more uses for whale products." As some species were threatened, conservation was more mentioned. In 1924, the *New York Times* warned that the days of this decadent industry were "numbered unless leviathan is protected by laws that can be enforced." In 1931, the League of Nations adopted the Geneva Convention for the Regulation of Whaling, but it was ineffective. Over thirty-seven thousand whales were killed in 1934, causing what was then "the greatest devastation of whale stocks in history." It only worsened thereafter. Over all, twentieth-century factory ships would kill almost 98 percent of all reported whales *ever* taken. Regarding itself as a historical society, not a conservation group, the ODHS glamorized the hunt.[54]

In 1935, the ODHS opened the Frank Wood Building, where many extravaganzas, including the "Pageant of the Sailing of the *Lagoda*," were staged, prompting complaints from traditionalists. The pageants had introduced, it was said, "the pulse of Hollywood," making the ODHS "more an exhibitionist than a 'historical' society." To attract more and younger supporters, Edward P. Alexander, a pioneering public historian, had urged extra measures such as pageants, radio programs, schools visits, and special exhibits. The museum gave free entry to everyday school groups and Sunday visitors, but other days it charged twenty-five cents, the same price as a movie ticket; free tickets represented about two-thirds of its 15,262 attendees in 1936–37.[55]

Nearby in Fairhaven was *Charles W. Morgan* (1841), which contrasted starkly with *Lagoda*. Built in New Bedford as a square-rigger, it was rerigged as a bark in 1867 and worked eighty years in whaling, the longest on record. In thirty-seven voyages, *Morgan* took nearly eleven hundred whales, earning gross revenues of $2 million. In 1915, Harry Neyland, director of New Bedford's Swain School of Design, proposed its acquisition, but Pease dashed the "vague and impractical" idea. So, too, did the Whalemen's Club. Though ship preservation was rare nationally, Neyland took a controlling interest in *Morgan* in 1924 and offered it to the city if it would be preserved as a museum. The ODHS and the city did nothing because *Lagoda* fit their needs: its expenses were nil and appearances shipshape. Memorialization, not preservation, set their agenda. Neyland approached Colonel Edward H. R. Green, whose forebears once owned the ship; his mother, Henrietta "Hetty" Howland Green, had died in 1916 and was reputedly America's richest woman. He took interest after seeing the ruins of *Wanderer* at Cuttyhunk. Immortalized in paint by Ashley, its crash left *Morgan* as the sole whaling bark afloat. In 1925, Green and Neyland formed Whaling Enshrined, Inc., to make it "a perpetual memorial." Committing $250,000, Green towed it to his estate, Round Hill, on Buzzard's Bay. Behind a breakwater, *Morgan* was set in sand, wrapped in a cement berm, and "securely moored in her living tomb until age rots her timbers." On the pier he piled oil casks and *Wanderer*'s gear. On shore, he placed the James Driggs shipsmith shop from New Bedford and planned to add (but didn't) an array of buildings.[56]

Neyland supervised *Morgan*'s rerigging and repair as a ship. It became, said historian George Sarton, "a complete and ideal whaling museum." Opened free of charge and year-round in 1925, *Morgan* drew record crowds. In the year after June 1, 1927, 189,851 people came aboard, which was almost twenty times the ODHS gate. From 1925 to 1938, 1,775,000 visitors walked its decks, three-quarters of whom hailed from out of state. Captain George Fred Tilton interpreted the ship but lamented, "There [was] no life in [*Morgan*], because there [was] no water under her keel." He flagged the vessel on its anniversaries and raised its sails on calm summer days. "He was all that a sea captain ought to be," journalist Cooper Gaw told the ODHS, "a spinner of yarns who never permitted a little matter like the truth to spoil a good story." But in 1936 Green died without making any provision for *Morgan*. Then in 1938, a hurricane damaged its rigging and hull and ruined the exhibits and roadway—*Morgan* seemed doomed. After Boston rejected acquiring it as a state exhibit, Tripp and publisher George Reynolds formed a "Save the *Morgan* Committee." Heading a subcommittee, former Navy secretary Charles Francis Adams III appealed to fellow yachtsmen. *Morgan* symbolized, he wrote, "an era that gave to this country the supremacy of the world in building and manning cargo ships, [and] an era that made an American port the whaling capital of the world." But that era was "now only a memory." Still, yachtsmen showed little interest.[57]

Newspapers from Portland to Philadelphia spotlighted *Morgan*'s plight. Estimating the cost of removal and repair at $30,000, the ODHS thought of relocating *Morgan* to Pope's Island in New Bedford, where tourists would fund its upkeep. But Whaling Enshrined stipulated that it had to raise the money first. With Europe at war in November 1940, however, the ODHS rejected a major fundraising campaign or the use of existing reserves. Yet it asked local residents: "The children of America, by their contributions, saved the frigate *Constitution*. The women of America likewise saved Mount Vernon. Will you help save the *Morgan*?" Little ensued. Then, in June 1941, Carl Cutler of the Marine Historical Association in Mystic, Connecticut, visited. *Morgan* was, he said, "cocked up on her bow; her stern high in the air; broken yards on deck, and her deck rotten and full of holes. Altogether, she was a pretty sorry sight. But she was not hogged; her lines were still good, and she was to that extent sound." Courting New Bedford, he praised its "public-spirited enthusiasm" but said later that "only a few people" there "had any real interest." On July 31, Neyland offered to transfer *Morgan* to Mystic. With Tripp as its "twenty-second and last skipper," it was towed to Mystic. "The day we lost the *Morgan*," said New Bedford mayor John K. Bullard fifty years later, "has always been the darkest day in our proud history."[58]

New Bedford still featured the world's "largest and most comprehensive" whaling collection. Premiering Hollywood's new *Down to the Sea in Ships* (1949), the museum held a gala and was, said the *New York Times*, "the pride of every last resident, including the bobby soxers." A remake of *Moby Dick* (1956) also debuted there, but because the city's landscape was so industrial, director John Huston built a set in Ireland. For Father Mapple, he created Melville's fictional ship's prow pulpit, which the Port Society replicated for its Bethel in 1962. Tourists and residents alike consumed that heady blend of fact and fiction. There the sculptor Anna Hyatt Huntington placed a ten-foot-high sculpture, *Memorial to Whalemen and Fishermen* (1962), while the Moby Dick Trail highlighted the museum. Visiting as a youngster was Peter Spectre, later *WoodenBoat*'s editor. "Everything on the *Lagoda* looked authentic," he declared. It was "one of the most stunning maritime museum displays" he had ever seen. Residents were equally impressed. As a local child, Kingston Heath regarded Pratt's *Whaleman* as a "symbol of the city." The imagery, he said, "reassured me of my regional identity." Later becoming a preservationist, he recanted, realizing that those images acted "as an agent of illusion and myth" through which "New Bedford's power elite" told "*their* view of history." He wanted to know the real story.[59]

"YOU DON'T NEED TO RIP OUT THE HEART OF AN OLD TOWN": WHALE, THE ODHS, AND A NATIONAL PARK

The real New Bedford was, like too many cities, facing urban renewal's wrecking ball. As waterfronts, city centers, and older neighborhoods economically declined, demographically shifted, and physically deteriorated, desperate city officials pushed to demolish and rebuild. A new preservation movement gradually arose. Through much of the nineteenth and well into the twentieth century, preservationists had embraced the patriotic and connoisseur traditions by primarily saving the homes of great men, the sites of history-making events, or expressions of great artistry. Protecting authentic streetscapes and neighborhoods began regionally on Boston's Beacon Hill through zoning (1924) and on Providence's College Hill through federal help (1959). At midcentury, the main remedy for ailing neighborhoods was still the bulldozer.

On its Johnny Cake Hill block, the ODHS demolished two early nineteenth-century boardinghouses, but a debate ensued. In 1958, wondering if the waterfront's decaying buildings could be saved, its Museum Committee persuaded trustees to fund a feasibility study. The report was positive, but ODHS trustees rejected it, believing that "it could not get bogged down in real estate." A small group dissented, wanting to blend "economic development and physical preservation." They were led by attorney George C. Perkins. As a boy from Upstate New York, he had visited his uncle on Buzzard's Bay and saw *Morgan* at Round Hill. After writing his Harvard honor's thesis on whaling, he thought that New Bedford's buildings "deserved better than to crumble away or fall to the wrecker." He allied with city planner Richard J. Wengraf, who was prioritizing the city's fishing economy by razing dozens of blocks to expand processing plants and erecting a hurricane wall (the world's longest at eighteen thousand feet).[60]

But to appraise its historic riverfront, Wengraf hired preservationist Antoinette Forrester Downing; she had used federal grants to create the College Hill Historic District in Providence. Her blueprint, said Senator Jack Reid later, became "a national model for using historic preservation as a means of community renewal." Surveying New Bedford's old-time waterfront, she ranked thirty-nine buildings (out of seventy) as exceptional. Unlike College Hill, however, this was a commercial district and, Perkins emphasized, they "had no intention of displacing the fishing industry." Emulating Providence's model, in 1962 Wengraf established the citywide New Bedford Redevelopment Authority (NBRA) and, as a district redeveloper, the Waterfront Historic Area League (WHALE).[61]

The league hired Corinthian Conservation Co. of Newport as a consultant. Endorsing preservation, Corinthian's Robert J. Kerr II said, "You don't need to rip out the heart of an old town" to renew it. Rejecting the prevailing practice of "colonializing or Victorianizing" old buildings, he stressed "the collective value of the historic district," not its individual structures, many of which reflected a vernacular tradition. Wengraf won federal funding to study a 190-acre site. It was a "first of its kind," explained journalist Ada Louise Huxtable. Focusing on an eleven-block area of "once-handsome granite, brick and wooden buildings of the 1820's through the 1850's," the study offered, she wrote, "recommendations on zoning, financing and enabling legislation expected to have countrywide application." Unlike Colonial Williamsburg's use of cutoff dates, demolition, and reconstruction, Huxtable praised the plan for treating "the city as a living 'continuum,' in which all periods and styles add up to the richest and most productive urban experience and design." Gentrification was an issue. While WHALE wanted to protect the district's fishing businesses, its boardinghouses included worrisome "grizzled characters right out of *Moby-Dick*."[62]

Neighborhood preservation and economic revitalization clashed when the NBRA proposed building a highway (Route 18) to link its processing plants with I-195. The road would have required the demolition of the

Custom House, the Benjamin Rodman House, the Third District Court building, and other whaling-era landmarks. Heading WHALE's opposition was Sarah Delano, widow of Clifford Ashley. The Waterfront Historic Area League persuaded the NBRA to move Route 18, but that led to the unexpected loss of the Rotch Counting House (ca. 1785) in the newly created Bedford Landing Waterfront Historic District. The district's small businessmen were suspicious, however, and claimed that WHALE and the ODHS were "in league against" them. This fear, albeit exaggerated, was "legitimately based," said John Bullard, then an MIT graduate student in planning and architecture. A descendant of town founder Joseph Rotch, son of a Whaling Enshrined leader, and later mayor himself, Bullard attributed those suspicions to class differences because the ODHS, Port Society, and WHALE were "composed of 'old families,' descendants of the whaling merchants who live in the suburbs and either appear to have relatively high incomes or don't appear to work." Those elite acted, he said, as if they knew "what [was] best for the district." Finished in 1975, the highway psychologically "put the waterfront a million miles away from the District."[63]

After finishing his MIT thesis, in which he proposed a plan for New Bedford that his adviser called "impractical and idealistic," Bullard focused on his increasingly troubled city, where race riots had erupted in 1970. While the NBRA addressed the needs of those turbulent neighborhoods, WHALE gained more latitude on the waterfront. After reading Saul Alinsky's *Rules for Radicals* (1971), Bullard asked landowners in 1974 to hire him as real estate coordinator. Emphasizing economic growth through tourism, he approached the museum, the key player, but it refused to hire him as it "feared becoming involved in real estate and politics." Instead, WHALE employed Bullard until 1985. With a $900,000 federal block grant, Mayor John Markey prioritized the waterfront, calling it the city's "worst neighborhood."[64]

Of all Massachusetts cities, New Bedford was unique in having its own Office of Historic Preservation, which Markey created with federal funds, and it put the largest share of its federal moneys into preservation. As the NBRA threatened historically worthwhile structures elsewhere in town, WHALE moved some into the district. Beginning in 1974, it not only remade the streets with cobblestone, period lighting, and bollards but also reintroduced trees. Bullard's so-called "Ten Acre Revival" saved both vernacular and exceptional structures. Overall, WHALE primed the waterfront's economic pumps with more than $3 million from 1965 to 1981. Said

Antoinette Downing, "New Bedford saved more of its architectural past and made it work perhaps better than any other city in the U.S."[65]

The 1960s were even more deadly to whales. "Poor old Moby Dick," tycoon Aristotle Onassis quipped. "In those days a whaler would be gone two or three years and had to go through horrors. Today my whaling fleet has nineteen units: a 'mother ship,' sixteen chasers, two tankers to supply fuel. It also has a helicopter to spot the whales, radar, and, for the men, a hospital, dentist, swimming pool and movie." From 1962 to 1971, industrial whaling killed three hundred thousand sperm whales, which equaled the estimated kill of *all* U.S. whalers from 1712 to 1899. Said marine scientist Robert Rocha, "One modern factory ship [could] take more whales in one season than the entire American whaling fleet of 1846 which number[ed] over 700 vessels." With the near extinction of the blue whale (the largest) in the early 1960s, a broader-based conservation movement arose, but the ODHS still glorified "the exploits of early American whalers." Antiwhaling groups asked for help, but the ODHS regarded conservation as "a scientific, marine biological problem," which it lacked "the necessary expertise to deal with intelligently."[66]

Instead, the ODHS was shifting its focus to the cross-cultural interactions of whaling crews. In 1974, it created the position of curator of ethnology and hired John R. Bockstoce, who redefined Arctic studies. After issuing his exhibit catalog, *Steam Whaling in the Western Arctic* (1977), the ODHS expanded its Bowhead Project with federal and National Geographic Society funding in 1978. Using its logbooks, which numbered over a thousand, Bockstoce extrapolated the size of the nineteenth-century bowhead whale population to establish modern hunting limits. Though commercial whaling was banned in 1986, it continued under renegade nations. By the early 1980s the ODHS, which was calling itself the New Bedford Whaling Museum (NBWM), showed its strengths and limitations through Bockstoce's scholarship. He authored his principal work, *Whales, Ice, and Men: The History of Whaling in the Western Arctic*, before leaving the NBWM in 1986. But, as a reviewer noted, he "duck[ed] today's issues of conservation." That same year the museum debuted a one-hundred-foot mural of a white sperm whale. Drawn by Richard Ellis, a marine conservationist gaining renown, "Moby-Dick" won acclaim. For the NBWM's new entrance in 2000, he also created a mural of a life-size head of a blue whale and dolphins. The loving work of Ellis was a shift from Bockstoce's scholarly pose.[67]

Meanwhile, New Bedford had kept its goal of preserving a *living* and *working* fishing industry. In 1978 a national reporter concluded that it was "not the fantasy land of so many restorations." The waterfront included *Ernestina*, which arrived at State Pier in 1982. Launched as *Effie M. Morrissey* (1894), thus being the nation's second-oldest Fredonia-style schooner, it had fished the Grand Banks, explored the Arctic, and worked as the last wooden transatlantic packet. In 1982 the Republic of Cape Verde gave *Ernestina* to the Commonwealth of Massachusetts. After parading in Op Sail 86, it was designated a National Historic Landmark (NHL) and the state's official vessel. Yet, with 60 percent of its economy based on fishing, New Bedford was about to strike twelve again because Georges Bank, east of Cape Cod, was nearing exhaustion. With a jobless rate double that of the state, Mayor Bullard and WHALE formed a Citizens Advisory Committee to promote economic diversification. Boston proposed creating a Heritage State Park, but it pulled funding in 1989 because of a recession. The Waterfront Historic Area League pushed for a national park, prompting a critic to warn: "The real thing doesn't sell," while "phony seaports" like Mystic were "raking in the visitors."[68]

In the midst of that recession, the Whaling Museum tried to diversify. Thirty-two miles away in Plymouth, which annually attracted seventy-five-thousand whale watchers, it opened the $1 million Whale Discovery Center in 1991. "Like nothing else in New England," its high-tech exhibits gave "kids of all ages a chance to discover what life as a whale would be like." With an Ellis-designed, life-size sculpture of a humpback whale on its roof, it was built without artifacts. The center, said NBWM director Anthony Zane, an environmentalist hired in 1988, was "dedicated to the whale as a barometer of the planet's health and to the need for the species' preservation." The *Standard-Times* of New Bedford said that it would demonstrate that the NBWM was not an "irrelevant historical side trip." Attracting only 36,000 of a projected 140,000 tourists over a two-year span, however, it closed.[69]

Meanwhile, WHALE was predicting that New Bedford's tourism would quadruple to five hundred thousand annually with a national park. After Senator Edward Kennedy and Representative Barney Frank (D-MA) legislatively interceded, the National Park Service (NPS) hired WHALE to undertake a special resource study to determine its eligibility. In 1993, the study concluded that New Bedford best illustrated U.S. whaling history. Introduced in 1994, a $10.4 million bill included *Ernestina* and the existing Bedford Landing NHL district. After passing the Democratic-controlled

House, it died in the Senate with election-year politics. The 1994 "Republican Revolution" changed everything, bringing in ideologues who targeted the proposed park. Arguing its case twice before committees was Anne Brengle, who left WHALE to become NBWM director in 1994. Serving until 2007, she was a skilled manager and fundraiser, which reflected a national trend "to put fund raising and business acumen high on the list of job qualifications for museum director."[70]

In 1995, Brengle became the city's lead spokesperson for the park. As a "unique private-public partnership," she said, it was "a model for future urban parks." After the city increased its financial commitment, WHALE sought support from Barrow, Alaska, where early homes were built from whaling hulks. An amended bill included Alaskan natives by funding an Iñupiat Heritage Center. In 1996, as the bill was faltering, Kennedy logrolled with Majority Leader Robert Dole (R-KS) so that each received a park. The Omnibus Parks and Public Lands Management Act of 1996 was signed by President Bill Clinton. The New Bedford Whaling National Historical Park (1998) became the 375th national park. After Congressional Republicans rejected any land purchases or unfunded mandates, the park's small staff relied on the city to manage the twenty-acre district.[71]

While the *Standard-Times* asked, "Does the National Park signal New Bedford's rebirth?" the president of Downtown New Bedford, Inc., called it "the most important engine for economic revival that this wonderful old city" had seen since the Depression. As the park's cornerstone, the museum expected visitation to triple. More lucratively, the community thought that Washington would fund dredging the harbor, beautifying Route 18, permanently berthing *Ernestina*, repairing the fishing wharves, and building a world-class aquarium. Said WHALE's executive director Antone G. Souza Jr., a descendant of Azorean whalemen, "The National Park is a symbol of hope. Hope that has been lost for so long." The NBWM followed with a capital campaign to update its six-building complex. More directly, the park enhanced the museum experience. The park's Visitor Center was located in the former Third District Court building, which was donated by Fleet Bank to WHALE and turned over to the NPS. There, the park staged maritime craft demonstrations and musical programs; its free walking tours were, said a columnist, "important to folks who live here and want to understand this great city better." With a Kennedy earmark of $1.5 million, which was matched by state and private funds, the museum renovated the Bourne Building in 2010.[72]

"WE'RE NOT JUST A HISTORY MUSEUM ANYMORE": REVERSING THE MUSEUM'S COURSE

"Let me describe New Bedford as I see it," Souza wrote the *Boston Globe* in 2000. "This is a city of hard-working multicultural people, who look very different from each other, speak English and dozens of other languages, and practice many different customs. New Bedford is the real America." It was all that, and more. Its economic plight aggravated long-festering racial and class divisions, as well as unemployment, drugs, and problem schools. Its harbor was "one of the most polluted in the nation," because the hurricane wall blocked the flushing of pollutants. Consequently, the NBWM was encouraging a more "active and responsible citizenry" through the state's science and technology curriculum. In 1998, for example, a fourth-grade program introduced the working waterfront, whose five-hundred-plus boats matched whaling's peak. Visiting *Lagoda* and *Ernestina*, students compared their own lives with those of the crews.[73]

More important, Kennedy, along with Senators Daniel Inouye (D-HI) and Ted Stevens (R-AK), inserted the Education through Cultural and Historical Organizations Program (ECHO) into a larger bill in 2001. Promoting cultural exchanges between Alaskan and Hawaiian natives with the mainland, it included the former whaling ports of New Bedford and Salem. In 2002, a three-year grant (later extended) funded the NBWM and the New Bedford Ocean Explorium, a then-developing, kids-oriented science center. Through ECHO, the NBWM became a pathbreaking institution. Focusing on a "very underserved, multicultural, multiethnic" student body, the program funded new curriculum development and experiential programs. "Without ECHO," admitted its education director, "that level of programming would [have been] difficult to achieve." In 2005, after the Bush Administration opposed ECHO's renewal, Kennedy and Stevens added Mississippi's Native Americans to a revised (and successful) bill. Quite fittingly, the museum called Kennedy its champion. But with his death in 2009, his Republican successor opposed ECHO, which ended in 2011.[74]

The NBWM accelerated its whale conservation program through ECHO. It began with the debut of the Jacobs Family Gallery (2000) and its sixty-six-foot skeleton of a juvenile blue whale. After being killed by a supertanker in 1998, "an intense battle to claim the bones" erupted between federal agencies, but Kennedy and Frank prevailed. A student named the unlucky whale KOBO (King of the Blue Ocean). Concurrently, over a million passengers were taking whale-watching cruises in the Bay State alone. Entering the museum through a new atrium, a visitor's first sight is not *Lagoda*, which was symbolic of the hunt, but the hanging skeletons of the blue whale and a thirty-five-foot humpback. With KOBO, the whale had bested the whaleship; as did Moby-Dick with Ahab's *Pequod*.[75]

Through ECHO in 2004, the NBWM hired Robert Rocha, a marine science educator, to develop programs and tell, he said, "the whale's side of the story." The number of skeletons tragically increased after a pregnant right whale was killed in 2004. By displaying the forty-nine-foot mother and her eleven-foot, unborn calf, which was unique worldwide, "we have an opportunity, and a responsibility," he said, to help. But, living within fifty miles of shore, only one hundred breeding female right whales remained in 2018, as ship strikes, fishing nets, seismic air guns, and a changing habitat created the possibility of extinction. For years the museum has also annually homeported the meeting of the North Atlantic Right Whale Consortium and staged a Right Whale Day during school vacations. "We're not just a history museum anymore," Rocha said, though most exhibitions and programs were still in the humanities.[76]

A long-planned core exhibit opened in mid-2009, *From Pursuit to Preservation: The History of Human Interaction with Whales*. Funded by ECHO, the National Endowment for the Humanities (NEH), and museum members, the $2.75 million exhibit traced the evolution "from the whale as monster to the whale as symbol or metaphor, from source of survival to source of commercial wealth, from the first gropings toward scientific inquiry to contemporary methods of observation and study." Centered round a forty-eight-foot sperm whale skeleton and a whaleboat, it displays photographs, maps, paintings, tools, and weapons (fig. 11). *From Pursuit to Preservation* separates industrial whaling from subsistence and communal hunting, which is depicted by an Iñupiat display. One image caught the attention of a *Globe* reporter. The 1830s painting, "Cow Whale Trying to Save Her Calf," shows a sperm whale protecting her youngster as the whaleboat goes in for the "fiendish" kill. The reporter remarked: "The word 'treachery' haunts the whole business. So, too, does 'courage.'" A copy of the story was attached to the exhibit to create a teaching moment. Apparently, younger visitors have difficulty understanding old-time whaling as whales have been anthropomorphized through pop culture, as with Keiko in *Free Willy* (1993) or Pearl Krabs in *SpongeBob SquarePants* (1999–present).[77]

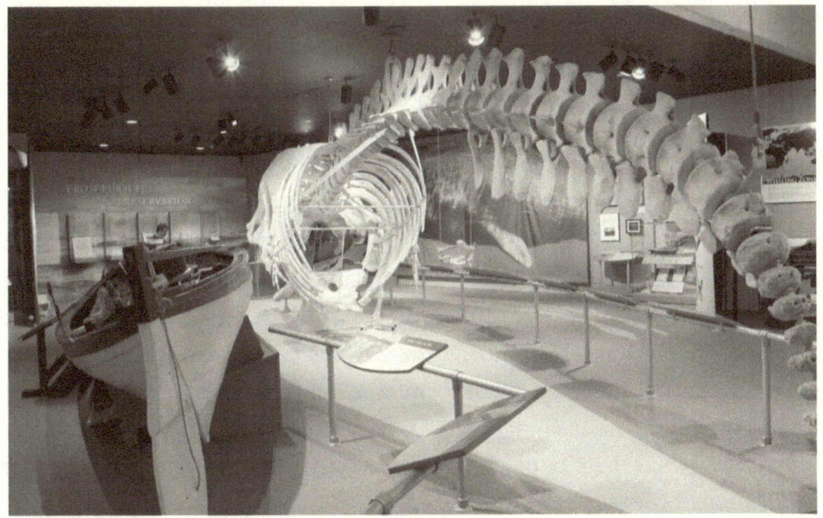

FIGURE 11. *From Pursuit to Preservation*, showing a sperm whale skeleton and a Beetle whale boat; the exhibit closed in 2018. *Photo by author, 2014.*

In 2001, the museum also acquired the holdings of the Kendall Whaling Museum (Sharon, Massachusetts) after its benefactor's death. Covering international whaling, its 72,000 artifacts were added to New Bedford's 125,000 items of mostly American provenance, thus forming an unrivaled collection. Creating space for Kendall's gift, which included a fifteen-thousand-volume library, required purchasing an uptown building and putting the NBWM in debt. Still, said the *Standard-Times*, it was "a marriage made in heaven." Long-running Kendall programs continued, including its Biennial Whaling History Symposium. Kendall's holdings allowed the NBWM to better blend history and environment, as when it used local painter William Bradford's *Arctic Regions* (1873) to stage *Arctic Visions: Away Then Floats the Ice-Island* (2013). Citing rising ocean temperatures, the exhibit offered, said its curator, "a prophetic prelude to news of the Earth's current climate situation, as these frozen regions . . . may yet vanish in our lifetime, never to be seen again." Still permeating the museum, whaliana grew after 1996 with an annual reading of *Moby-Dick*.[78]

The museum experienced another sea change with its coverage of race and ethnicity. In the 1950s and 1960s, every elementary school child "made the class trip" to the museum, recalled attorney James J. Lopes.

"We learned about scrimshaw and saw oil paintings of stern old whaling captains and their wives. Merchant Captain Paul Cuffe was not in their company. In fact there was not a single black or brown face to be seen." Beginning in the 1960s, however, the nation's identity was being slowly democratized by not only the civil rights movement but also the new social history, which explored the perspectives of previously neglected or underrepresented groups. Facing the city's social and economic problems, the *Standard-Times* accordingly called on local leaders in 1972 to formulate a new city image and revitalize community spirit. That led to the creation of the Black Heritage Trail during the U.S. Bicentennial. By 1980, teachers were asking the museum for information on "minorities in the whaling industry." While the trail included Cuffe, it largely missed everyday people until 1987, when the city placed a bronze statue of Lewis Temple near *The Whaleman*.[79] (See fig. 12.)

But the Whaling Museum was distracted by its troubled financing. With declining admissions, memberships, and income, museum director Brengle left in 2007. James P. Russell, vice president of Newport's Museum of Yachting, became president in 2008. The South Coast's yachtsmen were affluent and influential, and Laurie Bullard, wife of the former mayor, invited Newport's boaters to visit. She was told, "Jesus, no one goes to New Bedford." Some did and were welcomed. But, with the wealth disparity between a town like Westport and New Bedford, John Bullard told the *Globe*, "You've got the best and worst right next to each other. Are there any connections?"[80]

There was: Paul Cuffe of Westport. In 2009, the museum belatedly sponsored a symposium on the 250th anniversary of his birth. Russell admitted that it had missed his story. A Cape Verdean descendant, James Lopes had first heard Cuffe's name when he left town for college. The *Standard-Times* conceded that many residents had not heard of him, but it ranked him above Frederick Douglass as "the greatest African-American leader connected to the city." Cuffe had been a peer of the Rotches and the Rodmans, but there was, said Lopes, "not a single street, school, park or plaza" in the city named after him. In 2010, Lopes became an NBWM vice president and "was stunned to hear" that its colonial kitchen, which once comforted Yankee ladies, had wallboards from Cuffe's farmhouse. After dedicating a Cuffe Gallery (with those boards) in 2011, the museum opened an exhibition and later an expanded park in 2018.[81]

Today, the Portuguese (Azoreans and Madeirans) and Cape Verdeans are a majority in the city and included in its official history. But the NBWM

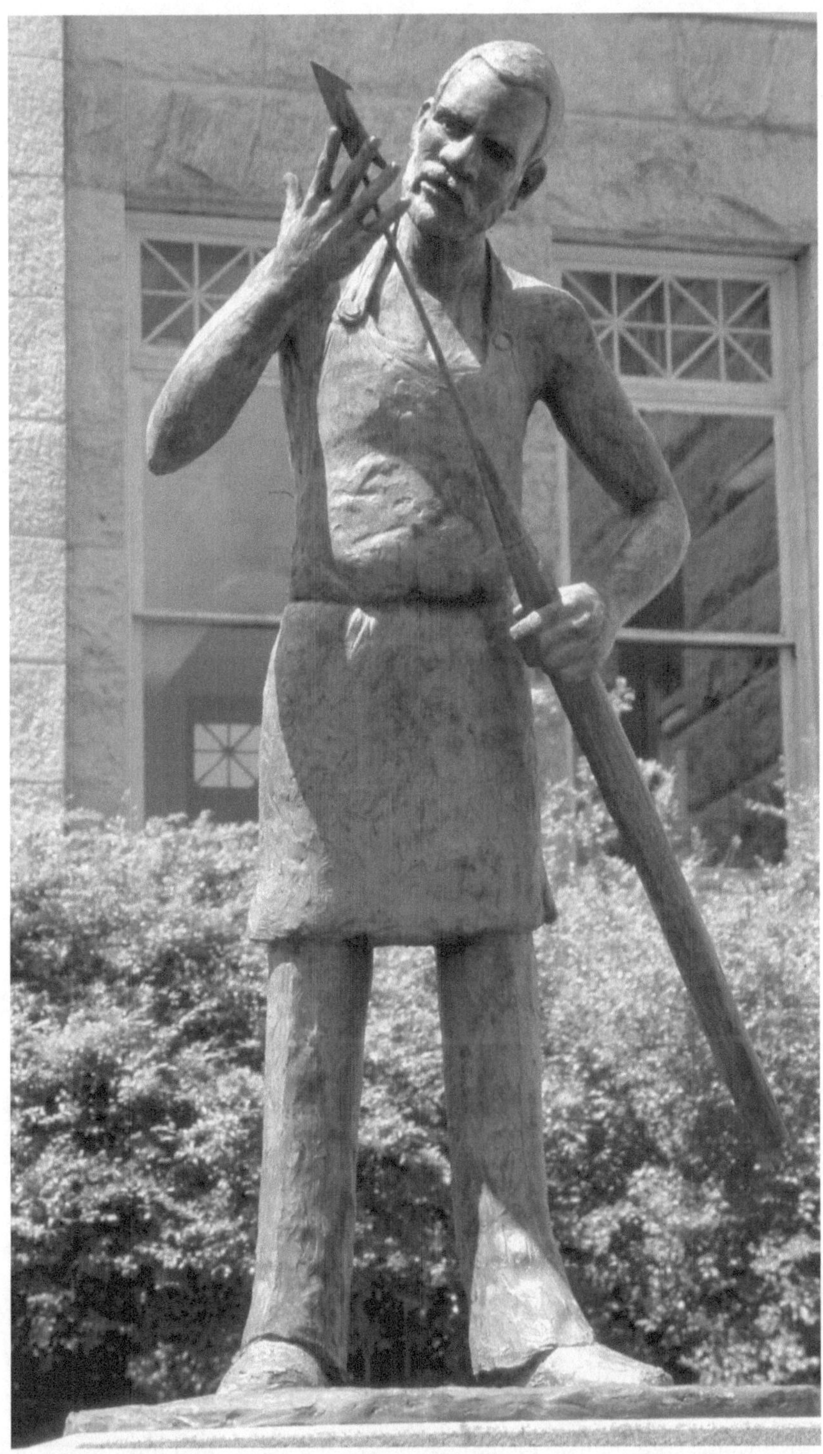

FIGURE 12. Lewis Temple, designed by John Toatley. *Photo by author, 1998.*

only slowly recognized their ranks. In 1989, Mary T. Silvia Vermette, a professor at the University of Massachusetts at Dartmouth, staged a conference and produced *Azorean Whalemen*, a ten-week NBWM exhibit that mostly focused on the officers. Pushing the NBWM, she established the Azorean Maritime Heritage Society (1997) and persuaded the mayor and museum to seek $500,000 from the Portuguese government in 1998 to fund a permanent exhibit. Because Luso-Americans made up "an estimated 65 percent" of New Bedford, Lisbon wanted to increase their visibility. Portugal's foreign minister visited the NBWM to make its donation. Still, a local politician suggested: "I don't think the museum's Yankee image is ever going to be truly shed. But it can be told along with the Portuguese experience." It took another nine years—and a visit by Portugal's president in 2007—for the NBWM to open its permanent *Azorean Whaleman Gallery*. A long-needed corrective, it was the nation's "only permanent exhibition space" on the Portuguese and Azorean diasporas. Thereafter the Azorean Maritime Heritage Society and Whaling Museum partnered with exhibits, festivals, and programs. The gallery revealed Luso-American political power; Governor Deval Patrick attended and noted that, while white nativists were fomenting much "agitas around immigration," the exhibit showed America's "best civic values."[82]

The museum likewise recognized Cape Verdeans. Since the 1970s, Cape Verdeans had held an annual celebration in town, and the museum opened a six-week exhibit, *The Cape Verde Connection*, in 1977. But many Cape Verdeans regarded the Yankee institution as stuffy and elitist. Shifting a generation later, Russell hired James Lopes to head the education department. The resulting *Cape Verdean Maritime Exhibit* depicted their homeland, community, and ties with America. Opening in July 2011 and previewed by Cape Verde's president, the gallery's "inspiring narrative" showed, said Russell, "how the Cape Verdean people overcame [the many] challenges." Its planning typified changes in the profession. Unlike a top-down process of development, curators convened public forums and, because the collection was mostly Yankee-based, asked for the loan or gift of family treasures. After an address by the Cape Verdean ambassador, the exhibit opened with traditional music and dance; a later program introduced the *Crioulo* dialect.[83]

This shift fulfilled an NEH recommendation that the museum "transition from a scholarly organization to a public one, serving a diverse and low-income community." Pledging to work "at a deeper and more systemic level," Russell said in 2009, the museum would be knitted "into the cultural fabric of our community and provide an inclusive and open stage for community participation and dialogue." Yet curators sidestepped fuller accounts of whaling's exploitation and lasting scars. The question is: To what extent can the museum tell a frank, sometimes disturbing, story and still win the support of the descendants of whaling's masters *and* their fo'c'sles? By calling whaling "a gateway for many immigrant groups in their quest for a better life," was it also dodging long-simmering racial and class tensions, which are tied to the city's poverty and limited opportunity, and thus propagating another "illusion and myth," as Kingston Heath wrote about Pratt's *Whaleman*? The NBWM fits a pattern whereby U.S. maritime museums, unlike many in Great Britain, generally avoid the issue of structural inequality and, echoing America's core ideals, emphasize an individual's mythical capacity "to transcend class, to make the most of the opportunity provided by the frontier of the sea." Historian Phyllis Leffler suggested that U.S. museums are "more congratulatory than apologetic" with their "celebratory stories of diversity, opportunity, and cultural enrichment."[84]

Meanwhile, the NBWM was evolving into that community-oriented museum. In 1903, the ODHS had discriminated against those immigrants, but decades later, it recognized the city's problems and encouraged civic betterment. The challenge for New Bedford leaders, said the *Globe*, was "to prove to the city's residents, again and again, that New Bedford [was] not destined to lose." One exhibit, said Russell, was to be "designed to inspire our youth by telling the stories of great accomplishments, discoveries, and entrepreneurial initiatives wrung out by men and women of this region." But are such inspiring tales typical of what historian John Bodnar sees as an attempt to shape immigrant memory and blunt working-class identity?[85]

Tied to its transition, the museum was going through "a paradigm shift." Not only had ECHO's sunset in fiscal year 2011 caused "government funding to drop from 36 percent of the museum's $3 million operating budget to 0.8 percent," but Congress had also changed with Kennedy's death, Frank's retirement, the attack on earmarks, and state redistricting. When the resulting cuts and dissent led Lopes and three others to resign, one trustee feared its commitment to diversity was failing. Still, the museum was touting its community service. Besides opening its auditorium to civic discussions, it offered a three-tiered apprenticeship. The top two tiers (for college and postgraduate students) were typical elsewhere, but the third targeted low-income, eleventh- and twelfth-grade ethnic teens. Funded first by ECHO and then by private and city money, the program was praised by the

American Alliance of Museums, the renamed national accrediting agency. Through it, students gained "positive role models and unique opportunities," as well as "pride in the city."[86]

With this overall shift, the museum set a "new vision" and recalibrated its mission. Vice president Gregory Galer called whaling "one manifestation of [New Bedford's] entrepreneurial spirit," while also identifying banking and finance, textiles, manufacturing, and commercial fishing. Emphasizing those themes, the museum offered some forty programs linked to the Massachusetts K–12 curriculum frameworks; using its volunteer docents, it annually served upward of twenty thousand students. Sometimes these activities or displays were a student's only introduction to a key topic, such as the city's industrial history. Visitors from elsewhere, however, were still attracted by whaling. They contributed most of the admission fees, which accounted for 15 percent of the revenue, while sales and rentals brought the total to 30 percent. The museum relied on grants and fundraising for the rest. By 2013, it was in the black and was running (successfully) a $10 million capital campaign for its endowment and expansion. In 2015, it opened an $8 million, twenty-thousand-square-foot education center.[87]

The museum was also taking ownership of its neighborhood. Like many city centers after commuters left work, the area became a ghost town. Small steps began in 1999, when the museum helped form AHA! (art, history and architecture), a coalition of downtown groups that sponsored free, early-evening events. By 2015, there were over sixty partners. Every dollar invested in AHA! generated nine dollars in consumer spending. Yet issues arose trying to meld a cultural revival with a working waterfront and its many bars. Rowdy behavior ensued, but a museum spokesman shrugged, "It was a problem a hundred years ago."[88]

In the summer of 2014, "the single biggest event" to exalt the city's stature occurred with *Morgan*'s return. Billed as its thirty-eighth voyage, it stayed nine days. The museum called it "a homecoming story," but few compared *Morgan*'s $7.5 million, five-year restoration with the plight of cash-starved *Ernestina*, whose skipper claimed it was (next to USS *Constitution*) "the [nation's] most significant wooden sailing vessel." Its saga spoke volumes about New Bedford's ambivalence toward ship preservation, especially as *Ernestina* was forced to quit the city. After a two-year restoration, funded by state and private money, the sail training vessel found a berth at the Massachusetts Maritime Academy on Buzzard's Bay.[89]

CONCLUSION: "AN EPIC CITY IN EVERY SENSE OF THE WORD"

When, in 1916 and 1921, New Bedford rejected *Morgan*'s preservation, *Lagoda* fit the bill for remembering global whaling. At the time, spindles and looms dominated the city. Yet museum leaders worried, as did tradition-minded White Anglo-Saxon Protestants elsewhere, that their region's founders and legacy were being forgotten. Through artifacts and programs, they preserved a history that blended family pride, hero worship, antimodernism, and cultural exclusion. Reversing the unsavory reputation of their whaling forebears, the Old Dartmouth Historical Society spotlighted saltwater heroes who made New Bedford known worldwide. They idealized an "old type of manhood," which was embodied in the bronze *Whaleman*, and a "golden era" that were every bit as exclusionary as the 1920s xenophobia, because real whaleship crews had been mostly exploited men of color.

But after New Bedford struck twelve again with textile's decline, its self-esteem and viability were questioned. The *Standard-Times* claimed, "We are heirs to a civic tradition that is self-denigrating and self-defeating." After World War II, the Whaling Museum still depicted whaling positively, displayed Yankee history, and catered to a limited audience. But as the museum's own whaling-era neighborhood deteriorated in the 1950s, some pushed the ODHS, unsuccessfully, to save whaling's architectural legacy. In 1962, those dissenters founded the Waterfront Historic Area League (WHALE). Melding economic betterment and building preservation, WHALE's leadership and success, more than anything else, pulled the ODHS along.[90]

The city recognized the many benefits of preservation, leading to an energetic public-private drive to create a national park. Think again of the federal role in helping New Bedford through not only urban renewal funds but the NPS, NEH, ECHO, and earmarks from Frank and Kennedy. In 1996, when the park bill passed Congress, preservation became a cornerstone of New Bedford's future. It was, said the head of its Economic Development Council, "a vital tool that helps us maintain the unique character of New Bedford while also serving as a catalyst for job creation, heritage tourism, and stronger, safer neighborhoods." Still facing chronic problems, New Bedford opinion makers questioned their ability to compete in the modern global economy. The museum was pressed by community leaders, diverse professionals, and its own financial needs to remake itself. With the help of federal grants, foundations, philanthropists, and even foreign governments, its former focus on Yankee whalers gave way to more inclusive, multicultural exhibits. Its focus on the glories of the hunt gave way to a broader understanding of whaling and an embrace of science and whale conservation.[91]

The Whaling Museum is still remaking itself by promoting local history, exhibiting the fine arts, and supporting marine science. But it has asked out-of-towners to cover more of the costs: they pay more for membership, while nonmembers pay a daily charge to use the library. Meanwhile, it also prioritizes community service, particularly school programs. Partly because of the city's deeply rooted social and economic maladies, as well as what *Standard-Times* editor Ken Hartnett called "the negativity that so enshrouds New Bedford in a soul-numbing fog," the museum has become a social service agency. In a neoliberal mold, it celebrates individual accomplishment, builds ethnic self-esteem, fashions cultural anchors, and establishes links between underrepresented groups and the larger society. In those cases, it promotes what the scholar David Lowenthal calls *heritage*. That term is often conflated with *history*, but heritage typically lacks the analytic, self-reflective, and timely questioning inherent in the discipline of history. The exhibits on the Azoreans and Cape Verdeans, for example, leave visitors with an inspiring response, one that is similar to the intent of the early ODHS. What needs more emphasis and analysis is how whaling (or any industry) fits into a bigger picture, such as the dynamics of global capitalism or the play of racial and ethnic prejudice.[92]

Still, by showcasing the many groups, picturing their communities, and building on the fishing economy, the museum and the national park have deservedly won friends and admirers. While the National Trust named the city one of the Dozen Distinctive Destinations in America in 2011, a *Boston Globe* reviewer called the museum "an extraordinary place with which no New Englander should be unfamiliar." Because the locale has experienced a whirlwind of change, a *Huffington Post* writer concluded, "New Bedford was and is an epic city in every sense of the word—something that cannot be said of many other prettier, more popular Coastal New England destinations—and the very reason I love visiting."[93]

CHAPTER 3

"STOUT HEARTS MAKE A SAFE SHIP"

Individual and Community at Mystic Seaport

On November 5, 1941, one hundred spectators sadly watched as the 113-foot-long *Charles W. Morgan*, the sole survivor of twenty-seven hundred wooden, U.S.-flagged whalers, left Round Hill, Massachusetts, for its new home. "An old friend was departing forever," said a reporter. Three days later, the century-old, badly leaking vessel arrived at Mystic, Connecticut, towed in the nick of time, free of charge, by the U.S. Coast Guard; a month later Pearl Harbor pulled the nation into the two-year-old world war. A newsman reported optimistically that *Morgan*'s rescue heralded "the revival of an American maritime supremacy." Acquired for $1 by the Marine Historical Association (MHA), it reportedly symbolized the "vigorous root of Americanism known as the 'New England Character.'" With a band of Sea Scouts, Captain William Tripp presented it to MHA founder Carl Cutler. Referring to the decade-long Depression, Cutler suggested that *Morgan*'s "cramped, primitive quarters and crude equipment" would teach an "inspiring lesson of what our forefathers endured and achieved." Yet battered by a hurricane, "superficially, she looked hopeless."[1]

Cutler feared that his hometown and museum were in worse shape. The village of Mystic, which straddles the towns of Stonington and Groton, had withered when its shipyards closed after World War I, and its factories stagnated with the Depression. The MHA was founded two months after Wall Street's 1929 crash, and it barely survived the 1930s; Cutler said it seemed to be "a dead cause." When he broached the idea of acquiring

Morgan, several directors countered that the MHA "ought to fold up for the [war's] duration." But Philip R. Mallory, a Gotham businessman who had just succeeded his deceased brother Clifford as MHA president, put his "weight on the line" by fronting $7,500 to accept the ship. That became the turning point of the MHA and the ship preservation movement, as no other on-shore museum had successfully saved such a ship. In 1942, *Morgan* was berthed in a bed of sand and became the postwar centerpiece of an invented village, Mystic Seaport.[2]

Cutler launched a movement and a mission. He inspired Karl Kortum to not only establish the San Francisco Maritime Museum in 1951 but also rescue *Balclutha* (1886) three years later. Similarly, he prompted Frank G. G. Carr of London in 1957 to save *Cutty Sark* (1869) and later found the British Maritime Trust with HRH Prince Philip, Duke of Edinburgh. Cutler's mission was equally ambitious. Thinking that 1920s America was adrift, he was troubled by its big corporations, materialism, and merchant marine cuts. In the 1930s, he deplored big government. In counterpoint, his MHA rekindled the mythical spirit of a small Yankee town whose mid-nineteenth-century Puritanism and face-to-face community were antithetical to metropolises in Boston and New York. Hoping to re-create the spirit of that seaport and its globetrotting ships, he pronounced: "Stout Hearts Make a Safe Ship." His museum became, moreover, an advocate of maritime expansion, forming common cause with the U.S. Coast Guard Academy in New London and Groton's submarine base and Electric Boat Company.[3]

But as Mystic Seaport boomed with postwar tourism and Cold War nationalism, the MHA became, in Mallory's hands, less of a maritime advocate and more of what Cutler called a soulless business with hierarchical management, bottom-line thinking, and an ideology of growth. He quit as a corporation superseded his Yankee community. By the 1960s, Mystic Seaport included sixty imported, rehabilitated, or new buildings. It was Connecticut's most popular attraction, drawing over a half-million visitors in 1968. As the village mushroomed, however, the ships and collections suffered. But change for the better slowly began in 1965. Though some difficult times followed, Mystic emerged with exceptional strengths: its fleet, research center, programs, and shipyard. In 1997 it began calling itself "the Museum of America and the Sea." Besides building *Freedom Schooner Amistad* from 1998 to 2000, it began restoring *Morgan* in 2008; the ship made its thirty-eighth voyage in 2014. Today Mystic Seaport is the nation's preeminent maritime museum.[4]

"THE OLD STANDARDS WERE RAPIDLY GOING INTO THE DISCARD": RIGHTING THE NATION'S WRONGS

Descended from Puritans, Carl Custer Cutler was born in Kingston, Michigan, in 1878. When he was six, his family returned to New England where his father, who had spent ten years at sea, served as a Baptist chaplain for the Seaman's Friend Society. His father and seafaring uncle were, Cutler said, "the objects of my youthful emulation." Yearning for adventure in 1898, Carl sailed out of New York's South Street on the bark *Alice*. "I earned my first A.B. in a ships fo'csle on a voyage around the world," he boasted; he failed to mention, however, that the duress led him to jump ship in New Zealand. After receiving his BA summa cum laude in history and economics from Brown University in 1903, he entered Columbia University but left before earning a law degree. He joined the New York bar in 1906.[5]

Working on Wall Street, he was afflicted by neurasthenia (nervous prostration). In 1909 he escaped to the Pacific Northwest, where he worked as a lawyer while recuperating through logging, hunting, and prospecting. In 1913 he married Helen Grant Irving, whose father had been a Mystic shipbuilder; two years later they returned to the East. While he worked in New York, she raised two adopted children on her ancestral homestead overlooking the Mystic River, a tidal estuary. He absorbed the romanticism of mid-nineteenth-century sailing. "The memories of the ships!" crowed one native, who like many spoke of them "with kindness in their voices, as men [did] of their own children." Cutler wanted more than memories. Disillusioned by Gotham's "business methods and morality," as well as by America's changing values, he thought that "the world was going wrong." Shaped by antimodernism, he delved into maritime history.[6]

Cutler believed that a cancer was metastasizing. "Property, profit, and privilege had been calling the turn with slowly increasing frequency," he wrote, but it was industrialization's "steam and telegraph" that changed the nation. "The modern machine" did "for America what the slave machine had done for Greece and Rome." Men were no longer men, he thought. "Broadway Dudes" began to "ape the fops and voluptuaries who had comprised the bulk of decadent Rome's ruling class." Industrial workers became "creatures who spent their lives in monotonous, robot-like repetition of simple, all but effortless operations." They were no better than "human jellyfish." With the "new" immigration of southern and eastern Europeans beginning in the mid-1880s, moreover, "the birthright of the nation

[had] passed to alien hands, and with it [had] dissolved a mass of fact and tradition that was implicit in the mental background of yesterday." Like Yankee nativists elsewhere, he wanted to restore the fabled traditions of individualism, responsibility, and honest work.[7]

After twelve years, Cutler quit Gotham, settled down in Mystic, and finished *Greyhounds of the Sea: The Story of the American Clipper Ship* (1930). His prodigious research led historian Samuel Eliot Morison to call it "the most ambitious history of the clipper ship yet written." Believing that the sea was "that great breeding place of the strong free races of every age," Cutler regarded its mid-nineteenth-century clippers as "the flower and symbol of all that was true and great and fine in a passing civilization." United States ships declined after the Civil War, he lamented, and were "manned largely by the sweepings of Europe." In a foreword, Navy Secretary Charles Francis Adams III thought *Greyhounds* would help restore "a once well-nigh universal maritime interest" in an industry that "profoundly affected the civilization of the Eastern States." Book reviews varied. While the *New York Times* called *Greyhounds* "a definitive history of the era," Morison said the story, despite its ambition, dripped "with sentiment and slush." But Cutler told his publisher it was "dramatic, romantic" and "especially timely" as "there is a large, powerful body in America fully convinced that it is vital we develop a strong merchant marine, and which is seeking to stimulate a popular interest in nautical matters."[8]

Maritime advocates were sailing against the tide, however. The navalist Alfred Thayer Mahan had argued that national security required U.S.-flagged commercial hulls, but the nation's shippers emphasized profits and relied on cheaper foreign vessels. With World War I, America was "brought to the verge of defeat," said Cutler, "for want of ships." In 1916, the nation reversed course, quickly becoming "the world's greatest shipbuilder." Yet with war's end, a shipping depression led the government to sell eleven hundred ships at a big loss. Cutler denounced that as "extremely unpalatable," but a Mystic Seaport study later concluded that there were "too many ships for the business." Meanwhile, naval disarmament, which began at the Washington Conference (1921), was being discussed at Geneva (1927) and London (1930). Groton's Electric Boat was hit hard, producing no submarines from 1925 to 1931. Cutler published *Greyhounds of the Sea* in this charged context.[9]

In 1928, Cutler met Charles K. Stillman, a Mystic physician and model collector. A 1904 graduate of Columbia University, he had practiced in New

York but moved to Mystic in 1911 after a "breakdown in health." In recovery, he researched local history. In 1837, his grandfather Clark Greenman, along with his brothers, George and Thomas, had founded a shipbuilding firm at Mystic's Adams Point. Later called Shipyard Point, it became the museum's future setting. In 1849, they also built a woolen mill nearby. By the 1860s, Greenmanville was "a small feudal establishment" with four hundred workers, a company store using scrip, and a Seventh Day Baptist Church promoting moral reform, pacifism, and temperance.[10]

While Massachusetts, Maine, and New York dominated the shipbuilding industry, Mystic's fourteen yards launched twenty clippers at midcentury. The Greenmans built the 1,679-ton *David Crockett* (1853), which made twenty-five round-trip Cape Horn voyages. As Stillman bragged, it was "one of the most successful ships ever launched from an American shipyard." Its success benefited from the protectionist Navigation Act of 1817; as a result, U.S. vessels carried almost three-quarters of American trade by 1858. With small holds, however, clippers became unprofitable. The Greenmans launched their last ship in 1878. After their textile mill passed to foreigners in 1897, the German-owned Rossie Velvet Mill opened across the street in 1898. As mills gradually waned, however, tourism waxed. Still, some locals regarded sightseers "as a nuisance."[11]

With retired silk manufacturer Edward E. Bradley, Stillman and Cutler talked of founding a marine museum with artifacts "from Connecticut to Philadelphia." At Stillman's expense, Cutler searched for models in the Connecticut River valley, once known for its yards. Most had been discarded, but collectors, including the Ship Model Society of New York, competed for the rest. The three men met symbolically on Christmas in 1929 to sign the Marine Historical Association's articles of incorporation. Cutler became secretary, Bradley president, and Stillman vice president, treasurer, and general manager. Recruiting supporters and trustees, Cutler thought that the MHA would mostly attract "the descendants of [Mystic's] early ship builders and owners." They included "relatives of two of the wealthiest families in America." One was shipping entrepreneur Clifford Mallory, and the other, Harriet Greenman Stillman (mother of Charles), whose niece Mary (granddaughter of Thomas Greenman) had married Edward S. Harkness, an associate of John D. Rockefeller.[12]

In 1929, Stillman and Bradley directed Cutler to draft a *Statement of Plan and Purposes*. With a "marine research, educational and experimental center," it hoped to draw select young men because "the first requirement of an adequate merchant marine and defensive naval force [was] keen, alert, intelligent material for officers." Unlike other maritime museums, which Cutler called "a mere tomb of the past," the MHA would be "of practical help" in making America once again "the first maritime nation of the world." In 1929, those other museums were focusing on collecting, not advocacy. The nation's oldest, Salem's Peabody Museum (1799), was primarily a hall of ethnology, but it had opened a Marine Room in 1905. Whaling museums in New Bedford (1903) and Nantucket (1930) were Yankee remembrances. The Marine Museum of the City of New York (1928), which developed from the Ship Model Society, displayed mostly models and artwork. While the Smithsonian Institution (1846) in Washington, D.C., likewise showed ship models, the Naval Academy Museum (1845) in Annapolis, Maryland, resembled Cutler's plan to "stimulate a practical as well as theoretical interest in marine affairs."[13]

Just where to put its museum was the first issue. Stillman promised to donate a seven-acre tract at Shipyard Point, but it lacked street access and the donation was long delayed. So, in 1931, as "people began to lose interest" with the deepening depression, Mary Stillman Harkness contributed $30,000 to acquire instead the adjacent two acres, on which stood the closed textile mill. The MHA converted the land's three brick buildings but demolished the three-story wooden structures. Across the street, Rossie Mill, which was Mystic's largest employer, contrasted with Cutler's mythical past, especially its tall smokestacks, foreign workers, and labor strife. Planning his first exhibit of models, he asked MHA members to help monetarily. They had "more millions than I have dollars," he grumbled, but they showed little excitement, treating him "with the same amused tolerance they accord to Fido." Debuting in September 1931 with forty-two borrowed models, the museum was, reported the *New York Times*, "a memorial to the men who once raised America to the position of the first maritime nation of the world." Briefly opened in July and August thereafter, a mere eighty-nine visited in 1937.[14]

The MHA attracted navalists, such as Captain Wilson Brown, who commanded Naval Submarine Base New London (Groton), and Rear Admiral Herbert Omar Dunn (USN, ret.), who succeeded Bradley as president in 1934. But they lacked the necessary big money. Through *Greyhounds of the Sea*, Cutler met members of the New York Yacht Club, including Clifford Day Mallory Sr. Born in Brooklyn, he was the grandson of Charles Henry Mallory, who had founded a Mystic shipping dynasty, and the son of Henry

Rogers Mallory, who left behind the second largest shipping business in the nation in 1915. After Clifford managed the U.S. government's burgeoning merchant fleet during the war, he headed the largest and most successful independent U.S. shipping house by 1941. Politically conservative during the turbulent 1930s, he fought government planners, corporate competitors, and labor unions. Through him, New York's India House, an elite club that promoted foreign trade, hired a cash-strapped Cutler to catalog its collection in 1935. In 1937, Mallory became MHA president.[15]

Because Franklin D. Roosevelt had been assistant secretary of the Navy under Woodrow Wilson, Cutler had hopes for his presidency; in addition, FDR had been Cutler's law school classmate, fraternity brother, and one who had invited him to seek an appointment. Yet, as the economy sank, said Cutler, FDR turned to "theorists and radicals" to address "the problems of distribution." He propagated "the old, vicious idea that the State and not the individual came first—the very doctrine our ancestors . . . came to America" to escape. Roosevelt's Social Security Act typified the decline of personal responsibility, he thought. With the New Deal, FDR had "done more to set class against class in America than all the other presidents put together." But, dispirited by the MHA's inactivity and his father's passing, Cutler left Mystic for Texas wildcatting. After Stillman died in 1938, he returned to help Mallory, but with Clifford's death in 1941, "the bottom dropped out of everything."[16]

Mallory's brother took the helm, influenced, he said, by Cutler's "vision & inspiration." Born in Brooklyn and educated at Yale University and then Columbia University's law school, Philip Rogers Mallory was MHA president for two decades and chairman for a third. His service was an act of contrition. Since the nineteenth century, the Mallory shipping family had two unwritten rules, wrote a biographer: "The business existed to make profits but also to be improved and passed on to succeeding generations; and, the sea was not to be abandoned for the farm, factory, or forum. To violate these precepts was unspeakable." But, in 1916, Philip quit the sea to found the industrial P. R. Mallory Co. Because of the stress, however, his physician ordered him to "lead a more detached life." Thereafter, the museum became, he said, "an avocation that [dominated] most of my thinking and spare time." Calling himself "an ordinary businessman," he not only held that corporations must "obsolete the old" but also condemned the New Deal.[17]

Mallory's support enabled Mystic to acquire *Morgan*, which Cutler called "the last real American ship, outside of the old *Constitution*." No

U.S. clippers survived, but he had considered buying the 244-foot *Benjamin F. Packard* (1883), the last square-rigged Down Easter; it represented, said historian Howard Chapelle, "the highest development of the sailing ship." Owned by a Rye, New York, amusement park, *Packard* had failed as a pirate ship and aquarium. But it was too dilapidated and big for Cutler's river, though he acquired some furnishings before its scuttling in 1939. In contrast, *Morgan* was one-sixth the tonnage, less than half the length, and in better condition and came with over $8,000 from New Bedford's failed preservation drive. With only 225 MHA members, however, the MHA was stretched to raise $40,000 for its repairs.[18]

World War II saved both the MHA and *Morgan*. After war began in Europe in 1939, Cutler gave talks on preparedness, telling one assembly that stoutheartedness was "the quality most needed today." It fostered "courageous, unselfish and complete cooperation of neighbor with neighbor for a common purpose and the common good." Ironically, fascist nations similarly sought consensus by limiting individual freedom. As the Battle of the Atlantic intensified in 1941, he opened an MHA meeting to an English speaker who donated an eighteen-foot jolly boat covered with U.S. and British flags. It came from the British steamer *Anglo Saxon*, which was reportedly sunk by a German U-boat. The men in its lifeboats were murdered, but two in the jolly boat survived a seventy-day trek to the Bahamas. "Believe it or not" creator Robert L. Ripley hyped it as "the greatest epic in the history of the seas."[19]

With the Japanese attack in 1941, Mallory suggested "using Pearl Harbor" to publicize the museum. Cutler broadcast his call for stoutheartedness locally and via shortwave to England. *Morgan* became a main platform. There, a USN officer repeated one of Woodrow Wilson's Fourteen Points, telling cadets that the United States had to ensure that the oceans were "a right of way" for all. Mallory, meanwhile, echoed *Time* publisher Henry Luce and warned that "America can never return to isolationism and still survive as a first class nation." That meant "new responsibilities, new opportunities for service, for trade, for leadership." During the war, while museum attendance jumped, Mystic became a suburb of Groton, where Electric Boat employed twelve thousand.[20]

After the conflict, Cutler and the MHA prioritized commercial shipping. In 1946, he sent members a pamphlet issued by defense contractor Westinghouse Electric Corporation, which stated that the merchant marine secured America's defense, exported its surplus products, and buttressed a seafaring tradition. At an MHA meeting, he urged members to lobby Congress, as did Frazer A. Bailey, former president of Matson Navigation Company. "If history teaches us anything," said Bailey restating Admiral Mahan, "it is that no nation can long remain a leader in world affairs unless it maintains its own sea trade." But as the number of Americans working at sea "declined precipitously," Cutler told the *Saturday Evening Post* that Mystic served "as a training ground" for mariners. Congress acted otherwise, disposing of almost two thousand ships from 1946 to 1951.[21]

The Marine Historical Association also focused on the perceived Communist threat. While MHA trustee Francis Vivian Drake, a *Reader's Digest* editor, was telling members that America was "the most vulnerable target in the world," Republicans were charging that it was being subverted by internal enemies, implicitly New Dealers. Cutler saw a grave conflict between statism and individualism. As he claimed before the Newcomen Society, an Anglo-American group promoting applied science and unfettered capitalism, the theory of statism rejected personal responsibility, while individualism was being undercut by aliens. For Mallory, statism was advancing under President Harry Truman, who "sugar-coated and honey-phrased" his agenda, including his proposal for national health insurance in 1945, to woo support. New Dealers were "like noxious insects," griped Harold H. Kynett, MHA director (1941–73). He was the philosopher behind Mallory, who explained in his autobiography, which was partly written and thoroughly edited by Kynett, "Over a period of more than thirty-five years, 'Doc' Kynett has probably had more to do with my 'education' and thinking than any other person." An archconservative who fumed over welfare, the Left, and mass society, Kynett wrote lengthy books, self-published as Christmas greetings, including *Fireside Admiral* (1950) on the MHA.[22]

In the hands of Kynett and Mallory, a right-wing nationalism shaped heritage preservation. Historic sites such as Mystic and Williamsburg, said Mallory in 1945, had a "part to play in continuing America's growth and avoiding an early decay." As such, Mystic's "priceless relics," the MHA declared, were "of Americans, by Americans, and for Americans." While critics of capitalism idealized common seamen, Kynett conceded that "the radicals, the Leftists of tradition, trespass occasionally" at his museum. But curators rallied "to repel boarders" using "relics of the past," such as the swords and pistols displayed in the Navy Corner. Mallory regarded those heirlooms as weapons "in our fight against the Godless materialist creed of Communism." To better convey that message, Mystic produced an "indoctrinal film," *Origins of Freedom* (1955). Reflecting his ideological thrust, Kynett "conceived and supervised" the movie, which was scripted by curator Edouard Stackpole. So unlike the real world of whaling, it depicted *Morgan*'s wholesome crew, their valorous hunt, and the freedom-minded port.[23]

The Cold War fueled an interest in exploring the heavens and seas. Concern spiraled after the USSR launched Sputnik (1957), and the space (missile) race prompted Henry B. du Pont to fund a seaport planetarium. Devereux Josephs, an education adviser to President Eisenhower, used Sputnik to suggest at the 1958 MHA meeting that Americans needed more science and a better use of their free time. "We run the risk of being undermined by leisure," he warned. Meanwhile, Explorer's Hall showed an exhibit on the Groton-built USS *Skate*. Proving the Arctic's strategic value in 1959, Commander James F. Calvert surfaced *Skate* at the North Pole, the first submarine to do so. Invited to speak at the museum, he recounted the adventure but also noted the desperate world situation posed by diminishing fossil fuels, an exploding population, and the "prospect of atomic annihilation." Surprisingly, he added that America's overconsumption created more "international friction than [did] political ideologies." He wanted to promote peace by raising "the world's living standards." Shipping mogul James A. Farrell Jr. rebutted by hawking America's "maritime strength."[24]

"DEDICATED TO THE PRESERVATION OF INDIVIDUAL RESPONSIBILITY": CREATING A VILLAGE BEFORE 1965

Inspired by Colonel Green's planned backdrop at Round Hill, Cutler proposed "the re-assembling along our waterfront of an early seaport street—wharves and ships on one side; lofts, shops and stores on the other, equipped in working order." Its "architecture and, as far as possible, the majority of the collections" would be limited to the period from 1820 to 1860. Green's dock had included the derelict James Driggs shipsmith shop of New Bedford, for which Cutler paid $50. Refusing to pay a mover $3,500, Cutler and assistant MacDonald Steers disassembled and trucked the shop and heavy equipment to Mystic. Hard work was Cutler's pride. With Steers, he loaded eighty tons of salt into *Morgan*'s hold, which he called "the toughest job I have ever struck since my going to sea." He had also watched MHA officers and members arrive in yachts and cruisers, stoking his resentment of upper-class dandies. "It is hard to get the brass tacks stuff over to our idle rich," he told a friend, and such work was "about all the old whaleships and the merchant marine signified."[25]

As attendance reached 23,000 in 1947, Cutler had second thoughts. "Whatever is done," he wrote Mallory, "we should avoid any tendency to a large and pretentious development." But tourism pushed the village's creation. First, a river bulkhead raised the ground level four feet. When a two-hundred-foot dock was built in 1948, the New York Yacht Club loaned (until 1999) its Station No. 10, a seashore Gothic Revival structure attributed to Alexander Jackson Davis. Needing "a snappy moniker," the MHA began calling itself Mystic Seaport. With 1,000 members in the MHA, "it takes a broader term to express a haven for yachtsmen, a port of call for the old salts, and a nostalgic hour or two for anybody, with 2200 feet of real salt water frontage from the new yacht dock to the farthest point of the Old Seaport Street. Seventeen acres of land redolent of hemp and tar, steeped in history, and dedicated to the ideals of individual enterprise, and the dignity of Man. 'Museum' won't do any more. We've grown beyond that."[26]

Second, Cutler wanted to include a sail loft, a working shipyard, and shops for a boatbuilder, rigger, cooper, and chandler. Another street was placed inland not only for a church and school but to "cut off" adjacent, modern backyards. Otherwise, he said, it would "be hard for the visitor to preserve the illusion that he has been transported back into the past," when "life was slow but satisfying and sure." That required a considerable remaking of history, as in 1944 when the museum acquired its second building, the Old Mystic Bank, the state's second oldest. It was purchased by Cora Mallory Munson, Philip's sister and widow of Frank C. Munson, whose steamship company ironically relied on foreign vessels before its bankruptcy in 1934. Formerly in Old Mystic, two miles northward, it was chartered in 1833 but failed in the late 1880s downturn. Reconstructed on Seaport Street with a portico that existed only in a sketch, the stone Greek Revival bank was dedicated in 1950. It was recast as a nexus in global commerce and, said the guidebook, "fitted out as an old-time shipowner's counting house. . . . Over the mantel is a painting of Hong Kong harbor, indicating that he is engaged in the China trade."[27]

Good press followed, as when the *Saturday Evening Post* spotlighted the Seaport in 1948; the story influenced Karl Kortum to found the San Francisco Maritime Museum. This "maritime Williamsburg" was, the *Post* reported, "a charming memorial to the romantic seafaring days." Its half-dozen photographs included Cutler and crew with officer's caps and tobacco pipes, surrounded by adoring children. Mystic reprinted ten thousand promotional copies. As tourism jumped to 36,505 in 1949, Cutler worried, however, that "the taste of the multitude" would trump his stoutheartedness. Kynett reassured him that, unlike Coney Island, it did not attract "those who seek 'thrill' entertainment." But tourism was ballooning with a national increase in family size, suburban homes, leisure time, and car ownership. Mystic was 55 miles from Hartford, 95 from Boston, and 135 from New York City. Though Kynett noted in 1950 that its "badly paved roads" deterred modernity, Esso's 1953 state road map featured the Seaport and *Morgan* on its front and back covers. To keep cars and busses away from the exhibit buildings, the museum opened a parking lot.[28] (See fig. 13.)

That, together with Harriet Stillman's donation of Shipyard Point, pushed the village's expansion. In 1949, the Seaport acquired the locally built Fishtown Chapel (1889) and relocated it behind *Packard*'s three-ton anchor. It invented, in addition to gravestones, a spire for its Gothic board-and-batten walls and arched door. Made into a "seamen's bethel," where clergy held Sunday vespers, it became the "most photographed" building. In 1950, the Seaport also dedicated the one-room Little Red Schoolhouse, which was attributed to 1768 and used in Griswold, Connecticut, into the 1920s. It included the original blackboard, master's desk, and stove. With their

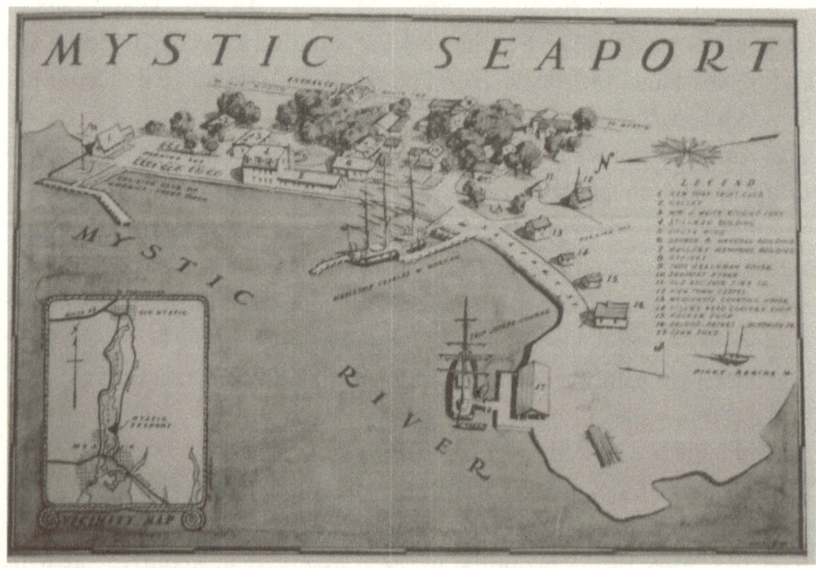

FIGURE 13. Map, 1950. *Courtesy of Mystic Seaport Museum.*

"meager but sound education," the guidebook noted, its students built "the ships that made their country's flag respected around the world."[29]

Nearby was placed the Samuel Buckingham House (1768). Donated in 1951 by the state highway department, which planned demolition, its three parts were barged from Old Saybrook. With a huge central chimney, framed timbers, and a 1690s wing, the house captured Connecticut's history: its denizens had founded Yale College, won the Revolution, and governed the state during the Civil War. Once at the Seaport, however, it was transformed into a shipmaster's house, as it engendered, said Kynett, "a feeling of snug harbor and stout security." Of all the exhibits, it appealed to women. While many sailors longed for the sea, which affirmed their manliness, such a house was a wife's bastion. Radiating a "quiet, stable charm" that was "so seldom in evidence nowadays," the kitchen served tea. The 1850s-style garden embodied the era's eco-imperialism; ships had brought its plants "from the far corners of the earth."[30]

Though Cutler launched the village project, its development was overseen by his successor, Edouard A. Stackpole, who served as curator from 1953 to 1966. Descended from a Nantucket whaling family, Stackpole had worked as associate editor of the island's weekly newspaper and as president, curator, and librarian of its historical society, which operated a small whaling museum. He sharpened Mystic's ideological thrust, claiming that the village was "an historical reincarnation rather than a restoration." Adjacent to the schoolhouse, Stackpole placed a building from nearby Pawcatuck to house the Geo. H. Stone & Co., Groceries and Hardware. Attributed to circa 1850, it was refurbished as a general store by Stone, who stocked it with his own collection. In the 1950s there was nothing more fabled than a general store, though it soon disappeared with Main Street's decline. Melding capitalism and democracy, the guidebook called it "the coffee house, the caucus, the chautauqua and lecture platform of the smaller community." Thus, when the Buckingham House, chapel, schoolhouse, and general store were ideologically joined, said Stackpole, they represented "the four bulwarks of our American Freedom—the Home, Church, School and Free Enterprise System." Frank Capra's propaganda film, *Why We Fight* (1942), used similar cornerstones.[31]

After unwanted antebellum residences were demolished, the village necessitated other inventions. Besides acquiring Greenmanville's Seventh Day Baptist Church in 1951, which Mallory moved and remade into a town hall, it created Spouter Tavern. In *Moby-Dick*, Melville wrote of

New Bedford's Spouter-Inn and its "heathenish array of monstrous clubs and spears" and its "cracked glass cases, filled with dusty rarities." Unable to find a real tavern, Mystic invented one with neatly decorated ship models, pewter mugs, and paintings. It was, said Stackpole, "the type wherein people of a seaport town met to discuss mercantile affairs, political events and regional happenings." Dedicated in 1956, it was donated by Rudolph J. Schaefer III, whose brewery underwrote its costs. But in a case of real preservation, the MHA saved in situ on Greenmanville Avenue the Thomas Greenman House (1842), which was given in 1945 by his granddaughter, Mary Stillman Harkness. Built in the fashionable Greek Revival style, its first floor was restored to reflect a well-to-do, mid-nineteenth-century shipbuilder. A visitor admitted, "If you're an addict of Victoriana, the interior will be a feast."[32]

Imitating Colonial Williamsburg, the Seaport showed period crafts but faced limits. In 1950 the Plymouth Cordage Company of Massachusetts donated its oldest ropewalk (1824). Originally 1,050 feet long, it was clipped to 262 feet because of the museum's limited money and space. In 1951, the museum barged to Seaport Street the two-and-a-half-story Charles Mallory Sail Loft (1832). Like the Mallory Exhibit Building, it illustrated the family's hold on Mystic's museum. Its keeper "was a white-haired mariner who joined his first ship when still a boy," noted a *House & Garden* writer in 1967. "This is typical of many of the Mystic Seaport craftsmen—ships and the sea have been their whole lives." Nearby were exhibits of a ship carver and a shipwright. Stackpole idealized their "simple work habits," telling docents that old-time America was "uncircumscribed by labor-management relations." Suspicious of his era's union shop, he praised an earlier day "founded on the right of the individual to select his own life."[33]

Seaport Street became, admitted Kynett, more "a stage setting" than "a museum piece." In 1952 Cutler sought Mallory's assurances that he was "definitely opposed to adding another row of buildings on [Shipyard] point." He warned that more development would make the Seaport "a swollen caricature of the primitive simplicity we set out to represent." Still, the museum grew. After the New Shoreham (RI) Life Saving Station (1874) was threatened with demolition, for example, the museum built a copy and swapped it for the original, which it placed on Shipyard Point. At a time when critic Ada Louise Huxtable was equating the removal or reconstruction of such structures with fakery, others championed the practice. The fact that the village was fabricated, opined *Popular Photography*, put "it on anybody's list of highly photogenic sites." Not only had fake become appealing, it passed for the real thing, as when *Museum* magazine concluded, "Everything is just as it was 100 years ago."[34]

Interpreting the Seaport was a necessity. What began in the 1930s as a one-man operation slowly attracted a corps of female hostesses, Girl Scouts, and Sea Scouts. Knowing that Colonial Williamsburg had a department of interpretation, Mystic placed costumed female interpreters, mostly local retirees, at exhibits in 1955. Period clothing for men became available in 1963. Stackpole also placed button-activated recordings at some sites, but he stated his message on a large billboard at the gate. It first read, "MYSTIC SEAPORT IS DEDICATED TO AN UNDERSTANDING OF THE ORIGINS OF YOUR AMERICAN FREEDOM," but he sharpened it as, "Dedicated to the Preservation of Individual Responsibility." Making sure that his "activists" were on cue, he asked in his training manual: "Why did a Democratic or Capitalistic system of business result rather than a Socialistic system?" While stressing that "free enterprise" insured a "vigorous and wealthy" society," he cautioned activists to stress not capitalism's material success, though unevenly distributed, but "our gain in cultural and spiritual values."[35]

"AS INDIVIDUAL AS WORKS OF THE PAINTER OR SCULPTOR": ARTIFACTS AS CURIOS, STORIES, AND TEACHING MOMENTS

By the 1950s, the village had overwhelmed the indoor exhibits (fig. 14). Collecting had started in the early 1930s when Mary Harkness and her sister Charlotte Stillman went antique shopping in Boston. Harkness funded the remodeling of the three-story mill (1862), which opened in 1939 and was named the Stillman Building after her deceased cousin Charles. Their tastes were not those of Cutler, who considered most paintings or prints inadequate in revealing a ship's "essential characteristics" and "remarkable individuality." His discernment applied to models. Most collectors, who included FDR in the Ship Model Society, romanticized full-built models, but the MHA called them faulty. It favored builders' models, which were half-hulls contoured to estimate maneuverability, speed, and capacity. By the 1950s, it had the world's "largest collection," but the public wanted full-built models.[36]

Knowing of the success of the Mariners' Museum, Cutler concluded that "the principal criterion by which [people] judge a museum" was its figureheads (fig. 15). Once removed from a derelict bow, however, most rotted

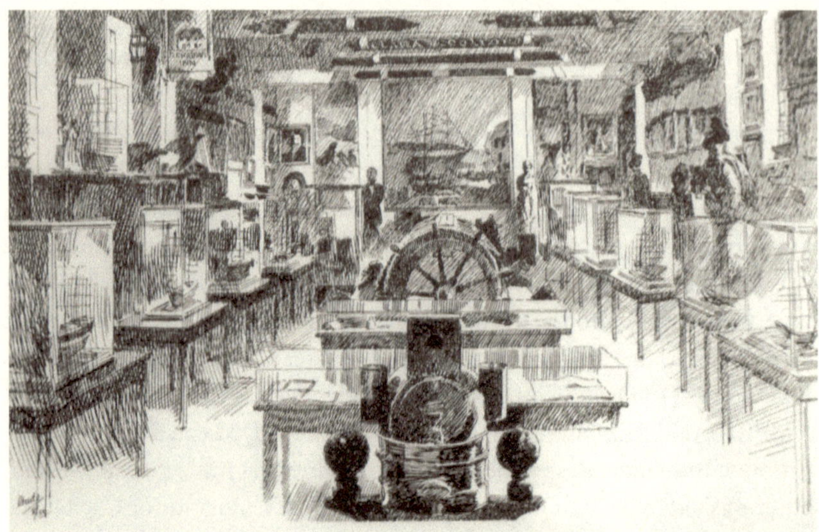

FIGURE 14. Stillman Building, south wing, in Harold H. Kynett, *Fireside Admiral* (1950), sketch by F. Wade Lane. *Courtesy of the Nantucket Atheneum and Edna G. Kynett Memorial Foundation.*

away. After Kynett donated his collection (and a room was named in his honor), Mystic possessed the nation's most extensive holdings. The Indian figure on *Seminole* was the only one from a Mystic-built ship. Ironically, the Pequots lived in Mystic; *Seminole* depicted an inland, not coastal, native. Female figures ranged from a matron to a goddess. Fixed on the rudderhead of a British coaster, *Saucy Sally* flaunted a "low-cut bodice" and "proper breasts." "The unabashed Miss *Sally*," said Stackpole, "never failed to arouse interest." By the 1950s the Stillman Building was overflowing with a hodgepodge of items, though Cutler had pledged to focus on the "crude, homely, everyday things" of American seamen. For young visitors, the Seaport had "a live Museum," where a child could "see, handle and feel" the artifacts. With an "early 16th century" Spanish chest, for example, they were told, amazingly, to "turn the key and see the complicated mechanism work."[37]

As Mallory prioritized the village, the Seaport's research program also suffered. In 1930, it published its first pamphlet, and fifteen by 1941, but Cutler wanted more and brought Walter Muir Whitehill to speak. An *American Neptune* founder and later managing editor, he told the audience that a museum must publish to be "vital and creative." In 1947, Cutler launched a quarterly journal, the *Log of Mystic Seaport*. Wanting "a definitive history

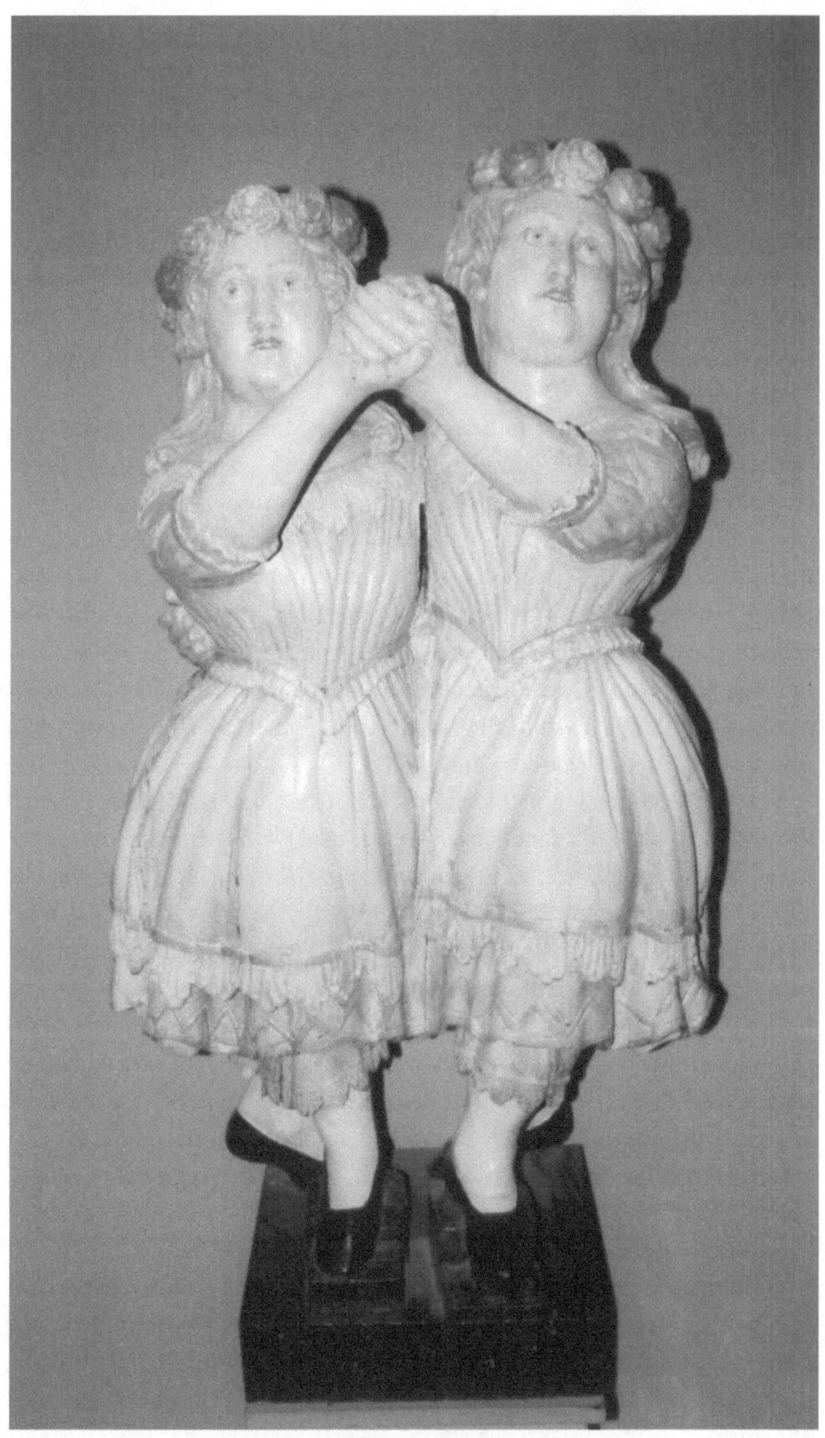

FIGURE 15. Figurehead, Sisters. *Photo by author, 1998.*

of America's sea record," he sought more details of "everyday life at sea in the old sailing ships," including vulgar expressions and manly chanties, which were unlike his day's "panty-waist radio and barber-shop chanties." Research required support, and in 1949 Harriet Stillman bequeathed her father's 1841 house. It became a curator's office and library until 1965. By then, major history museums had accepted Whitehill's advice that they were required to preserve their manuscripts and printed resources, "make them available to qualified users," and publish "as much as an institution's means permit."[38]

In 1954, Mystic added a fourth role with the Munson Institute of American Maritime Studies. Endowed by Cora Mallory Munson in 1955, it offered graduate students a five-week, six-credit course through the University of Connecticut. Examining the "development of the nation's leadership in world trade," it fit the day's commercial expansionism. Directed by Stackpole, it was coordinated by Harvard University's Robert G. Albion, who tried to steer the curriculum between "the nitpickers and the b.s. artists." Initially, most faculty were "members of the Naval Institute," but lecturers included Frank Braynard of the American Merchant Marine Institute and Ernest Dodge of the Peabody Museum.[39]

The MHA's collecting included boats. In 1931 Charles Stillman donated the first, a Mystic-built sandbagger, *Annie* (1880). Once cumbersome work boats, sandbaggers became "the fancy of New York yachtsmen in the late 1800's." Only twenty-eight feet long, but with large sails, *Annie* had fourteen crew members who shifted the ballast, carried in thirty fifty-pound bags, from tack to tack. As such, said Cutler, *Annie* needed "the ablest and most active young sailor men." But, when Yankees lost interest, sandbaggers waned. Meanwhile, museums were considering what other boats to save. Whitehill had advised curators to "emphasize primarily the activities of [their] own region." But, he admitted, some museums would develop "specialized collections which are national rather than regional in scope." Though he urged Mystic to focus on the Connecticut coast, Cutler boasted in 1948 that Mystic was the first to "be national in scope."[40]

Linking its region to the vast Atlantic Ocean, Mystic acquired some one-of-a-kind craft. Depicting the Grand Banks fisheries off Newfoundland, the forty-two-foot *Regina M* (1900) was purchased by Clifford Mallory in 1940, restored in 1958, and called (incorrectly) New England's last pinky schooner. The thirty-four-foot Friendship sloop *Estella A.* (1904) had fished off Maine but had been converted to a yacht. Arriving in 1957, it reportedly became "the most authentically restored Friendship sloop to be found anywhere." In 1956, Mystic superintendent James Kleinschmidt saved a nineteen-foot Kingston Lobster Boat (1892) rotting in a field. It was "one of an all but vanished type." Anchored in the Mystic River was the 123-foot *L. A. Dunton* (1921), which was purchased in 1963. Though it hardly resembled its original make as a Gloucester fishing schooner, a type that succeeded the smaller pinky, it was "the last of her kind to be constructed without an engine." Originally equipped with ten dories, whose workers had toiled under the lay system, it had worked the Grand Banks, with each dory catching up to eighteen hundred pounds of cod. Arriving in 1964, it was rerigged, but the story of its workers' bleak lives was told only later.[41]

Mystic even accepted a remembrance of FDR, which was endowed by his friends. "To breed [his children as] real sailors," Roosevelt had acquired the twenty-four-foot sloop *Vireo* (1914) for Campobello Island in 1920. But he was soon struck by polio. Cutler and Stillman shared FDR's interest in sea training. After the U.S. Maritime Commission (USMC) bypassed Mystic and established its academy at Kings Point (1943), however, the MHA focused on adolescents, first with Sea Scouts during the war and then, in 1947, when it hired Marion Dickerman to establish an education department. Best known for her work on behalf of the Democratic Party and less so for an intimate relationship with Eleanor Roosevelt, who later came to speak, her politics were antipodal to those of Mallory or Cutler, but she was an accomplished educator. By 1951, five thousand children were participating in the Seaport's program annually. It stressed "cooperation, tolerance, loyalty and high aspiration," which were prized by the era's corporate culture.[42]

Enhancing the Mariner Training Program, the USMC's square-rigged *Joseph Conrad* was given by an act of Congress. Built in Copenhagen as *Georg Stage* (1882), it had trained five thousand boys for the Danish merchant marine. Constructed of "sturdy Swedish iron," it survived a collision in 1905, but twenty-two mariners perished. In 1934, adventurer Alan Villiers renamed it *Joseph Conrad* under British registry. With a crew of teenage boys he sailed around the world—57,800 miles in 555 days. Only 110 feet long, "she looked almost as if she had sailed out of a bottle," he said. After becoming a U.S. training vessel, it was discarded and almost "relegated to the graveyard," having "grown a crop of grass and barnacles a foot and one-half thick." In August 1947, the MHA accepted *Conrad* at its annual meeting, which drew seven admirals, two members of Congress, and a one-thousand-strong audience. Recalling his training aboard similar ships,

Pacific War hero Admiral William F. Halsey Jr. (USN, ret.) did not omit the day's politics. President Truman had announced his containment policy, and Halsey declared that the "whole war was futile" if the nation stood down against communism. But, unfit for sailing, *Conrad* stood down and bunked thousands of youngsters over the years.[43]

While students practiced sailing aboard nineteen-foot dhows, in 1950 the Seaport initiated its Dyer Dhow Derby, which still continues. To introduce at-sea experiences for advanced mariners, it accepted, in 1953, the sixty-one-foot auxiliary schooner *Brilliant* (1932). Gifted by trustee Briggs Cunningham, a local industrialist, it was "one of the finest yachts of her size ever built in the United States." By 1992, *Brilliant* had trained more than five thousand youth, carrying up to ten students aboard weekly summer cruises.[44]

Unique for its day, the Mariner Training Program broke the gender barrier. Girl mariners had first come to Mystic through the scouts program in 1945. Besides learning swimming and sailing a dhow, they lived aboard *Conrad*, where they enforced their own laws, each of which was represented by a nautical symbol. Seeing the anchor, for example, they repeated: "I will face life with steadfastness and courage." That was needed, as their "final entertainment of the evening" in 1949 was a nightmarish "atom bomb test movie." Girl scouts who could not make the trip received "the loan of a sea chest" with pictures and films. By 1961, over 7,300 girls and boys had joined the program; by the early 1970s, the number was almost 19,000.[45] (See fig. 16.)

After Kynett claimed that *Conrad* showed off "the virtues of rugged masculinity," Villiers was startled to see "teen-age young women in blue uniforms" scrambling up *Conrad*'s companionway. A biographer depicted Villiers as a misogynist, but he reacted positively when the oldest woman, a Vassar graduate, bragged about her four-day cruise aboard *Brilliant* with nine sixteen-year-old girls. "We were no sissies as we scraped knuckles furling sail and working lines," she boasted. Like Cutler, she said: "So much of what is finest in America dates from the days of sailing ships. That's why we have these courses: to teach interested teenagers real, living history with real ships." Those courses—during the spring, summer, and fall—had a gender imbalance. On average, for every one hundred boys who attended, more than five hundred girls enlisted. To lodge them, *Conrad* was thrice hauled from 1960 to 1967 for hull repairs; its exterior was sprayed with polyester resin and fiberglass, while the interior's "dangerously thin"

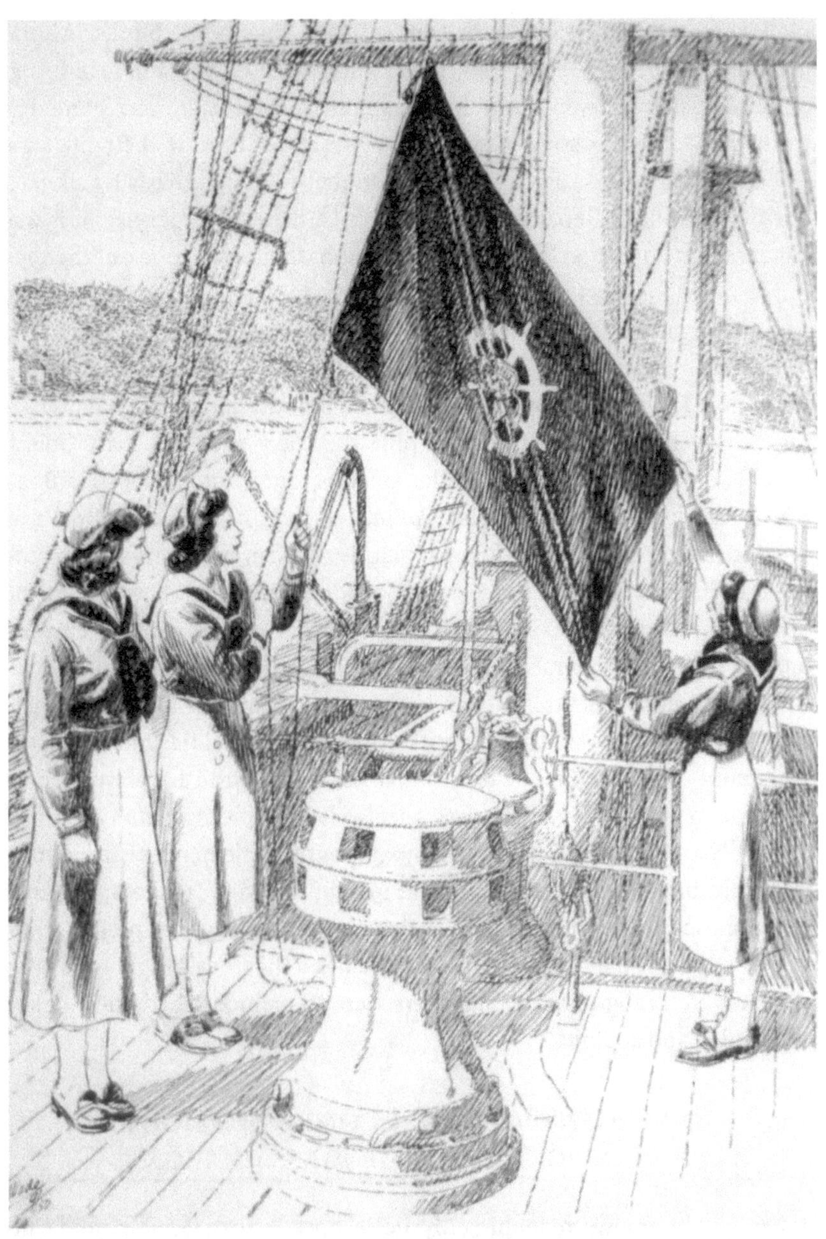

FIGURE 16. Girl Mariners Hoisting Colors aboard *Joseph Conrad*, in Kynett, *Fireside Admiral* (1950), sketch by F. Wade Lane. *Courtesy of the Nantucket Atheneum and Edna G. Kynett Memorial Foundation.*

plating was covered with ferro-cement. Needing more bunks, Mystic accepted the seventy-seven-foot coasting schooner *Australia* in 1951. Listed chronologically as twenty-fifth in U.S. shipping records, it was regarded as the nation's oldest existing commercial vessel afloat. Prior to their gift, Mrs. E. Paul du Pont and sons wanted to trim its two rotted masts by six feet, but Cutler balked. Repaired under Howard Chapelle's supervision, it was "in excellent condition." With girl scouts aboard, it even rode out the 1954 hurricane as four feet of water flooded Seaport Street. After its provenance was investigated and reset to 1862, however, *Australia* told the story of the West Indies trade.[46]

Of all MHA ships, *Morgan* was the most famous, but in disrepair. Offering help were personnel from not only the Navy and the Coast Guard, which were well represented in the exhibits, but Groton's Electric Boat, which also helped regularly with *Conrad*. In the 1930s, Electric Boat was accused of war profiteering, but by 1940 it was firmly integrated into the naval-industrial complex. Its Seaport work proved its bona fides. But the Seaport needed more corporate sponsors because gate receipts covered only 41 percent of operating costs. Sponsoring an exhibit aboard *Morgan* in 1956, for example, Archer Daniels Midland Company marketed whale products like steaks and oil, despite an increasing public interest in the mammal's conservation. In the vein of New Bedford's hero worship of Yankees, moreover, Mystic leaders selectively pictured *Morgan*'s crew and history. "Not too many authentic photographs of whalemen" existed, Kynett ironically, but inaccurately, claimed in 1950. If they did, "reality might mar tradition and that would never do." Evincing an upper-crust prejudice, he suggested that some men were so dark and hairy that they "might have been mistaken for orangutans," while others were so malnourished, they looked "slab-sided and anemic."[47]

"DIVERGENT VIEWS ARE COMING TO LIGHT": A CORPORATE REGIME TAKES CHARGE

The tourist boom was redefining Mystic Seaport. In 1949, Mallory told Cutler that the Seaport "had become a 'big business' and should thenceforth operate as a big business." Shocked, Cutler realized he was "on a strange ship with a crew that [spoke] a different language." In a 1950 essay, "The Future of Mystic Seaport," he told members that "divergent views are coming to light." While the MHA's founders had wanted to show, unlike "any other museum on earth," an old-time community, Mallory was worrying about money, having a budget of $85,000 and twenty full-time employees. To raise revenue, he had opened the Seaport Store and hired part-time manager Charles Brooks in 1948. Cutler instead proposed limiting growth and building an endowment; he argued that the store "violated the spirit of non-profit associations." Mallory overruled him, knowing that Colonial Williamsburg had created revenue-producing subsidiaries.[48] (See fig. 17.)

At an executive committee meeting in his New York office in late 1951, Mallory proposed giving Brooks full-time standing, more authority, and a higher salary. Cutler saw it as his make-or-break issue. As secretary, he crafted the minutes, amplified his perspective, and mailed a draft copy to the larger board of directors. Outraged, Mallory refused to accept them. If the controversy became public, he warned, it could "promote pointless discussion." Cutler considered quitting and told his brother that the Seaport had "become a sort of nightmare." He opposed Brooks's salary, which was "more than the [combined pay of the] five next most highly paid members of the organization," and his "sliding scale" commission based on profits. The latter, Cutler told Mallory, was "quite illegal." Angered, Mallory threatened to

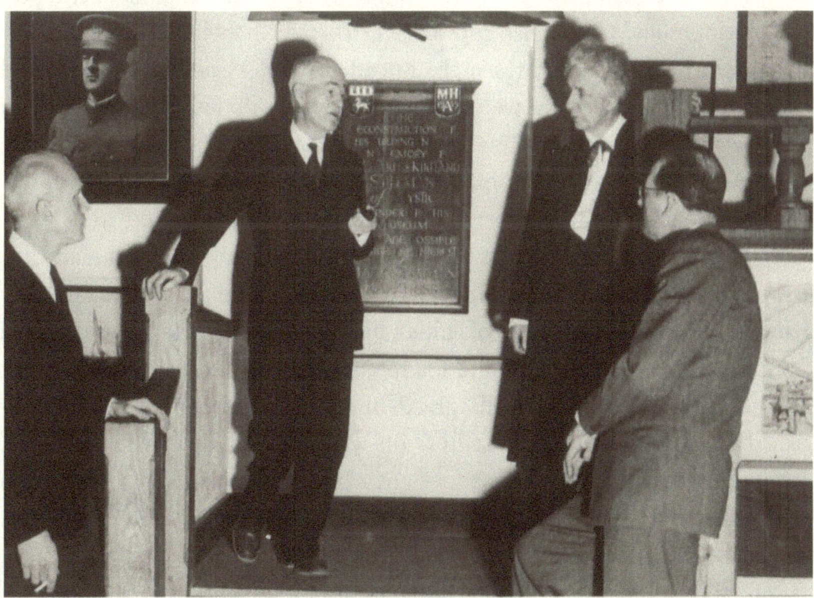

FIGURE 17. From left to right, MacDonald Steers, Carl Cutler, Marion Dickerman, and Charles Brooks. On the wall is a photograph of Charles Stillman. *Courtesy of Mystic Seaport Museum.*

"withdraw from the organization," but he and Kynett personally covered the profit sharing. Those "secret contributions," Cutler told Marion Dickerman, "approximately doubled" Brooks's earnings.[49]

Cutler also objected to Brooks's augmented responsibilities managing nonstore spending. Like Mallory, Brooks privileged business operations and revenue creation. When the souvenir shop failed to reap expected profits, he cut Cutler's staff and drafted the museum budget "without any consultation with curatorial, educational or library departments." Their personalities aggravated the rift. Cutler was a proud puritan, scholar, and rugged individualist. Brooks was, he thought, "a glib talker and a smooth cocktail companion." When Mallory was living in Miami Beach or New York, Brooks had "a strangle hold." Cutler wrote long letters to family and friends, complaining that Mallory had adopted "the methods and practices of a soulless modern corporation."[50]

Distraught, Cutler tried to line up his replacement. He thought Villiers had the right traits: "a pioneering spirit, a vision and plenty of practical experience." In 1950 and 1952, he proposed hiring Villiers, telling him he was "troubled by the fact" that marine museums were slipping "into the pattern of an ordinary business." But Kynett warned Mallory that he would make Mystic nothing "more than a Villiers' shrine" and undercut his "leadership and policy development." Cutler also considered Howard Chapelle, "the top ranking man in the field of nautical research." But after a Cutler briefing, Chapelle told the search committee: "If I were to assume responsibilities," the emphases on the village and the business manager "would have to be changed." Rebuffed, Chapelle soon moved to Washington, D.C., where he overhauled the Smithsonian's late nineteenth-century National Watercraft Collection.[51]

In 1952, Mallory and Kynett took charge of the hiring and excluded Cutler. They brought in Edouard Stackpole, who, said Cutler, had three faults: he had "no practical knowledge of ships"; his newspaper work was "no school for a serious research man"; and his reputation was based on local history and juvenile fiction. Mallory disagreed. In 1950, the Newcomen Society published Stackpole's adulatory address on whaling capitalist William Rotch, whom he praised as "America's first great Internationalist." In 1951, he also received a fellowship to study whaling, which led to *The Sea Hunters* (1953). Kynett backed "an unknown like Stackpole" because he had "to make a reputation" and would be malleable. He served as curator until 1966.[52]

Cutler was ill equipped to retire. Sacrificing his "family for so many years," he lived "on a very poor scale." Seventy-three years old, he hoped to spend his future writing. Repeating his complaints, he told Mallory he would resign as of December 31, 1952. The letter shocked Mallory. "Neither I nor any of your associates have sold their souls to Mammon," he protested, while defending his policies "to promote efficiency." He warned: "Under no circumstances is anything to be gained by an open breach which can only serve to encourage gossip and create schisms." He asked him to stay on as curator emeritus with "a retirement allowance."[53]

Cutler resigned quietly. With only his wife's modest wealth, he became curator emeritus and took the hush money, which was initially $2,375 per year but subsequently reduced by Mallory. It was a bitter pill to swallow for a rugged individualist who attacked social security but lacked a pension. He bared his soul privately, griping that the museum was being subverted by "a feverish concern for high pressure salesmanship." In 1953, the Mystic grapevine buzzed, but the local *New London Day* let Mallory respond. "What's the inside story on Mystic Seaport?" the *Day* asked. Was it "squandering money" and relying on a "rich patron"? Mallory replied, "Decidedly not." He even denied that "some officers or employees [were] subsidized by private gifts from the directors." He blasted the "malicious gossip" and "misinformation." Meanwhile, Brooks was rising. In 1957, after he appointed his wife to head the store, he became general manager with a full-time staff of sixty, and in 1964, managing director with a doubled staff. Reacting to criticism, Mallory created a new, but half-time, position of director, which was filled in 1956 by Vice Admiral James Fife Jr. (USN, ret.). Coincidentally, the Mariners' Museum had just hired a retired admiral. Wanting civilians in those jobs, Howard Chapelle thought both museums deserved censure.[54]

Cutler's criticism of "high pressure salesmanship" anticipated Stackpole's equation of visitors with shoppers. "We should be continually aware," he said in his training manual, that "the public comes to 'buy' or reject" the Mystic story. To boost revenue, it opened every day except Thanksgiving and Christmas and, in 1953, doubled the adult ticket to a dollar. With one hundred thousand annual sightseers, it became "Connecticut's No. 1 tourist spot" by 1955, and three years later, the gate had doubled. While the Mystic River Drawbridge (U.S. Route 1) was "the busiest bridge in the state," the bridge tender sometimes warned approaching boats, "No more room at Mystic Seaport!" In 1963, I-95 opened one mile north of the Seaport, spurring development.[55]

The Marine Historical Association developed a pyramidal hierarchy, with visitors to Mystic Seaport as the base, annual members in the middle, and major donors at the apex. Though 5,885 had joined the MHA by 1958, its leaders appealed to metropolitan and corporate elite. Complaints followed, especially during the Cutler imbroglio. One volunteer quit in 1951, alleging that it was "bowing to the great dog dollar" and "forgetting our great mass of supporters who have limited means." So, too, did a former MHA secretary allege that Mallory noticed visitors only if they were "in Dun & Bradstreet, or possibly the Social Register." Mallory countered that "large contributions" were its future, claiming that the MHA would have "fold[ed] up" long ago if left to local people. His strategy fueled expansion, as big donors were, he admitted, "very loathe to contribute for endowment and even more for salaries." They wanted a dramatic "physical improvement," such as a building. As a result, from 1961 to 1966, operating expenses rose 94 percent, while attendance jumped 80 percent. By 1968, the budget had passed a million dollars. Full-time staff reached 150, but a museum CEO soon conceded that many employees were hardly paid "a living wage."[56]

For its thirtieth anniversary in 1959, first-year president Franklin Cole invited Cutler to address the annual meeting. Not only had the Naval Institute Press just reissued *Greyhounds of the Sea*, but it had also published his *Queens of the Western Ocean*, for which Admiral Chester Nimitz (USN) wrote a foreword. Alienated from the MHA, Cutler was surprised when Cole welcomed "any kind of constructive criticism." Cutler told his audience, "I offered him some very fine constructive criticism and he wouldn't even listen to it." Yet, ever the gentleman, he said nothing of the flare-up with Mallory, who shared the dais, and accepted a standing ovation. An MHA pamphlet, *The Three Founders* (1965), dodged Cutler's critique. The Seaport ignored him, even after his death in 1966. But Stonington named a school in his honor. A later museum president ambiguously described Cutler's era as "a difficult maturation."[57]

"WE WERE THE LAUGHING STOCK OF THE MUSEUM WORLD": SETTING A NEW COURSE

In 1965, the Seaport began to change course as U.S. museums and preservation organizations were gradually introducing more professional regimens. Though Mallory stayed on as chairman (until 1970), Stackpole as curator (until 1966), and Brooks as managing director (until 1966), Waldo C. M. Johnston took the helm as its first CEO and director. With a bachelor's degree from Yale University and a master's from Harvard, he had taught at an elite academy, served as a World War II lieutenant colonel, and handled Yale's admissions. Though he lacked training in museum or historical studies, he was a sailor in the New York Yacht Club and cultivated upper-class circles. In 1967, for example, he added to his board Thomas J. Watson Jr. (IBM chairman) and Jakob Isbrandtsen (shipping baron). Henry du Pont was vice president.

In 1965 Mystic was, said Johnston, "more of a theme park" than a museum. "It wasn't very professional, in my book. It had some good collections and a good location—it was a fun place to come to, but . . . we were sort of the laughing stock of the museum world." The public was having fun. Imitating Williamsburg, the guidebook (1965) copied its graphic design and reiterated its traditionalist values. In 1968, after Villiers contributed a flattering, nineteen-page essay in *National Geographic*, Mystic "broke all previous attendance records" with a count of 548,139. But the staff were overwhelmed. Half-hour lines were common to board *Morgan* or see exhibits. Even the fictional Hardy Boys visited *Morgan* in one of their teen-audience mystery books. Senator Edward Kennedy brought his schooner and nephew John, son of the martyred president. As the *Wall Street Journal* reported in the bloody summer of 1968, it was an escape. "Get in a small boat," it said, and "when the fog closes in, what's happening in Jordan, Vietnam or the streets of Detroit is of small consequence." While the "embalmed" village seemed more real "than its Colonial counterpart in Virginia," it "kept its character . . . as a living port."[58]

Believing that the Seaport had been mismanaged, Johnston developed a wish list, which included his hope for leaders "who clearly understand the difference between a true museum and a business conglomerate." With that he initiated a sea change and, said a successor, "turned Mystic Seaport into a bona fide museum." Meanwhile, its operating budget "tripled in eight years." He hired Edmund Lynch as curator in 1966; when he resigned in 1969, J. Revell Carr came in, only to discover the stored collections in "deplorable shape." Once Brooks stepped down, the board created the Ships Committee. On it was the legendary captain Irving Johnson, a trustee since 1953, who called Mystic "the only thing of its kind in the world." Later, he added a voice-over to his film *Around Cape Horn*, which he donated to Mystic; it sold over eighty thousand copies in its first six years.[59]

When Waldo Johnston inspected the ships, he was appalled. As he told the First National Maritime Preservation Conference, "I knew something about wooden boats, but not much about dry rot and fungi—and never before had I seen what appeared to be stalactites and stalagmites between the decks of a number of sick ships." He climbed *Morgan*'s rigging, after which curator John Leavitt scolded him that it was "likely to come down." He told him, "The whole fleet [was] a mess." In 1969, Johnston hired marine engineer Maynard Bray as shipyard supervisor. Bray advised, "Lack of good routine maintenance [was] without doubt the biggest cause of sickness and death among old ships everywhere." Setting its course, Lynch ordered, "We must never compromise the one reality—Maritime History is ships."[60]

The fleet had been long suffering. For one, *Australia* was hauled for restoration as a mid-nineteenth-century centerboard coaster in 1961. Discovering extensive decay, workers realized that the hull was "held together literally by paint." Said Johnston, "Some bad mistakes" followed, and the hull "turned to punk." Prohibitively expensive to rebuild, *Australia* became "an example of all the things not to do." He conceded: "We did not know how to preserve ships in those days yet the museum had accepted all kinds of ships and small craft over the years, most of which were in bad shape." That was the pattern nationally. *Australia* was placed in a shed to show its skeleton. For another, *Annie* was "a rotting hulk" outdoors; the sandbagger was rebuilt in 1967. Over Cutler's objections, Mallory had even acquired the double-nosed steam ferry *Brinckerhoff* (1899), boasting that it was "the only one [of ninety-five thousand American steam merchant vessels] to have been preserved intact." Mallory wanted to headline its rare Fletcher walking beam engine, but he balked at the $60,000 repair and decided to scrap it. Facing criticism, in 1961 Mystic gave it to an auto wrecker who promised (but failed) to turn it into a restaurant. Grounded in the Pawcatuck River and damaged by vandals, *Brinckerhoff* was burned by court order in 1965.[61]

Johnston inherited other problem-filled ships, including the Baltic ketch *Gundel* and the Chesapeake Bay bugeye *Dorothy A. Parsons*. Amid Cold War tensions in 1961, the Seaport had accepted *Gundel* because it had brought anticommunist refugees to America in 1948. A bill, sponsored by Representative John F. Kennedy, gave citizenship to its "modern Pilgrims." But it nearly sank at its berth in 1964. Also housing youngsters in the Mariner Training Program was the eighty-four-foot *Parsons*. According to "a story widely circulated at the Seaport, quite possibly apocryphal," said Johnston, it was, in 1960, "simply sailed in, anchored and left there." Because neither related to "the 19th century New England maritime scene," Mystic sold them in 1968 to the Harry Lundeberg School of Seamanship in Maryland. But *Gundel* fell apart before its transfer. In 1968, Mystic also sold the schooner *Bowdoin*, which had been ceremoniously welcomed in 1959, to a Maine sail-training group. More apropos, in 1969 it accepted the forty-seven-foot *Emma C. Berry* (1866), built in nearby Noank. It was restored in 1971 under Chapelle's oversight, but only partially as little was known about its top deck. It was the last wet-well smack, which allowed outside water into the hold to keep its catch fresh.[62]

In 1955, while *Morgan* was reproduced as a plastic, ready-to-assemble Revell model, the real ship was receiving insufficient attention. Fitted with a new upper hull and weather deck in 1961, it was described as "almost completely restored" in its sand berth. But, in 1965, fears of below-the-sand rot prompted desperate "talk of sawing off her bottom and putting her upper hull in a house ashore." A brighter spotlight came with the National Historic Preservation Act (1966), and *Morgan* became the first merchant vessel named as a National Historic Landmark (NHL, 1966; USS *Constitution* was the first naval vessel in 1960. In 1971, the U.S. Post Office featured *Morgan* in a four-stamp set on preservation. Said writer Peter Benchley, "It radiates as much magic as if it were still pounding around the Horn."[63]

That's what Johnston wanted—to feel waves rocking *Morgan*. In preparation, he inspected the clipper *Cutty Sark* (1869) at Greenwich and Lord Nelson's *Victory* (1765) at Portsmouth, both in dry display, and the warship *Vasa* (1628) in a Stockholm museum building. He envied the care and money each received. But before hauling *Morgan* and, if necessary, rebuilding its hull, Lynch wanted to construct a shipyard because comparable facilities were rapidly disappearing. That was a game changer because no other museum had such a facility. It would not only have a "magnetic influence," drawing skilled artisans and perpetuating their threatened crafts, said Johnston, but "add greatly to the museum's stature." Bray was directed to build a shipyard and maintain the fleet, whose number of wooden hulls was unmatched by any U.S. museum. By 1975, he set ship preservation's "guiding principles," which, he said, "sound straightforward enough: put back the same material in the same configuration with the same standards of workmanship and above all make whatever you do reverseable [*sic*]." But, he joked, "if only doing it were as easy as saying it!" He warned, "Saving ships is expensive business," while experimenting with what Johnston called "the study of ship geriatrics."[64] (See fig. 18.)

Building a shipyard was costly, but Henry du Pont stepped in. An MHA trustee and executive of a company under fire for its Vietnam War–era chemical weapons, Henry died in 1970. But, reaping good publicity, his

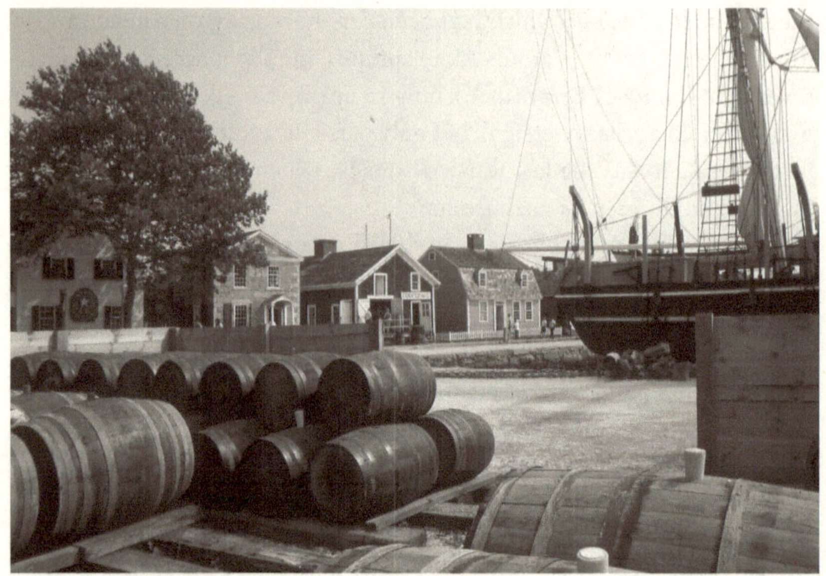

FIGURE 18. *Charles W. Morgan* and the whaling-era waterfront. *Photo by author, 1991.*

family came forward philanthropically. Removed from the village, Mystic's three-acre yard was on deeper water and the site of the former Charles Mallory Shipyard. It included spaces for painting, welding, rigging, and a lathe. Capable of hauling *Morgan*'s 313 gross tons (and similar-size ships), the lift-dock connected via rail to a shed, which included a visitors' gallery. Finished in October 1973, it hauled *Morgan* the following January, when, unexpectedly, Bray found no appreciable hull rot or leakage because "the mud in her seams helped keep her tight." Rerigged as a double-topsail bark (its configuration from 1867 to 1921), *Morgan* returned to a new stone wharf akin to old-time New Bedford. It was guided there by the forty-five-foot tug *Kingston II* (1937), which Electric Boat donated.[65]

The Seaport's most unusual acquisition was *Sabino* (1908). First named *Tourist*, the fifty-seven-foot, steam-screw wooden vessel served Maine's hotel-lined Damariscotta River until cars killed its passenger business. Renamed *Sabino*, it came to Mystic on a trial lease in 1973. Gambling that a U.S. Coast Guard (USCG)–certified passenger steamer would increase tourism, the Seaport finalized the purchase, after which it completed a five-year restoration and booked cruises on the Mystic River. Travelers enjoyed the sights, including coal being shoveled into its boiler. Attracting fifty thousand passengers annually by 1992, it was one of only two extant small steamers (once numbering 260,983 unlicensed vessels) in inland waters. Though only 40 percent of *Sabino*'s original fabric remained, it received NHL designation in 1992. Also recognized were *Dunton* (NHL, 1993) and *Berry* (NHL, 1994), the latter of which had "less than 10 percent" of its original fabric. In 2008, the Steamship Historical Society named *Sabino* Steamship of the Year.[66]

In 1997, Mystic bought the sixty-one-foot, diesel-powered *Roann* (1947), one of the last wooden Eastern-rig draggers for flounder, cod, and haddock. Old-time draggers were symbolic of Southeastern Connecticut because Stonington had once berthed them, while the *New Yorker*'s Joseph Mitchell wrote about the legendary dragger captain of nearby Noank, Ellery Thompson. Though Mystic Seaport had rejected publishing his autobiographical *Draggerman's Haul* (1950), which surprisingly became a Book of the Month Club selection, his ship paintings had become local folk icons. Numbering one thousand, they were hung in chandleries, saloons, and the homes, Thompson said, of nearly "every fishing captain from Point [Judith] to New London." Known also for his colorful yarns, he later became a popular Seaport interpreter. As *Roann* was potentially a National Historic Landmark, it was hauled in 2004 for a three-year, $1.1 million restoration, which was funded equally by the state and the museum. Besides its "lessons about climate change," *Roann* would tell, as did Thompson, "the story of the plight of modern fishermen, diminishing stocks and the regulation of fisheries." By 2008, there were only eighteen fishing and scallop boats, plus twelve lobster boats, left in the state's fleet, which homeported in Stonington.[67]

Mystic's collection of small craft, such as rowboats and dhows, received a boost with John Gardner's hiring in 1969. A tenth-generation Yankee, he learned the centuries-old art of boatbuilding in Calais, Maine. After earning a graduate degree in English and education in 1932, Gardner became, he said, "a full-time radical" on behalf of human rights, ecology, and crafts. "I'm not an antiquarian," he warned. "I have no patience with just collecting things, like a squirrel. They've got to enrich our lives in the present and in the future." As such, he remade Mystic's programs. Deploring "static exhibits," he compared their curators with "morticians embalming corpses." Instead of restoring a boat, which he called a sterile practice, he suggested using an old boat for reference and building a working copy. Keeping traditions alive would provide a creative task for Americans with leisure time.[68]

Impressed by the Antique Boat Museum on New York's St. Lawrence River, he held a Small Craft Workshop in 1969, and in 1970 the first-ever classes in boatbuilding (both still continuing). "History, thus activated, is transformed from an inert subject of scholarly contemplation to a socially constructive force," he said. "This is historic preservation. There is no other way." Adding a Rowing Workshop in 1970, he told the story of an elder craftsman who lamented: "If [the younger generations] can't do it with gasoline, they don't do it." But, facing hostile state and USCG rules limiting the use of privately built craft, Gardner began, in 1974, "waging a war with the Coast Guard and the boating industry." While the Seaport was staging an annual USCG tribute, Gardner called it "a puppet of the boating industry." The USCG reversed its policy. By 1988, Mystic was renting its newly built boats to visitors to ply the two-hundred-yard-wide river. Gardner's success led not only Maine's Lance Lee to open his Apprenticeshop in 1972 but also *WoodenBoat* magazine to begin publishing in 1974. By 2014 Mystic's unparalleled collection of 450 small craft was housed in Rossie Mill, which it had acquired in 1973. While Gardner credited Chapelle for arousing public awareness, they both favored traditional Anglo-American vessels. John Sands of the Mariners' Museum called Gardner "the acknowledged guru of an entire generation of lovers of small craft" but noted his bias against native craft and modern boats.[69]

Differing perspectives explained these programs' success. Facing worldwide crises in 1967, including the Vietnam War and the youth rebellion, Johnston voiced his unease. By 1973, however, as Watergate's corruption compounded the national misery, he seemed despondent about America's drift from its "religious conviction," faith "in government," and belief in "personal integrity." He wanted the Seaport to help "restore [America's] faith in individual enterprise and rekindle the dignity of man." But master woodcarver Willard Shepard attributed such unease to a boom in nostalgia. Suggesting that many Americans were still under the spell of mythmakers, he thought that they were "trying to convince [themselves] that we're really living in the 19th century when things were [reportedly] safe." Boatbuilding did have "a nostalgic appeal," Gardner conceded. But he attributed its popularity to "a revolt against commercialism" by Americans who wanted "a simple, wholesome, relaxed life style."[70]

Expanding its audience, Mystic offered a range of sailing classes, including some for women. In 1969, a female staffer joked, "Men are walking on the moon; but most of those left on earth won't let their wives take the helm of their boats for a split second." Its classes evolved into a Community Sailing Program and training in maritime skills, such as Basic Celestial

Navigation. Imitating South Street Seaport Museum, whose Mayor's Cup schooner race began in 1967, Mystic's annual Schooner Race (1968) even included a prize for the boat with the most crew members under age eighteen. Sail training included Sea Squirts (two- to three-year-old children), teens aboard *Conrad* and *Brilliant*, and adults.[71]

"MAKE THE HUMANITIES MORE MEANINGFUL, MORE URGENT": THE MUSEUM OF AMERICA AND THE SEA

In 1969, Johnston hired J. Revell Carr. Growing up in Baltimore, where he learned to sail, Carr earned a BA in art history at Rutgers University in 1962. After naval service, he entered a U.S. civilization graduate program at the University of Pennsylvania, finished his master's degree, but applied at Mystic before beginning a PhD program. He became, in a whirlwind, chief curator, director (1978), and president (1989). By 2000, when he retired, Mystic was the nation's preeminent maritime museum. But he credited Lynch and Johnston for jumpstarting the process. During Carr's tenure, Mystic's endowment rose from $3 million to $43 million, while its membership nearly doubled to twenty-five thousand.

But its remaking was difficult. As Johnston had warned in 1978, the Seaport faced significant threats: falling attendance, increased costs, and the necessity of raising a lot of money. Meanwhile, after the opening of Disney World (1971) and its imitators, he cautioned that Mystic's "values [were] being eroded by the thrill-seekers and the super-spectaculars." The Seaport's visitation reached 555,164 in 1969 but fell, rebounded, and peaked at 577,978 in 1976. By 1979 it had dropped to 434,059 and bottomed out at 265,000 by the twenty-first century. In 1980, a *Wall Street Journal* front-page story asked, "Is History Outdated? Outdoor Museum Are Having Trouble." When Colonial Williamsburg's gate was overwhelmed in 1979 by Busch Gardens (0.98 million versus 2 million), its staff blamed the "repetitive, dull and routine" presentation. As a lure, Mystic played its nostalgia card, introducing, for example, Camera Day in 1982 with costumed models and pictorial setups. "When people feel disenchanted," said a former director of the American Association of State and Local History, "they turn to a sanitized past that never existed."[72]

Local tourism became highly competitive. In 1980, the Seaport was the state's "largest single tourist entity." But an aquarium, which opened a mile away in 1974, beat it by 1982. Tourists were also flocking to Groton's free-admission USS *Nautilus*: Submarine Force Museum, which opened in 1986 and buttressed the Reagan-era arms buildup. By 1995, its visitation had reached 304,000. Additionally, the USCG agreed in 2013 to build a free-of-charge national museum on the New London waterfront; it is currently in the fund-raising stage. Even more popular was gambling. In 1992, the Mashantucket Pequots expanded their operation, eight miles north of the Seaport, as the Foxwoods Resort Casino. Said a town historian, "Resentment against the Pequot ran high." By 1995, it was the state's top attraction, drawing fifty-six thousand tourists daily. In 1996, the Mohegans opened their own competing casino fifteen miles away.[73]

Sinking in red ink, the Seaport resorted to layoffs, budget cuts, and using its endowment. It worried about "its own future," but Gardner warned that it would be "a fatal mistake" if Mystic, or any museum, tried "to compete with commercialized mass entertainment." Still, he feared it was already "beginning to happen." Then the Town of Stonington proposed not only a ticket tax on, but annual payments by, the aquarium and the Seaport for services. While Johnston had bemoaned the fact that the Seaport spent "enormous energies dealing with the town and state governments on matters of zoning, sewers, taxation, pollution, [and] traffic control," Carr used a University of Connecticut study to show that it yearly generated 1,234 jobs and $36.5 million in salaries and wages. Noting that its real costs were "*three times* what the visitor" paid, he called the Stonington plan devastating. It never passed, but, to enhance revenue, the Seaport introduced even more events, which still continue, such as Lantern Light Christmas Tours, Halloween's Nautical Nightmares, and Chowderfest. Meanwhile, demonstration squads showed visitors everything from climbing rigging, to lowering dories to cooking in the galley.[74]

While continuing the Munson Institute for graduate students and educating thirty thousand school-age children annually, the Seaport established a middle-tier program for undergraduates in 1977. The Williams College–Mystic Seaport Program in American Maritime Studies became the most innovative curriculum of its kind in the nation. It was conceived by Benjamin W. Labaree, who succeeded Robert Albion as Munson director in 1974. A Harvard-trained historian who headed the program until 1989, Labaree worried that the nation's youth had a "poorly developed overall sense of the sea." Beginning with twenty-one students from thirteen eastern colleges, the semester-long participants resided at the Seaport and took four Williams College classes: maritime history, sea literature, oceanography or marine ecology, and contemporary marine policy. They also learned a practical skill (such as sailing or boatbuilding), and made a weeklong, schooner voyage. By 1985, the program attracted two women for every man. They became, Mystic boasted, "better stewards of the planet." By 2012, it had graduated 1,478 students.[75]

In the meantime, Carr had shifted the museum's interpretive program from a nationalistic expansionism to a cross-disciplinary, scholarship-based approach. A hint appeared in a 1966 symposium, when panelists pushed it to find a broader audience. While Stackpole urged historians to study coasting and fishing crews and communities, his approach differed from the emerging "new social history" of Jack-tar. Setting a future course, the Seaport published *New England and the Sea* (1972), written by the Munson Institute's Robert Albion, Benjamin Labaree, Marion Brewington (Kendall Whaling Museum), and William Avery Baker (*Mayflower II* designer). In 1978, an eponymous permanent exhibit followed. Funded in part by the National Endowment for the Humanities (NEH), it was Mystic's "largest and most comprehensive exhibit" to date. Curated by Stuart Parnes, it blended materials on the three-century bond between "the people of coastal New England and the sea." Including a rare look at "the female sailor," it ended ecologically with "You and the Sea Today."[76]

Staff historians filled in gaps, often in the "New Social History of Seafaring," which explored the often gritty, exploitative environment. To encourage the study of African Americans and Native Americans, the Seaport established in 1989 the Paul Cuffe Memorial Fellowship. Its first recipient, W. Jeffrey Bolster, recognized it as the only grant coupling maritime and minority studies. In its first decade, it offered thirty-four fellowships, whose work helped reinterpret *Morgan* and the Seaport. Consequently, the museum broadened *Morgan*'s interpretation for its 150th anniversary—socially, economically, and technologically—to show it "as a reflection of America." In 1995, it also held the first National Conference on Race, Ethnicity, and Power in Maritime America; others followed in 2000 and 2006. But women were usually a sidebar in maritime exhibits, despite the publication by Mystic Seaport of *On Land and on Sea: A Century of Women in the Rosenfeld Collection* (2007).[77]

Those efforts led to rethinking the institution's purpose. In 1991, Carr launched a two-year study to explore an expanded mission. Knowing that the Smithsonian Institution only superficially covered the nation's maritime history, Mystic glimpsed an opening. Its village pictured the nineteenth century, but its programs and collections were broader, especially with the wider audiences promised by newer technology. After approving a revised scope in 1994, Mystic announced a future exhibition, *Voyages: Stories of America and the Sea*. With that, it began calling itself "the Museum of America and the Sea," though Congress controversially designated South Street Seaport Museum and the Mariners' Museum jointly as "America's National Maritime Museum" in a 1998 appropriations bill.

The opening of *Voyages* was preceded by an impressive book, *America and the Sea: A Maritime History* (1998), which became a Book of the Month Club selection. Noting that "North America is the most maritime of the world's great continents," it regretted that few historians and even fewer citizens realized its importance. Written by a half-dozen Munson Institute scholars, two of whom were endowed with NEH assistance, it was meant for "the ideal visitor to Mystic Seaport: an intelligent member of the general public, not ignorant of American history but keen to be fully informed about the maritime part to it." As such, said a reviewer, it "triumphantly succeeds." It did, at times, picture a mythical past, downplay business expansionism, and even gloss over whaling. Undercutting its commitment to research, however, the museum ceased publishing the *Log of Mystic Seaport* in 2005, just as the Peabody Essex Museum had deep-sixed *American Neptune* in 2002. As such, the nation lost its only active scholarly journals on U.S. maritime history.[78]

In 2000, the six-thousand square-foot exhibit, *Voyages*, took center stage. Preceding Op Sail 2000, when tall ships attracted almost a million visitors to New London, *Voyages* filled the renovated Stillman Building. Costing $2 million and funded partly by the NEH, it was "the largest new exhibit in the museum's 71-year history." With an eponymous book, an online exhibit, and a ninety-minute TV documentary (*Connecticut and the Sea*, narrated by board member Walter Cronkite), it was sectioned in seven themes, each of which presented past and present stories that were, noted a reviewer, "largely absent elsewhere at the Seaport." *Voyages* opened with "Coming to America, Immigrant Passages." Most tellingly, it began not with Plymouth's *Mayflower*, but with the Cuban boat *Analuisa* and its nineteen refugees who fled from Mariel to Florida in 1994. "It's as dramatic a story as we have in the exhibit," said project director Parnes, who wanted museums to "make the humanities more meaningful, more urgent." Its sympathetic portrait sent "the most important message," concluded a reviewer: "Things are changing at Mystic Seaport." Stating that newcomers had been treated "as outsiders who threatened the success of those who came before," a display asked, "When did you or your immigrant ancestors arrive in America. How welcome was your family?" Other sections creatively dealt with such topics as global trade and travel, naval service, the sea's natural resources, and recreation. Extended through 2013, *Voyages* was the Seaport's most important exhibit over an eighty-year history.[79]

In 2000 the Seaport also launched its re-created *Freedom Schooner Amistad.* In 1839, enslaved Africans had rebelled aboard *Amistad* but were captured and jailed in New London. After John Quincy Adams won their freedom in court, *Amistad* became "an icon representing the struggle for equality for all Americans." Anticipating its sesquicentennial, a movement started, stalled, but was revived by a $2.5 million Connecticut bond. Partnering with the Connecticut Afro-American Historical Society, the Seaport documented the ship, secured more funding, and created Amistad America, Inc., a nonprofit organization to own, operate, and endow the seventy-seven-foot ship. It was, said shipyard director Quentin Snediker, "the first major vessel" that the museum built "from scratch." Construction started in March 1998, and its $3.1 million budget included exhibits, interpretation, and programming, which was, noted Carr, "aided by virtually every department in the Museum." Fueling the publicity, Hollywood's Stephen Spielberg had filmed his *Amistad* (1997) partly at the Seaport: "You just can't re-create this [scene] on a sound stage," he admitted. Ten thousand attended the ship's launch, including twenty members of the U.S. House of Representatives and dignitaries from Sierra Leone. With that, said a local editorial, Southeastern Connecticut took "enormous pride in the important role played by Mystic Seaport." In 2002, membership reached a high of 27,536. Besides an exhibition, Mystic created an *Amistad* website, partly to correct the film's inaccuracies. While the shipyard maintained the vessel, which was named "the state's official flagship and tall ship ambassador," the independent, but mismanaged, Amistad America, Inc. was later taken over by the state, which had spent $8 million on it by 2013. The ship is now managed by Discovering Amistad, a nonprofit educational organization.[80]

Critical for the success of *Amistad* and *Voyages*, Mystic's research holdings were, said Carr, "the core of the institution." That led to the creation of the American Maritime Education and Research Center (AMERC) in the former Rossie Mill. Seen partly as a long-term solution to falling attendance and revenue, its first phase was opened in 2002 by Mystic's new president, Admiral Douglas H. Teeson (USCG, ret.). The center was, added

Congressman Robert Simmons, "a hell of a good investment for the federal government," which underwrote $5 million of the $16 million cost. Using one-third of the 153,000-square-foot building, AMERC housed the many artifacts and an exceptional library and archives, including the Rosenfeld Collection, "the world's largest assortment of photographs documenting maritime history from 1881 to the present." Eventually costing $40–$50 million, AMERC's future plans include a conservation workshop and a Watercraft Exhibit Hall.[81]

Those two years after the terrorist attacks of 2001 were, however, the worst ever for living history museums, reported the *Boston Globe*. Before 9/11, Mystic's attendance was over 400,000, but it fell to 320,000 by 2005. To fund shortfalls in its $20–$22 million budget with 315 paid staff, it again tapped its endowment, tried buyouts and budget cuts, and used more volunteers, whose number increased by 50 percent over 2002–7. By 2009, full-time positions had dropped to 147. With the Great Recession and stock market collapse, however, its endowment shriveled from $57 million to $30 million, and its remaining funds were restricted. Pinching visitors, Mystic raised admission to $24 because gate receipts accounted for half its income. In this midst of the Great Recession, a new president took the helm in January 2009. A former preparatory school headmaster, Stephen White lacked museum experience but had "dramatically increased [his school's] endowment and raised 20 million for its strategic campaign." Those two tasks, reported the *New London Day*, "await[ed] him at Mystic Seaport." Besides slashing winter operating hours, he sought big donors, as with a $600-per-plate gala that presented its *America and the Sea Award* (est. 2006) to billionaire William I. Koch, a libertarian conservative who fought environmental regulations, promoted competitive sailing, and owned an enviable maritime art collection.[82]

With those hard times, "a near caste system" marked the local community, wrote historian Leigh Fought, a former museum staffer. Like the waiters and retail clerks in the tourist-oriented economy, many "museum professionals" and craftspeople worked in fields "with low salaries nationwide, [and] found themselves in the same economically precarious position." The average annual salary for historic interpreters was between $12,000 and $14,000. After the Seaport closed for six winter weeks and cut its spending, discontent rose. When the museum began to turn a profit in 2012, a drive to unionize its workforce followed. It was an uphill battle because nationally "less than 13 percent of workers at museums, art galleries and historic sites" were unionized. But, according to the labor federation AFT Connecticut, which was organizing the drive, the complaints stemmed more from the staff's frustration with administrators than actual pay and benefits because they "truly love working there." Said one, "We want management to see us as partners." The most active union proponents were restoring *Morgan*. Coincidentally, its shipwrights in 1841 had demanded a ten-hour day and stopped working. "Some of [that] bad blood" was passed down, reported the *New London Day*, which noted "the disparity between big six-figure salaries for top museum management and the modest pay for rank-and-file workers." Fifty percent of eligible employees signed a union card, leading to a National Labor Relations Board vote. But as the museum community's psyche fractured, workers rejected unionization.[83]

Restoring *Morgan* was one solution to the psychological and financial dilemma, but advance steps were necessary. First, the Seaport replaced the thirty-year-old, unreliable lift-dock in 2007. Costing $6.4 million, of which the state gave $2.5 million, the new dock (with a five-hundred-ton capacity) also enabled the shipyard to earn outside revenue (as when it later restored *Mayflower II*). Second, the Mystic River's depth was an issue. While *Morgan* drew twelve-and-a-half feet, the low-tide depth north of the drawbridge was twelve feet. It had not been dredged since 1941, but only partial federal funding was allocated in 2007. Dredging was only finished in 2015 after the passage of a state bond. Third, after Hurricanes Hugo and Katrina ravaged the South's woodlands, shipyard director Snediker acquired three hundred tons of live oak and yellow pine, including an eight-hundred-year-old tree. He even received oak that had been buried for a century in the briny mud of Boston. It was "manna from heaven." In 2008, he hauled *Morgan*.[84]

After the Seaport's membership had plunged to 17,000 and attendance to 275,000, Stephen White introduced a plan in September 2009 to reballast the museum. As fundraising faltered, he admitted, "We're trying to think big . . . [and] do things that inspire people to become a member, inspire people to come and visit, and inspire people to be philanthropically supportive." Once restored, *Morgan* was initially scheduled to go down the river and back, but White and his board approved a symbolic trip to the National Oceanic and Atmospheric Administration's Stellwagen Bank National Marine Sanctuary, off Cape Cod. Whales were once hunted there, but now watched. Having raised $3 million, he needed at least $7 million more for the work, programs, and endowment. But he said, "We're not going to go into debt to do this." The *New London Day* judged that if the museum could "pull it off," it would become "a restoration wonder, a public relations bonanza and a romantic sea experience." Visiting Stellwagen Bank would also give *Morgan* a chance "to make peace and complete the circle." The NEH chipped in $450,000.[85]

In addition to a keel-to-waterline rehabilitation, nearly all of *Morgan*'s sails and rigging were replaced. That meant, said sailmaker Nathaniel Wilson, "restoring the skills," as well as "the living memory of it sailing." The 2008–13 work returned the vessel to its 1895–1905 (and best documented) era. Before 2008, 30 percent of the ship's material was original, but replacing its deterioration left only 15 percent. While Snediker melded period tools with state-of-the-art technology, visitors followed the work via a cell phone audio tour, which was funded by state and federal grants. *Morgan* was launched on July 21, 2013. The five-thousand-strong audience included Governor Daniel Malloy, who announced a $500,000 grant, and filmmaker Ric Burns, who had produced the PBS whaling documentary *Into the Deep* (2010). In his keynote address, Burns acknowledged that ships like *Morgan* "have always been powerful metaphors for us humans—metaphors for experience, for existence, [and] for the human community."[86]

For its thirty-eighth voyage in mid-May 2014, *Morgan* was temporarily equipped with modern safety and navigation equipment, a sanitation system, and a working galley, but not with watertight bulkheads or engine. Captained by Richard "Kip" Files of Maine, who had skippered *Elissa* in Galveston, *Morgan* was cheered as it was towed down the Mystic River. The advance planning was intricate, with 140 staff and 105 volunteers ashore or aboard. "We gave those spaces to you," White told those aboard, "so that you could help us interpret this experience and shed your personal light on it so that generations to come will all know how you saw it." One participant optimistically cast that as an attempt to give "the public a greater stake in [the museum's] interpretation of the past." Receiving its sails and ballast in New London, it opened to visitors and readied for its eight-week trip to New Bedford, Provincetown and Stellwagen Bank, and Boston, where it docked next to *Constitution*. Accompanied by *Roann*, its traveling exhibits showed the changing perception of whales held by not only the larger society but the Seaport, as it had once sold scrimshaw in its museum store. Helping to repair the fractured museum community, the voyage led to, according to White, "a psychic transformation of the Seaport village." CBS Evening News used the voyage for its upbeat, closing segment. As *Morgan* returned, it was greeted by thousands. One admitted: "I have goose bumps all over my body." Others began talking about a thirty-ninth voyage.[87]

CONCLUSION: "MYSTIC SEAPORT IS AN IMAGINARY PLACE," OR IS IT?

One voyage was missed in the tally—from Round Hill to Mystic in 1941. As *Morgan*'s guardian, Carl Cutler was a pioneer among world preservationists. In 1929, he called for a "marine research, educational and experimental center." Besides his advocacy of U.S.-flagged commerce, his Marine Historical Association became a museum to save discarded models and figureheads, a library to encourage neglected studies, a port to dock obsolete ships, and a center to resurrect a once-common but waning culture. It's often said that history is made by committed actors, and Cutler was one—a dyed-in-Yankee-wool advocate of maritime culture. Mallory tacked from his course, but Johnston and Carr, reflecting contemporary professionalism, returned to Cutler's design. Today, Mystic is the nation's standard-bearer.[88]

The jury is out on Mallory's corporate principles that continue to shape the movement. Decrying them, Cutler represented an older school catering to maritime devotees and scholars. Mallory wanted to "obsolete the old" and, said Cutler, "put me and all I stand for, further in the background." As in corporate ledgers, Mallory maximized new initiatives and acquisitions. But his bottom-line management, which he introduced allegedly "to promote efficiency," neglected the fleet, library, collections, and even local residents. By expanding the village and pushing its nostalgia, he catered to day-trippers but so stretched real history that Johnston called Mystic "the laughing stock of the museum world." Like his own company, which became Duracell, Mallory embraced a grow-or-die philosophy. For major history museums, bigness defined "progress."[89]

While Cutler's and Mallory's historic village was an invention, it continued what had begun at Round Hill. Critics of such creations, notably Jane Jacobs and Ada Louis Huxtable in the early 1960s, urged preservationists instead to value real over imagined communities, in situ work over removal, preservation over reconstruction, and streetscapes over isolated buildings. When Mystic was building its village in the late 1940s and 1950s, however, criticisms were rare. Many of those moved structures, moreover, could have been lost. The museum's recent guidebook admits in its first line: "As picturesque and well established as it looks, Mystic Seaport is an imaginary place." Tourists can visit real working ports, but how many little communities want swarms of sightseers interrupting their daily lives? Yet Labaree also joked, "Inviting upwards of a half-million people to tramp all over your last wooden whaleship is hardly the best way to preserve it!"[90]

Is Mystic Seaport imaginary? Or is it a place alive with all things maritime that most would not otherwise experience? As the exhibit *Voyages* reminded visitors, America is a nation dependent on the sea, but most don't realize it. Nor do they realize that the museum's gate covers less than half of its operating costs. Preserving ships is particularly expensive, though in recent decades Mystic has set national standards. With four wooden-hulled ships registered as National Historic Landmarks, its fleet may be smaller in tonnage than that of San Francisco Maritime, but the port's nineteenth-century roots and shallow river set the limits. Still, its holdings are qualitatively unmatched. To repeat Lynch, "Maritime history is ships."[91]

When nature is rough on New England, Mystic Seaport's village, ships, and programs draw too few visitors to pay the bills. Though a state tourism official said, "When people think of Connecticut, they think of Mystic first," the nineteen-acre Seaport had long needed an all-weather facility. In 2015, it began work on the $11.5 million Thompson Exhibition Building, its first major new building in fifty years. Doubling as a visitor center for the north end, it opened in September 2016; after New Year's Day, when much of the campus closes for five weeks, its five-thousand-square-foot gallery (the largest of seven venues) defines the museum. With its space and better security, said vice president Paul O'Pecko, "We'll be able to really get some drop-dead [traveling exhibits] here now." Meanwhile, the Seaport's increased web presence will earn revenue, boost its stature, and teach about America and the sea. By 2013, while elementary students in the nation's heartland were making "a virtual field trip" to Mystic, regional educators competed for its Orion Award, which was established in 2005 to recognize their use of the museum's collections in their curriculum.[92]

Will that be enough? In the end, it must be programs—enriching, immersive, interactive, and empowering—that attract and hold a younger, more diverse audience. While a Seaport CEO called the aging baby boomers "a great market" and thought, in 2001, that "lifelong learning [had] the greatest potential," what must first be kindled, as Gardner stressed, was a personal appreciation of the sea. It's a way of life so different from land-based experiences or computer-generated activities. If Cutler was correct that the sea builds stouthearted characters, then once engaged through a dyer dhow derby, a boatbuilding class, a Williams-Mystic experience, or a memorable *Morgan* tour, individuals will perhaps, as Cutler dreamed, reconnect land and sea in their own lives.[93]

CHAPTER 4

"TO MAKE THE AMERICAN PEOPLE MORE SHIP-MINDED"

Shipbuilding and Sea Culture at the Mariners' Museum

In 1930, and while Mystic's Marine Historical Association was formulating its plans, Archer Milton Huntington was creating the Mariners' Museum in Newport News, Virginia. It was seven miles from the troubled shipyard he inherited in 1927. With an initial commitment of $1 million, it was expected to dwarf John D. Rockefeller Jr.'s ongoing restoration of Williamsburg, twenty-three miles to the north. Huntington decreed, "This Museum is devoted to the Culture of the Sea and its Tributaries, its Conquest by Man, and its Influence on Civilization." It was also devoted to his Newport News Shipbuilding and Dry Dock Co. (NNSDD). Shipyard head Homer Lenoir Ferguson had proposed it and served as first president, and his staff designed and managed the operations. Improving the yard's tarnished reputation, its goal was to make Americans more sea minded or, Ferguson said, ship minded after their retreat from the seas.[1]

In his post–World War I "return to normalcy," President Warren Harding had pushed to cut spending, downsize the world's competing navies, and act independently overseas. At the Washington Conference in 1921–22, world powers agreed to big cuts in battleship tonnage and a ten-year suspension of new construction. The Big Three contractors (Newport News, Bethlehem Shipbuilding, and New York Shipbuilding) feared for their future. "Over night seventy million dollars of work in the Newport News plant was stopped," NNSDD reported. The company town "entered the darkest economic period of its history." Facing a simultaneous depression in commercial shipbuilding, the Big Three conspired to stymie the next round of negotiations at Geneva, Switzerland, in 1927 to reduce cruisers. Hawking U.S. naval supremacy and stoking mistrust of Great Britain, their lobbyist, William Baldwin Shearer, took credit for the failure of negotiations at Geneva. While employed by the Big Three, he wrote *The Cloak of Benedict Arnold* (1928), picturing a conspiracy by internationalists and pacifists "to weaken America." The NNSDD rebounded when the navy awarded contracts for two cruisers, and the Merchant Marine Act (1928) led to a dozen passenger liners. But clergy, journalists, and politicians condemned the intrigue. That led Senator Samuel M. Shortridge (R-CA) to hold hearings in 1929–30. Threatening to punish the contractors, President Herbert Hoover promoted more reductions at London in 1930 and Geneva in 1932.[2]

Newport News marched to a different drummer. Ever since Collis P. Huntington founded the city in the early 1880s and his Chesapeake and Ohio Railroad energized the sleepy peninsula, its docks and shipyard (1886) had driven the economy. The NNSDD grew with the emerging naval-industrial complex. With his death in 1900, the nation's largest private yard reverted to his nephew, Henry Edwards Huntington, and Collis's second wife, Arabella (Belle), a former Richmond barroom hostess. The story varies as to whether Archer, who was born out of wedlock in 1870, was fathered by Collis or another man. Regardless, Collis married Belle in 1884 and treated Archer as his own. Widowed, she was one of the world's richest women and married Henry in 1913. With World War I, the NNSDD became the navy's top contractor. Belle's death in 1924 and Henry's in 1927 left Archer in charge.[3]

As president of both shipyard and museum, Ferguson combined naval expansion with local development, building not only "the world's largest private shipbuilding business" but also Mariners', which became the yard's alter ego and was compared with Britain's National Maritime Museum in Greenwich. Archer Huntington resigned from the museum board in 1935 and sold the yard in 1940, but thanks to his largesse, Mariners' assembled one of the nation's best collections of global small craft, marine fine and folk art, and maritime scholarship. With the outbreak of World War II, it spotlighted the yard's ships, hosted NNSDD ceremonies, hailed sea power, and stoked patriotism. Championing its region, it opened a Chesapeake Bay Room in 1957 and a major wing in 1989. That began "a new era" in its history.[4]

It quickly tacked, however. Facing stiff competition from Norfolk's trendy Nauticus, a maritime-themed complex that opened in 1994, and anticipating the expiration of Huntington's endowment in 2002, Mariners' remade itself. In the 1990s, it downplayed its scholarly roots and beckoned a popular audience. Anchored in the naval-industrial complex of Hampton Roads, it intensified its focus on sea power with a permanent gallery in 1997. Exercising its federal muscle, it won not only codesignation in 1998 as "America's National Maritime Museum" but also the right to open in 2007 the USS *Monitor* Center, which showed the salvaged remains of the pioneering warship. After neither brought the necessary support, it replaced its Chesapeake Bay Wing in 2013 with a family-oriented ocean science exhibit and theater. With a rich maritime collection and setting, it is today seeking a wider, more financially supportive constituency.[5]

"EACH STEP IN THE PROGRESS OF MARINE ART AND SCIENCE": HUNTINGTON, FERGUSON, AND THE MUSEUM'S BEGINNINGS

Archer Huntington was a poet and scholar—unlike Collis, who wanted him to administer the shipyard. Sheltered by Belle, Archer so wrapped himself in erudition that he became a recluse. With a keen interest in Iberia, he founded the Hispanic Society of America in 1904; over his lifetime he created another dozen museums and libraries on diverse interests. But, absorbed in his scholarship, his wife left him, leading him to despondency and gluttony. In 1924, however, he married Anna Hyatt, a gifted sculptor who rescued him from despair. Yet, in 1927, she developed tuberculosis, and thereafter they lived mostly at Brookgreen Plantation in South Carolina. He visited Newport News infrequently, arriving in his private train or a chauffeur-driven van. His fortune attracted attention. But as the economy collapsed in the early 1930s, he "felt that all he could or should do [with his inheritance of $150 million] was to provide the opportunity for cultural development." Though most U.S. museums were focusing on public education after losing the battle with universities over the control of scholarly research, many of his institutions advanced scholarship. Ferguson persuaded him to blend research and education at Mariners'.[6]

Born to a North Carolina judge, Homer Ferguson entered the Naval Academy at fifteen. After sail training aboard USS *Constellation* (1854), he studied construction, finished with honors in 1892, and completed graduate work in Glasgow under a dreadnought designer. Joining "the naval aristocracy," an elite band pushing U.S. fleet and commercial expansion, he served as an assistant naval constructor at private and government yards.

He became NNSDD superintendent in 1905, general manager in 1912, and, after its chief executive went down with *Lusitania*, president in 1915. With war, Ferguson "inaugurated a program of vast plant expansion." After the armistice and Harding's big naval cuts, Ferguson condemned disarmament, as in a speech at the U.S. Chamber of Commerce, for which he had served as president. While his yard built yachts, passenger-cargo ships, and tankers, often at a loss to keep afloat, he was active in the naval-industrial complex's Society of Naval Architects and Marine Engineers (SNAME). America was left powerless, he warned SNAME in 1922, but "our future lies largely upon the sea."[7]

After serving as SNAME president in 1928–29, he deplored Hoover's acceptance of the London Treaty (1930), which limited the fleet further. His objections mirrored those of the Navy League, a lobbyist group which preached Admiral Alfred T. Mahan's doctrine that a global navy and infrastructure were necessary to advance trade and national power. But in the Senate, which ratified the treaty, Arthur Capper (R-KS) called the Navy League a "greedy commercial organization . . . seeking to make excessive profits from the government for steel and shipbuilding companies under the plea of super-patriotism." In the *New Republic*, Professor Charles Beard warned that policymaking belonged "to disinterested citizens, not to navy leagues, navy bureaucrats, armament profiteers and facile journalists paid by concerns with dividends at stake." Praising Ferguson, Huntington was happy that it was "the trained business man who runs the country, not the professors."[8]

Launching three years of museum planning in 1930, Ferguson sent NNSDD naval architect Harold F. Norton to inspect London's Science Museum of South Kensington (later, the Victoria and Albert Museum). Its maritime department consisted "almost entirely of a quite marvelous collection of models of small boats [and] sail boats." Norton then visited Munich's Deutsches Museum. Its chronologically arranged shipbuilding section was, he thought, "marvelously well calculated to instill ship mindedness into [its] visitors." Huntington instead ordered Mariners' to show models in reverse chronology; prioritizing NNSDD ships would advertise their success. During the Depression, the yard's staff made those models to keep local jobs. Because it wanted to show "each step in the progress of marine art and science," NNSDD vice president Roger Williams told Groton submariner Captain Wilson Brown that Mariners' was "mainly for the use of students of Naval architecture." For experiments, it also wanted a model testing tank, but William Gatewood, a shipyard engineer reassigned to manage the museum, knew it would not "prove attractive to the public." Because the museum's charter stipulated a nonprofit operation, it transferred land to the yard, which built a hydraulic laboratory.[9]

Science writer Waldemar Kaempffert asked Ferguson to consider a more ambitious mission. While praising those museums in London and Munich, he wanted Mariners' to show less engineering and more of the social and economic influence of ships and the sea "in different parts of the world." Past editor of *Scientific American* and *Popular Science*, Kaempffert had also directed Chicago's Museum of Science and Industry but was fired by executives intent on corporate restructuring. He resultantly wanted scientists, not businessmen, in charge. He further warned Ferguson that "the dullness of the average museum" could be avoided if the displays were pictured as a "great pageant," which was typical of progressive history. As the current science and engineering editor of the *New York Times*, he suggested that such museums "belong to the people," not special interests.[10]

Out of deference, Ferguson called it the Huntington Mariners' Museum, but the philanthropist replied that it was "not my Museum as you call it, but yours." While Huntington was titular chairman, shipyard managers comprised the museum's trustees and officers, who served without pay and first met in Huntington's New York home on June 5, 1930. Mariners' was governed "through a self-perpetuating Board of Trustees" representing "professional interests in shipbuilding and in ship operation." Huntington ordered, however, that if the board diverged from its educational charter, the property would revert to the University of Virginia. He also set its financial structure. It would be "free to the public" and would not fundraise. So, when shipyard employee Alexander Crosby Brown suggested forming a financially supportive friends' society, Ferguson declined. But he was impressed by Brown, who had circumnavigated the globe with four Yale classmates in a schooner. Reassigned from the yard in 1934, he became the museum's corresponding secretary and chief of publications. Meanwhile, Huntington's personal financing was obscure. In 1936, reported *Fortune*, Mariners' endowment consisted of 22,233 shares of the privately held shipyard. Royalties from his West Virginia gas and coal holdings also became an endowment covering the museum's work.[11]

The first issue was choosing a site for the museum. Ferguson suggested locating it near the yard and downtown. But Huntington chose a Warwick County setting, seven miles northward, which his father had bought as a watershed. There on the James River, an 880-acre wooded park wrapped the museum. Before a spellbound Chamber of Commerce audience, Ferguson envisaged building "a vast structure of white marble." Huntington disagreed. Thinking that the yard's idled engineers could design it, he wrote that a classical edifice would "clash entirely with the exhibits, which are purely scientific and mathematical." Ferguson's picture, however, held the media's eye. In 1931, the Virginia Chamber of Commerce predicted (with much hyperbole) that it would cost $24 million. As "the world's finest maritime museum," said the *Baltimore Sun*, it would rank among "the most ambitious public benefactions of the twentieth century."[12]

First creating a nature preserve, which cost $300,000, shipyard workers built a five-hundred-foot stone dam to raise Waters Creek ten feet. The freshwater, 167-acre lake was named after Matthew Fontaine Maury, the Virginian who wrote *Physical Geography of the Sea* (1855) and transformed the U.S. Navy's Depot of Instruments and Charts. "Virtually inventing modern oceanography," he won the epithet, "Pathfinder of the Seas." Six years later, it became the epithet of a traitor, as his Confederate treachery was denounced by (among others) the Salem Marine Society, which hung his portrait head down and backward (and still thus hangs). The museum redeemed his legacy, but his lake became treacherous with water moccasins, rattlesnakes, and so many pollutants that the public was warned of "the possibility of contracting poliomyelitis or typhoid fever by bathing or swimming in the waters." The adjacent woods and gardens attracted visitors from all over, but a shipyard director asked the scruffy neighbors to "make every effort to clean their properties."[13]

The park included sculpture by Anna Hyatt Huntington. A student of Gutzon Borglum, she was, said journalist Ida Tarbell, "one of America's five ablest women." Distressed by the machine age but hired by its overseers, she crafted nine monuments for the grounds. Rising thirty feet above its base, *Conquering the Wild* depicted a man, allegorically Collis Huntington, subduing a rearing horse. Its pedestal was flanked by four male figures representing the art of shipbuilding, literature, art, and labor. The figures picturing the manly pursuits of shipbuilding and labor were "anatomically overwhelming." Yet, this statue and others were vandalized, leading trustees to blast the "dim-witted, undisciplined" culprits, whose gunfire left chips and pockmarks. Collis's shadow loomed large in other ways. While *Fortune* admitted that his empire was built "on the backs of Chinese coolies . . . [and] Virginia Negroes," the museum produced a two-volume biography.

Reassigned from the yard, Cerinda W. Evans was, said the *Richmond News Leader*, a "hagiographer" who "closed her eyes to [Collis Huntington's] ruthless business methods," which (as elsewhere) generated the money that became "the endowment of libraries and museums."[14]

Mariners' had imperial ambitions. Unlike national museums in Europe, it was "free from any limitations of time or place." With scale models, scientific drawings, and "every type of small hand and wind-propelled boat known," Ferguson told Governor John Garland Pollard, scholars, engineers, and everyday folk would learn their sea traditions. For the $1 million Huntington had spent by mid-1932, however, it had only one building, a warehouse that his agents filled. With the Depression, many people sold their treasures for a song. Traveling to eleven countries with his wife Nola, Frederick F. Hill, for example, "found more marine material" in New England than anywhere else. Ferguson's buyers scoured the Gulf Coast twice and, in 1935, launched the first of two expeditions to the West Indies and the Spanish Main. He even hired Captain Irving Johnson, an adventurer circling the globe. On Pitcairn Island in the South Pacific, he met Parkin Christian, a descendant of HMS *Bounty*'s mutineer, and acquired "a vise, bench anvil and a piece of her rudder." In 1937, agents in Europe completed "the most profitable expedition yet undertaken," while others searched U.S. auctions and antiques sales. By 1945, Mariners' holdings, 70 percent of which had been purchased, were valued at $2 million.[15]

Shipping companies and yards gave old records and materials. While the NNSDD donated its half-hull models, Ferguson sought help from Representative Schuyler Otis Bland (D-VA), whose advocacy of the fleet prompted the U.S. Merchant Marine Academy to name its Kings Point library after him. In 1933 he authored legislation allowing Mariners' to receive the Navy Department's unwanted books, manuscripts, drawings, models, and obsolete property. Invoking the law, the museum asked the navy to donate a model of the NNSDD-built battleship *Illinois* (1901) "and/or other models not needed." When the navy balked, Ferguson appealed to Navy Secretary Claude Swanson, another Virginian, but little followed, because the navy wanted to establish its own museums.[16]

Work with the National Park Service was more productive. York River oystermen had long complained about submerged hulks from the Battle of Yorktown (1781). At the request of Colonial National Historical Park (est. 1930), the museum joined its investigation. Using a shipyard tug and barge and a museum-paid diver and crew, they explored the site, but with little sense of scientific archaeology. With a high-pressure hose, they removed mud from the submerged ships in 1934–35 but failed to refloat the forty-four-gun HMS *Charon*. They dredged "cannon, articles of rigging and iridescent bottles in considerable quantity." One rum bottle was sent to Interior Secretary Harold Ickes, who gave it to President Roosevelt. Ickes wrote: "I have rarely seen him so interested"; FDR appreciated "the public spirited cooperation" of Ferguson, who needed a boost because he would soon testify before a Senate inquiry. The museum split the booty with the park and published Ferguson's archaeological report.[17]

In late 1933, Mariners' opened its doors without ceremony. By 1936, it added a main display room (50 feet by 150 feet), later called the Great Hall of Steam. The bronze double door was striking. Sculpted by Herbert Adams, whose credits included two doors at the Library of Congress, it featured panels depicting sea themes since the ancient Greeks. Worked by the Gorham Manufacturing Company in 1935, the panels included a mariner, a mermaid, and historic watercraft in bas-relief. On each side were single doors, one etched with Huntington's founding decree. Also depicted were the Eastern and Western Hemispheres, thus challenging President Hoover's and Professor Beard's proposals to defend only the Western sphere. The doors were topped by Adams's conception of the modern navy; he highlighted battleships, though General Billy Mitchell had proven them to be highly vulnerable to air attack in 1921. In the distance was an aircraft carrier—the navy's future, as when the NNSDD launched USS *Ranger* in 1933 and laid USS *Yorktown*'s keel in 1934.[18]

Entering those doors, visitors saw figureheads and paintings, as well as curios atop sawhorse tables (fig. 19). After a few items were stolen, wires were attached to hold articles in place, and the shipyard made aluminum display cases. Curator Harold Sniffen, a Hampton native and Middlebury College graduate, thought it had the feel of an old attic. But, said a visitor, it was not cluttered by "a lot of junk," as was Henry Ford's Dearborn museum, which Ferguson claimed was "quite incoherent." Superintendent Joseph T. Holzbach greeted visitors. He had, said the *Washington Star*, "a rollicking sense of humor and a deep-set love of the sea." In 1935, the American Automobile Association called the museum the "Most Unadvertised Place in America," saying that its abundant materials required a day's visit.[19]

With free admission, attendance increased through the 1930s, but the weekday hours of 9:00 a.m. to 5:00 p.m. meant that working people could attend only on Saturday or three hours on Sunday. In 1934, attendance

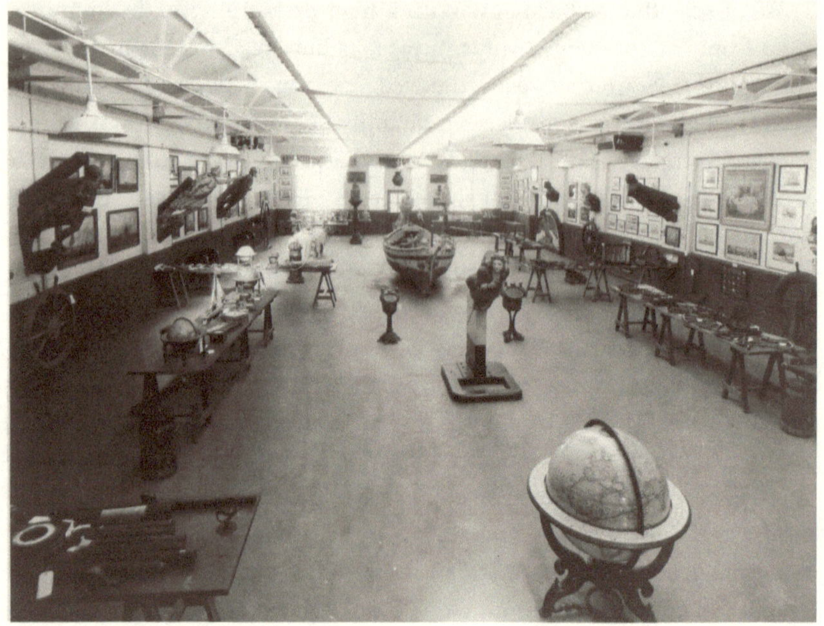

FIGURE 19. Artifacts were placed on tables prior to the installation of glass cases. *Courtesy of the Mariners' Museum, Newport News, Virginia.*

reached 40,000; by 1937, 96,000; and by 1940, 132,400. In 1939, visitors came from every state and forty-five foreign countries or dependencies. In the segregated South, where Newport News upheld Jim Crow until the late 1960s, groups of blacks did visit separately, but there was little in the museum on African American history. It displayed, without explanation, a "sea chest from the brig *Sultan* of New Orleans, 1853"; its interior lid depicted a loin-clothed African male whose neck chain was held by a white man. Regardless of race, residents of Hampton and Newport News who lacked a car were accommodated only in 1938, when regular public bus service began on weekends.[20]

"THE INCOME PRODUCER FOR GRAY-HAIRED CURATORS AND LIBRARIANS": THE SHIPYARD FROM THE DEPRESSION INTO THE COLD WAR

Meanwhile, a political drama was unfolding in Washington. Initially encouraged by FDR, a U.S. Senate committee chaired by Gerald Nye

(R-ND) investigated in 1934–36 contractors accused of not only price fixing, collusion, and profiteering during U.S. neutrality in 1914–17 but also blocking postwar disarmament. Public suspicion heightened. In 1934, the Book of the Month Club offered *Merchants of Death* on the arms industry, while *Iron, Blood and Profits* exposed the munitions trade; both mentioned Newport News. Big Three lobbyist Shearer testified before the committee. Focusing on the naval-industrial complex, including the NNSDD, the *Christian Century* suggested in a 1935 editorial: "Not a dollar of the nation's money should be spent on naval shipbuilding until it has been clearly proved that this business, avowedly a patriotic effort to provide for the national defense, is not in reality a sordid racket conducted in such a way as to mulct the public while pouring millions into the pockets of a little clique of insiders." Ferguson played the card of national defense. "Having the world's second-best navy," he testified, "is like holding the second-best hand in a poker game." The committee nonetheless called the contractors' record disgraceful.[21]

With fascism rising in 1936, the tide changed. Roosevelt, who had been assistant navy secretary in 1913–20, was a friend of the Navy League and had even met Shearer. In April, Eleanor Roosevelt toured the museum, celebrated NNSDD's fiftieth anniversary, and christened *Yorktown*. In October, Mrs. Claude (Elizabeth) Swanson officiated at a ceremony for USS *Enterprise*. The Merchant Marine Act also gave generous subsidies to the yard. Called by *Fortune* the "dean of U.S. shipbuilders," Ferguson saw "signs now of having the heads of our own government very much interested in the sea . . . [and] making the youngsters feel proud" of the yard's work. *Fortune* hailed the NNSDD as the "most solidly established shipyard." With $70 million in contracts, it was the navy's "indispensable No. 1 customer." It had also, oddly, become "the income producer for gray-haired curators and librarians." Concluding that a global "naval race [was] imminent," *Fortune* saw "a golden opportunity" for shipbuilding, but citizens had to be educated on its importance.[22]

The Navy League, for one, was educating the public. In 1935 it resumed publishing its magazine, *Sea Power*, and its director went on a national tour. But *Variety* magazine called his presentation "unadulterated propaganda in favor of the steel companies and shipyards." Ferguson wanted a more respected voice, he said, "to make the American people more ship-minded." His Mariners' Museum fit the bill. In the *Nautical Gazette*, columnist Captain Felix Riesenberg urged a visit to the museum; Sea Scouts and cadets could "profitably spend a month" there and "come away informed and inspired." He declared: "This is the great American Museum of the Sea." Similarly, Washington, D.C., residents, whose Smithsonian Institution had only a small maritime collection, were told that Mariners' had "the most complete record now in existence of the stirring drama of man's progress on the ocean." The *Washington Star* advised that "every American" should see it. "A large delegation from Congress," led by Vice President John Nance Garner, "seemed much impressed," though Mariners' lacked "the historic tapestries, oils and ship models which the British have in their Maritime Museum."[23]

Opening the National Maritime Museum in Greenwich, in 1937, King George VI urged Britons to emulate Sir Francis Drake and Lord Horatio Nelson. Like Mariners', its principal benefactor was a shipbuilder, and its founders, including the British Navy League, mixed history and empire. Ferguson wanted a similar audience. While school groups were "more necessary . . . than almost anything else," he told naval architects, Mariners' also advanced "the interest of our profession" because U.S. universities lagged behind Europeans in promoting applied marine science. Championing that goal was the Newcomen Society, an organization of British and American corporate leaders and engineers who popularized history while defending free-market capitalism.[24]

That Anglo-American friendship intensified with war in 1939. The day before the German blitzkrieg in Poland, Mrs. Roosevelt christened SS *America*, the largest passenger vessel built in the nation. The naval architects society held its 1940 meeting at the museum to inspect the liner (and the museum's fifteen-foot model) before it became the troopship *West Point*. In 1940–41, the yard delivered eight passenger liners, which were similarly converted. In 1940 it also launched USS *Hornet* (a flattop) and built the battleship *Indiana*. Though the United States only entered the war after Pearl Harbor, the preceding months were hardly ones of neutrality for the yard or its museum. In May 1940, FDR donated a sixteen-foot model of the Holland-America Line's *Rotterdam*, whose namesake city had just been bombed by the Luftwaffe. Soon after, he gave a large model of the Swedish-American Line's *Gripsholm*, which the United States chartered as a neutral-flagged mercy ship. When Great Britain's ship models were stranded at the 1939 New York World's Fair, Mariners' offered to buy two, but Britain loaned all five. The thirty-foot RMS *Queen Elizabeth* was moved by railcar. In 1941, as the Battle of the Atlantic raged, Mariners' sympathetically exhibited the fair's *Century of British Transatlantic Shipping*.

The impending war hit home in other ways. In July 1940, FDR visited Hampton Roads and shared a platform with Roger Williams, whom he described as "one of my Navy boys in the old days" when they "used to cruise together." The president called the NNSDD "not only one of the most successful Yards but also one of the happiest." Roosevelt regretted, however, not having time to visit the museum, which he said had "all kinds of models, but more Merchant Marine than it is Navy." In September, he transferred fifty old destroyers to Britain to protect its convoys; twelve had been built at the yard. By mid-1941, the U.S. Navy was escorting convoys to Iceland, whose importance the museum stressed by placing a Leif Erikson statue at its entrance. Made for the New York World's Fair, the original was crafted by A. Stirling Calder. With the Nazi conquest of Denmark (Iceland's motherland) in 1940, however, the statue was loaned to the museum. Similarly, Mariners' inherited from the Dutch their World's Fair exhibit, a galleon wind vane, measuring six feet from bowsprit to transom, that it placed atop its main entrance.[25]

In 1940, Huntington decided to sell the yard. Fearing that it would be commandeered by the government, Archer said he would let "the gray-haired curators . . . worry about the value of an armament's business, not he." *Newsweek* valued it at $100 million, but a group of speculators paid $19.5 million. Holding 77,109 out of 100,000 shares, Huntington sold his stock and those in his philanthropic trusts, which he reimbursed. In 1943, Mariners' total assets were $7 million. By then, it included three display rooms, a model shop, and a library around the building's open court. With twenty thousand volumes, the library, which Huntington stipulated would "be equal in importance with the museum," reflected the interests of shipbuilders, shippers, and the navy. It held everything from logbooks, including that of John Paul Jones and his *Ranger*, to movies documenting the construction of ships, to Samuel Clemens's pilot's license (1859). While the leadsman's cry "By the mark twain" had inspired his nom de plume, the license was given to the museum (to the chagrin of Missourian and federal archivists) by a mother who likely wanted to insure her son's shipyard job in 1932. It became "one of the [museum's] most valuable possessions."[26]

Acquired in 1940, the Edwin Tappan Adney Collection included 121 models of Eastern Woodlands canoes, mostly made to one-fifth scale. It was later called "the most valuable single resource for the interpretation of native North American watercraft." While touring a Montreal museum, Mariners' agents Frederick and Nola Hill saw the Maliseet birchbark models, which were valued at $25,000 and acted as collateral for an Adney loan. Mariners' bought the group and hired Adney to write a book, which was finished after his death by Howard Chapelle. Adopting New Brunswick's outdoor life, Adney had published "the earliest detailed descriptions of a birch-bark canoe, with instructions for building one." Ruing that native youth had forgotten their culture, he had tried to regenerate a tradition.[27]

With such acquisitions, attendance reached 150,750 visitors in 1941. It fell dramatically in 1942 and 1943 with war and gas rationing. Though curators Sniffen, Brown, and Robert Burgess joined the navy, the museum maintained regular hours and attracted military personnel, convalescents, and even Boy Scouts who camped in the woods. With a free bus from nearby Fort Eustis, Sundays boomed. Its patriotic message was "of paramount importance," but a visit was also regarded as desirable recreation, as opposed to the scandalous Hampton Roads bars and brothels. In 1943, Mariners' staged an unusual form of entertainment. As bystanders watched, home defense forces with gas masks and smoke screens simulated a battle. Their enemy was not Nazi invaders but "a fancied mob on mischief bent," as had occurred in Los Angeles, where mobs of sailors and soldiers, like "storm-troop thugs," attacked people of color for four nights. Outbreaks occurred in Norfolk and other military towns where the color line was breached.[28]

To symbolize a steadfast Americanism, Mariners' displayed a massive carved eagle, sculpted by John Haley Bellamy, under a gigantic U.S. flag (fig. 20). With an eighteen-foot wingspan, the figurehead had been removed from USS *Lancaster*. After Mystic's Clifford Mallory sent a photo in 1933, Ferguson inspected it in a Boston junk dealer's shop. Said to represent the national ethos, it later appeared on the covers of *Life* and *Newsweek*. Meanwhile, visiting English mariners were urged to see the figurehead of HMS *Formidable* (1825), an eighty-four-gun warship, as it was "stern, resolute, [and] determined." Lord Nelson's materials were more familiar. Reinforcing the British Navy League's cult, Mariners' displayed a bronze bust and an ivory model of his flagship *Victory*, which was a shrine in Portsmouth, England.[29]

Those relics inspired the war effort. Reaching thirty-one thousand jobs in April 1943, the NNSDD, which ran for a mile and one-quarter along the James River, delivered forty-six ships to the navy during the war and repaired another 1,483. In 1945, *Time* called Ferguson "the best builder of warships in the U.S., if not in the world." Mariners' contributed to the

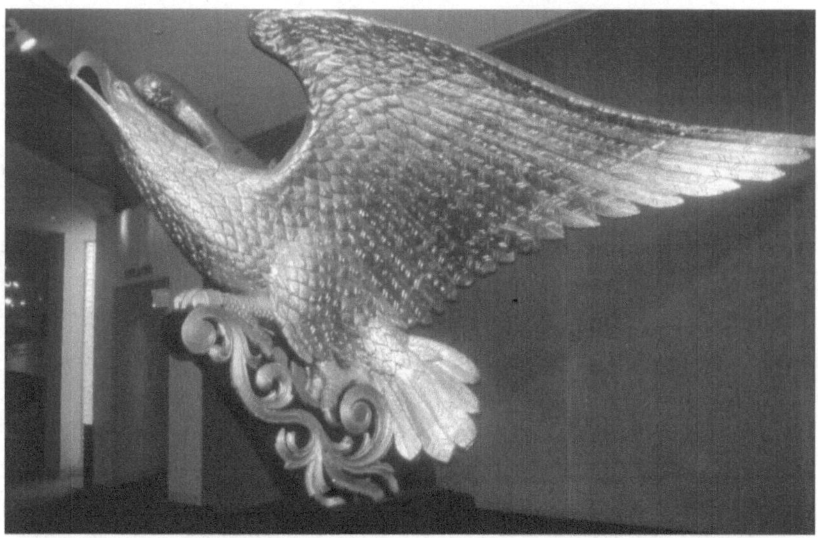

FIGURE 20. USS *Lancaster* figurehead. *Photo by author, 1998.*

making of those ships paradoxically by donating fifty tons of relics, including ten Revolutionary War cannons, to a scrap drive. Because the yard was so busy, the museum acted as its surrogate, often hosting the "sponsor and launching parties." In a retrospective, it published *Newport News Ships: Their History in Two World Wars*, which led Alexander Brown to suggest that "Virginia's most famous product, renowned the world over," was not its tobacco or hams but its ships.[30]

The yard's wartime boom, however, was followed by another peacetime bust. As *Time* noted, "What the yard will do when its war contracts all run out, some time in 1947, is anybody's guess." In 1947, Ferguson retired from the yard but still captained the museum. The future of Hampton Roads, said a labor leader, was in global shipping. Ferguson served on the board of the National Foreign Trade Council, and curators coordinated a radio program, "What the Mariners' Museum Means to Foreign Trade." According to Frederick Hill, who became director in 1946, the museum showed the necessity for new construction by emphasizing changes in technology. But as capitalists opted for foreign-built freighters, Mariners' stressed Admiral Mahan's concept of sea power. Coming to town was Joseph L. Kochka, an adviser to the U.S. Merchant Marine Cadet Corps. Calling Mariners' "the best source" on the merchant marine, he said that it was a "diamond the value of which" locals failed to appreciate. He emblazoned his message on his trailer: "A MODERN MERCHANT MARINE MEANS: JOBS, INDUSTRIAL ACTIVITY, TRADE, NATIONAL SECURITY, SEAPOWER." True to Mahan, another placard preached: "SEAPOWER = NAVY + BASES + MERCHANT MARINE." A third echoed Westinghouse Electric's drive, endorsed by Carl Cutler: "THIS TIME—LET'S KEEP OUR MERCHANT MARINE."[31]

The city's leading paper, the *Newport News Daily Press*, scolded the Chamber of Commerce for being "indifferent to [the museum] if not neglectful." Drawing 134,500 visitors in 1947, Mariners' imparted "honor and distinction upon us," said its editor, and the community should appreciate "this fine local asset." Given that generation's experiences, as well as the intensifying Cold War, naval themes permeated the museum. In 1947 it celebrated Navy Day, which, since October 27, 1922, the Navy League had observed on Theodore Roosevelt's birthday. As the air force waxed and the navy waned, the NNSDD warned "that our *first* line of defense [must] be kept strong." In 1947, Mariners' launched a bicentennial observance of the birth of John Paul Jones. Recognized as the first "to gain national and lasting recognition of his outstanding use of sea power," Jones's propaganda value was recognized by Teddy Roosevelt (and Mariners') by ignoring his years as a slave trader, a brawler, and a Russian mercenary. Though not a citizen, he was called the "Father of the United States Navy." Also, in 1947, Mariners' marked the sesquicentennial of USS *Constitution*'s launch. It symbolized "the might of American sea power in both war and peace," but after its restoration (1927–31) Mariners' ironically showed no interest in purchasing its salvaged main mast and bowsprit as relics.[32]

The paintings of Thomas C. Skinner Jr. stressed another angle of shipmindedness. After studying art in New York and Spain, he was employed by the yard when his sister married Ferguson. Assigned to the museum in 1932, he was given a studio at the yard, where he recorded construction and repair. In addition to ten large murals in the Great Hall, a special exhibit in 1948 featured sixty paintings. Some proudly showed NNSDD ships, but combat's grisly side was missing. One of the best paintings (ten feet six inches by six feet six inches), *Entering Dry Dock, S.S.* Maltran *at Newport News, December 14, 1934*, showed a small freighter, bellowing smoke, with a crew of African Americans working the ropes. It disclosed their labor's grime, sweat, and toil (fig. 21). Of NNSDD's 8,400 employees, 23 percent were blacks, who, *Fortune* noted, got "exactly the same pay as whites for the same work." But the Congress of Industrial Organizations called a strike,

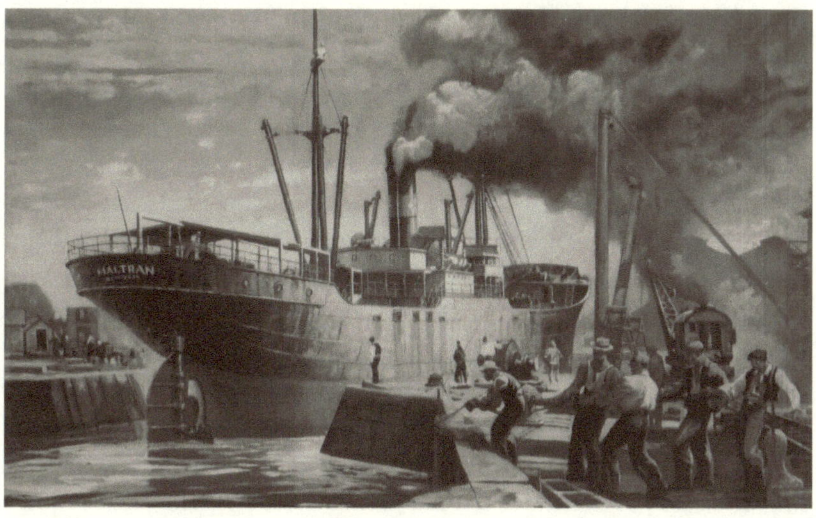

FIGURE 21. *Entering Dry Dock, S.S.* Maltran *at Newport News, December 14, 1934*, by Thomas Skinner, 1934. *Courtesy of the Mariners' Museum, Newport News, Virginia.*

which failed; a company union replaced it. Skinner's paintings helped sell the yard. As a curator said, "Any shipyard worker viewing these pictures ceases, at least while he stands there, to be a clock puncher, a boss hater, or a man-who-does-more-than-he's-paid-for, and he becomes a shipbuilder, a fashioner of a mighty thing of steel which can cope with the sea in all its violent moods." When Ferguson died in 1953, the NNSDD was "the greatest shipbuilding plant in the world."[33]

FOSTERING A "SPIRIT OF SEA-CONSCIOUSNESS": FIGUREHEADS, MODELS, SMALL CRAFT, AND CURIOS

In 1948, the budget of $150,000 included 10 percent for acquisitions, which it highlighted in *The Mariners' Museum: A History and Guide* (1950). With 250 pages of text and photographs, the guidebook was compiled by Brown, also a founder and associate editor of the *American Neptune*. He showed, for instance, the entry's two Spanish cannons. Arriving in Havana in 1935, museum agents had been befriended by strongman Colonel Fulgencio Batista, then the target of a general strike. To curry favor, Batista allowed them to excavate Cabana Fortress, where they found the rare bronze cannons. Richly decorated, they dated to 1721 and 1746. Visitors entering the

Great Hall also glimpsed paintings, ship models, freestanding instruments, and diverse curios.

While the *Richmond Times-Dispatch* regarded the figureheads as "most memorable," their popularity increased after they became anachronisms. Mythological figures were common, such as the sea nymph aboard the clipper *Galatea* (1854). Typical of male fetishism, those "bare-breasted beauties" reflected, said a reporter, an old adage "that the waters could be calmed by a woman uncovering her body at sea." Equally seductive was a mermaid figurehead, which was found in St. Thomas. Yet "disaster and evil nearly always follow in the wake of the legendary mermaid," noted librarian John Lochhead, who left it to psychologists to explain why seamen "regarded their motives as deceitful and their purpose to lure the reckless and infatuated to destruction." Another carving was the Queen of Sheba. From an unknown ship, the cabin ornament raised Jim Crow's eyebrows. The biblical queen had been Ethiopian, but a reporter described her complexion as "slightly Negroid." According to Virginia's Racial Integrity Act (1924), that category only required "one drop" of black blood. Sexually crossing the color barrier was taboo, but common. "As a scantily clad, winsome foreign woman," said a later writer, "she subtly implied potential liaisons in distant ports," a topic that few museums discussed. But for the straitlaced, she implied religious conversion, as in the story of Solomon. By 1945, Mariners' had eighty-five figureheads, triple Mystic Seaport's fold.[34]

More central to the museum's mission were its ship models, which by 1949 numbered over eight hundred and represented almost every craft once afloat. Models had been stereotyped as "a happy icon for a gentleman's study," but a Ferguson classmate at Annapolis reported that school children who visited his New York museum couldn't "get enough of models and their parents and teachers [were] the same." This "irresistible appeal," reported the American Association of Museums, was explained psychologically by childhood dreams of adventure, romantic exploits, and heroic combat. To foster that "spirit of sea-consciousness," Mariners' inexpensively sold the plans and material to build a thirty-inch model racing yacht. Young and old shipbuilders alike were reportedly "never so happy as when in [their] own 'dockyard.'" Like New York's natural history museum, Mariners' developed a model-making facility. In 1932 Sumner Besse, a yard supervisor, became head model builder. An MIT graduate in marine architecture and engineering, he and his five-man crew crafted twelve models until war forced the shop's closure in 1939. Eight were NNSDD ships. Made for the 1939 world's fair, NNSDD's *America* was seven hundred pounds and fifteen feet long. Using a uniform scale of 1:48 (one-fourth inch to one foot), the model stressed the engineering and design but missed its cozy interior, styled by and for women.[35]

August Fletcher Crabtree depicted the evolution of ships in sixteen miniatures. Hoping to find a buyer or display space for his work in 1947, he visited Mariners' but was rebuffed. It later purchased part of his collection for $75,000 and hired him to carve and lecture on Sundays for a dozen years. His exhibit opened in 1955 (permanently in 1971). Said a reporter, "Had Faberge been building ship models rather than crafting Easter eggs, his work would surely rival Crabtree's superlative virtuosity." His model of a thirty-foot Venetian gondola, for example, was seven and one-half inches long. Asked if his ships would sail, as his wife had sewn operable rigging and canvas, he replied: "Give me a crew that's small enough!" The *New York Times* called them one of the ten best collections of miniatures in the world.[36]

Mariners' also developed a small-craft collection, which reportedly had "never been done before" in the nation. Its creation depended on the whims of agents, curators, and the founder. Though Huntington "was not really interested in nautical things," a staffer explained, some craft became his "private toys." He built the museum around a fifty-one-foot Portuguese sardine boat with a "phantasmagoric design"; as the museum expanded in 1940, its extraction required knocking a hole in the wall. Congressman Bland called it "the most arresting single exhibit." Huntington vetoed acquiring larger ships, including *Royal Savage*, a Revolutionary War schooner whose submerged hull was found in Lake Champlain near the gunboat *Philadelphia*, which the Smithsonian displayed. In addition, Brown asked Ferguson (unsuccessfully) in 1935 to fund a Polynesian expedition to buy fast-disappearing craft and objects. Through agents, Ferguson instead acquired native boats or commissioned the building of others, as in the case of a twenty-foot Santa Anna Island Bonito canoe.[37]

Those boatbuilding traditions were also being lost in America. In 1939 Mariners' hired Crow's Heart, who lived with North Dakota's Mandans, to build two bullboats, which were round, covered with hides, but extinct. He was "one of the last" to ride them across the Missouri River. After whites had slaughtered the buffalo, Indians substituted cowhide. The museum showed one of each. Surprisingly left unmentioned by a generation familiar with Rosie the Riveter was gender. Bullboats "usually came under the purview of women," noted historian Elizabeth Fenn, but were built by men and women alike. The death of Crow's Heart meant the end of a tradition. But, applauding Mariners' inclusion of "the work of primitive peoples," an engineering-minded naval officer similarly admired the Alaskan kayak's "workmanship and design," especially its "ratio of hull weight to deadweight." Reflecting his present-minded use of the past, he suggested that shipbuilders examine such craft to solve the industry's "pressing problems."[38]

Craft even floated on Lake Maury. There "in absolutely untouched condition" were a Greek sponge sloop from the Gulf of Mexico and a Chesapeake Bay sailing canoe. Exposed to the elements and lacking maintenance, however, some "sank at their moorings." While smaller boats were moved to the courtyard, larger ones sat unprotected under pine trees. The middle display room centered round a thirty-foot whaleboat. In 1933, Mariners' had commissioned New Bedford's Charles Beetle "to build what was probably the last whale-boat ever made by this prolific builder." With a shipbuilder's pride, Ferguson said, "If there had been a better boat designed and built the world over than the old Yankee whaleboat, I haven't heard of it." Still, some locals wondered why a southern museum spotlighted a Yankee trade! Ferguson toured museums in New Bedford, Nantucket, and Salem. He bought whaling art from Clifford Ashley and displayed his painting of the "Sail Loft," where Beetle had worked and which the Bourne Museum re-created in its gallery. Thus, with eighty-five boats by 1978, Mariners' had "the largest small craft collection in a North American museum." But it would be outpaced by Mystic.[39]

To represent its own region, Mariners' exhibited the oysterman's Chesapeake Bay log sailing canoe. Museum manager Gatewood ironically saw his first one at the New York Boat Show. After an inquiry, he heard that the nearby hamlet of "Poquoson made the best one," but "the old hands" were "passing rapidly [and] leaving no written accounts of how they did their work." So, in 1934, he acquired the twenty-six-foot *Maggie E. Smith* (1891), but the museum again neglected maintenance and lost it. More comfortable with scholarship, Mariners' published Marion Brewington's *Chesapeake Bay Log Canoe* (1937). A Philadelphia banker, antimodernist, and later curator at Salem's Peabody Museum, Brewington also studied the bay's bugeye, a multi-log-hulled vessel with two masts and three sails that developed after the Civil War for oyster dredging. None had been built since 1918. Brewington's writings exposed the "brutality, starvation, [and] murder" faced by those oystermen, but museum curators instead depicted in a color movie the less exploitative modern fleet. Yet Brewington deplored the oysterman's "oily, grimy motorboats" that Virginia, but not Maryland, allowed in its waters.[40]

Meanwhile, the theme of sea power was becoming more conspicuous with the intensifying Cold War, the navy's local prominence, and the presidency of Captain Roger Williams, who succeeded Ferguson. A direct descendant of Rhode Island's founder, Williams was an Annapolis-trained engineer who served in the navy (1901–20) but then headed operations at International Mercantile Marine Co., America's largest shipper. He became NNSDD vice president in 1930 but kept a corporate office in New York. There he was "the naval gentleman personified," said *Fortune*, and "a familiar figure at the quaint, conservative India House." During the war, he headed an NNSDD subsidiary in North Carolina that built 243 merchant ships and employed 20,959.[41]

Williams anchored Mariners' more firmly in the naval-industrial complex. In 1955, he replaced director Hill with Rear Admiral Evander Wallace Sylvester (USN, ret.), whose advanced degrees in naval architecture and business matched Williams's focus. As Mystic Seaport went through a similar change, Howard Chapelle told Carl Cutler that civilians should be heading such museums. The museum's military orientation was evident in its programs. During Jamestown's 350th anniversary festival in 1957, for example, Sylvester helped organize Freedom of the Seas, Hampton Roads' first international naval gathering since the Great White Fleet of 1907. In tandem, Mariners' mounted the *International Naval Review Exhibition*, for which the navy presented a twelve-foot model of the NNSDD-built carrier *Forrestal* (1954), while the Electric Boat Company gave a model of USS *Nautilus* (1954). Described as "one of the few display models on exhibit," *Nautilus* was relatively secret to all but the Kremlin. Also, after the USSR launched Sputnik in 1957, which showed the Soviets' ability to deliver a nuclear warhead, Edward Teller claimed that America had lost "a battle more important and greater than Pearl Harbor." An emissary of Sperry Gyroscope Company reassured a Mariners' audience that NNSDD's first nuclear-powered ballistic submarine, *Robert E. Lee* (1959), had a perfect missile guidance system and the ability to retaliate.[42]

Thoughts of nuclear Armageddon perhaps prompted the museum to ask artist John Hawkinson to craft "an exact replica of the Ark." He replied, "Heck, nobody in the world could do that." Still, he reportedly built the first-ever museum model. Using Genesis 6:14-22 and a scale of 1/16 inch to one foot, he portrayed "a barn-like structure, on a huge raft." He chose a raft because, "after considerable research and thought," he figured that "Noah did not possess the knowledge, manpower, nor equipment to construct a typical ship's hull." Sylvester concurred, adding: "Noah had only three sons, who, like most sons, probably weren't too interested in working. He was not going to do anything he didn't have to do. . . . It was built on the principle of least work." Its diorama was realistic "to the minutest detail." Said Sylvester, it was "one of the most important pieces in carrying out our educational mission."[43]

With Sylvester's death in 1960, the museum again turned to a navy retiree. In the midst of heightened United States–Union of Soviet Socialist Republics tensions, it surprisingly chose an individual known for international cooperation. Since graduating from Annapolis in 1925, Rear Admiral George J. Dufek served as the navy's "top 'cold weather' expert," having taken six expeditions to the Antarctic and two to the Arctic. In 1939, for example, he navigated Admiral Richard E. Byrd's steam barkentine *Bear* in Antarctica, which Thomas Skinner depicted in a museum painting near its figurehead. Dufek became "senior U.S. adviser to the President" on the Antarctic program. Under the admiral, the *First International Antarctic Exhibition* opened on October 28, 1962. Occupying over eight thousand square feet, it ran six months and featured models of Antarctica (given by Walt Disney Productions) and the U.S. atomic power plant at McMurdo Sound (loaned by the Martin Company). It showcased the International Geophysical Year (1957–58), when, as Dufek explained, scientists worked together, "regardless of national affiliations and political views." Yet, his exhibition was jeopardized by Cold War politics when the USSR and three Soviet bloc states boycotted it. Shortly before its debut, President John F. Kennedy announced the discovery of Soviet missiles in Cuba. As the crisis unfolded, a U.S. commander was hoping a Soviet misstep would justify JFK wiping "them off the face of the earth." But, said a local writer, the world took "a step back." Before the debut, the Russians relented by sending four large panels, but because Hampton Roads was a closed military zone, Dufek retrieved them from the Soviets' Washington embassy. Dufek used the Antarctic exhibitions to hawk his agenda of constructing a modern icebreaker fleet because the U.S. Navy had "commitments near both poles." While Americans were worrying about a missile gap, he warned of an icebreaker gap. The United States had nine, but "they have 31."[44]

Dufek also staged *Sea Power in the Civil War*. Hampton Roads was best known for the Battle of Ironclads of March 9, 1862. It revolutionized not only "the navies and the naval policies of the world," a colleague told Ferguson, but "the colonial policies of all nations, and hence the commercial policies of all nations" because advanced metallurgy became a tool of imperialism. Such shipbuilders as Sumner Besse were not impressed by CSS *Virginia*, which was the iron-plated USS *Merrimack* (1855), but USS *Monitor* (1862) was "an inventor's dream." Mariners' had earlier shown a painting of the clash, which prompted neo-Confederates to ask Huntington to display their flag. "Personally, I think the idea is idiotic," he wrote Gatewood, "but if it is popular, and expresses the sentiment of our neighbors, I have not the slightest objection."[45]

The Civil War's centennial mixed neo-Confederate politics, sea power, and tourism. Expecting "a second massive invasion" by Yankees armed only with billfolds, Richmond suggested that Virginians follow Alabamians who discovered "that a tourist was equal to three bales of cotton and was a darn site easier to pick." Long claiming that Yankees had distorted the ironclads' battle, a Newport News editor called in 1959 for a reenactment to establish "a correct historic version." Many expected Mariners' to sponsor the event, but Sylvester wanted nothing "shoddy" to make it "ashamed and disappointed." In 1962, however, tourism-driven Norfolk staged the battle, twenty-two times. As Mariners' admission was still free, it drew over a million centennial visitors to a new wing touting "the largest single display in its 33-year history." It included fifty models, Confederate and Federal, built and donated by the yard. Funded by the state's Centennial Commission, Mariners' also created an animated diorama of the 1862 clash, which debuted with a military band, uniformed Confederates, and remarks by historian Lyon G. Tyler Jr. of the state commission. Dodging contemporary issues, Tyler focused on the soldiers' "generosity in victory and their serenity in defeat." His die-hard Confederate father and grandfather (a former U.S. president) had been anything but serene.[46]

Depicting the Union attack on Mobile Bay, where USS *Hartford* engaged CSS *Tennessee*, another diorama enlivened the federal vessel. United States admiral David G. Farragut was known for his order, "Damn the torpedoes! Full speed ahead!" In 1957, a decommissioned, neglected, and thus damned *Hartford* sank, however, at its Norfolk moorings; Mariners' acquired and displayed its trailboard and billet head. Though Newport News had been a Confederate bastion, Mariners' prized Farragut for inspiring Admiral Mahan, who saw, said curator Harold Sniffen, that "never in history did seapower play as important a part as during the Civil War." Glimpsing modern lessons, he added that the Confederacy had suffered because it did not maintain its navy. In all, said the *New York Times*, Mariners' showed "an unequalled collection."[47]

Watching from afar, the African American historian John Hope Franklin asked, Why was Virginia committing "so much of its meager resources" to mark a war that "all but destroyed the nation [Virginia had] done so much to establish?" He knew that neo-Confederates were politicizing the centennial. According to the Virginia Travel Council, tourists would learn a "greater understanding of the historical truths Virginia is trying to present." Those truths revolved around what State Senator and Centennial Commission chairman Charles H. Moses called the war's "primary cause," a state's right to defend slavery. As federal authorities and civil rights activists pressed desegregation, he warned that the South's ability to maintain white control was "being siphoned off by an ever more powerful central government." Neo-Confederates regarded their control of public history similarly, as when Alexander Brown proposed placing a marker at Camp Butler, where refugee slaves had encamped outside the Yankees' Fort Monroe in Hampton. "A civil war of ideas" erupted. Calling Brown's proposal "blasphemous," they blocked it and declared that Virginia "should not commemorate 'Yankee' events." While visiting the Mariners' exhibits, the state commission's director dodged the issue and diplomatically shifted to anticommunism's "lessons of patriotism and heroism." In 1961, after the Soviets put the first human in space and the United States faced recession and overseas setbacks, he said, "Similar attitudes are needed today as America faces cold war losses in science, the world market and on battlegrounds of Laos and Cuba."[48]

After its Civil War Centennial boom, attendance fell, even during the U.S. Bicentennial, and Mariners' began to shift. In 1973, Harvard-educated William D. Wilkinson, former registrar at the Metropolitan Museum of Art and a Mariners' curator since 1971, became its first professionally trained director and served until 1991. Midway in his tenure, the American Association of Museums (AAM) called it "one of the leading museums of its kind in the world." To maintain that prominence, Mariners' needed better facilities, funding, and attendance. One long-discussed stratagem was headlining Chesapeake Bay. As part of Virginia's 350th commemoration in 1957, which drew 217,141 museum visitors, it had opened the Chesapeake Bay Room; it featured a diorama of the Jamestown settlement and, later, others by John Hawkinson on native boatbuilding and mid-1600s shipbuilding. The room's curator, Robert Burgess, emphasized fishing, shipping, and commerce but focused little on slavery, its so-called "peculiar institution." Likewise sidestepping the centrality of slavery was the museum's scholarly *Tobacco Coast: A Maritime History of Chesapeake Bay in the Colonial Era* (1953).[49]

In 1989, Mariners' opened its largest expansion to date. The state funded a third of the twelve-thousand-square-foot, $4.5 million Chesapeake Bay Gallery, and the *Newport News Daily Press* spurred the museum's "first-ever fund raising drive." Drawing forty-six hundred visitors its first day, it was dedicated by Governor Gerald Baliles and, at his side, Lieutenant Governor L. Douglas Wilder, soon to be the first elected black governor of Virginia. While the fifty-seat theater showed *Mariner*, an eighteen-minute prize-winning film about global maritime activities, the Public Broadcasting Service was airing a sixty-minute version. Covering the early 1600s to the present, the lower-level exhibits began with a spectacular Fresnel first-order lens from the Cape Charles Lighthouse and a seventeen-foot by fifty-eight-foot mural of skipjacks oystering in Maryland, which (unlike Virginia) forbade power boats. Accompanying a native dugout canoe (1630s) were a half-dozen fishing boats, but the text's mention of the Bay's "replenishable resources" missed a brewing environmental crisis. In addition to Antonio Jacobsen's iconic steamboat paintings, the upper level showed photographs by the *Baltimore Sun*'s A. Aubrey Bodine; held by Mariners', they constituted "one of the great pictorial archives of the Chesapeake." A commissioned diorama of Norfolk International Marine Terminal was also featured, as Hampton Roads was the East Coast's second busiest cargo-handling port. In all, curators said, the wing was "the beginning of a new era." But not new enough. While its catchy actor-interpreters included a James River explorer, a pirate, a lighthouse keeper, and a steamship passenger, they omitted the ever-present black fisherman.[50]

Mariners' was simultaneously promoting Chesapeake-related events. In 1984 folk-rock singer John Townley developed a music program that soon reached 16,325 students annually. His group also issued *A Chesapeake Sailors' Companion: Four Centuries of Maritime Music on the Chesapeake Bay* (1986). In search of African American work songs, he went in 1989 to the still-undeveloped Eastern Shore, but the oyster shuckers weren't singing. "We're just livin' in a different age," one explained. "The young generation is not like the old generation way back." Boatbuilding had an up-and-down story too. Besides illustrating a Poquoson boatyard in a diorama, the museum produced an award-winning film, *Billy Moore, Chesapeake*

Boatbuilder (1981). In 1985 Mariners' launched the Deadrise Project, when Moore and high school students began building up to forty-two-foot-long deadrise oyster boats. After Governor Baliles visited the museum's facility, it became the state boat in 1988. But, within a generation, the museum's boatbuilding waned, as education programs were redesigned for school funding and state standards.[51] (See fig. 22.)

By 1994, the Chesapeake Wing had failed to boost the museum's admissions. A convergence of threats posed an ominous future. First, Huntington's trust fund, which provided $2.5 million yearly in the late 1980s, was inadequate as the institution grew, even after the museum imposed an admission fee. Second, Mariners' faced rising costs, necessary expansion, and deferred maintenance of its facilities, including its long-ignored park. Retaining a seventy-five-acre border, as per Huntington's rule, it gave one hundred acres to Warwick County for a Virginia Living Museum emphasizing wildlife conservation, which created a third threat. In 1994, the

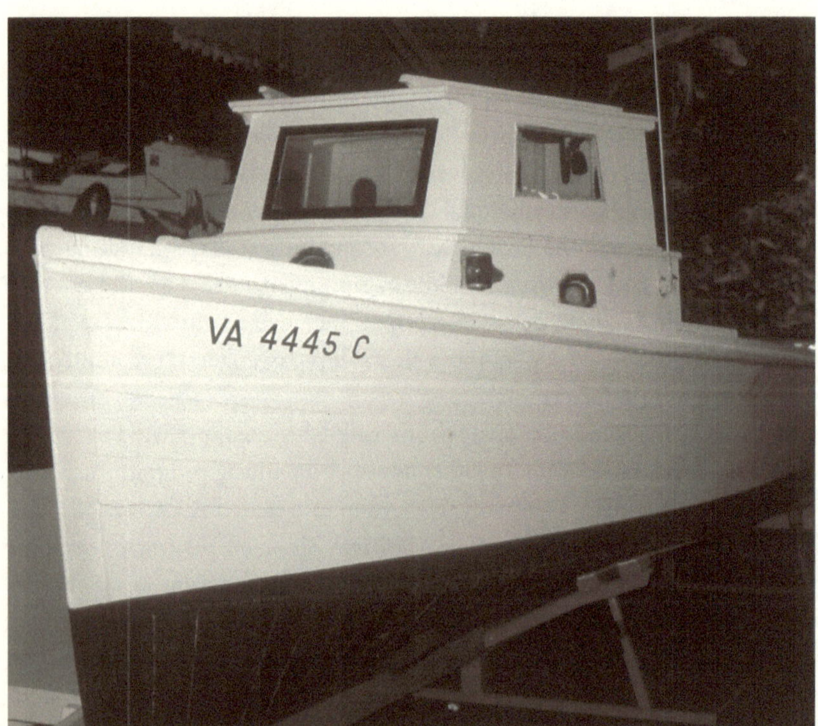

FIGURE 22. Deadrise boat, ca. 1955, acquired 1987. *Photo by author, 1998.*

Living Museum drew 540,000 visitors, which exceeded Mariners' gate by sixfold. More competition ensued with the opening of the Virginia Air & Space Center in Hampton in 1992. Mariners' attendance fell further with the opening of Norfolk's Nauticus in 1994.

Divided by Hampton Roads—only three and a half miles apart, but culturally wide—Norfolk and the Peninsula had long been rivals, but that intensified in 1983 after James Rouse's Enterprise Development Corporation opened Waterside, a festival marketplace in Norfolk. Next door and costing $52 million, the 140,000-square-foot Nauticus National Maritime Center opened in 1994. Touting interactive exhibits, its head dismissed Mariners', saying, "We will appeal to those people looking for action." It drew 436,139 visitors in 1994. Timothy J. Runyan, editor of *American Neptune*, hoped that its visitors would "discover the drama, the excitement, the skill involved in humanity's mastery of the world's seas and waterways." But others questioned its hybrid, entertainment-oriented qualities. In 1997, the *Daily Press* opined, "Quite simply, Nauticus is not a museum." By then, Nauticus was showing modern naval warfare on its first floor, while its Hampton Roads Naval Museum occupied the second. But, as the gate fell to under 200,000, a new director added a science center upstairs. After USS *Wisconsin* (1943), one of the largest battleships ever built, was docked there in 2000, attendance jumped to 459,000 in 2001. Given to the city, the battleship was included in the admission fee. By 2007, Norfolk was contributing "$700,000 annually to [Nauticus's] operating budget, besides more for maintenance and debt service payments." Being outpaced, Mariners' had hired John Hightower as president in 1993 to remake the museum. Though he had been fired by the South Street Seaport Museum, his subsequent success creating the Norwalk Maritime Center in Connecticut (with an aquarium, IMAX, and exhibits) was convincing. He told reporters he'd double Mariners' attendance by 2000. One means was a return to its roots.[52]

"THE UNIFYING THEME OF 'SEA POWER'": LINKING THE NAVY, THE YARD, AND THE MUSEUM

To boost Newport News Shipbuilding, the U.S. Navy, and its own turnstile, Mariners' underscored sea power. With the end of the Vietnam War in 1973 and the breakup of the Soviet Union in 1991, the nation's defense budget had fallen, generating fears in the military-dependent local economy. Opening in February 1977 in a sixty-five-hundred-square-foot space, a permanent exhibit traced sea power since the 1588 Spanish Armada. As the "largest single exhibition yet undertaken," its five elements were, said director Wilkinson, "the ships, their weapons, the men who sailed them, the strategy and tactics of their use in combat, and the support facilities that have kept them afloat." Each element was developed through four epochs: the Great Age of Sail (1588 to 1814); the Period of Transition (1815 to 1865); the Rise of the Battleship (1866 to 1916); and the Age of Global War (1917 to the present). The Rise of the Battleship, for example, showed how "an expansionist policy . . . led directly to the Spanish-American War and the acquisition of major bases in Cuba, Puerto Rico and the Philippines." But, curators admitted, "technical progress in guns, armor, engines, and hull design was so rapid that it was not unusual for a ship to be obsolescent by the time she was commissioned." One lesson was "the need for continuing development of a more flexible naval force," while another was, as in the 1930s rise of fascism, that "both arms limitation and collective security had proved pathetically ineffective deterrents to aggression."[53]

In 1986, that continuing development was illustrated in *A Century of Shipbuilding*, which a curator called "the largest [temporary exhibit] we've ever done." It honored the shipyard that had been sold in 1968 to Houston-based Tenneco Inc., which quickly removed a plaque quoting Collis Huntington's vision for the company: "We will build good ships, at a profit if we can, at a loss if we must, but always good ships." Tenneco was ironically buying loss-prone companies and forcing profit-oriented changes. The exhibit was accompanied by an attractive book commissioned by the yard and published by the museum. Costing Mariners' upward of $100,000 to mount, *A Century* showed the yard's long bond with the navy. Author William L. Tazewell called the museum "a good neighbor," but it was actually a surrogate hosting yard festivities and developing exhibits.[54]

A Century also spotlighted the yard's great liners. While the museum had displayed a large model of SS *United States*, it saluted its architect, William Francis Gibbs, by devoting a gallery to his work in 1972 and, in 1990, tripling its size to mark its own sixtieth anniversary. Called the "dean of American naval design," he was responsible for more than six thousand naval and commercial vessels, including twenty-seven hundred Liberty ships. But his greatest achievement, *United States*, was idle at a nearby dock. Said retired curator Burgess, it was on par "with the Pyramids or the great cathedrals of the Middle Ages," but in 1969 it was another casualty of transatlantic aviation. In 1984 its interior was auctioned. From its first-class dining room,

Mariners' acquired not only a sixteen-foot-high wall sculpture for display (*Expressions of Freedom* by Gwen Lux) but also the regal china and place settings, which the gift shop sold to status-minded consumers of the neo-Gilded Age.[55]

In 1995, Mariners' mounted a six-month-long exhibit, *Carriers, Codes, and the Silent Service: World War II and the New Navy*. Its launch was fun—a cocktail reception with dancing "in a setting reminiscent of a World War II canteen"—but also serious. Besides writing an explanatory scholarly tract, naval historian and consultant Carl Boyd organized a colloquium. Paying tribute, he noted that America's wartime ability to produce aircraft carriers showed "the decisive weakness of the Japanese shipbuilding industry." Since 1960, the nation's sole contractor for flattops was Newport News. Unique for Mariners' publications, Boyd offered pointed analysis. Questioning America's "exaggerated naval presence around the globe" and implicitly the contracts so necessary for Newport News, he called for a "judicious down-sizing" to reflect the changed circumstances of the Cold War after the Soviet Union's dissolution. Thinking that the Seawolf-class submarine then being built by Groton and Newport News was "too expensive," he suggested more affordable "quiet diesel-electric submarines." Similarly, while Ronald Reagan had wanted fifteen carrier-battle groups, Boyd thought that even twelve were too costly and could resemble "the dreadnought-like mentality that governed U.S. naval policy at the outset of the [twentieth] century." The exhibit showed that "adaptability and agility—not bigness per se—will be the watchwords in the prudent application of naval force."[56]

The board ordered Hightower to introduce more permanent exhibits on sea power. After citing Huntington's founding decree, he decided that a second "guiding principle" would be Mahan's "concept of sea power." Expanding Wilkinson's definition, Hightower included "all the commercial, military, economic, political, artistic, scientific, and social elements that make up the fabric of a nation's maritime affairs and, ultimately, its national strength." Transformative in purpose, curators began to "refocus and integrate each of the Museum's permanent exhibitions around the unifying theme of 'Sea Power.'" The new guidebook condensed it to five parts: Age of Exploration, Art of the Sea, Paths of Commerce, Art and Science of Shipbuilding, and Commanding the Sea. The first three were used at other museums, but the last two showed the influence of the local yard and the navy. Commanding the Sea was imperial, beginning with Sir Walter Raleigh: "Whoever commands the sea, commands the trade, whoever commands the trade of the world, commands the riches of the world, and consequently the world itself." A seventeen-minute film, *Sea Power: Beyond the Horizon*, introduced the museum.[57]

Opening in a permanent, sixty-one-hundred-square-foot venue, *Defending the Seas* featured the U.S. Navy up to 1999. With music by the U.S. Atlantic Fleet Band, its debut included remarks by Admiral Jay L. Johnson, chief of naval operations, who called the yard, museum, and community "a maritime home for this global Navy." Praising the museum, he said, "As soldiers walk old battlefields with their grandchildren, so shall we walk this gallery and explain where we sailed and what our Navy's contribution to history has been." Museum director Claudia Pennington also spoke. Formerly head (1993–97) of the U.S. Naval Museum in Washington, D.C., she was recruited by Hightower to double attendance, which reportedly caused staff complaints. *Defending the Seas* was organized by chief curator William Cogar, who formerly taught at the U.S. Naval Academy and headed its museum. They put Mahan at the philosophical helm of the museum. The exhibit showed, for instance, the navy's "important role in increasing the flow of commerce around the world, and therefore influencing our nation's economy." With *Defending the Seas*, Mariners' launched, in 2000, a website, Battle of the Atlantic, that drew 1.2 million (free) visitors in a year. A similar program for ticketed visitors at Nauticus relived the World War II Atlantic conflict.[58]

Sea power exhibits included many on Lord Nelson. Boasting that it was "the premiere American repository for Nelsonia," Mariners' staged a gala in 1986 to open *The Immortal Memory: Admiral Horatio Nelson, 1758–1805*. A "watershed event" that had piqued interest in Nelsonia, said curator Richard C. Malley, was Mahan's biography, *The Life of Nelson* (1897), which emphasized "a new aggressive battle philosophy." A long-term exhibit in 1992, *Engage the Enemy More Closely*, was followed in 1998 by *Nelson: A Time for Heroes*, also curated by Malley. With more than two hundred paintings, costumed interpreters, and a mock-up of Nelson's flagship *Victory*, it showed, said the museum's education director, how his use of raking fire made "naval warfare much more horrible than it was before." Mariners' concurrently sponsored a handful of children's programs exploring "life aboard a navy ship in the 1800s," but without the horror.[59]

Hightower's plan to double attendance by 2000 was iffy at best. Though Mariners' holdings were praised, critics questioned "its ability–and its willingness–to communicate the importance of that collection beyond the specialized realm of maritime enthusiasts and scholars." But, Hightower claimed, museums only thrived by "constantly reinventing themselves." Hemmed in by rival museums, competing against home-based media, and facing budgetary hell with the end of Huntington's endowment in 2002, he needed traffic from the northeast corridor. To offset declining federal support, many museums had been trying to boost their gate. As Norfolk's *Virginian-Pilot* reported, Mariners' began moving "to more family programming and educational events." By 1997, over half of its one hundred thousand visitors were from afar (one hundred miles or more), while a quarter were local. Among many plans, it wanted a real fleet to attract attention.[60]

That led to the National Maritime Museum Initiative. In 1996, former Mariners' trustee and New York shipping magnate John J. McMullen suggested that it merge with South Street Seaport Museum. Since that was forbidden by Huntington's charter, the two agreed to share resources. While each remained autonomous, they were, said Hightower, "blending our collections, our operations, and our missions across the board." In what the *New York Times* called "a match made in museum heaven," Mariners' rich collection and the Seaport's impressive fleet and half-million visitors would be shared. National funding was expected. "Museums talk about collaboration a lot," said Ed Able, AAM president, "but I haven't seen anyone do it with this kind of creativity and imagination." The 1997 agreement, signed with Seaport president Peter Neill, pledged collaborative exhibits, schooner visits to Virginia, and shared publications. In praise, the *Newport News Daily Press* observed: "A museum must be continuously evolving. Just opening the doors every day is not enough."[61]

More newsworthy, the two partners staged a coup when, at Hightower's request, Senators John Warner (R-VA) and Daniel P. Moynihan (D-NY), inserted a last-minute amendment into a defense spending bill that designated the two museums as "America's National Maritime Museum." Signed by President Bill Clinton in October 1998, the provision put them ahead of others if and when federal funding became available. But it only reaped derision from the Council of American Maritime Museums (CAMM). Led by Mystic Seaport, CAMM lobbied the Senate to amend the law and co-designate all CAMM members, but Warner blocked any revision. Still, other than a few shared exhibits and much self-aggrandizing, the designation yielded little.

The epic story of RMS *Titanic* yielded more. Since 1980, it had occupied a corner of the Great Hall, and an expanded exhibit in 1985 followed the wreck's discovery twelve thousand feet below the surface. Mounted in the wake of Hollywood's megahit *Titanic* (1997) was a nine-month blockbuster exhibit, *Titanic: Fortune & Fate* (1998) (fig. 23). To pique interest, Mariners' staged high- and low-brow parties. With guests attired in tuxedos, evening gowns, or period attire, the lavish "Last Dinner" sold out, while "The Real Party" featured "lively dancing and revelry" for would-be steerage passengers. With that, said Hightower, Pennington had shown "the marketing savvy of P. T. Barnum." Attendance in 1998 tripled to three hundred thousand, while over one-half million accessed the web version. With "a never-before-assembled collection of rare artifacts, personal effects and memorabilia," it was accompanied by parallel exhibits, such as *Building the Titanic*, and a one-hundred-thousand-print-run book, which mostly focused on high-and-mighty passengers. Visitors felt the drama. Besides receiving a ticket with the name of a passenger or crew member,

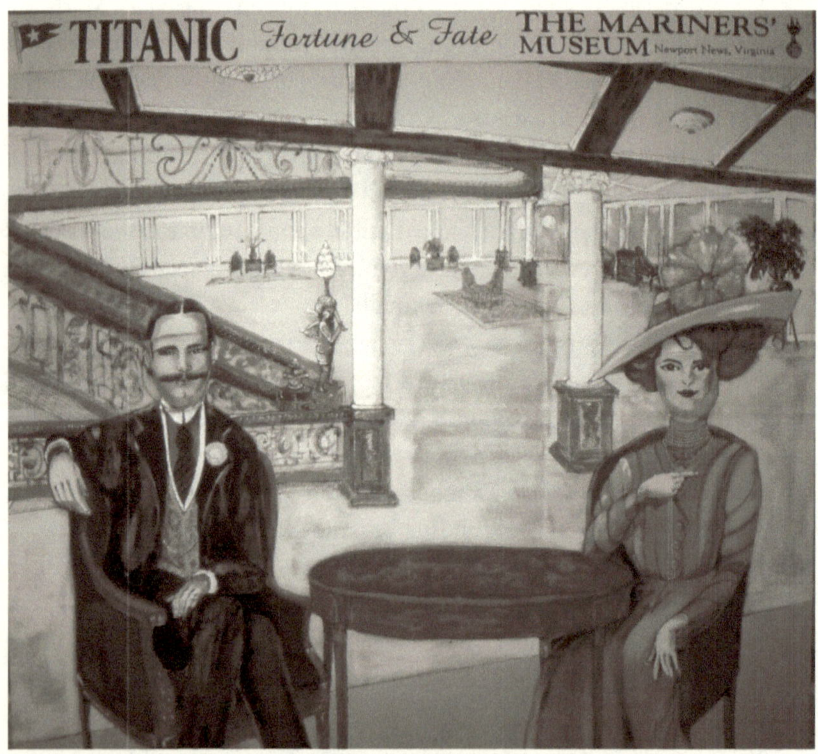

FIGURE 23. *Titanic* exhibit. *Photo by author, 1998.*

whose life and fate they followed, visitors could send a Morse code message or immerse their hands in twenty-eight-degree-Fahrenheit water. Such romanticism was fun but missed contemporary ocean disasters still taking less-privileged souls.[62]

Significantly, Mariners' excluded the archaeological trove (six thousand items) salvaged by RMS Titanic, Inc. that was traveling to *Titanic*-hungry museums. With the salvage company facing hard times, and because museum professionals considered "the plunder of shipwrecks a mortal sin," their sale or even showing was controversial. The Council of American Maritime Museums forbade its "members from exhibiting anything that was obtained improperly from a shipwreck." The International Congress of Maritime Museums (ICOMM) acted similarly. Yet, museums flouted the ban; in 1994 and 1995 Greenwich "drew record crowds, but also universal condemnation from museum professionals." The largest U.S. show, in Memphis, was denounced by ICOMM, but to no avail, as *Titanic* mania overwhelmed museum ethics. Later, a federal court ruled that the insolvent salvage company could not sell its trove, and Hightower negotiated (initially in secret) to acquire it as a donation. He knew that the curatorial cost would be immense. But a judge balked, ruling that the proposed donation did not adequately reward company investors.[63]

An ocean apart was *Waters of Despair, Waters of Hope: African-Americans and the Chesapeake Bay*. Curated by Benn Trask in 2000, the eight-month display, whose travel was funded by the National Park Service, included reenactors and singers. It examined the Bay's influence since 1750 on "the average person," whether in slavery, oystering and fishing, or cargo handling, as in Skinner's *Entering Dry Dock*. Trask hoped *Waters* would become "a springboard for other exhibits" on race because, said a reviewer, "Truth need not be hyped or simplified; it speaks volumes by itself." *Captive Passage: The Transatlantic Slave Trade and the Making of the Americas* (2002) followed; it was Mariners' most significant (and wrenching) exhibit ever. It was inspired by a 1994 exhibit at Liverpool's Merseyside Maritime Museum, which Hightower and Neill realized was "inextricably tied to race relations today." Like newer affective exhibits, it immersed its visitors; poet Maya Angelou could "smell the blood and hear the chains" of the Middle Passage. Hightower and Neill resolved to develop a similar exhibit. South Street drafted a script but lacked funding. So, Mariners' took charge. Hightower faced "strong negative reaction" from his own community. Still, the National Endowment for the Humanities contributed almost $300,000.[64]

While Merseyside presented an Afrocentric perspective that worked for reconciliation, observed a critic, the Mariners' exhibit emphasized how the pursuit of economic gain led to moral turpitude. Mariners' staging was provocative; some reviewers told children and the faint-hearted to skip its almost overwhelming Middle Passage scene. Yet, while Merseyside developed an International Slavery Museum, U.S. museums opted for temporary shows. The *New York Times* praised the exhibit in a long review. When *Captive Passage* traveled to the Anacostia Museum, located in a historically black neighborhood of Washington, D.C., its Smithsonian curators showed the hypocrisy of America's fight for freedom, which Mariners' had soft-pedaled, but the show generated right-wing complaints. Before traveling elsewhere, *Captive Passage* was promised a New York showing, but Hightower wanted to drop his partner at South Street and add the more prestigious New-York Historical Society. His move failed but torpedoed the alliance (see chapter 6).[65]

The long-standing female presence in maritime history was also a deserving, but neglected, field. Pitched to a popular audience in 2001, the nine-month show *Women of the Sea* covered three centuries and included female singers, speakers, and costumed interpreters. Besides a re-created cabin depicting a captain's wife at sea, the show included other roles that women undertook for economic need, patriotism, or adventure, as in the case of pirate Anne Bonny, a USN WAVE (Women Accepted for Volunteer Emergency Service) during World War II, or Gertrude Vanderbilt sailing in the America's Cup. As a syndicated columnist noted, men might "be less judgmental if they knew women had been 'cutting it' at sea for years." Yet, the exhibit had none of the pizzazz of *Titanic*, and after 1999, Mariners' was facing "a significant drop in attendance, diminishing revenue from endowments and staff layoffs." Backing away from blockbusters, as did many other museums, Hightower sought a permanent remedy.[66]

"ONE OF THE WORLD'S MOST IDENTIFIABLE AND HISTORIC SHIPS": FROM SMALL CRAFT TO USS *MONITOR*

In the early 1970s, the museum's small craft collection needed a large boathouse where its eighty vessels could be better interpreted. In 1974, it built a 17,400-square-foot facility, but surprisingly without a modern, artifact-protecting heating, ventilating, and air-conditioning (HVAC) system. Lacking a real fleet, curator John Sands wanted more small craft because they were "preeminently personal creations" generating empathy in his audience. Warning preservationists of the bias inherent in the privileging of traditional Anglo-American craft, he urged them to collect, maintain, and perhaps model more diverse craft. By the mid-1980s, Mariners' had nearly one hundred small craft, which, with such vessels as a Brazilian jangada and African canoes, it billed as the nation's "largest international small craft collection." But the overcrowded, poorly designed warehouse was a problem. Most interested in "the evolution of small boats," whereby visitors could see "the various hull forms, construction, [and] rigging," the museum prioritized, as did its founders, technical considerations that defined shipbuilding's progress. "Opening the door," said the *Daily Press*, "is like cutting the bonds of time and space. Once inside you can skip through centuries in less than an hour. And you can stride across continents with no more trouble than taking a casual walk." That was the issue: lacking historical context, viewers had difficulty understanding cultural and geographic influences.[67]

Extending its holdings, Mariners' added *Simokon* (1929), a thirty-eight-foot Chris-Craft commuter yacht given by the Stroh brewing family. In 1987, it acquired the Chris-Craft Corporation's sixty-year-old archives, which were called "one of the most complete and important collections of records documenting the pleasure boating industry in the United States." Founder Chris Smith was, explained a curator, "probably the first to adopt the advertising concept of family enjoyment in motorboating." Many shows followed. *Chris-Craft: The Affordable Dream*, which first ran in 1999, showed a wooden dock and four boats. "These beautiful yet affordable mahogany boats whispered of the Social Register," the museum noted, but they "gave the growing American middle class an opportunity to realize its dream of social status." Other nooks displayed fishing gear and picnic baskets, reminding viewers that, even during the Depression, the company "stressed the less frivolous pleasures of family life and outdoor living."[68]

After the board ordered a new fifty-thousand-square-foot facility, Hightower opened in 2003 the International Small Craft Center, which cost $1.4 million. Unlike the hot and dusty warehouse, it was visitor- and artifact-friendly with modern HVAC. "From the outset," said curator N. Lyles Forbes, "we wanted to get beyond technical descriptions of how the boats are built." Displaying about 75 of the 125 boats, they were clustered to show how the environment (such as Arctic cold or open seas) shaped their design. Visitors learned more at audiovisual stations and websites, while a walkway enabled them to see inside the boats.[69]

The one boat that Mariners' wanted was what Confederates had called a "Yankee cheese box on a raft." After sinking in a Cape Hatteras gale on December 31, 1862, USS *Monitor* rested, upside down, 230 feet below the surface, until its discovery in 1973. As the default guardian of offshore sites, the National Oceanic and Atmospheric Administration (NOAA) planned to let it rest in peace, but fearing pilferage, it reconsidered. In 1985, it reached "a cooperative agreement" with the National Trust's Maritime Office, headed then by Peter Neill, for its documentation and possible recovery. Peter Spectre of *WoodenBoat* warned, however, against federal involvement, as it "had a damned poor record" of ship preservation. A contest over ownership ensued. Newly hired as South Street's president, Neill claimed *Monitor* as "a New York ship" built on the East River.[70]

In 1987, NOAA chose Mariners' for two reasons. First, it had "an existing facility capable of preserving and interpreting the existing collection," plus "an excellent staff, . . . demonstrated management capabilities and a sound financial base." At a 1987 ceremony with museum president Thomas Downing, NOAA transferred nearly one hundred artifacts, but the fate of the real prize—the submerged ship—was uncertain. Second, though Downing asserted that Mariners' exerted no "political pressure," it had clout after the Virginia congressional delegation had chosen its committees wisely. Before retiring in 1977, Downing had served nine terms in Congress, where he was chairman of NOAA's principal oversight body, the oceanography subcommittee. In 1987, Senator Paul Trible Jr. (who had succeeded Representative Downing) and Representative Herbert Bateman (who succeeded Trible) also sat on managing committees. While Norfolk wanted *Monitor* for Nauticus, the *Daily Press* called the idea "positively silly."[71]

In 1992, *Clash of Armor: USS* Monitor *vs CSS* Virginia was the first Mariners' exhibit to feature its collection. With a twenty-minute film on the wreck, which left the "viewer with a sense of awe," *Clash of Armor* was, reported *Civil War Times Illustrated*, the museum's main attraction in 1997. Yet, more pertinent, the issue's cover story asked, "Can We Ever Raise the *Monitor*?" Because of navy budget cuts and delays, archaeologist John Broadwater, who managed NOAA's *Monitor* sanctuary, conceded: "We are not convinced that recovery is the best option, especially with our limited funding and resources." A writer concluded that the $11 million recovery would take a miracle.[72]

In 1997 Congress acted after NOAA asked only for funds to lift about a quarter of the ship, "including the engine, the propeller, the massive iron turret, two nine-foot guns and some of the heavy armor belt that still girds the sunken warship." The cost of that virtually unprecedented effort had risen to, reported the *New York Times*, "more than $22 million, making the venture a hard sell financially and politically." The National Oceanic and Atmospheric Administration sought "public and private allies to contribute money, gear and enthusiasm." The help of the Pentagon's Legacy Resource Management Program was critical. When some scholars questioned if *Monitor* was "worth the cost," the success of Sweden's *Vasa* was mentioned. Sunk on its maiden voyage in 1628, the warship was recovered in 1961, treated with chemicals, and housed in its own museum in 1990. *Vasa* generated national pride and became Sweden's top museum for tourists. NOAA wanted its artifacts displayed, not lost in storage.[73]

Hightower saw an opportunity. Receiving a $500,000 planning grant from Newport News, in 2000 he proposed creating a USS *Monitor* Center, which could draw 250,000 annual visitors. Besides a conservation lab, it would include a copy of the 173-foot vessel, multiple exhibits, and theaters. Predicting it would become "one of the premier Civil War tourist attractions in the South," it would make, claimed museum vice chairman Lloyd Noland, "Newport News a tourist destination." As "one of the world's most identifiable and historic ships," said Hightower, its funding would mostly come from state and federal grants.[74]

As part of a $30 million capital campaign, Mariners' received a congressional earmark of $5 million in 2003, which the *New York Daily News* called pork. Because marine archaeology had been neglected by top-tier museums, except in San Francisco, NOAA contributed $9.5 million, as it wanted to create "a nationally prominent showcase for its cultural resources and sanctuary programs." All told, nearly $19 million came from federal, state, and local governments. The shipyard (then, Northrop Grumman Newport News) gave $250,000. It also donated the $1 million *Monitor* replica, which more than one hundred employees built using Navy-donated materials (fig. 24). At the time, the yard sought more congressional friends and consistent funding. In the conservation lab, the large iron artifacts, such as the two-hundred-ton turret (minus the remains of two sailors who were buried in Arlington National Cemetery), were placed in yard-built tanks filled with chemicals where, through electrolytic reduction, the metal was stabilizing. It was, said center director David Krop, "the largest marine metals conservation project in the entire world."[75]

After breaking ground in 2004, the 63,500-square-foot USS *Monitor* Center opened on March 9, 2007, the battle's anniversary. Mariners' still had $3 million to raise. With a crowd of one thousand admirers, Governor

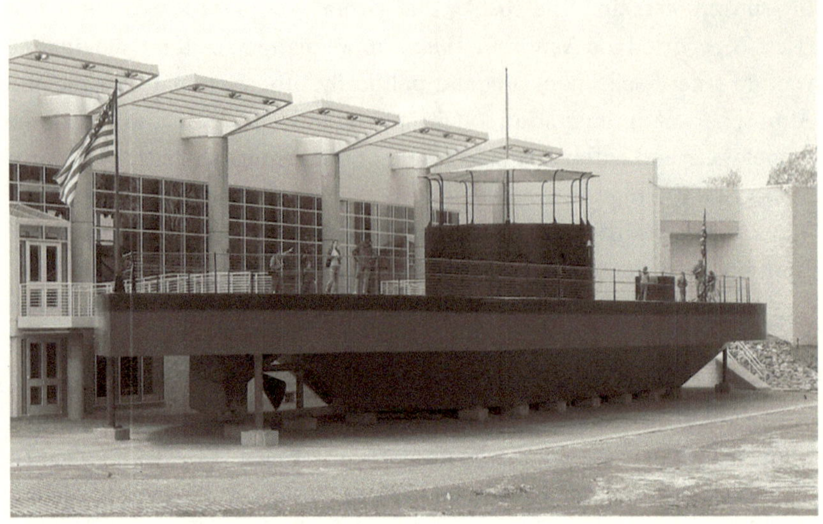

FIGURE 24. Replica of USS *Monitor*, adjacent to Monitor Center, 2007. *Courtesy of Mytwocents at English Wikipedia.*

Timothy M. Kaine noted that the educational facility reflected the Old Testament adage of beating "swords into plowshares." The $31.5 million wing had an eighteen-thousand-square-foot exhibition space, a twenty-thousand-square-foot conservation lab, classrooms, and theaters on the battle, sinking, and recovery. Re-creating the time and place of each event, its goal was, said curator Anna Holloway, to make history "exciting to students so they will understand it and learn from it." Those lessons fit the concept of sea power. The exhibit pictured—in display and in the theater—the March 8, 1862, battle in which *Virginia* destroyed two Union wooden warships. *Monitor* intervened on March 9, thus saving the Union and showing that navies must modernize to prevail.[76]

The center also showed the human story. Through eight interactive, personal story stations, a re-created living quarters, and video games, the exhibit told of *Monitor*'s crew. The two-story gallery displayed the world's first revolving gun turret, the twenty-ton steam engine, and the archaeological expedition. Because the real 120-ton turret would be undergoing conservation in a ninety-thousand-gallon tank for up to twenty years, the museum created a full-size replica with a cutaway view of the eleven-inch Dahlgren guns and eight-inch armor. The nine-foot-tall, twenty-one-foot diameter re-creation was, said NOAA's historian, so good, "it's going to be permanent." The public viewed the lab's tanks, whose conservator admitted, "This is a dream project for me."[77]

The dream was more folly for administrators, however. Calling the center "a transformational moment for the museum and Tidewater Virginia," Hightower was overly optimistic (as he had been at South Street) when he predicted it would draw an additional 250,000 visitors. Eyeing that popular audience, the museum deemphasized its scholarly roots, as in 2007 when it decided to relocate its library, which was the third largest maritime collection in the world with seventy-eight thousand volumes, one million manuscript items, and six hundred thousand photographs. Because the National Archives and Records Administration set standards for NOAA's *Monitor*-related materials, the museum balked at building a costly facility and instead persuaded nearby Christopher Newport University (CNU) to include its holdings there. When the CNU library opened in 2009, Mariners' staffed its portion and controlled its materials. But, in 2015, CNU's expanding needs required the Mariners' unit to close for two years and eventually find space near its own galleries.[78]

During the Great Recession, the museum's budgetary problems were glaring. Late in 2009, William Cogar became president. Reallocating resources "to a rapidly growing Internet presence," he cut public access from seven to five days, saying "this is the way that museums are going to have to operate in the future." Yet the million web visitors did not pay the admission fee of twelve dollars. After Cogar quit in late 2011, the board hired Elliott Gruber, a psychologist praised for fundraising at nonprofits. With the Civil War's sesquicentennial, he hoped to attract an *additional* one hundred thousand visitors. But in 2013, only sixty thousand *total* visited. Making matters worse, NOAA funding evaporated. It had signed two agreements, whereby the museum agreed to conserve and display the NOAA-owned artifacts, but amazingly there were no dollars-and-cents stipulations. Ending in 2013, the agreement's renegotiation was stymied by the ascent of Tea Party conservatives, constraints on federal spending, and the slow national recovery.[79]

While history museums were facing duress across the board, Mariners' budget was millions in the red from 2010 to 2013. Out of $9 million spent in 2013, for example, it lost over $2 million, which was covered by its $130 million endowment. In 2014, the industry giant, Colonial Williamsburg, reported an operating deficit of $42 million. While NOAA awaited its own spending package from Congress, Gruber said, "These are federal government artifacts. . . . Providing the funds for their well being should be the responsibility of the federal government." The museum shuttered one of the labs—closing it to visitors, placing a tarp over the tanks, and making its needs known to friends. James Delgado, director of NOAA's Maritime Heritage Program, insisted that "the artifacts [were] not at risk."[80]

But Mariners' was. In 2015 it established the USS *Monitor* Foundation to raise its profile, recognizing that NOAA was privatizing a public obligation. As attendance was dropping, the museum tried again to reinvent itself. Gruber was tasked with establishing the Family Exploration Gallery, which included Explorers Theater, a multiuse facility for lectures and 3D, high-definition films. One element revolved around the JASON Project, a nonprofit subsidiary of the Sea Research Foundation and the National Geographic Society. Through a video link to museums and kindred institutions, its audience followed the undersea explorations of Robert Ballard, who had discovered *Titanic* in 1985. To make Explorers Theater fit, Mariners' scuttled the Chesapeake Bay Gallery in 2013. As such, Mariners' was not only emphasizing edutainment but ceding some of its regional coverage to Maryland's Chesapeake Bay Maritime Museum and the Calvert Marine Museum.[81]

In so doing, Mariners' was seeking a larger demographic: the younger generation and its school programs, a popular interest in ocean exploration, and a bigger (yet still undefined) maritime community. Seeing his tide recede, Gruber resigned in early 2016. As its next president and CEO, the board hired Howard Hoege III in October 2016. Besides serving as its strategic planning consultant in 2015, he had roots in public policy, leadership training, and even the U.S. Senate Armed Services Committee. Believing that the museum had to bring in a more diverse audience, in late 2018 Mariners' began offering a flat admission fee of one dollar, reportedly *forever*. Hoege admitted, "We are focused like a laser beam right now on defining who those people are and then trying to define what value we provide to them." A West Point graduate whose tour of duty included a life-shaping stint in Iraq, he regarded his job, partly, in therapeutic terms. "Personally, there is no more important task in the world right now," he said, "than trying to be a force that binds communities together."[82]

CONCLUSION: THE FUTURE IS "NOT WHAT IT USED TO BE"

"One of the world's outstanding repositories of sea culture" in 1997, Mariners' was trying to reballast its load in 2018. From 1930 to 2002, its endowment had been a blessing and a curse. Such moneys allowed it to acquire world-class holdings without having to worry about attendance. With his advocacy of global shipping and defense, Ferguson and his yard had set its agenda. As Mariners' boomed, it rode the swell of Cold War internationalism and Virginia's love of its history. During the Civil War Centennial it attracted over a million visitors, but only a fraction visited during the sesquicentennial. It is now dependent upon the public, but Virginia has changed. The museum's last two decades have been filled with ambitious attempts to find an audience to replace Huntington's royalties: blockbusters such as *Titanic*, the National Maritime Museum Initiative, and the *Monitor* Center. Mariners' simultaneously searched for a theme to solicit continuing support: shipbuilding, the Chesapeake Bay, sea power, and oceanography. Those themes are important to Hampton Roads, but they have not been enough. Realizing the need for a diverse following, it expanded from scholars and sea power advocates to include Civil War buffs, pop culture trends, and now children. Museums stress community building, but as Hoege was asking, Which communities? What message?[83]

Almost a century old, Mariners' evolution shows, again, how museums are forced by circumstance to reinvent themselves. Huntington's fortune first shaped the institution, enriching the gallery, library, and park. Yet Ferguson was the practical builder, not simply of ships, but also of institutions like his yard, museum, and city. It was recently claimed that "perhaps the most remarkable person to have lived in Newport News was Homer Lenoir Ferguson." A British commentator called his museum the "one true gem" in that "dreary industrial" town. From the start, his Mariners' Museum stressed an ideological message. During times of disarmament, it emphasized a strong navy; if commerce retreated from the sea, it sounded the importance of global trade; if the shipbuilding business was in jeopardy, it taught its members to take pride in their work, professionalize their ranks, and educate the public; if its general audience did not understand the sea's importance, it spotlighted Lord Nelson, USS *Monitor,* Crabtree's miniatures, and Norfolk's navy to make its message more appealing; and now, as the world is fracturing, it stresses building a community around the sea. Whether it was Huntington's goal of making the public sea minded or Ferguson making them ship minded, one common denominator was the museum's advocacy of sea power.[84]

Their concept of the sea was that of the twentieth century: Huntington's railroad, Ferguson's shipyard, and Norfolk's navy base. Along the way, the U.S. government made it possible by expanding the navy, creating a global empire, and recognizing its interests as those of the yard and museum. The museum became an integral part of the naval-industrial complex. All the while, there was an abundance of artifacts because it had applied, said Director William Wilkinson, "the most catholic criteria" for building a collection. What curator John Sands called "a strange mish-mash of things" enabled it over the years to display more dimensions. At the same time, however, museums were moving from an emphasis on curating objects to cultivating communities. For the Hampton Roads community and its economy, Mariners' pictured a historical progression leading to modern technology, larger navies, and bigger ships in ever more distant ports, vessels often docked at nearby quays carrying the Old Dominion's trade.[85]

Yet, for the museum that glorified the conquest of the sea, its future in the twenty-first century is, as Hightower said (quoting Paul Valéry), "not what it used to be." The museum's wealth of artifacts and documents still contributes to the audiovisual, interactive, computerized presentations inherent in real and virtual exhibits and educational presentations, but the "real" artifact has less value in a world of 3D printers, IMAX films, or internet hits. Despite its wealth of artifacts, its turnstile did not turn. The old question is how to capture a new audience. According to criteria set by museum consultants, Mariners' sustainability is at risk because of its financial instability and weak attendance. Yet "strong relationships with the community," as through its one-dollar admission, might be its saving grace.[86]

Offering some hope was the showing of *Turtle Vision 3D* in Explorers Theater. An animated children's film following Sammy the turtle over fifty years of climate change, it targeted, as all museums must in some way, its future audience. While it was shown, the *New York Times* was publishing a four-part series, *The Outlaw Ocean*, in which reporter Ian Urbina noted how little understood the vast seas were to landlubbers. As many Americans were troubled about environmental degradation, he noted: "Ships intentionally dump more engine oil and sludge into the oceans in the span of three years than that spilled in the Deepwater Horizon and Exxon Valdez accidents combined." Those ships also "emit huge amounts of certain air pollutants, far more than all the world's cars." Mark Young, a retired United States Coast Guard commander, told Urbina that the world's oceans were "like the Wild West. Weak rules, few sheriffs, lots of outlaws." So, if *Turtle Vision 3D* and the accompanying Mariners' exhibits and programs can raise interest, address problems, and promote action, the museum's story of shipbuilding, natural conservation, and recreation can be told in a broader context of a living Chesapeake Bay and global oceans.[87]

CHAPTER 5

"A SAILING SHIP STIRS THE GENERAL PUBLIC LIKE NOTHING ELSE"

Remaking San Francisco's Waterfront and Identity

In 1949, the success of Mystic Seaport was on the mind of Karl Kortum as he readied a lunchtime presentation at San Francisco's Bohemian Club. Scott Newhall, a budding editor at the *San Francisco Chronicle*, had invited the city's newspaper publishers to hear Kortum's proposal to create a maritime museum. Showing a large sketchbook, he outlined his vision for Aquatic Park. On a lagoon, a museum would occupy a stylish, but empty, Works Progress Administration (WPA)–built bathhouse. Alcatraz Island and the Golden Gate provided a scenic backdrop for various West Coast vessels. Emphasizing a square-rigger's "beauty and romance," Kortum suggested: "A sailing ship stirs the general public like nothing else." A weed-filled tarmac and railroad tracks would be replaced by Victorian Park; it was ringed by old, red-bricked factories, including Ghirardelli Chocolate. His plan was game changing because urban renewal elsewhere was erasing Victorian landscapes, while the world's fleet of commercial square-riggers had dwindled to a score. By highlighting oceanic commerce, Kortum was also remaking California's historical identity, which had been defined by Spanish missions, forty-niners, and overland pioneers. Newhall guessed, "If anybody could put the program over," it was Kortum, "a stubborn and an enthusiastic young man."[1]

After sailing aboard the bark *Kaiulani* around Cape Horn and the Cape of Good Hope in 1941, Kortum committed his life to global maritime preservation. But Newhall had more immediate goals after a bitter waterfront strike in 1948. A museum could mend San Francisco's reputation as an "insecure port," he thought, by creating a "common meeting-ground" for employer and laborer. The publishers agreed that it could heal "the faltering spirit of San Francisco." Newhall assured Clarence Lindner, publisher of the top-selling *Examiner*, it would be, like Mystic, "self-supporting from admission charges or donations."[2]

The San Francisco Maritime Museum (SFMM) opened in 1951. Needing revenue in 1954, Kortum acquired the globetrotting, square-rigged *Balclutha* (1886). Anchoring the SFMM through tourism, it recalled San Francisco's presence in distant ports. He then persuaded Sacramento to open the adjacent San Francisco Maritime State Historic Park. Thus in 1963, the state completed his 1949 proposal by building Victorian Park, preserving the red-bricked Haslett Warehouse, and purchasing the lumber schooner *C. A. Thayer* (1895), steam schooner *Wapama* (1915), and scow schooner *Alma* (1891). While the fleet symbolized San Francisco's standing as the North Pacific's capital, Kortum transformed its north waterfront by fighting insensitive development and promoting a maritime revival. In so doing, he created an integral part of the city's identity.

But success was his undoing. By 1963 he had assembled the world's largest museum fleet of historic, commercial vessels, but no one had anticipated its huge expense. Under Governor Ronald Reagan, Sacramento tried (unsuccessfully) to unload the state park onto the city; the governor then starved it in an early case of Reaganomics. The state park and museum were almost broke. Recognizing their absolute importance, however, Representative Phillip Burton (D-CA) intervened, and Congress established the National Maritime Museum, which merged the institutions in 1976–78 under the National Park Service's Golden Gate National Recreation Area. Kortum expected federal money to underwrite his work, but the overcommitted, underfunded, and nature-oriented park service was ill prepared to take on its first fleet and full-spectrum museum. Outraged and outgunned, Kortum fought back. In turn, Congress created today's freestanding San Francisco Maritime National Historical Park (SFMNHP) in 1988. While central to understanding America's past, present, and future on the Pacific, the park now struggles to maintain the nation's most complex, publicly owned museum fleet.

"THE SHINING MULTITUDE OF YELLOW SPARS STAYED IN MY MIND'S EYE": KORTUM ENCOUNTERS THE SEA, SPRECKELS, AND NEWHALL

Born in 1917 and raised in Petaluma, forty miles north of San Francisco, Karl Crouch Kortum descended from a Donner Party survivor and a Napa Valley vintner. Both shaped his character. His father raised chickens after Prohibition, which instilled Karl's distrust of arbitrary authority. But those chickens set his future because such scow schooners as *Alma* came up Petaluma Creek to its poultry ranches. Karl was pulled seaward, joining the Sea Scouts, building ship models, and reading tales by Alan Villiers and Carl Cutler. While visiting family in Alameda in 1928, he saw the Alaska Packers Association's "Star" salmon fleet; it included nineteen of the Bay Area's fifty-plus square-riggers (out of seventy-six nationally). "The shining multitude of yellow spars stayed in my mind's eye," he recalled. The scene was "unextinguishable."[3]

Harrison Dring became his friend in the mid-1930s. Whether alone on his Harley or with Karl on the back seat, Harry rode to Oakland Estuary's "Rotten Row" to see its old ships. In the late 1930s, they attended meetings of the Pacific Marine Research Society in San Francisco. Sometimes Kortum hitchhiked alone, took the fifteen-cent Sausalito ferry, and glimpsed some of the Bay's 175 steamship lines. Begun in 1925, the society discussed the history of ships and trade, while its founder, shipping executive Edward Clark, told stories of sailing with Howard Chapelle, drinking with Searsport Captain Lincoln Colcord, and visiting Salem's Peabody Museum, Colonel Green's *Charles W. Morgan*, and museums with ship models in New York and Annapolis.[4]

Meanwhile, during the Depression, the Port of San Francisco was traumatized by a war between capital and labor. Both sides influenced Kortum. After the Roosevelt administration guaranteed collective bargaining, fifteen thousand West Coast longshoremen struck in 1934. Harry Bridges, the Australian-born strike leader, regarded the city's working conditions as among the world's worst. He picked Norwegian-born Harry Lundeberg to lead the Sailors' Union of the Pacific. His sailors were, *Fortune* warned, "the true proletariat of the Western world." The turnout became "the largest and most powerful maritime labor strike in American history," but it was broken by an anti-union "newspaper oligarchy."[5]

The Golden Gate International Exposition (1939–40) bettered the city's image and boosted its tourism. Situated near the Bay Bridge (1936) and the Golden Gate Bridge (1937), which undercut the income of many ferries, the expo was held on Treasure Island. Historian Robert Rydell has shown that the fair advanced "America's long-standing imperial ambitions" along the Pacific Rim, but Kortum was thinking of the empire's roots by suggesting (unsuccessfully) that planners fill a lagoon with historic ships. A few models were shown, but the crowds flocked to the Chinese opium den or Sally Rand's Nude Ranch. To present more maritime history, Clark assembled a committee, which included Mrs. Alma de Bretteville Spreckels, the city's grand dowager, and they added models of *Balclutha*, *Wapama*, and others. Once the fair closed, a larger exhibit opened downtown at the Merchants Exchange, but the *San Francisco Mission Merchant News* advised: "The city [should] obtain one of the few remaining square-rigged ships on the Coast, berth it at the Embarcadero," and illustrate "the complete nautical history of the community."[6]

In 1941, Kortum found rigging work in Oakland Estuary. In a life-shaping decision, he volunteered aboard *Star of Finland*. It was, he said, "paradise on earth." Launched in Maine as *Kaiulani* (1899), it was the only extant, U.S.-built, steel merchant bark. Operated by the Alaska Packers after 1910, it was mothballed in 1930 but appeared in the Hollywood thriller *Souls at Sea* (1937). With a war raging in Europe and China, Kortum and Dring were hired on the renamed *Kaiulani* to carry lumber to South Africa. On the voyage, they learned of Cutler's rescue of *Morgan* and Japan's attack on Pearl Harbor. But while carrying munitions from South Africa to Australia, its skipper refused to set in for repairs. What followed was a strike or, as a reporter claimed, "the only U.S. ship to undergo a mutiny during World War II." The ringleaders—Kortum and Tom Soules—were acquitted on a procedural error. Before *Kaiulani* was converted into an army collier, Kortum ordered the sails lowered on what he called "the last Yankee square-rigger." While Dring served in the wartime merchant marine, red tape kept Kortum from becoming a navy second lieutenant, but he served as a uniformed civilian in the Army Transportation Corps.[7]

Back home, Spreckels controlled the Clark exhibit. Kortum humorously called her "a fairly statuesque babe," knowing that, as a young, nude model, Alma was the bronzed goddess atop the Dewey Monument at Union Square. Then she married Adolph Spreckels, whose father was the

West Coast's richest man. In May 1941 she financed the exhibit's move to the Aquatic Park bathhouse. Attributing the collection's inspiration to Munich's Deutsches Museum, which included Nazi propaganda, her lawyer and business manager solicited the help of William Randolph Hearst, reputedly "Hitler's man in America." After Pearl Harbor, however, the army commandeered the venue. Four years later, with war's end, she pushed to establish a science and industry museum there, but the city refused to lend its building.[8]

Upon his return home, Kortum saw the square-rigged *Pacific Queen* (formerly *Star of Alaska* and *Balclutha*) docked at Fisherman's Wharf and imagined imitating Cutler's ship-and-shore museum. But after failing to interest Spreckels or Mayor Elmer Robinson, he approached Scott Newhall, who edited the *Chronicle*'s Sunday magazine and had an adventurous streak. Descended from prominent merchants, he had quit the University of California at Berkeley in his senior year, where he studied philosophy and art, and bought a forty-two-foot ketch, which he and his wife sailed to Mexico in 1936. His trip ended disastrously—with a wrecked ship and an amputated leg. Still, he served as a wartime correspondent. From 1952 to 1971, he was the *Chronicle*'s executive editor, moving it to first place. He was called the city's "best editor" in the twentieth century.[9]

In 1949, after Newhall reviewed Villiers's *The Set of the Sails* in the *Chronicle*, Kortum wrote him about his vision. Including a *Saturday Evening Post* story on Mystic Seaport, he claimed that Aquatic Park was the nation's dullest waterfront. He proposed a dramatic change. As cable cars were descending Hyde Street, he thought, the sight of its red-bricked buildings "created an enclave with a mood of its own." They included the Ghirardelli factory (1889) and the Cannery and Haslett Warehouse (1907–9). He proposed adding not only a Victorian-style park and cable car station but also *Pacific Queen*, *Thayer*, and *Wapama* to the lagoon and *Alma* at "an old time shipyard." That image, he predicted, would inspire "Come to San Francisco!" advertisements. Unlike most museums, which he derided as "institutions by and for experts," the bathhouse's upper floors could display public-oriented exhibits. Though he was inspired by maritime museums in Mystic, Newport News, and Salem, he knew them only indirectly; he liked their melding of collecting, research, and publishing. Excited, Newhall sent Kortum's proposal to his editor Paul Smith, who was trying to reestablish "national confidence in San Francisco's [strike-torn] waterfront."[10] (See fig. 25.)

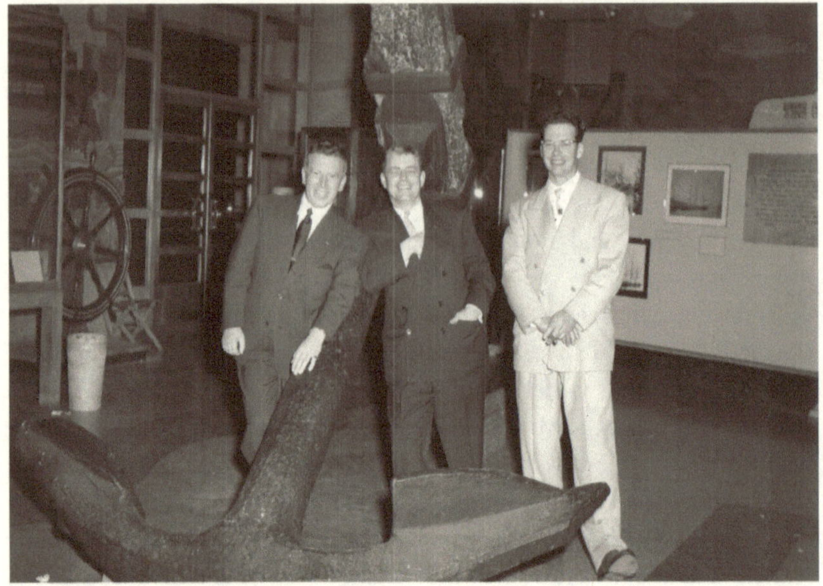

FIGURE 25. Paul Smith (left), Scott Newhall (center), and Karl Kortum (right) at the museum in 1951. *Courtesy of the San Francisco Maritime National Historical Park.*

Worrying about Spreckels, Newhall sent reporter David Nelson to her mansion. Becoming the whiz who made Kortum's plan happen, Nelson was the son of a Swedish immigrant who, after being shanghaied in Boston, ended up as an Oakland shipwright. After interning at a public affairs institute, David joined the newspaper. His genial demeanor complemented Kortum, who came across as blunt, if not overbearing. For the next forty years Nelson directed the museum's friends group and worked in public relations for the *Chronicle*, museum, or shippers. In 1949, he asked Spreckels to donate her collection, give financially, and join the museum board. "Afraid of dying," she had "one scotch and water," he remembered, and "promised us her entire maritime collection." But the sixty-eight-year-old widow mixed "senility and energy in a dangerous way."[11]

By 1949, San Francisco's port was facing a "complete breakdown of employer-employee communication." Smith wanted both sides involved in Kortum's planning. At the Bohemian Club luncheon, Newhall reminded the publishers that shipping was shifting to the Gulf Coast, but he predicted that Kortum's project would ease "ill-will along the Embarcadero." The *Chronicle* jumpstarted the plan: its artist drew the ink-and-pastel sketches,

Newhall provided the connections, and Nelson handled logistics. To avoid "an inter-newspaper battle," Newhall told publishers, "If you don't like it, at least don't knock it." They agreed. More visionary than manager, Kortum wanted John R. Lyman or Harold Huycke to head his museum. All three were self-taught historians. Graduating from the California Maritime Academy in 1944, Huycke went to sea and, as a "boilersuit maritime historian," spent off-duty hours writing. Lyman was a chemical oceanographer by education but became "the cornerstone of West Coast maritime history." Yet wanting Kortum in charge, Newhall covered his expenses for a year and assigned Nelson to help.[12]

Smith wanted the San Francisco Maritime Museum Association's (SFMMA) board of directors to "include the president of each steamship company, the head of the Sailors' Union, the publishers of the four newspapers and representatives from both the Waterfront Employers Association and the Longshoremen's Union." He specified Lundeberg of the Sailors' Union because steamship owners were pursuing a divide-and-conquer strategy of red-baiting Harry Bridges and negotiating with Lundeberg. The two labor leaders warred bitterly as the former syndicalist Lundeberg became a Republican. Incorporated on January 6, 1950, the SFMMA temporarily headquartered at City Hall, which loaned its bathhouse for one dollar a year.[13]

Aquatic Park's history shaped the museum. Waterfront parks had been proposed in North Beach in 1866 by landscape architect Frederick Law Olmsted and in 1905 by architect and planner Daniel H. Burnham. Both were blocked by military and industrial interests. Then in 1906, the city was destroyed by an earthquake and three-day fire. After sporadic rebuilding there, the WPA erected the $1.5 million bathhouse in 1939. Designed by William Mooser III in the Streamline Moderne, it contrasted with what *Time* magazine called the "excessively ugly background" of the Ghirardelli factory, designed by Mooser's father, and his grandfather's Fontana warehouse. The WPA's "Palace for the Public" resembled "a luxurious ocean liner" with "rounded ends, set-back upper stories, porthole windows and ship rails." With a beach-level entry from its quarter-mile-long shore and an 1,850-foot semicircular seawall, called Municipal Pier, the building's street-level space was briefly leased in 1940 to a casino, the Hot Jazz Club, which Kortum visited. After the military's wartime use, the city created a senior center there, which exists to this day, but the rest was "as opulent and as empty as a Mayan temple."[14] (See fig. 26.)

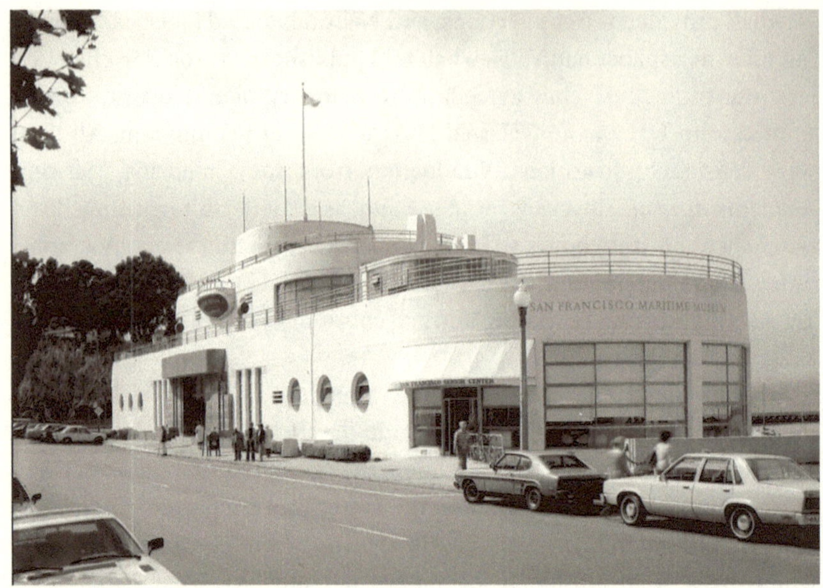

FIGURE 26. Aquatic Park Bathhouse and Casino transformed into the museum. *Courtesy of the Historic American Buildings Survey, Prints & Photographs Division, Library of Congress.*

The SFMM opened on May 27, 1951, as part of the fourth annual World Trade Week. Over five thousand attended, many bringing a floorplan printed in the *Chronicle*. At an opening night bash, said Nelson, "socialites sipped champagne with labor leaders, maritime magnates mingled with walking bosses, political big-wigs cornered publishers and [all] took note of the impressive turnout." That included Spreckels, who became its principal patron. She gave "$65,000 in cash" before 1955 and ran a flea market in her massive garage, which brought in "$500 every month." She initially gave Kortum $150 a month and a free apartment, which he shared, after December 1951, with Jean, his bride and volunteer secretary. Pressed by Newhall, the city put Karl on its payroll in January as director, but, said Jean, "he had no one to 'direct.'"[15]

Though three hundred thousand visited in its first year, the museum had an empty treasury because the city ruled that admission could be charged only on two weekdays, and the SFMMA did not fundraise during the Korean War (1950–53). Yet, it needed $225,000 for Kortum's planned fleet and Mystic Seaport–inspired re-creation—variously called Argonaut

Bay, Gold Rush Plaza, or Project X—that was predicted to draw 1.5 million visitors annually. Like Mystic's anticommunism, it promised to teach "the principles of self-reliance, ingenuity, individual responsibility, and the worth and dignity of the individual." The museum expected corporate funding, but the elite were, said a state historian, like the pioneers—"a little cheap." The SFMMA tried radio ads. One related Argonaut Bay to "fabulous, wicked, alive San Francisco." Another asked: "Did you know that in San Francisco, forty cents out of every dollar . . . comes from world trade?" After three failed pitches, the doldrums set in.[16]

"'The Last Great Sailing Ship Left on the Coast": Acquiring *Balclutha* and a Fleet

Kortum regarded ships as the museum's raison d'être. Sitting in his third-floor office, he stared at Richardson Bay where *Pacific Queen* was "decaying on the Sausalito mud flats." He knew that the 1,716-ton, steel-hulled square-rigger could enliven his drive. Earlier called *Star of Alaska*, it was "the fastest and the last of the famed Alaska Packers fleet." He inspected the rusty, pockmarked hull and found that "to enter her dark hold was like a visit to a planetarium." Its purchase was, however, "a semi-crazy piece of business for a small-time historical society." Frank "Tex" Kissinger, a former carnival performer, had bought the ship, which he renamed *Pacific Queen*, for $5,000 in 1933; he painted its hull silver, masts and spars red, and figurehead gold. Wanting tourists, but failing with a tween-deck aquarium, he remade it as a pirate ship. Villiers spurned such "maritime buffoonery" but admitted, "If it brought the boobs aboard [who paid twenty-five cents], it was good." Meanwhile, *Pacific Queen* worked as an extra in *Mutiny on the Bounty* (1935), but Hollywood began using models in tanks for sea movies. With war, the military wanted it for scrap, but Lundeberg intervened, saying that it had too little metal. After Tex had a fatal heart attack, his widow demanded $75,000, but the Museum Association had only $25,000. She threatened to sell it for target practice. When Kortum pretended that he had decided instead to buy San Diego's *Star of India* (formerly *Euterpe*, 1863), she signed an option in 1954.[17]

Newhall reconvened the publishers to reaffirm Kortum's plan because Spreckels opposed the purchase. A clash ensued because, said Newhall, "Karl ran this thing very much as you would expect Chancellor von Bismarck to run a museum." Some board members were glad when she quit. But gender was important. As Spreckels remarked, "Ships are not for women." Nor were maritime museum boards apparently. Still, Karl knew, "at least half [the board were her] dilettante" friends. The decision came in April. Kortum pressed Lundeberg, who seldom attended meetings, and briefed him. When a Spreckels ally referred to its scrap value, Lundeberg replied in a firm, but soft, voice that the junkyard's offer was "no way to set a price for the last great sailing ship left on the Coast." The board was stunned. None of the executives, said Kortum, "was going to quarrel with Harry [because] he controlled the [working] conditions on their vessels." It okayed the purchase, and the board contributed the purchase price. After the harbor commission denied it a berth at Fisherman's Wharf, Kortum telegrammed the governor (using Lundeberg's name) to reverse the decision.[18]

What to call it was an issue. If *Pacific Queen* was kept, Kortum told SFMMA president (and shipping company executive) John Cushing, Tex's hucksterism would be "a subject of derision in the museum world." Cartoonist Hank Ketcham reinforced that fear in *Dennis the Menace.* Arriving at its pier, the rascal yelled, "Look! A PIRATE SHIP!" Cushing wanted to use the name *Star of Alaska*, but Kortum pushed for the original *Balclutha*, derived from the Gaelic *Bal* (town) and *clutha* (Clyde River). Built in Glasgow, its figurehead depicted a Scots noblewoman. The 256-foot ship, which carried 2,660 tons of cargo, sailed around Cape Horn seventeen times. That was, said Kortum, great "come-on material to get the public on board." Regarding the Horn passage as the maker of real men, he claimed that "*Star of Alaska* and *Pacific Queen* had almost effeminate careers by comparison." *Balclutha* became official with its 1955 rededication.[19]

Pacific Queen's rescue spotlighted global shipping. In 1954, San Francisco's Democratic congressman John F. Shelley was challenging the Eisenhower administration's "failure to support our merchant marine," equating its neglect with "national suicide." Such rhetoric shaped *Pacific Queen*'s campaign. Kortum estimated its repair bill at $120,000, a prohibitively expensive sum. But "eighty shipping companies chipped in $55,000 worth of material," reported the *Saturday Evening Post*, which pictured the ship on its cover. Three shipyards carried out free repairs worth another $12,000. Its image appeared in the *New York Times*, *Baltimore Sun*, and *Seattle Times*. It was, claimed Nelson, "the greatest community effort since the earthquake and fire." Led by American Federation of Labor tradesmen, the 555 volunteers represented eighteen unions and provided thirteen thousand hours of labor. That would have "cost $250,000 in cold cash," said Villiers. Typical for consensus history, Nelson stressed that "the spirit of the old full-rigger" prevailed as "man, boss and owner pulled together." But unity required pressure. A shipfitters' leader organized weekend workers, but he "coerce[d] his members" by saying if you "work for free on weekends," you would get "work in the shipyard during the week." Nelson also conceded, "We certainly manipulated" the press, but "it was for a good cause." For the yearlong restoration, Kortum was technical director, while Huycke and Lyman researched its history. Equally important were older tradesmen such as chief rigger Jack Dickerhoff, who later superintended work on *Star of India*, *Falls of Clyde*, and *Wavertree*. He and Kortum asked Dring to help when his ship docked in 1955. As Dring's family waited in the car, Harry scolded Karl, "I've had enough ships to last me forever." He relented, spending the next quarter-century maintaining the state and federal fleets.[20]

With a fireboat escort, a regatta, and the civic band's oompah, *Pacific Queen* was towed in July 1955 to Pier 43½ at tourist-dominated Fisherman's Wharf. Rechristened *Balclutha*, it was a ten-minute walk to the museum. The restoration was trumpeted in a half-hour film, *Saga of a Ship* (1955), which was, recalled Nelson, a "love story" pitched at "TV stations across the Nation." Few took the bait, however. Charging 50¢ for adults, the SFMMA earned $93,000 in its first year, but *Balclutha* cost $80,000 annually to maintain. Spurred partly by a hawker with a sandwich-board sign, a million toured the ship in the first half-dozen years. Meanwhile, the museum drew "a quarter million people annually—the largest attendance at any [U.S.] maritime museum."[21] (See fig. 27.)

Balclutha appeared on national television, as in 1955–56 on ABC's *Disneyland* and NBC's *Wide Wide World*, which "reached 32 million and 18 million viewers respectively." For a ten-minute piece, NBC wanted "the right guy with the right face" to convey sailing's dangers. A heavily tattooed Swede, Fingal Larson, warned, "Your best chance to come through a storm was to have a Captain who knew what he was about." As the camera panned to the captain's deck, the narrator opined that his "absolute authority . . . was necessary—for the ship was the body, the crew were the hands, and the master was the head that made body and hands work together." Reflecting the country's hierarchy, Americans learned to heed proper authorities. In a longer live broadcast, for which Nelson wrote a script, Arthur Godfrey visited. His show attracted eighty-two million viewers and pictured San Francisco as a "good port." Yet Kortum was no fan of TV, claiming that youth were better served by sail training than "peering into the end of a cathode-ray

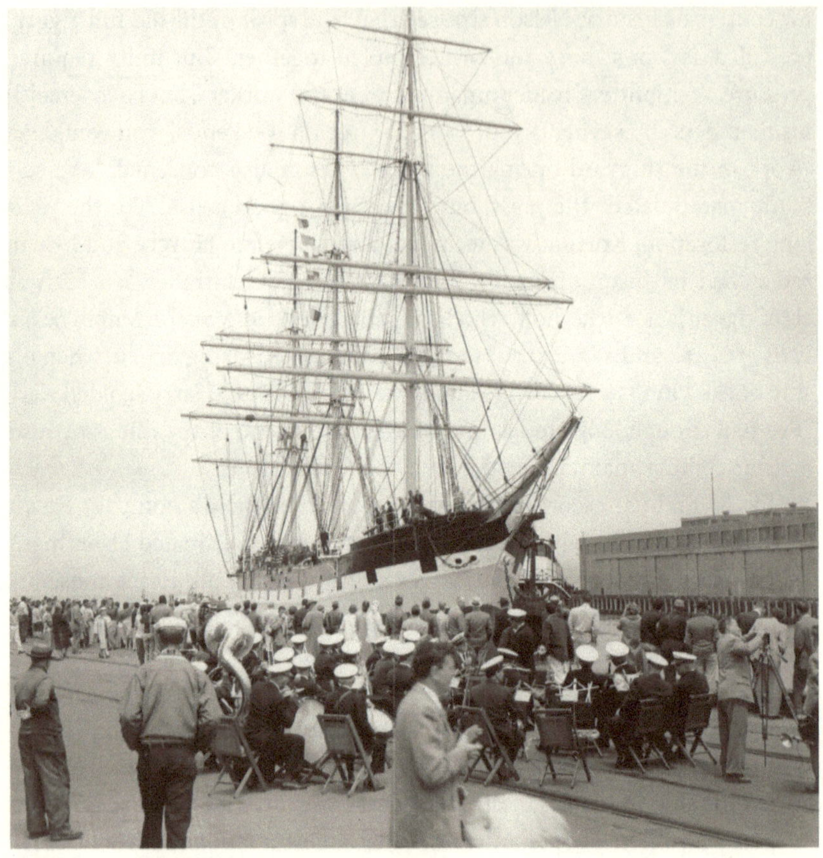

FIGURE 27. *Balclutha* rededicated at Fisherman's Wharf Pier 43½, 1955. David Nelson in center foreground. *Courtesy of the San Francisco Maritime National Historical Park.*

tube." Gazing into *Balclutha*'s large binnacle, Dennis the Menace said, "Gee a ROUND telebision! Wonder how ya turn it on?"[22] (See fig. 28.)

To avert "institutional claustrophobia," Kortum wanted more ships. Congress was giving away USS *Olympia*, Dewey's 1898 flagship, but he felt that "our first duty" was "to celebrate the traditions of the merchant marine." Rejecting replicas, Kortum chose vessels to represent the port's history, but he needed money. Hearing that Washington, D.C., was returning $65 million in oil royalties to California in 1955, he asked Sacramento to buy two schooners, *Thayer* and *Wapama*. Legislators okayed $200,000, but Governor Goodwin Knight balked. Using Harry Lundeberg's name, Kortum telegrammed Knight, who had "a soft spot in his heart for Harry" but

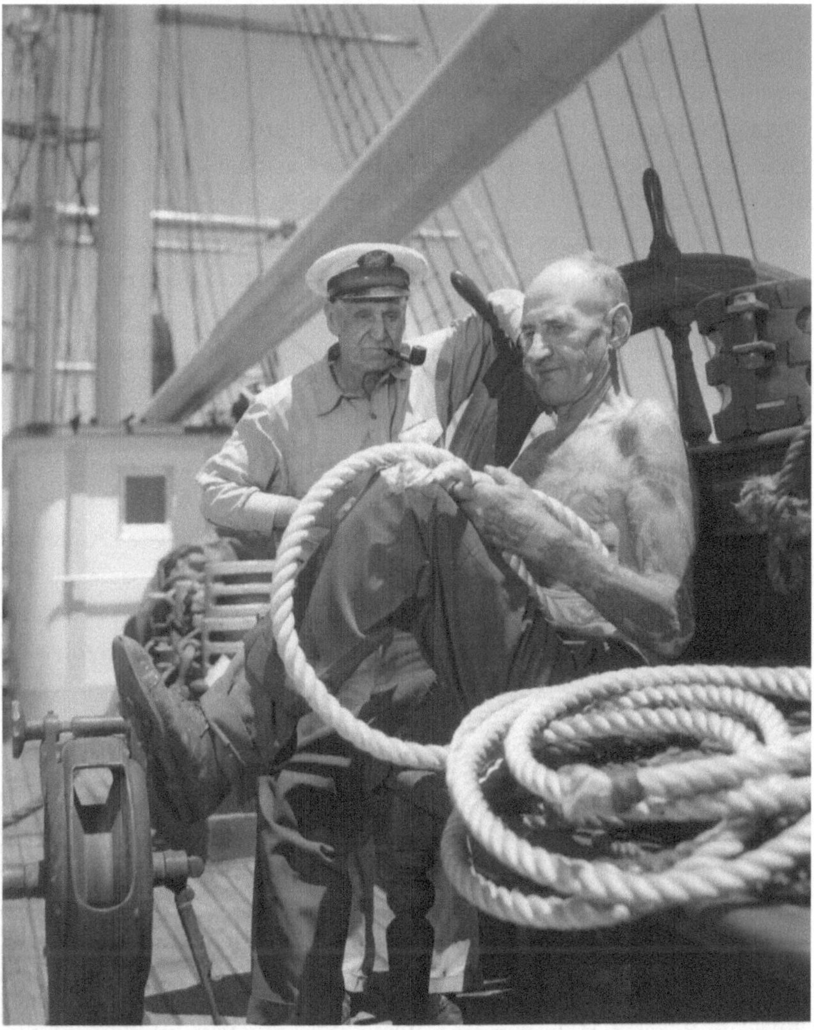

FIGURE 28. Old Salts aboard *Balclutha*: Captain John Rankine and Fingal Larson. *Courtesy of the San Francisco Maritime National Historical Park.*

wanted the Park Commission to fund the schooners. Kortum warned that the commission seemed interested only in Spanish missions and Gold Rush towns. Stanley Dollar then intervened. Former head of the Dollar Shipping Lines and current SFMMA president, Dollar asked his friend and commission chair, Joseph Knowland, for help, as he also controlled an additional $2 million in royalties directly allocated to San Francisco.[23]

After the publishers agreed, Kortum presented his Project X to the commission and the city in 1956. But the mayor instead proposed using those royalties and ships for a Ferry Building State Park, which abutted his own lagging real estate development. Outraged, Kortum wrote telegrams for Lundeberg to send, and the SFMMA leaked its plan, comparing it with one-year-old Disneyland. Project X would be, Kortum promised, "a good deal more sedate, and certainly more historically accurate." After Knowland rejected Ferry Park and state parks head Newton Drury endorsed Project X, the mayor relented. Kortum's 1949 vision was nearing reality. He optimistically told England's Frank G. G. Carr, who directed the National Maritime Museum at Greenwich and was saving the famed clipper ship *Cutty Sark*, "State preservation should guarantee [the park's] existence ad infinitum."[24]

A victorious Kortum joined a Seattle crew readying *Thayer* (1895) for its sail to San Francisco. A three-masted, bald-headed schooner of 452 gross tons, it was, he said, "the last commercial windjammer to fly the American flag." Built to carry 575,000 board feet of lumber, its life expectancy had been twenty-five years. But after World War I, *Thayer* worked in the Bering Sea, supporting cod fishermen in dories, and then as the stereotypical pirate ship. Acquiring *Thayer* for $25,450, the state hired Huycke to make it "fundamentally sound," which cost another $60,000; that was, he said, "my best job ever." With a crew composed of Huycke, Dickerhoff, Dring, and Kortum, Captain Adrian F. Raynaud served as skipper. He had first rounded Cape Horn in 1909 and worked on old ships for most of his life. *Thayer* embarked with newsreel cameras whirling, but after a storm hit and the vessel floundered, Kortum admitted, they scrambled "to save the schooner—and our necks." The United States Coast Guard (USCG) provided an emergency tow. Though restored, *Thayer*'s work was "never finished," the state conceded, as it was "often impossible to draw the line between maintenance and restoration." As SFMM curators were preparing its displays, the state asked Kortum to target the "education level of viewers in their teens." He refused, noting that a major defect in "the American character" was its attempt "to reduce all operations down to the level where they can be performed by a 12 year old child." While Kortum illustrated *Thayer*'s workmanship to a more discerning audience, the National Park Service (NPS) later pitched its interpretive program to students and "visitors with a seventh-grade education."[25]

Afterward, Kortum proposed acquiring the last Pacific steam schooner to show how technology had obsolesced Thayer's sails. In Seattle, the

205-foot, 905-ton *Tongass* (formerly *Wapama*, 1915) had been junked with a rotted hull and broken boilers. In 1958, Drury okayed its purchase, though he called it "a wreck and a monstrosity." Its type was unique to the West Coast, where 225 had been built from 1884 to 1923. Named after a graceful waterfall, *Wapama* carried a million board feet of lumber; its sixty passengers admired the elegant interior. The 825-horsepower, triple-expansion steam engine could maneuver into doghole ports to load wood from clifftop chutes. Its donkey (auxiliary) engine thus "made clearcutting the efficient way to log." Steam schooners also transformed business. Whereas a sailing schooner had been owned by a group of investors, steam schooners not only were operated by powerful corporations but also made service more regular and reliable. Yet by the late 1920s, they were obsolete and struggled to find work. Only later was a story told of the Prohibition-era *Wapama* mixing booze, gambling, and "wayward women" when the crew lashed "down the wheel of the ship to keep it going around in circles during the bacchanalia." After the state's "thorough restoration," it was rededicated in 1963.[26]

In 1959, Drury also agreed to Kortum's emergency request for $500 to purchase the fifty-nine-foot, forty-one-ton scow schooner *Alma* (1891), which he retrieved from the mudflats. Gaff-rigged with two masts, it looked like, said a writer, "a cross between a sailing yacht and a floating cigar box." Carrying everyday goods, scow schooners were "unpretentious, practical, and hard-working." Some four hundred had been built before 1906, but only two existed "in the public eye." Like steam beer and cable cars, they symbolized the Bay Area, said Roger Olmsted, whom Kortum hired as SFMM librarian and curator. After *Alma*'s business was taken by trucks and bridges, the much-altered schooner worked as an oyster-shell dredge until abandoned in 1957. Hoisted onto Hyde Street Pier, but lacking accurate plans for its restoration, *Alma* was, said *WoodenBoat*, "a very poor example."[27]

Alma's work was delayed by the acquisition of *Eureka* (formerly *Ukiah*, 1890). The 299-foot, 2,420-ton ferry was "the largest floating wooden structure on earth." Built in Tiburon, it (but not its engine) was rebuilt in 1922. Workers joked that they "jacked up the whistle . . . and slid a new boat underneath." After 1941, it operated from Hyde Street Pier for the Southern Pacific Railroad, which ran over forty ferries on the Bay. *Eureka* was its largest, carrying 120 cars and twenty-three hundred passengers, including Kortum. All were amazed by its twin twenty-seven-foot-diameter, side-mounted paddle wheels and its single-cylinder, four-story-high walking-beam engine. Only one similar engine exists—in *Ticonderoga*, which sits on land in Shelburne, Vermont. But in 1957, *Eureka*'s crank pin snapped, and Southern Pacific president (and SFMMA head) Stanley Dollar offered Kortum either *Eureka* or the ferry *Berkeley*. Kortum was enthralled by *Eureka*'s engine. While *Berkeley* was gifted to the Maritime Museum of San Diego, *Eureka* debuted at Aquatic Park after the SFMMA gave it to the state in 1962. Nostalgia was kindled with ten antique vehicles aboard, including a Dodge truck restored by Newhall.[28]

"THE BEST EXHIBIT OF ITS KIND IN AMERICA": VICTORIAN PARK AND *BALCLUTHA*

Kortum was consumed with Victorian Park's creation. After he had blocked the mayor's sale of the weed-choked parking lot in 1955, the state leased the four-acre plot and began work in 1961. He complained, however, that the landscaping proposed by the state's modernist architects would give visitors the sense of a suburban "bourgeois barbecue." He persuaded the state instead to copy Mystic's cobblestones and New Bedford's bollards. Though Knowland told his Park Commission "staff [to] make things happen" for a new pier replicating old Meiggs' Wharf, he refused Kortum's request that it also build an early shipyard. Even before the park's completion, its maritime setting and plan won the praise of the trendsetting urban critic Jane Jacobs. Opened in October 1963, San Francisco Maritime State Historic Park encompassed Victorian Park, Hyde Street Pier with its four ships (*Eureka*, *Thayer*, *Wapama*, and *Alma*), and Haslett Warehouse. Projected to draw two million sightseers annually, it was, according to state planners, "one of the most ambitious, and certainly the most difficult and different projects [they had ever] undertaken." However, it was a pyrrhic victory for Kortum's museum, which invested $100,000 from 1955 to 1960. In protest, Roger Olmsted resigned, telling Kortum that the museum was left "in an intolerable and potentially ruinous position" with "large liabilities" but "no clear-cut path to significantly increased revenue."[29]

Meanwhile, not willing to waste his "time on temporary shows," Kortum relied on permanent exhibits. During the Cold War, he admittedly tried to give the public "a feeling of being rooted and secure." Yet antimodernism ran deep. Scott Newhall, for one, was "a real artist who," a reporter noted, "created a world of his own." His office had bric-a-brac from the Irrawaddy Steam Navigation Co. of Asia, for which, noted *Who's Who*, he was chairman of the board. But this company and its artifacts were a hoax that he created to spoof modernity. Paradoxically, he dismissed most Americans as wanting only "fairy tales to fit the American fantasy." More fundamentally, Kortum believed that the late nineteenth-century world was better than his own: "Everything went slower; there was, consequently, more interaction between human beings." Museum librarian David Hull recalled that "working for Karl was like living in the 19th century." In the 1950s other San Franciscans were escaping suburban and corporate culture. The iconic columnist Herb Caen called them "beatniks," and North Beach was "the capital of Beatdom."[30]

The museum immersed visitors in a one-of-a-kind world between Beatdom and suburbia. Unusual for the Federal Art Project, the building's nautical surrealism had been fashioned by Hilaire Hiler, who was, said *Time*, "one of the wonder boys of modern decoration." Depicting a sunken ship and the lost continents of Mu and Atlantis, his interior walls had the only murals "worth talking about in the United States," declared writer Henry Miller. "Few people" had ever seen his brilliant fish and sea creatures "unless they [were] lucky enough to enjoy delirium tremens." In addition, Sargent Johnson, one of only two black artists in California's WPA, carved smiling fish into Vermont slate, and Italian-born sculptor Beniamino Bufano crafted a black frog and a red seal. Unique for the state's WPA, the art made everyone smile. *Time* called the whole "one of the most sophisticated WPA building jobs in the U.S."[31]

The murals were backdrops for Spreckels's models, paintings, and figureheads, worth $75,000, along with photographs and artifacts added by Kortum and crew. Most eye-catching was his novel use of ship remnants, which he learned from the National Museum of Nautical History in Stockholm. In 1951, for example, a Kortum expedition with "a psychologist, a singer, . . . a stevedore, and a designer" retrieved from Sausalito's mudflats the fifteen-foot-high carved bow of the schooner *Commerce* (1900). Atop a stand that Newhall welded, it dominated the main room. Kortum also showed a fourteen-foot stock anchor from USS *Independence* (1814). While Newhall called him "the best natural-born designer that he'd ever seen," Spreckels muttered, "Anchors belong outdoors!"[32]

She added the figurehead of Davy Crockett. The life-size rendering, from George Greenman's yard in Mystic, was acquired by Adolph Spreckels, but when Alma gave it to the SFMM, it drew little attention. In late 1954, however, Disney's *Davy Crockett, King of the Wild Frontier* television miniseries and film ignited a craze, which a scholar considered "one of the great popular culture events" of the 1950s. With his long rifle and resolute pose, it became a Cold War shrine and the museum's "number one attraction." Unlike the ever-vigilant Davy, however, the figurehead had been mounted only when the ship was safely in port. Visitors also saw a re-created nineteenth-century diver salvaging a wreck. Disney's *20,000 Leagues under the Sea* (1954) depicted the oceans as another dangerous frontier. But not for Dennis the Menace, who climbed atop the diver for a photo opportunity and gave the museum more publicity.[33]

Models were numerous. Spreckels gifted a fourteen-foot tanker from the global empire–building Bechtel Corporation and a twelve-foot *Queen Mary* built by longshoreman Knut Wulffschmidt. The five-masted, Hamburg-based *Preussen* (1902) was one of "the greatest square-rigged ships that ever sailed"; Eric Swanson spent five thousand hours in his Embarcadero tenement creating a ten-and-a-half-foot copy. It was, said Villiers, one of "the best models in the world." But while U.S. soldiers were fighting overseas in 1945, Spreckels's $5,000 purchase of the model so riled self-appointed patriots that they dynamited her mansion's gate. The blast eerily mirrored the ship's history, which curators overlooked. Named after Prussia as the arms race was intensifying, *Preussen* hauled nitrates for making explosives and fertilizers. Villiers spun a different story. He lamented in *The Set of the Sails* that *Preussen* was swamped in a "power-crazed" world pushing "the mechanisation of all seaborne trade" and the creation of "huge ships and great companies." That giantism worried Cutler, too, but it was the ship's raison d'être.[34]

Because the seven-thousand-square-foot bathhouse had limited space, *Balclutha* became "A Memorial Museum of Early San Francisco." The *New York Times* called it one of two "fascinating, off-beat exhibits" rivaling the "old stand-bys" of Chinatown and Fisherman's Wharf. Most alluring was its captain's quarters, but Kortum walked a tightrope depicting its notorious fo'c'sle. Not only were his financial backers shipping barons, but the SFMM was building labor-management consensus. Moreover, scholarly maritime history, said historian Jesse Lemisch, had ignored Jack-tar's exploited life and focused on ship models, trade, and the great explorers and navigators. Kortum tried to evoke "the intensity of [Jack's] daily experiences," but his displays could hardly match Cobweb Palace, a long-gone Meiggs' Wharf saloon featuring scrimshaw and models that sailors traded for rum. Still, the *Times* thought that *Balclutha*'s fo'c'sle and galley looked authentic, though both were spick-and-span. Other displays focused on the Gold Rush from 1848 to 1855, when San Francisco's population jumped from four hundred to twenty-five thousand. Calling it "one of the biggest movements of ships since the Crusades," Kortum showed the *Forest of Masts Panorama*, a five-part daguerreotype (1853) with hundreds of abandoned ships that became warehouses, bars, brothels, and stores. Such ships carried more forty-niners than did the wagons across the plains.[35]

Balclutha symbolized a global trade that San Franciscans hoped to emulate. It made the fifteen-thousand-mile trek from England around Cape Horn and returned with wheat, as well as guano mined on equatorial islands by coolies under deadly conditions. It was one of the last extant Cape Horners of Britain, whose merchant fleet in 1897 included 515 steel-hulled and 936 iron-hulled sailing ships. Homeported in San Francisco in 1902, it became "the last full-rigger which actually flew the American flag." Chartered to Alaska Packers, *Balclutha* ran aground in 1904; locked in its hold were desperate (but ultimately safe) Chinese workers. The horrifying story was among many told in tween-deck exhibits. Renamed *Star of Alaska*, it worked until 1930 for the Packers, which racially segregated its workforce in an extended poop deck, fo'c'sle, and tween deck. Conditions were awful. It was "the messiest ship I'd seen in many a day," said artist Gordon Grant on a 1925 voyage; his log and sketchbook unfortunately omitted the workers. To revise the record further, Kortum wanted (but failed) to strip off "every Alaska Packer vestige." If visitors imagined, said David Nelson, they "could hear long dead echoes of the sing song chatter of holds full of Chinese."[36]

The tween deck also exhibited *The Barbary Coast and Old Sailortowns*. For years, good San Franciscans had been "ashamed . . . and perhaps afraid" of the Barbary Coast, but Kortum displayed the district's anything-goes hippodrome. Besides a large bas-relief panel depicting anatomically correct satyrs chasing nymphs, there was a coupled mannequin of a grizzled sailor and woman. Years later, a curator sanitized the story as "a damsel in distress," but she was likely a prostitute who worked the city's five thousand bars in 1890. It was "the worst of all the Sodom and Gomorrahs," said Ambrose Bierce; in 1906, fire and brimstone devoured the Barbary Coast. Though rebuilt, it was demolished in 1935 for waterfront development.[37]

The Barbary Coast added to the lexicon "shanghaiing" and "Mickey Finn," which were romanticized by guidebooks but also called "fakelore." San Francisco was reputedly "the crimping capital of the world." If a seafarer drank a Mickey Finn or smoked an opium-laced cigar, he would be taken by a Whitehall boat to an outbound ship, perhaps never to return. The museum called its Whitehall boat a "water taxi." Thinking that the ship came first, Kortum said that "discipline had to be thrust upon these surly fo'c's'le crowds." Still, he displayed the sinister world of "hell ships," but the Merchants Exchange ignored mention when showing W. A. Coulter's painting of the hell ship *W. F. Babcock*. Kortum's exhibits resultantly won acclaim. *American Neptune*'s Walter Muir Whitehill praised *Balclutha* for avoiding commercialism, while *Atlantic Monthly* editor Edward Weeks called it "the best exhibit of its kind in America." So impressed, Frank Carr "started campaigning for the establishment of a [British ship] Trust." By the summer of 1967, *Balclutha* was open daily from 9:30 a.m. to 11:30 p.m.[38]

Balclutha was joined at Pier 43½ by a British tug with anachronistic side-lever engines, once familiar around San Francisco. Upset that Greenwich's National Maritime Museum wanted to remove an engine from *Reliant* (formerly *Old Trafford*), Kortum asked Carr to dismantle the partially scrapped *Eppleton Hall* (1914) instead. After he agreed, however, Carr was sacked, and his successor, Basil Greenhill, only dispatched a "downright insulting" refusal six months later. Having already planned an expedition to retrieve *Old Trafford*, Newhall and Kortum formed a phony business to buy it and, contrary to Britain's antiquities laws, secret it to America. Their agents were, however, met by the police. Greenhill wanted to press charges, but trustee Prince Philip "thought rather favorably of the Americans' enterprise." Still, Greenhill threatened to jail Kortum "if he dared show his face in England again." Meanwhile, Kortum's absence while on San Francisco's payroll led his critics to summon a grand jury, but without indictment. So Newhall bought *Eppleton Hall* for $6,000, spent $148,000 for its repair, and skippered the last extant, Tyne-built paddle tug across the Atlantic. It was greeted by eleven thousand fans in March 1970. Newhall's tale became a Book of the Month Club featured selection. While Newhall donated the one-hundred-foot *Eppie* to the Museum Association, the state park acquired the steel-screw, 135-foot tug *Hercules* (1907). Harry Dring struggled, however, to maintain the poorly funded state fleet.[39]

Kortum was drawn further to global ship preservation. In the Falklands, *Vicar of Bray* (1841) was the sole survivor of the Gold Rush's 777 ships. It was as important to the West, he said, as "the California missions, the Alamo, the Governor's palace in Santa Fe, Sutter's Fort and the Golden Spike." Though remade into a jetty, the bark was "surprisingly intact." Whereas 85 percent of its original fabric survived, only 15 percent remained of USS *Constitution*, for which the U.S. Navy had "a spare-no-expense attitude." As Sweden had honored *Vasa*, Newhall wanted *Vicar* as "a shrine [in Haslett Warehouse] to our early history." *WoodenBoat* countered, however, that such ships "should remain in the Falklands." It did and became a ruin. In Washington State, meanwhile, Kortum saved *Falls of Clyde* (1878), an iron four-master of 1,809 tons. In 1963, after a three-year effort, *Falls* docked in Honolulu, where the Bishop Museum created a maritime center. Captain Fred Klebingat tearfully remarked that his "dream [had come] true."[40]

Most dear to Kortum was *Kaiulani* in the Philippines. But overcommitted, he convinced a newly formed Washington, D.C., group to acquire the bark that Filipinos agreed to donate. At a White House ceremony in 1964, Kortum watched President Lyndon B. Johnson accept its deed and assign its preservation to the reconstituted National Maritime Historical Society (NMHS), which Peter Stanford and Kortum soon headed. While LBJ became preoccupied with the Vietnam War and the NMHS was searching (unsuccessfully) for a philanthropist, Filipinos complained that America was backsliding on its "moral obligation" to save *Kaiulani*. In 1967, Kortum testified before Congress that it was the last survivor of seventeen thousand U.S.-built merchant square-riggers. Congress guaranteed a loan, but red tape and inexperience hindered the NMHS. Finally, Senator Edward Kennedy interceded in 1975. While headlining *Kaiulani*, which was designated the Bicentennial Fleet's flagship, he proposed creating an independent National Trust for the Preservation of Historic Ships. The existing National Trust deflected his bill; exasperated, Kortum told a syndicated reporter that it dictated "how the bulk of federal funds for historic preservation [were] spent, without consideration for [other] views." Bitterness followed, but all came to naught as Filipinos stripped *Kaiulani*. Only a few pieces were saved. Had the sailor John Kennedy lived, said Kortum, he "would unquestionably have cleared paths in government for [its] return and restoration," but LBJ "couldn't have cared less."[41]

"WE HAD TO TURN TO THE FEDS": THE NATIONAL PARK SERVICE ENTERS MARITIME PRESERVATION

Kortum predicted that tourism would fund ship preservation, but Aquatic Park was itself threatened. In 1962, developers announced that a fifteen-hundred-unit apartment complex would replace the Ghirardelli Chocolate Company. Protecting the district's Victoriana, while resisting new high-rises and freeways, Kortum persuaded SFMMA trustee William Matson Roth, grandson of the shipping baron, to intervene; after an $18 million investment, he opened a trendsetting festival marketplace there in 1964. It was a "brick Xanadu," said environmentalist David Brower, but historian Alison Isenberg later called it a male space, as was the maritime museum. In 1963, Kortum also helped save the Cannery, built in 1907–9 adjacent to Haslett Warehouse. Investing $12 million, museum friend Leonard Martin remade its three stories as shops and restaurants in 1967. Both projects gained national awards, but slow profits. Meanwhile, the state park was underfunded, poorly attended, and in jeopardy. Park commissioner George Fleharty said, "Let's send for Walt Disney to tell us what he thinks." But reporter Harlan Trott feared commercialism. Calling *Balclutha* "the million-dollar waterfront beauty," he advised: "The city needs a diva more than a Disney."[42]

Kortum worried about Haslett. Under Ronald Reagan, Republican governor from 1967 to 1975, the parks were hit by California-style Reaganomics. In 1968, his director of state parks and recreation, William Penn Mott, proposed giving the park to the city. Mayor Joseph Alioto, who was the Museum Association's honorary chairman, wanted a no-cost deal, which failed to happen. Meanwhile, Mott created a railroad museum in Sacramento, thus killing Kortum's similar hope for Haslett. Still, Kortum eyed tourism's potential. "Our experience," he told architect Piero Patri in 1970, "is that a very substantial portion of the middle class public" wants tourism to be educational. But after Patri prepared a $26.5 million plan for Haslett and the SFMMA secured financing, Reagan's office tried to sell the building. "These people," David Nelson griped in 1971 to Dianne Feinstein, president of the San Francisco Board of Supervisors, "have planned, schemed and plotted for nearly five years" to offload the building. Supporting the SFMMA was San Francisco Tomorrow, an activist group in which Jean Kortum was prominent; its members fought back with injunctions and lobbied Mayor George Moscone and Representative Phillip Burton.[43]

While the Kortums campaigned for the community, their work against freeways and high-rises challenged capital. That tug between community and capital, said scholar Richard DeLeon, typified San Francisco's antiregime politics and restrained its pro-growth government. Karl helped to thwart construction of a nuclear power plant fifty miles to the north at Bodega Head, while Jean led a campaign against extending the double-deck Embarcadero Freeway. Its proposed eight-lane Golden Gate Freeway would have turned "Aquatic Park into a swirling tangle of freeway ramps, exhaust fumes, [and] automobile noise." Instead, the North Waterfront was, reported the *Chronicle*, "saved from the bulldozers by mass action." Mayor Alioto derided Karl, Jean, and other activists as a "nut house brigade" halting change "in the name of ecology and social progress." The Kortums were called "the Saul Alinskys of the waterfront."[44]

With opinions so polarized, Karl was either a savior or a demon. In 1965, *Venture* magazine opined that he looked "about as formidable as an aging Boy Scout," but he was, added Roger Olmsted, the "scourge of the Chamber of Commerce and the Building Trades Council." Retaliation followed. While threats forced the Kortums to get an unlisted telephone number, the city neglected his museum building, failed to remove its trash, and ignored the polluted lagoon. Facing hostile trustees and the mayor, Kortum admitted to Herb Caen that Scott Newhall "had to bail me out again and again." Pushing preservation beyond the connoisseur tradition of great men and buildings, and challenging modernist planners, his Victorian scenes were slowly appreciated. But, as worthy buildings still fell, he asked Caen: "Where is human scale? Where is Jane Jacobs? WHERE THE HELL is the Planning Commission?" As a "reasonable growth" movement gelled, the city was called "the best example of urban renewal in the country." In 1969, as Caen and Kortum were awarded the Silver Cable Car Award (even before Willie Mays and Seiji Ozawa), Jean and Karl were included in a "Gallery of Civic Heroes," which then numbered eight, for "transforming the northern waterfront into one of the great promenades of the world."[45]

North Beach's social ferment, however, grabbed more attention than did Kortum's Victorian sensibilities. In 1959, comic Jonathan Winters tried to climb *Balclutha*'s rigging, naked, and ended up in the psychiatric ward, while in 1965 "three bare young representatives of the Sexual Freedom League" liberated the lagoon. In 1969, "four homosexuals, undressed," were found cavorting in a museum supply room. The social revolution hit *Balclutha*'s crew, which included "hippie types." In 1971, a drug bust snared three, whom Kortum called "quite decent kids" earning $1.62 an hour. He blamed Alioto's city hall for the raid. As thousands migrated to San Francisco, Newhall thought that it had become "a melange of god-knows-what," thus earning Caen's moniker "Baghdad-by-the-Bay." Yet Caen was reassured by Aquatic Park, which gave meaning to a city that had "lost its way."[46]

By 1965 Aquatic Park's public image belied the not-so-public spreadsheets. *Venture* magazine offered a glowing appraisal. "How is it that, at a time when other historic American waterfronts, like those of Boston and New York, are being destroyed, corrupted or pinched off from the citizenry by the elevated concrete girdles of superhighways," it asked, was San Francisco "managing to do something scenically exciting and culturally valid with part of its port area?" It noted that Aquatic Park was motivated "primarily to benefit ordinary citizens." Yet, in 1965, the *Examiner* proposed placing the tenuous state park under the Museum Association. Many tourists could not differentiate the park from the museum. In 1966, Peter and Norma Stanford visited from New York; he realized that "part of it is owned by a museum corporation, and part of it (the marine park) by the state," but "oddly enough, nothing we have makes this clear." They copied the model for South Street Seaport.[47]

The deaccession of federal lands, including nearby Fort Mason, and inappropriate proposals for their development, finally forced that consolidation. Chairing the House of Representative's National Parks Subcommittee, Phil Burton told his aide William G. Thomas in 1970 to draft a bill creating the Golden Gate National Recreation Area (GGNRA). Thinking that Congress would reject the state-owned ships, his map included them without mention. A former *San Francisco Chronicle* reporter and Harrison Dring friend, Thomas admitted that, as parks were created, Congress "cared not a fig for the [NPS] opinion." But in creating a merged maritime museum, Burton's bill mandated gifts by the SFMMA, state, and city. The logistics took years. President Richard Nixon signed the bill on October 27, 1972. Six years later, Burton's $1.2 billion Omnibus Parks Act doubled the 115-square-mile GGNRA, which included parks, nature areas, and Fort Mason. Said NPS framer Horace Albright, the Burton Bill ranked "in importance with the law establishing the Park Service itself." So many parks were created or expanded, however, the NPS was overwhelmed. Free of an admission charge, GGNRA became "the most heavily visited and popular" NPS unit. But Caen joked that the acronym GGNRA sounded "like a social disease."[48]

After GGNRA superintendent William Whalen doubted if Haslett would become a federal museum, the Kortums opposed the state transferring the site. They countered that Sacramento should instead develop Haslett as a museum, restore its fleet authentically, and allow *Balclutha* to move to the Hyde Street Pier. Once that was accomplished, Karl predicted, the entrance fees "could gross the same kind of money as Mystic Seaport," a million dollars a year. The state nevertheless gave its fleet and Haslett to the NPS at the end of 1976. After a popular vote, the city followed with its bathhouse and park in 1978. Kortum recognized a fait accompli. So, lastly, the SFMMA donated its physical assets in mid-1978, but it received a contract to operate *Balclutha*, its chief source of revenue. Only association president Newhall dissented; quitting the board, he said, "Karl, you're going to get lost" in the federal system. Kortum rebutted, "We had to turn to the feds, because they were the only source for the big money" for more ships.[49]

The new National Maritime Museum (NMM) upset the Smithsonian, which had planned to develop a Hall of American Maritime Enterprise, partly from Howard Chapelle's collection. The name caused another stir, as it was done "so quietly that other museums," said *WoodenBoat*, "were caught standing still." Some questioned giving a national designation to a West Coast collection; others feared it would grab limited federal dollars. Thinking that Karl was six years shy of retiring, Jean asked Burton, and Mayor Moscone asked the interior secretary, if Karl could join the NPS. Thomas and NPS director Whalen objected, but Burton told Thomas: "Tell Whalen to hire Kortum." Burton then pushed Thomas into the NPS as public affairs officer for the GGNRA and, in 1981, for the NPS Western Region. The GGNRA hired Kortum ally David Hull and independent-minded Dring and Stephen Canright. A rift between Kortum and Dring widened.[50]

As executive director of the renamed NMM Association (NMMA), Nelson wanted to earn revenue by accepting the gift of USS *Pampanito* (SS-383). But a hearing was required to berth the World War II submarine at Pier 45. Labor leader Harry Bridges denounced the proposal as militaristic. His fears were real as the NMMA initially skirted the fact that in 1944 *Pampanito* had sunk *Kachidoki Maru* (formerly *President Harrison*) while carrying the British and Australian prisoners of war depicted in *The Bridge on the River Kwai* (1957). Over four hundred POWs perished. By 1982, when *Pampanito* opened, Fisherman's Wharf was swamped by twelve million tourists at the kitsch-filled Pier 39. The NPS moved *Balclutha* to Hyde Street in 1988 and enacted a pier fee. In turn, more visited Kortum's Aquatic Park, which Newhall dubbed a "Potemkin village." Kortum had predicted that "the historical museum movement [was] going to increase . . . in exact proportion to the degree to which the future looks less attractive than the past."[51]

With its first-ever fleet and full-spectrum museum, the NPS had difficulty getting its sea legs. Said James Delgado, who served as GGNRA historian from 1979 to 1986, the transition "was almost like a hostile takeover or, to phrase it better, a merger between two unequal partners, each more or less ignorant of just who and what their new colleagues were." At Kortum's request, the NPS hired Captain Eric Berryman (USN, ret.) to assess its holdings. Ranking it "among the top two or three such museum collections in the world," he proposed acquiring two square-riggers and a floating dry dock. "In San Francisco the extraordinary opportunity exists," he argued, to "re-create the 'forest of masts' described with wonder." But he knew that the decision to create a "west coast maritime Smithsonian" was "entirely political." Dring exploded: "Look at this! It's a shopping list for new acquisitions, and we are having difficulty enough taking care of the ships we already have." Implausibly, Berryman suggested that maintenance was "not a major factor" for metal-hulled ships because of newer technology.[52]

Kortum and the NPS had conflicting plans, but both were upended by the inauguration of President Reagan in 1981. Ushering in antienvironmental activists, it began the "dark period," noted the independent National Parks Conservation Association (NPCA). As ideologues slashed NPS budgets, they targeted Burton, who warned: "The National Park System, one of the major talismans of the United States as a civilized community, is in [desperate] trouble." Unexpectedly, Burton died in 1983. Meanwhile, the NMM suffered because placing a fleet under park rangers was, said Thomas, like "giving Yosemite National Park to the Navy." With its focus on natural and historic sites, "very few people in the park service really understood what we needed." An NPS assistant director conceded that it shied "away from ship preservation because of the great expense." Few rangers, added Delgado, "knew fore from aft and port from starboard."[53]

While Kortum and Dring only talked "to each other through Karl's secretary," Dring warred against the NPS. If its managers would not fund his ships, he said, they should "take them out beyond the Golden Gate and sink them." Further angering Kortum, he wanted to move the fleet to the tranquil China Basin, four miles southeast of Aquatic Park, to get "away from the politics and struggle for funds" in the GGNRA. The NPS rejected the move, prompting China Basin's advocates to suggest that the NMM primarily existed "for the benefit of Fisherman's Wharf tourist merchants." Dring quit in 1984 and was replaced, as historic ships manager, by an ill-prepared ranger. As a vendetta against Kortum, Dring allegedly won a "death bed promise" from Thomas that Kortum-acolyte Steve Hyman would never get that job.[54] (See fig. 29.)

Of all Dring's ships, *Wapama* was in the worst shape. Badly hogged and in danger of sinking, it was hauled in 1979, when he found a broken keel. In April, he struck "a good deal" with a shipyard and "funding was fully

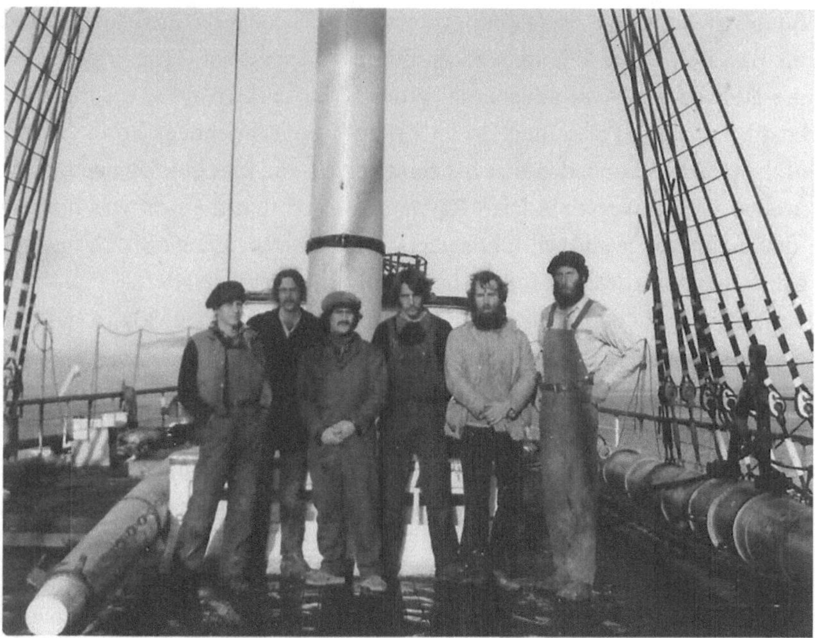

FIGURE 29. *Balclutha* crew, 1979, Steve Hyman (right) and Stephen Canright (second from right). *Courtesy of Steve Hyman.*

allocated," but the NPS "welched on the deal." He bashed the bureaucracy's "stupid bottlenecks." In 1980, *Wapama* was placed uncovered on an undersized, rented barge and towed to Alameda. Golden Gate National Recreation Area maritime-unit manager Glennie Wall said, "Harry, I promise you, we will restore *Wapama*, put her back in the water and return her to Hyde Street Pier." Wall reneged on that promise. Unfunded, its rot spread. Though it was designated a National Historic Landmark (NHL) in 1984, Interior Subcommittee chair Representative Sidney R. Yates reportedly would have been "content if she fell apart." By 1985, after spending $500,000 for the barge, estimates doubled to a seven-year, $7 million restoration. Surprisingly, *Wapama* then received the President's Historic Preservation Award, not for its conservation but for the restoration planning undertaken by a private consultant, White Elephant Management. *WoodenBoat* was harsh. Noting that *Wapama*'s "condition [was] significantly worse than it was 10 years ago," its editor Peter Spectre scoffed: "Ah yes. Make a mess, fix part of the mess you made, get an award."[55]

Meanwhile, *Eppleton Hall* was in limbo. In 1976, after volunteer Bill

Burgess reactivated *Eppie*'s supporters, the USCG recertified tug cruised the Bay. But, as the feds stepped in, Burgess stepped out. "The Friends and the NPS became two adversarial groups," he said. In 1986, a consultant heard that the NPS wanted "to let her rot." Superintendent Brian O'Neill of the GGNRA conceded that his eight vessels and pier quickly needed $33 million. Ship surveyor Adrian Raynaud alleged that the fleet was hurting "due to ignorance and willful neglect." Then *Thayer* sprang a six-thousand-gallon-per-hour leak in 1988. The usually supportive National Trust told the NPS that it "must commit the resources and move quickly to halt the deterioration that threatens this important collection."[56]

Kortum made waves in an organization that prized "peace at all costs," said Hull. Meanwhile, Reaganomics meant less money for the GGNRA's competing units. Wanting "a temple of excellence," Kortum told the NPS, which only operated visitor centers with limited displays, that it did not know how to run its "first full spectrum museum." His NMM had *one* curator, while Britain's NMM had over *twenty*. His NMM also suffered because the NPS did not actively collect artifacts or promote scholarship. O'Neill's predecessor as superintendent had earlier suggested to superiors that the NMM be placed under the Smithsonian, but his proposal went nowhere. Using Fort Mason, the NPS established the J. Porter Shaw Library in 1983. Kortum wanted more research and collecting, especially as maritime technology was rapidly changing, but the NPS instead emphasized processing its inherited 250,000 photographs, 120,000 vessel plans, and 1,200 shelf-feet of archival materials. Escalating the tension, Wall promoted John Maounis, who was hired temporarily in 1979 as a museum technician, to a new position, supervisory museum curator. Lacking any off-site museum or ship experience but holding the necessary college degrees, he leapfrogged over Chief Curator Kortum. The museum, said Delgado, "descended into personal insult and petty moves," leading to "a convoluted and sad web." Because of Kortum's renown, Wall praised him before professional audiences, but she acted in the opposite manner offstage, issuing a reprimand in 1985. At the NMMA, he became persona non grata.[57]

Balclutha became a battleground. At a national conference in 1985, Maounis claimed that Kortum's tween-deck exhibits were "so unrelated to the vessel that visitors remember the presentation," not the ship. He toed Wall's line by proposing their removal. But Wall had also hired White Elephant to survey *Balclutha* (NHL, 1985) before dry-docking because its hull was "so thin you [could] put a fist through [it] in places." The firm urged funding its repair, not revising its exhibits. Wall assembled an Interpretive Prospectus Team, whose intent, said member Glenn Gordinier of Mystic Seaport, was to "evaluate the programs . . . and advise on how to improve things." With Kortum as a self-invited guest, its meeting in February 1986 also included ship preservationist Michael Naab, GGNRA historian Delgado, and J. Scott Harmon from the NPS Harpers Ferry office. Gordinier said that the thirty-year-old displays were often "informative and intriguing," but artifacts were being damaged by rainwater leaks. Trends had also changed, he added, as "hands-on and interactive displays were gaining popularity and the static approach was losing ground." When Kortum was dismissive, Naab walked out, followed by Harmon, who took "credit for removing all [of *Balclutha*'s] junk." Years later, curator Richard Everett recalled, however, that the tween deck was "a wonderful and quiet world" and so "unlike any museum ashore." It "was heartbreaking for Karl," said White Elephant engineer Don Birkholz, as the artifacts went into storage and most panels were trashed in 1987.[58]

Haslett was entangled in the debate. Since it did not meet earthquake codes, Washington wanted to sell the half-block building, whose rents paid for most of the fleet's maintenance. After the Interior Department closed it, Kortum told *Examiner* columnist Warren Hinckle that the museum was "dead in the water." Superintendent O'Neill charged him with insubordination and imposed a five-day suspension. Kortum rebutted that the Interpretive Prospectus Team were "'extraterrestrials' who came to town on a 'junket' with 'idiotic' ideas." After that blast, he needed political cover. While assemblyman (and future mayor) Art Agnos wrote O'Neill, Mayor Feinstein complained to Representative Sala Burton about the NPS's "wasteful and insulting" treatment of him. After replacing her deceased husband in 1983, Burton was perhaps, said Thomas, the museum's only friend in Congress.[59]

Herb Caen and Hinckle led the Kortum chorus. "Crusty Karl Kortum," Caen wrote, "is under fire from the Feds again and may even lose his job, which would be a disaster. . . . Save Karl Kortum! And also the historic ships, most of which are in danger of sinking. Billions for bombs, nada for niceties." Hinckle fired a bigger salvo. Calling Kortum "the John Muir of maritime preservation," the former *Ramparts* editor deplored his demotion to ranger work. "To assign a man of Kortum's world stature to such guide work," he hammered, "is like ordering the director of the Metropolitan Museum in New York to sell trinkets in the museum gift shop." He blasted: "If the Park Service bureaucrats can't get along with Karl Kortum, they should be fired, not Kortum. We can always get more bureaucrats. We can't get another Karl Kortum." Cultural politics was also at play. Erasing the tween deck's stories of hell ships, worker exploitation, and the Barbary Coast opened the door to nostalgia. While no other museum in 1986 presented such a probing look at the port, the keelhauling of Kortum added to San Francisco's antiregime fears. The *Examiner* included him, along with author Bret Harte, scientist Linus Pauling, and computer whiz Steve Jobs, in its "One Hundred One Memorable San Franciscans." But he could not win under NPS rules and did not appeal his suspension.[60]

The battle exposed the profession's fault lines. Partly a philosophical clash, Kortum and Stanford were champions of "the large-ship preservation movement," which was assailed by friends of small craft, fine arts, and skills programs. The fracas exposed other divisions. For one, museum standards were increasingly cited, and the tween deck had (and still does have) rainwater problems. For another, the maritime community was not willing to bite the NPS hand that could coordinate (and perhaps feed) a more effective preservation movement. Kortum's once-praised attributes—conviction and determination—were now liabilities. South Street's Peter Neill suggested, for example, that Kortum's "fight with the Park Service [was] getting in the way." That clash was inevitable, stated the NPCA, "when you bring in people who are government bureaucrats and combine them with the independent and opinionated individuals who work on these ships." As sociologist Max Weber had warned, bureaucracies trumped individuals.[61]

The publicity brought some attention. Though he blamed his "limited resources," NPS director Mott (1985–89) conceded, "If the ships don't get proper maintenance, they are going to sink." Yet his past quarrels with Kortum and the 1980s culture wars also limited Mott's response. Only modest changes followed. In 1985, Congress created the National Maritime Initiative, which collected information, inventoried historic vessels, and designated vessels for NHL status because fewer than two hundred ships had been placed on the forty-seven-thousand-entry National Register. But money did not follow. After White Elephant drafted a fleet plan and stressed maintenance, Wall reported that she needed a waterfront staff of forty-two and an annual budget of $3 million but had only twenty-three people and under $1 million. In a limited response, the NPS persuaded Congress in 1987 to raise its profile by creating the Aquatic Park National Historic Landmark District and to give the NMM the unprecedented right to keep its gate fees.[62]

Hoping for more money and better press, a bill was introduced in

Congress to separate the museum from GGNRA. While the Museum Association hired William Whalen as its lobbyist, the bill renamed the bathhouse after the recently deceased Sala Burton. Drafted by Thomas and Whalen, the bill was contentious; GGNRA's O'Neill and Wall resisted; they also wanted to discard *Eppleton Hall* and *Alma*. After the Interior Department nixed a $33 million provision for the ships, the bill allowed Haslett's acquisition only after the park submitted an acceptable general management plan. To restrict Kortum, Thomas inserted a mandate that the park "shall not acquire any historic vessel" until its current fleet was maintained. As such, Thomas admitted blocking "a number of worthy donations." Recognizing a fait accompli, Kortum still griped that the title "park" would dodge museum standards. But the Interior Department told Congress that "national museum" could be used only by the Smithsonian. Ushered by newly elected Representative Nancy Pelosi, An Act to Establish the San Francisco Maritime National Historical Park was signed by Reagan on June 27, 1988.[63]

"LARGER THAN LIFE. I'M GLAD I KNEW HIM": THE PASSING OF KORTUM AND HIS DREAM

After the NMM received a poor evaluation, regional director Stanley Albright (Horace's nephew) appointed Thomas as park superintendent in 1989. He accepted—if "Kortum agreed to cooperate." But, as noted in *National Parks*, Thomas had "no experience managing a large staff, overseeing complex projects, or running a museum." In his diary, he admitted his inadequacies; as it turned out, personnel issues—resulting from his own inexperience, cronyism, and harassment—consumed much time and distracted from the ships. His truce with Kortum lasted two years, but as the fleet faded, said Nelson, "things went to hell in a handbasket."[64]

With SFMNHP's creation, expectations were raised that "desperately needed federal funding" would follow. But it didn't. Not only had a recession set in, but the much-expanded NPS also had constricted funds; meanwhile, expensive ship work required years of lobbying and special authorizations. After a year, Thomas conceded that "the resources [were] not equal to the task of saving all [the] ships and never [would] be." The House Interior Subcommittee made it worse in 1990. Regarding "the historic ships as a bottomless pit," members were frightened off by the "overwhelming amount" that was needed. But when the park received $2 million for *Eureka*, Thomas compounded the problem. "For the next year," he admitted, "I'll seek nothing more" for the ships. Consistent with a privatizing trend, he sought help from the friends association, which recruited volunteers, aided marketing and education, and helped fund projects.[65]

Complicating the fleet's work since the mid-1980s, the NPS had been drafting the Green Book (1990) on ship restoration. Like the secretary of the interior's recommendations for protecting architecture and landscapes, the Green Book suggested procedures to coordinate federal efforts. Compiled by Naab, who worked with White Elephant's Walter Rybka and Don Birkholz, as well as South Street's Norman Brouwer and Mystic's Maynard Bray, they put order into an ad hoc process. A larger problem was NPS's unfamiliarity with ships and what curator Stephen Canright called the "complex set of maritime skills and values." Referring to *Balclutha*, he thought that the NPS had facilitated "a passing [of those traits] from one generation to the next," but Kortum and his followers called it a failure.[66]

Thayer (NHL, 1984) became the most pressing case. Postponing its dry-docking in 1991, Thomas favored "vessels which [could] be fairly easily saved or kept up." Yet an advisory board warned him "very strongly" about "the poor quality of the maintenance of the vessels." It blamed the acting ships manager, whom Thomas allegedly had hired because of Dring's vendetta against Steve Hyman and Kortum. The advisers had given Thomas their proposals for *Thayer*, but he ignored them and brought in consultants (naval architects) with "no background or skills" with historic wooden ships. Ship surveyor Raynaud had advised: "Put one man in charge of the job, no committees, a fellow who knows what he's doing, and give him the money and authority to spend it." Challenging NPS procedures, Raynaud was accustomed to earlier, private practices.[67]

Bad press followed. While the NPCA placed the SFMNHP on a 1992 list of "parks in peril," Benjamin Labaree, head of Mystic's Munson Institute, excluded it from his compendium of "our best maritime museums." In 1993, the National Trust placed *Thayer* on its Eleven Most Endangered Historic Places, the first time a ship had made the list, and four years later listed the park itself. Supporting the NPS, the Museum Association readied a report (which it later mysteriously suppressed) that suggested scrapping *Wapama* and *Eppleton Hall*, the former because of its ruination and the latter because it was also deemed nonhistoric. In 1993, *Balclutha*'s crew sent a confidential letter, which eleven signed in the mutineer tradition of the round robin, to U.S. senator Dianne Feinstein. Asking Congress to investigate, the crew objected to another case of cronyism as Thomas promoted an unqualified foreman to acting ships manager. Contrary to law, the Interior Department released it and its signatories to Thomas, who retaliated against (among others) chief rigger Hyman, whom he called "Kortum's agent provocateur." He reprimanded, suspended (for five days), and demoted Hyman, but his actions were later overturned.[68]

The park's budget turned blood red after the "Republican Revolution" of 1994. National Park Service deputy director Denis Galvin took the unusual step of blaming Congress. "We just don't have the money," he said. "Give us the money and we'll keep the ships alive." While Republicans controlled the House of Representatives from 1995 to 2007, the SFMNHP's yearly visitation was almost four million, but its inflation-adjusted base funding dropped. As San Francisco's ships wasted away, Congress authorized $4.5 million to build a square-rigger for an empty wharf at Salem Maritime National Historic Site. Salem was "not a Park Service budget priority," reported the NPCA, but the earmark was funded anyway. Salem superintendent Steve Kesselman attributed San Francisco's shortfall to the fact that Thomas (or his superiors) failed to highlight their ships in a 1993 construction budget.[69]

"Things have never been worse," rued Kortum, whose performance Thomas rated "minimally successful." Exhausted and frail, Kortum retired in 1995 but acted, said the *Chronicle*'s Carl Nolte, like "a prophet denouncing the uncaring heathens." He died in September 1996. Without Thomas's authorization, the ships' crews lowered their flags to half-mast for a week. In long obituaries from London to Melbourne, he was eulogized like a decorated admiral. They echoed Walter Cronkite, who cast him as "America's foremost marine preservationist and historian." At a 1992 ceremony, Cronkite said, "By sheer determination, backed by what I call a kind of intellectual brilliance, he has made the case for historic ships clear to us all, and he has made it stick." In a service aboard *Balclutha*, a cannon salute, color guard, and speeches marked his death. The *Examiner* called him "an extraordinary man." A local writer deemed him "the greatest ship preservationist the world has known."[70]

"In retrospect," said a more critical Delgado, "it did take people like Kortum to succeed in a great initiative like founding that museum and saving those ships. It takes a tough as nails, hard driven son of a bitch with passion and ego and grit to overcome the nay sayers and the fence sitters and the seeming supporters who do nothing but bullshit and drain energy.

It takes a larger than life character to survive all that and get it done." But Delgado thought that he had stayed too long for his own good. Since 1949, Kortum had been sailing against powerful currents. He was a visionary and humanist who challenged standard-minded bureaucrats, TV-oriented suburbia, and profit-obsessed developers. At the *Balclutha* service, Bodega Bay colleague David Pesonen said he had fought "to keep the modern world from sinking into homogenized mediocrity." While Delgado thought that "in the end, no one—KK, the NMM, or the NPS—came out as a hero or the good guy," Kortum knew that heroes mattered less than preserving those ships and their culture. Some adversaries never forgave his alleged transgressions, but others have shown more balance. Kortum could come across as "egocentric, gruff, irascible, opinionated, [and] stubborn," Walter Rybka recalled, but he "was also warm hearted, generous, humorous, [and] eloquent." Unusual for his day, "he had a keen appreciation of beauty, craft, seamanship, and a large-minded poet's view of the maritime world." Said Naab in hindsight, "I'm glad I knew him." But Hyman resolved, "It is up to us to carry on."[71]

With him, a generation was passing. "I am a seafaring man," Kortum declared. "I loved every day I spent at sea. . . . I want to share it, so that other generations can respond the way I do." Like him, Newhall, who had died in 1992, felt that the "American culture as we've known it, is . . . disappearing rapidly." When rangers did not know port from starboard, Kortum mourned, as he also did watching San Francisco shipping migrate elsewhere, which was due in part to the policy of the same shippers who served on the Museum Association's board. In 1995, the Port of San Francisco operated at 3 percent of capacity. Tourism was, said Newhall, "the only thing that's kept [San Francisco] alive." But Nolte likened it to "industrial pollution." The loss of a working waterfront, said a union leader, made it "a one-dimensional city."[72]

With tourism, hopes brightened for Haslett. Though Thomas told the Museum Association that he would have liked "to tear it down," the NPS resurrected in 1996 a decade-old proposal to introduce a museum, visitor center, library, and archives. It wanted an entrepreneur to offset the $18.6 million cost and use the rest of the building. But when offered much less, the park kept only ten thousand feet, which became a Visitor Center funded by $2.5 million from the lease. The NMMA objected, claiming that the NPS was shorting the ships. Signed in 2000, the deal typified the era's lopsided public-private partnerships. The $40 million, 252-room Argonaut Hotel paid some $1 million annually for fifty-seven years. A guest said innocently, "How many hotels boast a National Park Service visitor center on the ground floor?" As the park receded into Fisherman's Wharf glitz, a guide sighed, "A lot of folks don't realize we're even here."[73] (See fig. 30.)

In 2002, Thomas retired, boasting that the hotel was "the largest historic leasing" in NPS history. Stressed out, he died in 2004, eliciting but one local newspaper tribute, and that from John Burton, an old friend, former congressman, and Phil's brother. Thomas's "first love was the sea," said state senator Burton. "His second [love] was politics. As superintendent of the [SFMNHP], he did an outstanding job of combining the two." A contrary view was offered, without media coverage, by the U.S. Office of Special Counsel (OSC). After investigating Hyman's complaint, the OSC concluded that Thomas had perpetrated "a lengthy pattern and practice of harassment and retaliation against a subordinate foreman who had disclosed to Members of Congress and the media, evidence of the superintendent's abuse of authority and gross mismanagement of the park's historical ships." Thomas privately called the OSC "the Gestapo of government." Once his guilt was decided, the law required his removal, but "in lieu of disciplinary action," he was allowed to retire. Had he appealed, the law required him to "pay his own attorney fees." Focusing only on Thomas, the OSC did not go up the NPS ladder. For Hyman, whose career was ruined, it was a "pyrrhic victory."[74]

The public knew nothing of the decision. Nor was there an open

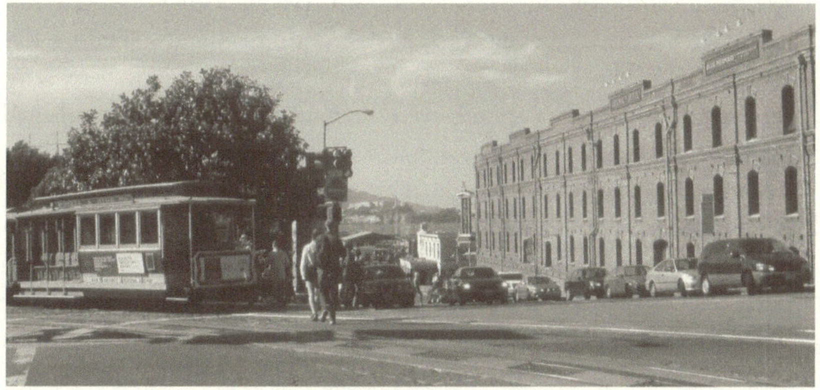

FIGURE 30. Hyde Street Cable Car Turnaround and Haslett Warehouse (with Argonaut Hotel and, at its left corner, the NPS Visitor Center). Alcatraz Island is in center background. *Photo by author, 2007.*

discussion of what went wrong or its remedy. Compounding the disarray, the Park Service replaced Thomas with Kate Richardson, a forest ranger from the Virginia woods. As one craftsman added, she wanted "to get the park in the NPS way." That meant reducing the museum, the library, and the number of curators and craftspeople. Her appointment led Hyman to complain, "There is not a single person in the Senior Management of this museum who has any experience with the restoration and preservation of historic vessels and they don't seek the advice of those who do have such experience."[75]

Addressed in the park's *General Management Plan* (1997), those ships required as much as $62 million. Two ships were listed as operational. First was *Hercules* (NHL, 1986). Submitting its historic structure report in 1990, Tri-Coastal Marine (formerly White Elephant Management) noted that the tug had not "been adequately stabilized" and "received little preservation funding." The surveyors recommended a $1.1 million restoration. Thanks to volunteer Harry E. Morgan, a lifelong chief engineer, its engine in 1991 was "running for the first time in 33 years." But Thomas fired Morgan for complaining about his mismanagement. Marking its centennial in 2007, *Hercules* was honored as "the only surviving steam-powered ocean tug in the United States." Second, the scow schooner *Alma* (NHL, 1988) was also operational. Maintained by the Friends of *Alma*, it even participated in the Master Mariners Regatta; it was the only extant vessel to have sailed in the original nineteenth-century event. After a three-year rebuild, it moved to Hyde Street in 1992. In 1993, Al Lutz, a retired chief bosun aboard USCG *Eagle*, became captain. Once *Alma* was USCG certified, Lutz trained a crew and regularly sailed, carrying cash-paying customers and attending Bay Area festivals.[76]

Meanwhile, *Wapama*'s friends were regrouping. No serious work had been done since 1990, and its estimated rebuilding exceeded $18 million (and by 2011, $61.4 million). In 1996, the newly formed Pacific Steam Schooner Foundation interceded. Headed by Rear Admiral Thomas Patterson (USMS, ret.), who had saved SS *Jeremiah O'Brien* (1943), the last unaltered Liberty Ship of World War II, the foundation needed $5 million to stabilize *Wapama* ashore under a roof. Knowing that the federal government had set aside $1.5 million to bury the toxic ship, Patterson asked (unsuccessfully) for help. The NPS scrapped the NHL-listed, last-of-its-kind *Wapama* in 2013. For Adrian Raynaud, its demise was "a heartbreaker."[77]

Eureka's fate was also in doubt. After a $2 million appropriation,

Representative Pelosi rechristened *Eureka* (NHL, 1985), but it was only hauled in late 1993, when a crew coppered and caulked its bottom until funds ran out. But, as the *Examiner* noted in 1996, its superstructure had "gaping holes," while the "passenger deck [was] a mess from uncaulked leaks." The NMMA raised funds by renting *Eureka*, and then *Balclutha*, for weddings and receptions, but the NPS ended the practice. Then, *Eureka* became the set for *Nash Bridges*, a CBS police action drama. Its star, Don Johnson, was looking for a place with, he said, a "beat-up look," and the ferry "was perfect." The rent ($210,000 by the third TV season), said a ranger, "couldn't have come at a better time." In 1999, *Eureka* was again hauled for $1 million in repairs, but its work was suspended because of scarce funds. With the discovery of past restoration errors and more neglect, its estimated repairs are, currently, as high as $30 million.[78]

Eppleton Hall's deferred maintenance had so exhausted Newhall's patience in 1992 that he endorsed its dry-berthing or transfer to a better steward. Two years later a lead arose when Mick Jagger of the Rolling Stones took interest. With his nine-year-old son, he dropped by Kortum's office. Though Karl "was not familiar with Mick's music," recalled David Hull, they talked about Jagger's "relatives in the fishing industry in England." Jagger later returned, called *Eppie* the "apple of his eye," but offered "no satisfaction." In 2010, the tug looked "as spruce as ever" from afar, said another English visitor, but close up, its neglect was obvious. Sightseers were "warned to keep away." For its centenary, *Eppie*'s hull was repaired, but it was closed to the public because of its problem-filled engine room and interior. Its future is uncertain.[79]

The sailing ships fared little better. When hauled in 1987–88, *Balclutha* became the first U.S. ship to illustrate "the new national standards for documenting historic vessels." But the NPS deferred its next dry-docking to 1998, when the NMMA mostly covered the $1.5 million bill for its main deck, foremast, and hull. The *San Francisco Chronicle* reminded the public that *Balclutha* was "a priceless artifact," not "a mere tourist attraction." It reportedly possessed "more original material than any museum ship in the world." Though it was billed as "the National Park Service's premier maritime resource," Steve Hyman asked if "the federal bureaucracy alone, subjected to the vagaries of political winds, will ensure her preservation." Skepticism was warranted. In 1996, the NPS had an overall $4.5 billion maintenance backlog; in 2017 it reached $11.9 billion.[80]

Debuting aboard *Balclutha*'s long-empty tween deck in 2005 was *Cargo*

Is King! It was billed as "a totally immersive environment, not [Kortum's former] exhibit gallery." Including simulated cargo and audiovisual displays, the exhibit reportedly showed visitors "how their own world [was] remarkably similar to the one this 19th century ship served by transporting cargoes that enriched the lives of people around the world." While such feel-good presentism was all too common at history museums, the display missed modern controversy, such as the increasing power of multinational corporations that were shifting global production, investment, and commerce, often to the detriment of those same "people around the world."[81]

Drawing more publicity was *Thayer*, "the last of a fleet of more than 400 West Coast lumber schooners." With its hull hogged, rotten middle mast removed, and timbers weakened by dry rot, it was taking on two feet of water daily; the bilge pump ran nonstop because twelve thousand students visited annually in the late 1990s. Finally, in 2004, it was moved to a seaplane hangar for restoration. By 2007, after nearly 85 percent of its original timbers had been replaced, the park reported that the $14 million work was "virtually unprecedented." But much work still awaited funding as of 2019. *Thayer*'s restoration won awards, but a debate ensued about its authenticity. Canright claimed that its integrity had been maintained, but Hyman disagreed, stating that without its realia, it was a poor replica.[82]

While the fleet deteriorated, the park was expanding. It acquired Municipal Pier in 2004, but its estimated repair bill was a jaw-dropping $68 million in 2010. It also launched a three-year, $13.8 million restoration of its Sala Burton Building. In 2006, thousands came for one last look because Richardson ordered that no artifact-based exhibits would be reinstalled. When completed, it was bare, and visitors angrily wrote in the guest book, "Where's the museum?" A half mile northward at Haslett's Visitor Center (also free), a long-term, interactive exhibit, *The Waterfront! Sailors Called It Frisco*, debuted in 2012. Curated by Richard Everett, the thirty-six-hundred-square-foot display had been announced in 2005 but awaited funding. Initially vetted by focus groups, it was mounted over a three-year span with a half-dozen re-created scenes and ambient sounds. Visitors encountered such old-time sights as Fisherman's Wharf, the Barbary Coast, and the pre-1940 Hunter's Point shipyards. At each, they heard recorded conversations, marveled at full-size artifacts, or inspected rare materials and photographs. To avoid using glass cases, designers tucked their 360 artifacts "into ship facades, store front windows, and even ship passengers' luggage." Showing the Port of San Francisco's decline, *The Waterfront!* included a film showing the 1201-foot containership *Fabiola* (2010) steaming "right by San Francisco on its way to Oakland." Like *Fabiola*, the sensation-filled *Waterfront!* was distant from *Balclutha* and its quiet tween deck, but it competed against Ripley's kitschy "Believe It or Not!" museum nearby.[83]

As the twelfth-most-visited NPS park, the SFMNHP drew 4.1 million visitors, of whom 30 percent were local. The Visitor Center encouraged sightseers to see Fort Mason's Maritime Research Center. But it is a mile away, inadequately staffed, and open only by appointment. Its J. Porter Shaw Library includes, among many holdings, John Lyman's materials, "the largest private collection in existence on Pacific maritime history." As "one of the four best libraries of commercial maritime history in the United States," it is aided by a friends group. But as Kortum had warned long ago, the NPS still fails to appreciate this unique resource.[84]

CONCLUSION: "THUS PASSES THE GLORY OF [SAN FRANCISCO'S] WORLD"

So, too, did Kortum's dream pass. Inspired by childhood memories, *Kaiulani*'s voyage, and Mystic Seaport's success, he was alarmed by the demise of the world's commercial sailing fleet. His SFMM and *Balclutha* showcased that past, as did the state park and fleet. By 1963, Aquatic Park berthed the world's largest museum fleet, though others later surpassed it. Along with Scott Newhall and David Nelson, he saved an endangered district that mixed fact, legend, and invention. Visitors learned of *Balclutha*'s global trade and realized that the nation's mythical western frontier had included sailors and distant empires. As ships swayed amid smells of tar, hemp, and saltwater, visitors found a lost world. Easing social and economic tensions, shippers and workers found common ground.

Kortum was a proud antimodernist. Set in Victoriana, he noted, "As a character reference I might point out that I have plowed with a horse, mowed with a scythe, and sailed around Cape Horn before the mast in a square-rigged ship." But he was no escapist. With Jean, he not only fought the construction of waterfront high-rises, freeways, and a nuclear power plant but also sought to remake San Francisco's strand in line with his history-minded, people-oriented interests. Said the *New York Times*, he "transformed the city's north waterfront." Yet his private museum and state park were not financially viable in the short term because the city and state failed to appreciate their long-term value. After Phil Burton stepped in,

City Hall, Sacramento, and the Museum Association donated their assets to the newly formed National Maritime Museum in 1976–78. But amid a record-breaking expansion, the Park Service was financially overwhelmed, bureaucratically resistant, and philosophically unprepared to govern its first-ever fleet and full-spectrum museum. Turmoil followed. With his high standards and even higher hopes, Kortum wanted *more* of what he started but slowly realized that the NPS was not his savior.[85]

Seeing the passing of an older maritime culture, Kortum acquired what the NPS calls its "largest museum collection," though it is now largely hidden in warehouses and underappreciated. Although the park is mandated to "preserve and interpret the history and achievements of seafaring Americans and of the Nation's maritime heritage, especially on the Pacific Coast," its implementation is constricted by the NPS's visitor center model and the lack of a meaningful acquisitions budget for collecting. Moreover, it has interpreted its mandate narrowly. By focusing on the century after the 1849 Gold Rush, the SFMNHP has tacitly made Kortum's museum *opening* in 1951 as its own *closing* date. Thus, the SFMNHP is hesitant to display and interpret the West Coast's more recent history, as production and commerce have shifted to distant corners of the Pacific Rim.[86]

Moreover, and like too many museums and preservation organizations, the NPS doesn't tell its own story well: how and why preservation began, and how that work was an act of interpretation subject to the era's cultural politics. It has even overlooked the preservationists; besides removing a 1950s *Balclutha* plaque that honored them, the park's curator of history ignored Kortum in a fiftieth-anniversary story on the ship's debut as a museum. While Phil Burton's statue commands Fort Mason's heights today, mention of Kortum is missing. Historian Alison Isenberg recently spotlighted Karl and Jean, however, in her book on the era's battles over San Francisco's landscape. In 1996, the Park Association honored Newhall by dedicating the veranda and a small exhibit at the Sala Burton Building. But a decade later, its plaque was "in ugly disrepair" and removed. At odds with the SFMM's founders, especially Kortum, the NPS has been reluctant to acknowledge anyone but the politicians who legislated the park. Today, most of the park's seventy-five employees have no memory of the full-spectrum museum. The Visitor Center, if practice prevails, will only revise its exhibits twenty-five to thirty-five years after their debut. Hence, the material and interpretation will grow stale over such a long span.[87]

Seeing the neglected plaque, Nelson lamented, "*Sic transit* [*gloria mundi*]." "Thus passes" also applied to the Port of San Francisco and its eight-mile waterfront. When Kortum spoke at the Bohemian Club in 1949, the port was facing stiff competition, but by the 1990s, it was, said former port director Tom Soules, "the only port in the country . . . willingly committing suicide" by ignoring its shipping. Newhall jabbed, "There are vast groups within our city here who do not relate to San Francisco as a maritime city at all." As such, the port's rise and fall begs for better historical explanation.[88]

Instead, San Franciscans were, by the 1990s, more susceptible to myth and romance. Herb Caen helped create the legendary San Francisco built before the Embarcadero Freeway. The town was, he joked, "full of nostalgics." The fabled city wrapped around Kortum's park and fleet. Looking for its "ghosts and legends," Caen admitted squinting "a bit on foggy nights at the *Balclutha*, imagining a masted forest of the waterfront." In 1997, his funeral procession ended, appropriately, at Aquatic Park. While Kortum believed that the nineteenth century was better in many respects, his *Balclutha* exhibits still undercut nostalgia, reminding all that sailors (like forests, whales, and other resources) had been exploited. That abuse did not end in 1951; it deserves a modern explanation.[89]

In its seven decades, San Francisco Maritime has undergone a major transition. Kortum was most interested in collecting artifacts. With a pathbreaking, multidisciplinary scope, he presented their technology, artistry, and humanity. As the world's fleet of old square-riggers dwindled to less than a score, he led the large-ship preservation movement worldwide. Standing above others in his field, he was a collector, campaigner, and advocate. In a different sphere, the NPS manages a wide-ranging empire. It speaks of being a good steward and educator, though its bureaucracy can be byzantine. When the NPS took over San Francisco's museum and fleet, Kortum's previous emphases were muted, but the transition to its own priorities was difficult and uneven. Although Kortum had underplayed educational programming, for example, the rangers prioritized it by often expanding the museum's focus on gender and ethnicity. Ideally, a museum or preservation organization should meld both approaches—that of the Kortums and the rangers—as it carries out its mission. But the Park Service is not only a massive government corporation with a distinct operating system but subject to Washington's changing paymasters and ideology. Thus, more than long-established private institutions, San Francisco Maritime, like ships in its fog-bound Bay, has a murky view of its fore and aft horizons.

CHAPTER 6

"THE STREET OF SHIPS"

Creating South Street Seaport

In 1963, while California was readying its maritime state park, three East Coast yachtsmen were persuading President John F. Kennedy to endorse a privately funded sideshow at the 1964 New York World's Fair. The expo was designed to spotlight emerging technologies bridging the planet, but these seamen wanted to honor the sailing ships and culture that had first bridged global markets. Operation Sail's procession of twenty-three tall ships was, declared the *New York Times*, "a spectacle probably never [to] be repeated"; its crews were feted in a grand ticker tape parade. But Op Sail was insignificant to JFK's Texan successor, who "stirred indignation" by ignoring his invitation. Others were dreaming, however, of a sea revival because, as sailing enthusiast Kennedy had said, a windship fostered "strong, disciplined, and venturesome men."[1]

Peter Stanford turned dreams into action. He had been "a seadog since the age of two," noted *Time* magazine, and at fifteen published his first of seven essays in the U.S. Naval Academy's *Proceedings*. In October 1965, the thirty-eight-year-old advertising executive and his bride, Norma, walked about San Francisco's Ghirardelli Square and Fisherman's Wharf. They were most impressed by Karl Kortum's privately run museum and its state park offshoot. Entranced by the schooner *C. A. Thayer*, Peter imagined "taking an old sailing ship to sea." Seeing the "brilliant" displays aboard the square-rigged *Balclutha*, he confessed: "We were swept off our feet." They took home "the idea of a New York sea museum."[2]

Early in 1966, as New York's harbor was being overtaken by West Coast ports, state legislators in Albany kindled interest in shipping by passing a bill to create a New York State Maritime Museum. Taken by surprise, the Stanfords then founded the privately run South Street Seaport Museum (SSSM), thus imitating Kortum's model of private and public museums side by side. The Stanfords wanted their museum to collect old ships to recall Gotham's once-dominant global commerce and to revitalize Lower Manhattan's decrepit East River waterfront. As middle-class residents were fleeing the city for suburbia, moreover, they cast their SSSM as a community-building movement. Unlike any other U.S. historical society, they declared, "This museum *is* people." But their consultants worried about the project's financing and suggested copying revenue-minded Mystic Seaport.

All the while, the SSSM was pulled into the cutthroat world of Gotham real estate. Seeing an opportunity to oust the shabby Fulton Fish Market, City Hall wanted to monetize its blocks around the early nineteenth-century Schermerhorn Row, where the state had proposed locating its museum. Designating the Seaport as sponsor of an urban renewal district, the city cast the museum as its proxy. One mile to the west, meanwhile, the 110-story Twin Towers of the World Trade Center were rising; in counterpoint, the block-long Schermerhorn Row was the city's oldest trade center. The two became pivots for Lower Manhattan's economic rebirth. The Seaport basked in the spotlight. But its arc dimmed after a real estate crash in 1972 thwarted a planned gift to the museum of over fifty revenue-earning buildings. Nearly insolvent, the SSSM was reportedly rescued when City Hall acquired those properties and leased them back to the organization. The district's landscape would thereafter be shaped by City Hall's agenda.

In 1975, as New York City and New York State were facing their own bankruptcies, however, they hurriedly capitalized the district to generate revenue. Albany abandoned plans for its still-undeveloped state museum, and City Hall, following the lead of businessmen who had taken over the SSSM, promoted a developer's plan to build a festival marketplace. Inspired by Ghirardelli Square, the James Rouse Company swayed its many skeptics by predicting that the profits of its mall would bankroll the museum; it promised further to protect the district's maritime authenticity. Championed by Mayor Ed Koch, Rouse's New Fulton Market (1983) and Pier 17 mall (1985) were spectacular but ephemeral hits. The museum received none of the promised bounty, while its district was swamped by glitz, which many

New Yorkers mocked but lured Donald Trump to propose (unsuccessfully) building the world's tallest tower there.

A dilemma ensued. The Seaport Museum had rescued a ten-block historic district and amassed the nation's largest fleet of historic commercial vessels, but its finances were precarious. Slowly, it rebounded in the 1990s, largely through educational programs that made it the city's third most popular history museum. But it was then floored by the terrorist attacks of 2001, its own administrative dysfunction, and Superstorm Sandy in 2012. After two Republican mayors tried to sink the museum, it stood at death's door. Only with a renewed citizens' movement, a political shift in 2014, and an improving economy has the museum begun to glimpse a better future.

"A RECREATIONAL ACTIVITY WITH A SOCIAL GOOD": CREATING "A STREET OF SHIPS" ON THE EAST RIVER

In the early 1960s Lower Manhattan was on the cusp of change. Its kingpin, Chase Manhattan Bank's David Rockefeller, wanted to replace its dreary East River warehouses with financial and trade exchanges. In the decayed blocks occupied by the 140-year-old Fulton Fish Market, he planned in 1960 to build there, under the auspices of the Port Authority of New York and New Jersey, a World Trade Center. But New Jersey instead demanded (and got) a Hudson River site. Still, Rockefeller's Downtown Lower Manhattan Association (DLMA) and City Hall planned to redevelop the Fish Market district. Instead, in 1966 Peter and Norma Stanford wanted to create a "historical marine park" with "old sailing-ship hulls," as in San Francisco. They called the Fish Market's docks "the last enjoyable bit" of the waterfront. As bulldozers razed a nearby area, they organized their campaign.[3]

Like a ship heading for the same port, state senator Whitney North Seymour Jr. had long been interested in the area. A lawyer with roots in Wall Street and historic preservation, he focused on saving Schermerhorn Row (1811–12). Built in the vernacular Federal style as countinghouses and warehouses on Fulton Street, it was Manhattan's largest and oldest intact block. With his proposed legislation in early 1966, the worn-down Row was to be rehabilitated as the New York State Maritime Museum. His proposal "caught Norma and me by surprise," Peter recalled. It also, added Seymour, "met with strong opposition from a real-estate group headed by powerful banking interests led by [Governor Nelson Rockefeller's] own brother," David.[4]

While David wanted to erect a "huge insurance complex" on the Row's land, he also suggested creating a park, like his father's Colonial Williamsburg, with relocated antique buildings around the Revolution's famed (but reconstructed) Fraunces Tavern a half mile away. Rockefeller's DLMA threatened Seymour, who sought help from Ada Louise Huxtable, architecture critic of the *New York Times*. Though surprised by the DLMA letter and "the violence of [its] attack," she was outraged by the park's fakery. Deriding the DLMA as "totally archaic in its viewpoint and real-estate oriented in its programs," she suggested instead that New York emulate New Bedford's preserved riverfront. Governor Rockefeller signed Seymour's bill, but only after its funding had been stripped. In late 1966, the Stanfords melded their proposal with Seymour's unfunded effort by forming a citizen-based Friends group.[5]

Historic preservation, meanwhile, was expanding its focus. Unlike Rockefeller's invented park or Seymour's indoor museum, the Stanfords wanted to re-create, Norma wrote, "a scene that once existed." Their "street of ships" would highlight real vessels and extant buildings on paving-stoned lanes. When critics worried about funding, however, Frederick L. Rath Jr., a founder of the National Trust for Historic Preservation, conjectured that "an urban Mystic Seaport" with eateries, shops, and active piers would be a solution. Huxtable endorsed the idea. By emphasizing architectural diversity, actual streetscapes, and working neighborhoods, she was challenging the connoisseur tradition in historic preservation, which prioritized buildings associated with great men and events. She was able, Peter said, "to disarm Rockefeller our most dangerous opponent."[6]

Active in the good-government City Club, Peter took fulltime leadership of the movement and predicted that the district would become "a recreational activity with a social good" for a million sightseers annually. Realizing that the demolition (1963–66) of the once-glorious Pennsylvania Station showed what the *Times* called the city's "tin-horn culture," a cadre of reformers, yachtsmen, and everyday citizens joined his cause. But City Hall's urban planners snubbed the Row. That tired not only Huxtable but Peter, who called them "snobs and belle lettristes." Moreover, Mystic Seaport, which relied on Gotham money, looked askance at this upstart. Yet maritime historians Robert G. Albion, Howard Chapelle, John Lyman, and Karl Kortum joined as advisers. Stanford also won over Frank Braynard, who had helped persuade JFK to back Op Sail and became "the dean of ocean liner history." Albany chartered Stanford's Seaport Museum on April 28, 1967, while the unfunded State Museum lived only on paper.[7]

Offering to help was Eric Ridder, an Olympic gold medal–winning sailor and publisher of the *Journal of Commerce*. But he warned, "No matter how you slice it, this venture is going to take a lot of money." He introduced Stanford to Jakob Isbrandtsen, a maverick shipping tycoon who was worth, according to *Forbes*, $125 million, but "held sway over $900 million worth of assets." He liked Stanford's concept because those East River piers had once berthed his fleet. As Stanford's "prize catch," Isbrandtsen became the Seaport's decade-long chairman. Pushing containerized shipping and thus undermining the old port that Stanford idealized, Isbrandtsen resembled earlier antimodernists by prospering in the new economy but finding reassurance in an older culture.[8]

Demolition threatened their old port. In the thirty-eight-acre Brooklyn Bridge Southeast Urban Renewal Area, the Friends focused on saving Schermerhorn Row and its adjacent blocks. As director of Mayor John Lindsay's Office of Lower Manhattan Development, Richard Buford, for example, favored Stanford's proposed purchase of old four- and five-story buildings near the Row, which would be funded by selling their air rights to permit construction of nearby high-rises for Wall Street's workforce. At his request, the museum issued *A Proposal to Recreate the Historic "Street of Ships"* in July 1967. Incorporated into Lindsay's Manhattan Landing Plan, the *Proposal* won broad political support, especially after the U.S. Conference of Mayors called preservation a tool for economic development. But, short of funds, Lindsay designated the museum as the *un*assisted sponsor of the Urban Renewal Area, the first such designation for a U.S. museum. Hence, it was expected to raise its own capital. Such "renewal" was, said a later scholar, the "knife-edge" of neoliberal urbanism, whereby private enterprise was expected to achieve city-sponsored goals. Richard Weinstein, who succeeded Buford, called the seaport "a business area" ripe for redevelopment. Along with David Rockefeller, whose park proposal had collapsed, Lindsay thus cast the museum as their proxy to introduce amenities for residents and tourists. As the Twin Towers broke ground in 1966, topped out in 1973, and represented Lower Manhattan's future, Schermerhorn Row symbolized its past. "Without the Rockefellers," sociologist Robert Fitch concluded, there would have been "no South Street Seaport. No World Trade Center."[9]

Their plans hinged on the Row, whose fate marked changing perspectives on whether owners had the right to demolish what the public regarded as its inheritance. Owned by influential developers Sol Atlas and John McGrath, it faced poor odds because old buildings nearby were falling like dominoes. Moreover, the newly empowered Landmarks Preservation Commission (LPC) was hampered by the connoisseur tradition. But with Lindsay's and Rockefeller's blessing and the Friends' popular support, the LPC designated the Row a landmark on October 29, 1968. While the legality of the city's landmarks law was being adjudicated, the developers cut a deal to save the Row, thus leaving the U.S. Supreme Court to affirm the law's constitutionality in *Penn Central v. City of New York* (1978).

The district's meaning was also being negotiated. In 1968, the Seaport's principal benefactor, the J. M. Kaplan Fund, called a planning conference to explore the issues. In a keynote address, Daniel Patrick Moynihan, who was crafting neoliberalism at a Harvard think tank, pictured the museum as an anchor in a storm-wracked society. Helping the museum was "not just a matter of cultural interest," he said, but of "concern for social stability." Yet the conference itself became stormy over the means to that end. While Stanford proposed returning the district architecturally to the sailing-ship era (1790s–1870s), others favored real preservation and authenticity. Moreover, Kortum and Chapelle suggested filling the planned state museum with artifacts, especially vernacular items ignored by connoisseurs. That was too much for John Hightower, head of the state's arts council, who retorted that it "should not be a club or warehouse for the wealthy or for scholars." A local businessman offered a counterpoint. "A museum *is* people," Joe Cantalupo suggested. "If the people don't go for this," he declared, "we might as well wrap it up." His declaration was rare within U.S. museums, but it became the Seaport's mantra.[10]

Acquiring a fleet was a priority. Kortum urged Peter Stanford to get "at least three large, deepwater, square-rigged ships." Both wanted the U.S.-built *Kaiulani* (1899). After Stanford expressed interest in the Fish Market's schooners, however, Kortum chided him: "Schooners are just spear carriers for square-riggers, which are divas." Yet, as in Greek mythology, divas sang the siren's song that drew ships to dangerous shoals; likewise, preservationists would realize that the bigger the ship, the bigger the headache. Still, any collection was a matter of chance, and its first ship became *Ambrose*, *LV87* (1908), a lightship that had marked the harbor's

Ambrose Channel but was discarded by the U.S. Coast Guard (USCG). For *Ambrose*'s debut in 1970, Stanford invited David Rockefeller, who bestowed the DLMA's imprimatur and called the museum "an important part of a vital and growing Lower Manhattan." Reciprocating, the museum participated in his World Trade Week.[11]

Next came the 125-foot *Lettie G. Howard* (1893), which was, said Stanford, "a remarkably graceful survivor of the vanished [Fish Market] schooner fleet." While Gloucester, Massachusetts, had acquired the schooner and hoped to center a museum round the partially restored, two-masted, gaff-rigged ship, its financial plan failed. Purchased with Isbrandtsen funds, *Lettie* sailed instead to the SSSM in 1968. After insurers forbade *Lettie* to sail, however, it displayed the crew's quarters and photographs from *Men, Fish and Boats* (1934), authored by Peter Stanford's father, Alfred. A second schooner, the 102-foot *Pioneer* (1885), arrived from Gloucester in 1970. Built as a wrought iron–hulled sloop for a Delaware River iron works, it was rerigged as a schooner in 1895 but repeatedly modified. Abandoned in 1966, it was restored by Russell Grinnell Jr., who descended from the New Bedford owners of the clipper *Flying Cloud*. After his death, *Pioneer* was spurned by Mystic Seaport because it was "replated, rerigged with non-authentic material, [and] the stern reconfigured." So the family donated funds to South Street to buy it for sail training. Grinnell's nephew, George Matteson III, captained *Pioneer* and became a trustee and benefactor. It was "the only remaining American-built iron sailing vessel" and the only USCG-certified ship owned by South Street for years.[12]

Mentored by Kortum, Stanford shared his belief that the yards of three square-riggers would "begin to catch the pier side mood of South Street as it exists in legend." As adventurer Irving Johnson proselytized "the religion of sail" and Kortum the square-rigger movement, Stanford became their disciple. For them, a square-rigger symbolized a world apart from modernity, whether in its daily work, craftsmanship, character building, or struggle with nature. They searched worldwide for them. Although wooden clippers and Down Easters had been lost, few of the more than three thousand iron- or steel-hulled merchant square-riggers survived of those launched in the British Isles before 1907.[13]

One of those square-riggers was *Wavertree* (1885). In 1966, Kortum found the disfigured hulk, shorn of its rigging and main mast and remade as a sand barge, near a Buenos Aires "slaughterhouse, floating in a veritable sea of lanolin which coated and protected her hull." Knowing that such ships had been lost in standard histories, just as sailors had been stereotyped as Jack-tar, Stanford recast them as globalizing the economy and society. *Wavertree*, *Balclutha*, and their kin, he said, "made history at the most basic level, moving the cargoes and people, and ultimately the ideas that shaped the world we know today." When launched in Southampton, however, *Wavertree* was already an anachronism: built of iron, not steel, and loaded by hand, not steam winch. In a traditional design, it was rigged with single, not double, topgallants. As such, it was labor intensive and dangerous. With 31,495 square feet of canvas and a 140-foot mainmast, said Captain Alan Villiers, "those ghastly deep topgallant sails, that brute of a great mainsail, and the enormous foresail were hell to set and murder to take in again." Still, it was "a *real* ship with a *real* history," Kortum told Stanford, because it had tramped between ports, including Gotham, on six continents and was dismasted in a Cape Horn gale in 1910. "This is the stuff of which sea romance is made."[14] (See fig. 31.)

Isbrandtsen funded *Wavertree*'s purchase. To ready it for a six-thousand-mile tow, the museum ran up a $290,000 bill at an Argentine navy shipyard. Its inability to pay, however, led the U.S. ambassador to warn: "There would be an international lawsuit embarrassing to the national interest." The brewer Rudolph J. Schaefer III and commodities dealer Jack R. Aron helped financially. Becoming front-page news, it arrived on August 11, 1970, which Lindsay proclaimed as *Wavertree* Day. He called it "the largest museum artifact ever brought to New York in one piece." Villiers headlined the effort, as he had done with San Diego's *Star of India*. For decades his sailing books and *National Geographic* essays had intrigued audiences, including a young Stanford and Kortum. He lectured repeatedly, hoping to foil the "schemes of real estate operators" who wanted East River high-rises, not square-riggers. Yet he idealized such ships, claiming that they had "sailed in peace under God," while missing the fact that *Wavertree*, like others, had carried nitrates for explosives. Sailor Archie Horka similarly believed that the "hard and inhuman" work "drew men to it, real men." Another admitted, however, that "all the hardships have slowly faded from my mind, leaving the proverbial 'Romance of the Sea' as a legacy from those far-off days."[15]

Realizing that what visitors saw was inscrutable, inaccurate, or off-message, the Seaport resolved that *Wavertree* "should be correctly restored and rerigged." Isbrandtsen estimated a five-year, $1 million effort, but it took much more to accomplish. The restoration generated so much friction between Stanford and Isbrandtsen, moreover, that Stanford pressed his

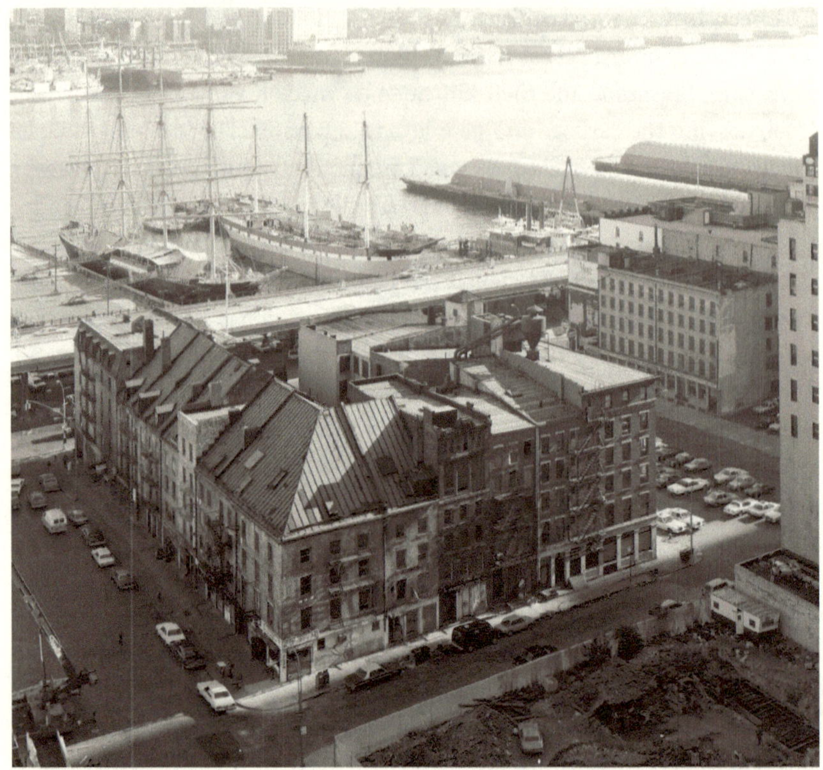

FIGURE 31. Schermerhorn Row (prerestoration), Fulton Street (left) and Burling Slip (also known as John Street, right). *Peking* is docked at Pier 16 (left) and *Wavertree* at Pier 15. Note the working waterfront across the East River in Brooklyn. Historic American Buildings Survey, 1976. *Courtesy of the Prints and Photographs Division, Library of Congress.*

board of trustees (unsuccessfully) to hire Kortum in 1972 to direct the work. Upon Kortum's recommendation, the museum hired ship historian Norman J. Brouwer and restoration manager Richard A. Fewtrell, who admitted, "No other ship I know of has been this far dismantled and brought back to sailing condition."[16]

Meanwhile, the Seaport added to its fleet the ferry *Maj. Gen. William H. Hart* (1925), the steamer *Alexander Hamilton* (1924), and the square-rigged *Moshulu* (1904). The Seaport typically acted as a shelter of last resort and worked with partners to keep ships from the breakers. Piers 15–18 were jammed, *Boating*'s Dick Rath griped, but if Stanford found another ship, "Peter would get it anyway." Yet, after the city discarded *Hart*, Seaport volunteers arranged its donation to the SSSM, recalled Matteson, "without any formal consent from the museum leadership." It arrived during a festival so that Lindsay, who was decked out in boating attire, created photo ops directing *Hart*'s docking and taking *Wavertree*'s wheel, thus giving credence to the Seaport's sanctioned role.[17]

The Seaport developed a partnership for the privately owned *Hamilton* in 1972. As the Atlantic Coast's last large sidewheel steamer, its work for the Hudson River Day Line ended in 1971. Its triple-expansion, inclined engine was, said an old-timer, "a sight never to be forgotten." Encouraged by City Hall, the museum partnered with California-based Specialty Restaurants. But the company failed to deliver promised repairs because, as the young son of the firm's president told the press, "I think this boat's a wreck!" *Hamilton*'s departure and decline clouded ship preservation over the next five years. Proposing the creation of a National Trust for the Preservation of Historic Ships in 1975, Senator Edward Kennedy urged action for *Hamilton*, *Kaiulani*, and others, but the existing National Trust fought the bill. In 1977, *Hamilton* sank at a New Jersey pier during a gale.[18]

As the Seaport considered saving the square-rigged *Charles Cooper* (1856) in the Falklands, a national debate ensued. *WoodenBoat* editor Peter Spectre blasted those who were "merely jerking [such ships] out of a backwater and putting them on display, hoping somehow that everything will come out OK in the end." As restorer of the bark *Elissa* (1877), which was retrieved from Grecian waters with the help of Kortum and Stanford, Galveston's Walter Rybka acknowledged that "most ship saves are started by ardent preservationists with little grasp of the technical problems." If they knew the issues beforehand, "they would be too discouraged to make the attempt." Still, he sighed, "You win some and you lose some."[19]

Hoping to profit from the shipboard dining fad, Specialty Restaurants bought *Moshulu* from the Walt Disney Company. Reaching "a tentative 20-year lease" with the Seaport, it brought the 335-foot steel barque, which was "one of the world's best known sailing ships," to South Street with much hoopla in 1972. The restaurant idea ran aground, however, as city inspectors debated, "Was it a building or a vessel?" After a bank loan failed, the lease fell through. "Many wept when she left" for Philadelphia, where Specialty cut windows to create a tween-deck dining space. It became a "four-masted salad barque," a craftsman joked.[20]

In 1975, the museum gained a different four-masted barque, *Peking* (1911). Donated by trustee Jack Aron, who with his son Peter established major Seaport collections in the fine arts and scrimshaw, *Peking* was built for the Cape Horn nitrate trade by Ferdinand Laeisz & Co. of Hamburg. In 1932 an English school for indigent boys, which later included Richard Fewtrell, purchased the renamed *Arethusa II* as a stationary ship. But the school moved ashore and consigned it to auction. Because *Wavertree* was an unrestored mess, Aron wanted to showcase *Peking* for the U.S. Bicentennial. Knowing that Seaport trustees were "scared to death of taking on another vessel," he created Peking Joint Venture representing his foundation and the museum; it placed the only bid of £70,000 ($165,000), which equaled its scrap value, and funded its preparation for a trans-Atlantic tow. Welcomed in November 1975, it was, said the *New York Times*, "roughly equivalent to the Metropolitan Museum of Art's finally acquiring a passionately sought-after Rembrandt." Yet, Rembrandts numbered in the thousands, while there were "perhaps 10 sailing ships her size left in the world." Taking the main berth at Pier 16, *Peking* pushed *Wavertree* to Pier 15, jeopardized its under-funded work, and angered Isbrandtsen, who claimed that the board had not been consulted.[21]

Peking became best known for a 1929 film shot by Irving Johnson in a Cape Horn gale. Inspired by Jack London's novels, he had signed on as a tourist for a voyage of eleven thousand miles. His book, *Round the Horn in a Square-Rigger* (1932), and later film, Peking *Battles Cape Horn*, defined the barque. Trimmed to ten minutes, the film with his taped commentary was continuously shown aboard *Peking* after 1980. Seeing it was "a must," said a reviewer, as it "makes all other kinds of sailing look like child's play." Mobbed by admirers at the Seaport, Johnson was, like Villiers, a living legend. Struck by the resilience of Cape Horn sailors, he contrasted their lives with the dependency of modern society. What he learned was "to lean forward into life." *Peking*'s rescue gave him a sense of permanence. "Can you imagine," he asked, "greater satisfaction to a sailor than having his old Cape Horner saved from the ship breakers?"[22]

Rounding out its fleet, the museum acquired the seventy-two-foot steam tug *Mathilda* (1899) and the steam lighter *New York Central No. 29* (1912). Tugs and lighters were the harbor's everyday work boats, but *Mathilda*, which was donated in 1970 by McAllister Towing Company, was an oddity because it had spent seventy years in Canada's fresh waters. It even flew a tattered Canadian flag, which was saved "by patching its frayed edge with a remnant of the perfect color red underwear." Not surprisingly, Canadians griped. Neglected, *Mathilda* sank at its berth in 1976, a week after *Hart*'s main engine room also flooded. With its smokestack almost submerged, *Mathilda* became the wrong kind of headline. The McAllisters coaxed the Seaport to send it to the Hudson River Maritime Museum as a shore exhibit. A sad fate also met *New York Central No. 29*, which was renamed *Aqua* and was "the last operating" steam lighter. Fearing that its weak hull would fail, the Seaport removed its prized Scots marine boiler and scrapped it. But, said historian Brouwer, there was no subsequent "effort to save the boiler."[23]

Despite the setbacks, "the most significant thing SSSM was doing in the early '70's," boasted carver Michael Creamer, "was saving ships. Period. Public awareness of the city's history right in your face; not hidden away in a glass display case" at the uptown Museum of the City of New York. Its eleven vessels represented "the largest historic fleet [then] assembled by any museum." But it had the largest headaches too. In 1976, Stanford confessed, "I am quite ready to step aside from what I regard as a deteriorating and sadly unseamanlike scene." He was rethinking Kortum's warning that "the ship end of things comes out second" when buildings took precedence. Manhattan land schemes, which were expected to fund his ships, had instead become the major threat.[24]

"SALVATION ON THE EAST RIVER": HOW A BLUE-COLLAR CULTURE WAS CHANGED

After Sol Atlas failed to block the Row's historical landmarking, he "wished us good luck with our hysterical buildings," Isbrandtsen joked. But he was not laughing when his strategy of buying nearby blocks for the museum began to unravel. He had huge loans, interest, and legal bills. The Seaport expected that the air rights would sell quickly to pay off the loans. But the city's bureaucracy stalled. Proposed in mid-1969, the sale was authorized only in 1973. Meanwhile, Manhattan's construction boom went bust when the World Trade Center came online and interest in the air rights evaporated. Stanford admitted, "I honestly don't think our own people understood" what to do.[25]

Intending to donate all or most of those properties to the museum, so as to generate revenue, Isbrandtsen had secretly purchased them through his Seaport Holdings, Inc. Meanwhile, his shipping empire was quaking, and shareholders forced his resignation in June 1971. *Forbes* asked, "Was Isbrandtsen siphoning off money?" His stake in the seaport district ran as high as $17 million because he had paid dearly for what the *Times* called "the most valuable commercial property in the world." Begging the banks to "make an investment in the port and buy the air rights," Stanford admitted to Kortum that "the bureaucratic and banking support for South Street of course flows from the Manhattan Landing project." The city also wanted the seaport as the Bicentennial's center stage; its designation, said Richard Weinstein, "would be like a hunting license to go after Federal funds."[26]

In 1972, New York State, a half-dozen banks, and City Hall saved the Seaport. The *Daily News* claimed that it would "not cost the taxpayers a penny," but the city bonded $8 million for its role. First, Lindsay purchased the Row and its entire block from Atlas-McGrath for its original cost of $3 million; in 1974 the city gave it to the museum, which resold it to New York State. Second, the banks and City Hall worked on the debt of Seaport Holdings. After the museum agreed "to pay $6 million to the banks," the banks bought the air rights. Isbrandtsen suffered big losses. Because the public knew few details, museum trustees could vote that the "land held by Mr. Isbrandtsen for Museum use, and further land purchased by the banks, will be donated to the City of New York." With more strings than the New York Philharmonic, the donation put a positive spin on a bailout in which the weakened museum became a lessee, not a landowner. The two-inch-thick agreement, which evolved from the 1969 air rights proposal, was completed in 1973. It was, said Lindsay, "the most complex lease" he had ever signed. In it, the city granted a ninety-nine-year lease to the museum, which retained its designation as developer of Isbrandtsen's former holdings and the waterfront (Piers 16, 17, and 18 and 15's north side). In 1978, a ten-block, three-pier area was designated as a historic district.[27]

That still-gritty neighborhood attracted a diverse lot as the Seaport shifted more to community development. With its mantra of "This Museum *Is* People," the SSSM included poet Allen Ginsberg reciting Walt Whitman, songster Pete Seeger encouraging reform, author Joseph Mitchell telling stories of the old port, and the museum promoting Earth Day every day. The Seaport mixed "crowds of suburbanites and public housing dwellers" with "hard hats and hippies." The *Times* approved, as on a July 1971 evening when a folk singer at Pier 16 drew an audience sitting on blankets and newspapers. As they joined a chorus, an editor felt an epiphany shared by many who worried that Gotham was hemorrhaging with social conflict and being smothered by soulless skyscrapers. Across the river, he saw a neon sign of the Jehovah's Witnesses that flickered "The Dead shall rise." He experienced his own "Salvation on the East River." "For a fleeting hour," he wrote, "one small segment of this great, troubled city was in harmony with itself, and with nature. It was the kind of experience that can help make New York more human and livable again."[28]

Seeger was a regular feature. Drawing three thousand fans at his first songfest in August 1967, he embraced controversy. In 1968, with over a half-million U.S. troops in Vietnam, he filled "the streets with peaceable antiwar songs." Conservatives griped, but Seeger remembered being reassured by Joe Cantalupo, who "came up and shook my hand warmly," saying, "We mustn't ever forget such things around here." The establishment soon joined. In 1969, for example, Seeger arrived in his newly launched *Clearwater*, a replica of a nineteenth-century Hudson River sloop designed to raise environmental awareness. At the tiller was Lindsay; all were singing chanteys. Drawing big crowds for two Earth Day concerts, Seeger served as the honorary chairman of the museum's first Environment Week in 1970. He beamed, South Street was "a nice informal place" with spirited people. A *Times* writer added that its "vision of love and joy and passion for life" seemed "to consume the museum's workers." Likewise performing regularly was the Seaport's X Seamens Institute. Heading the foursome was guitarist Bernie Klay, who, with John Townley on mandolin and concertina, belted out sailors' songs. Klay was reeducating listeners because, he said, most "people lead aimless lives, waiting for the television, the newspaper, for someone else to pleasure them." Instead, "people that learn folk arts and singing can always pleasure themselves." Performers also sang, as Stanford recalled, "a good mix of black liberation stuff which we welcomed as expressing the concerns of the day—AND because it was great music."[29]

The museum also promoted art and history. Held in 1972, for example, the Ninth Annual Avant Garde Show drew two hundred artists and eight thousand people to Pier 16. Yoko Ono installed a "conceptual sculpture," while Ay-O chose to hang, instead of signal flags on *Hamilton*'s rigging, "hundreds of pairs of women's lavender panties." Seeing the lingerie, Norma Stanford said, "I blew my stack." Celebrity George Plimpton had suggested the show, which Braynard approved because he believed that everyone should "be open-minded." That applied to Charlotte Moorman, who once played her cello bare breasted. At Pier 16, she donned a Day-Glo diving suit, and as photographers yelled "Push her down," she played her instrument submerged in a tank. The *Village Voice*'s Annette Kuhn lamented the "shallow avant-garde scene" but was thrilled by "the ship itself." Also, to present the district's history, the museum hired preservationist Ellen Fletcher

Rosebrock. First highlighting vernacular architecture, she added a grassroots look at its workers, sailors, and shopkeepers. As the Sidewalk History Project explored everything from "Waterfront Dives" to "Warehouse Cats," Norma wanted people "to see themselves as part of the stream of history" and thereby reverse her era's alienation.[30]

For the U.S. Bicentennial, New York hosted Op Sail 76, which was coordinated by Braynard, first through the Seaport and then independently. It showcased an eighteen-mile-long parade with 228 sailing ships, another eight hundred craft, and fifty-three naval units. It was viewed by over five million onshore. "Almost single-handedly," according to *Newsday*, Braynard "saved the Bicentennial from banal commercialism and gave America the most meaningful observance of its independence by far." But the Cold War almost froze East Bloc participation. Regretting the U.S.-USSR rift, Braynard said, "When people are at sea, you don't ask them what their politics are, you ask how they hoist their sail." Op Sail's inclusion of the USSR's *Kruzenshtern* (formerly *Padua*, 1926), which was aided by Walter Cronkite's personal diplomacy, created "a little bit of a crack in the Cold War." More contentious, and recurring in Op Sail 86, was the inclusion of Chile's *Esmeralda* (1953). After a U.S.-backed coup toppled Chile's democratic government in 1973, scores of political prisoners were tortured onboard. At *Pioneer*'s helm in the 1976 parade, Walter Rybka knew, however, that the regatta's sailors were "a pretty apolitical lot."[31]

Meanwhile, the Seaport's democratic movement was under attack as its board reverted to "yachtsmen and suburbanites." Objecting to "This Museum *Is* People," they derided Stanford's open process, while City Hall insisted on corporate-style leadership. The attack was led by James "Brass Knuckles" Shepley, chief operating officer of Time-Life. "He was truly a force of nature," said later museum president Christopher Lowery, and he "spoke in a perpetual growl that perfectly complemented his persona." He was well connected to City Hall, Albany, and Washington. In 1974 Shepley displaced Stanford (who became titular president) with his own appointee; in 1976 he pushed Isbrandtsen aside for a surrogate chairman.[32]

Shepley remade the struggling museum by introducing a hierarchical structure and accelerating development. But he worsened its finances, and his managers, including Buford, polarized the museum. "Everyone was expected to take sides," program director Philip Yenawine recalled. "The content people, historians, designers, educators, writers, basically sided with Peter," but "the board, funders, and the city sided with Buford; the power came to reside there." In 1976, the board axed Stanford, who fled across the East River to his National Maritime Historical Society. Shepley replaced Buford with John Hightower, a Rockefeller family protégé who had been fired at the Museum of Modern Art. The board asked Melvin Conant for advice. Blasting Stanford, the Fortune 500 executive argued that every "program, asset, and opportunity" must pass "three *inseparable* tests . . . *Tangibility, Fundability, Manageability*," which was to ask, does it relate to the whole, is it financially doable, and is it workable? He suggested downsizing the fleet and properties, hiring "a *manager–fund-raiser* with skills in *development* and *administration*," and replacing the volunteer staff with professionals to gain "Museum accreditation." That corporate model was the antithesis of the Friends' participatory democracy, but Conant warned that the Seaport was "in danger." Perhaps "in peril."[33]

Seeger claimed that Stanford was sacked, however, "for being more interested in boats than boutiques," because "business people wanted to make more money off the place." Shepley was a close friend of James Rouse, who, inspired by Ghirardelli Square, opened Boston's Faneuil Hall Marketplace (also known as Quincy Market) in 1976. With Mayor Ed Koch (1978–89), Shepley and Rouse predicted that the Seaport's empty coffers would be filled by a mall's profits. Hightower conjectured that the district would "become the most exciting and perhaps the largest development project in the City of New York," attracting up to thirty-five million visitors annually. Shepley put Rouse on *Time*'s cover, calling him the savior of depressed cities. The National Trust concluded that a festival marketplace would generate "the critical mass of visitors that [the museum] needs to survive." But a member of Community Board No. 1 predicted that "the museum [was] likely to become a sideshow."[34]

As the Seaport focused on developing a mall, its red ink was aggravated by the costly, unpredictable nature of ship preservation. Rescuing deteriorated ships, it had gathered a fleet quickly, but money was elusive. "The philosophy of maintaining these ships," Stanford said in 1976, "has been to try to make one or two fit for public presentation—and keep the rest in safe storage, against the day that they could be funded and brought up." But safe storage was difficult for ships in the water requiring regular maintenance. In 1979, for example, *Lettie* was "the last surviving" U.S.-flagged Fredonia schooner, but it was "rotten to the core," and the Seaport offered "to give it to anyone who would restore it." No one stepped forward. *Ambrose* was every bit as bad, as Spectre discovered in 1980. Said the former Coastie, it was "a discredit to the Coast Guard and an embarrassment to former and present servicemen." He preferred seeing it "go to the shipbreakers" than stay there. After donating *Peking* to the Seaport, the Arons mostly paid for its work. But because the elder Aron was, said George Matteson, "very impatient with the gobbledegook and fussy pace of marine restoration," he did it his own way.[35]

Wavertree became the flashpoint because, said Peter Aron, "nobody wanted to commit large amounts" of money to restoration manager Fewtrell, who "was brilliant but 'impossible'!" Yet, added Rybka, later director of the Erie Maritime Museum, Fewtrell "was always right about what you should do to a ship and how you should go about it," but he was "a poor fit with a management who knew nothing about ships but did think in timelines and budgets." After Hightower and Shepley fired *Wavertree*'s seven-man restoration crew, the *New York Post* charged that the museum was "seeking to trim sail before selling out to a real estate developer." They could have learned from Kenneth Reynard, who had just surveyed *Wavertree*. While restoring *Star of India*, Reynard had started one job but moved to another after obstructions arose. He admitted, "This procedure provoked criticism from some quarters as 'too much started, nothing finished' but this is indeed the nature of a restoration project." Isbrandtsen defended the ships, but Shepley growled, "Jakob, God damn it, shut up."[36] (See fig. 32.)

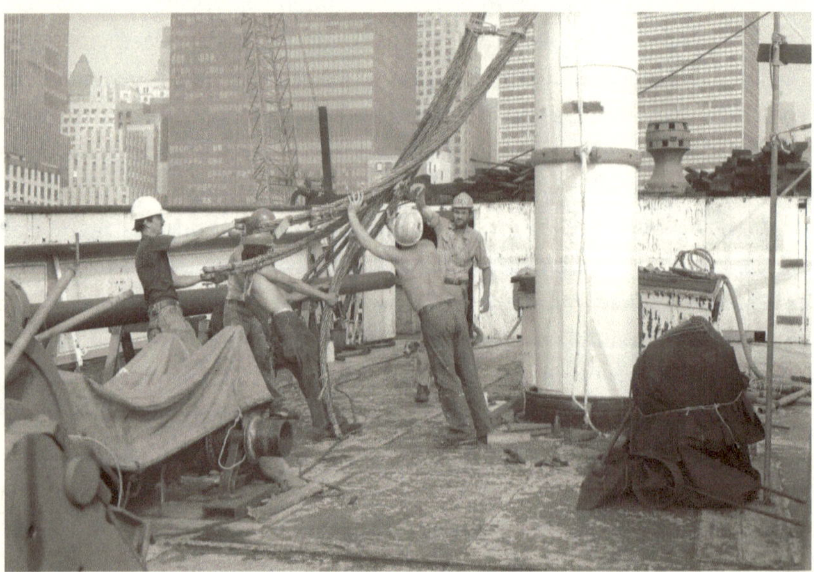

FIGURE 32. Stepping *Wavertree*'s foremast. Richard Fewtrell (right), ca. 1977. *Courtesy of Gerry Weinstein.*

A second victim of the mall was the Pioneer School, which was the brainchild of *Boating*'s Dick Rath. "An ardent believer in the Kipling story *Captains Courageous* and the sail training disciplines of Irving Johnson," said Matteson, Rath envisioned using *Pioneer* "as a social curative to the problem of inner city drug addiction and the racial biases which he understood to be their root cause." In 1971 the Pioneer Sail Training Program was funded by philanthropist Brooke Astor and the city's Addiction Services Agency. On two-week sails, over three summers, recovering addicts learned "to pull their own weight," said school head David Brink. Each voyage included a new batch of former offenders, approximately "50% black, 25% Hispanic, and 25% Caucasian." As such, their "afros, scars, funky inner city clothing . . . stuck out like a sore thumb" when they docked at nearby ports and yacht basins. But, as cook Shari Galligan added, the counselors taught them to handle their "boredom, loneliness and depression" without resorting to drugs. The national media praised the program, and the museum commissioned the documentary film, *Pioneer Lives*, with a narration by Stacy Keach and music by Fewtrell.[37]

But its graduates had "criminal records, little or no education, and no employment history or job skills." Knowing of boat manufacturers' need for technicians, Rath and Brink established the Pioneer Marine Technical School in 1972 aboard *Hart*. With a curriculum lasting nine hundred hours, its first graduates appeared on NBC's *Today* show in 1973. "Unlike a lot of the half-baked job training programs," said the *Daily News*, "this one has a waiting line of employers eager to hire graduates." Yet the Addiction Services Agency added students who were unable to read the engine manuals, which were "written on a third grade reading level," and on methadone, prompting critics to blast it as "a WPA for junkies." Lindsay rebutted, "Jobs work better than jails." But after funding cuts and a tabloid-hyped scandal, it closed in 1982. Rath and Brink blamed racism. Fearing that the school's minorities aboard *Hart* would deter customers, the Rouse Company had ordered, Brink alleged, "Get rid of the niggers."[38]

A third casualty of the mall was a visitor center, which Albany had promised but then abandoned. Awash in deficits in 1982, the Seaport gambled on another medium to introduce the district and leased a large exhibit building to Rouse and the Trans-Lux Corporation. Produced by Paul Heller, *South Street Venture* debuted in 1983 with $250, invitation-only tickets for the likes of Charlton Heston and Dustin Hoffman. Its state-of-the-art cyclorama showed such scenes as a clipper rounding Cape Horn. "Much as

I generally can't stand educational movies," said a *Daily News* columnist, it was "a painless way to learn history." It was later renamed *Seaport Experience* because, said Trans-Lux's chairman, "we did not want it to sound like an investment request to our patrons." Perhaps it should have; the show failed financially by 1990 because it reflected, said the museum's president, the "substitution of entertainment over education." It also backfired. After watching it, complained a Seaport program director, "many people seemed to feel that they had 'seen the museum' and, thus, had no need to visit the [revenue-earning] galleries."[39]

After two years of negotiations and hype, in which Rouse promised to retain the district's authenticity and underwrite the museum, a deal was reached in 1981 between the city, the state, Rouse, the Fish Market, and the museum's new real estate development arm, the quasi-independent South Street Seaport Corporation (SSSC). Because it relied on over $60 million in public funds, making it the most subsidized of all festival marketplaces, it was criticized as corporate welfare. Guided by the intricacies of the city's Uniform Land Use Review Procedure (ULURP), which had been established in 1975 to give communities more input into decisions over development, the 1981 lease cast the SSSC as the city's tenant and Rouse as its subtenant. However, the lease's provisions effectively privileged Rouse and hamstrung the museum for decades. The SSSC's head, Christopher Lowery, took over the SSSM itself. Opening in July 1983, Rouse's first phase included restaurants and upscale shops in Schermerhorn Row, on Front Street, and in the full-block, three-story New Fulton Market. The *New Yorker* showed the pedestrian mall on its cover. In 1985 an emporium opened on the rebuilt Pier 17. Said Koch, "This is one of the most important developments to have taken place over the last eight years of this administration." But the museum suffered, as admissions fell by 34 percent and foundation grants dropped 67 percent from 1984 to 1985. At a closed-door trustee meeting in 1985, Peter Aron questioned the "poor management" of Lowery and Shepley's surrogate chairman John Ricker. Instead of presenting a $300,000 donation, Aron tore his check in half. "On [Lowery's] recommendation," Ricker retorted that "the Museum should close its doors" and let Rouse run the district. A catharsis followed. After Stanford leaked the story, Lowery was forced out as museum head, the board was redefined, and the struggling museum committed its energies to its pre-Rouse mission.[40]

Former head of the National Trust's maritime program, Peter Neill became SSSM president in mid-1985. Only in 1989 did he take control of the

SSSC. He inherited what the *Wall Street Journal* called "a mess." Although the historic district had been saved from the wreckers, it was synonymous with the mall. The fleet, which was snatched from the breakers, was ridiculed as mismanaged. The museum's public face, which was called "a joyous jumble of exhibitions" in 1976, was reduced to one gallery with a borrowed exhibit. Neill called it "intellectually and financially bankrupt," but he stressed that "South Street Seaport is a *maritime* museum and the ships are both symbol and reality of the demands of our commitment." Peter Aron, who became chairman in 1987, strove to put its funding on four legs: an endowment, philanthropy, government support, and earned income, including membership and programs.[41]

The American Association of Museums had praised the Rouse deal, but Neill gradually realized that its critics were right. While paying the SSSC the minimum rent of $3.50 per square foot, Rouse achieved "a record-breaking sales figure of $560 per square foot" in 1987. But "there were always accounting ways" to hide the profits, Aron conceded, so that "the museum never got a nickel." Drawing some twelve million visitors annually, which was a third of Hightower's hyped predictions, the mall became the city's most popular tourist attraction in 1988. *Crain's New York Business* called the $375 million project "an astronomical success." But, because of its sugarcoated projections and a flawed business model, the faddish mall withered. As Rouse chased profits through out-of-control bars and tacky stores, the National Trust regretted "the 'Faneuilization' of waterfronts."[42]

To create a higher profile, the museum tried pier-side programs, often taking a cue from other museums. Aboard *Peking*, for example, it staged a Summer Sea Chantey series. But in 1999, Rouse simultaneously held events with "ear-drum-blasting music" that completely "drowned out" the chanteys. Relations with Rouse deteriorated on so many issues that Neill hired lawyer Stephen J. Kloepfer to lobby their landlord, the Economic Development Corporation (EDC), a quasi-public agency that manages city-owned properties. But the EDC was unresponsive as it privileged commerce. That led to long EDC delays funding the Row, whose exterior the state had restored before deeding the building to the city in 1983. While Rouse rented its lower two floors, the museum leased its upstairs, awaiting funds for restoration and exhibits.[43]

At smaller venues, the museum displayed the port's history. The exhibit *Harbor Witness*, for example, centered on the working waterfront that most New Yorkers ignored. Sketching abandoned wooden ships, John A.

Noble had built a floating studio, which *National Geographic* once featured. Though snubbed by mainstream museums, his "technical prowess in lithography was unsurpassed," admitted critics. Also distant from the mainstream were Long Island's seine fishermen, as shown by Peter Matthiessen's *Men's Lives: The Surfmen and Baymen of the South Fork* (1986). His photography depicted their struggle against nature, but three lesser forces caused their undoing: environmentalists protecting the striped bass, bureaucrats catering to sport fishermen, and shore elite wanting marinas. Matthiessen showed seine fishermen at work, but their passing meant "the end of a surfboat tradition that began when the Atlantic coast was still the frontier." *When Cod Was King* explored another controversial topic, overfishing. The exhibit was funded by Norway, which, flush with oil money, rehabilitated one Seaport gallery, while a second venue focused on Newfoundland, where, as in New England, fishing had collapsed. Norway's industry survived, said Neill, because of a century-old government policy of managing catches. A critic praised the show, as it "challenged viewers to assess" root problems, including free market capitalism.[44]

Those loaned exhibits exposed the limits of the Seaport's collection. In 1990 an opportunity arose when the Federal Deposit Insurance Company seized the insolvent Seamen's Bank for Savings (1839), which owned an "irreplaceable 2,000-piece collection of ship models, ships in bottles, nautical paintings, prints, scrimshaw, ship's clocks, barometers, captain's spyglasses, oil lamps and ship's logs." It was "worth $10 to $15 million," said an auctioneer. Neill "pulled a couple of influential strings," but New York's congressional delegation couldn't deliver. A trustee then wrote Prescott Bush, the brother of President George H. W. Bush; the note then went to "the administrator of the FDIC/savings bank bail-out." The museum received "the exclusive right to bid on the collection," which was conservatively appraised at $3,412,500. When news broke, one buyer blasted the "closed backroom deals." But the *Maine Antique Digest* defended the museum, while U.S. courts ruled that the FDIC had served the public good. Peter Aron's foundation donated the purchase price.[45]

Questionably in the public good was tattooing, as it had been outlawed in Gotham in 1961. But, by 1995, thirty million Americans had at least one, and the exhibit, *The Devil's Blue: American Tattoo Art and Practice through the Port of New York (1840–1961)* raised, said critic Michael Kimmelman, "issues of social marginality, fetishism and anti-establishmentarianism." Capitalizing the controversy, Neill invited the Hells Angels to the debut, and their leader rode "his bike up the stairs." Museum goers, including elderly ladies, posed with the 150 heavily tattooed bikers! *Vogue* covered the show, and bourgeois slumming swelled when the *Times* judged it "an excellent historical survey." With lectures and workshops, the needlework was further gentrified with a program "For Children & Families: Tattoo Arts–make your own!" While Gotham legalized tattooing in 1997, the Seaport's forays into pop culture fizzled with *Under the Black Flag: Life Among the Pirates*, especially after the *Washington Post* warned that real pirates were "as romantic as slave traders." The *Times* and *Daily News* ignored the ten-month exhibit.[46]

That was an inauspicious start to the Seaport's 1998 affiliation with the Mariners' Museum (see chapter 4). Sharing programs, including *Under the Black Flag*, their National Maritime Museum Initiative was initially set for eight years. The Seaport, which was stalled at 30 percent of its $27.5 million capital campaign, needed Mariners' artifacts for moneymaking exhibits, particularly after Neill learned that its ticket buyers came "expressly to visit the Museum," not the mall. Through a backroom deal in 1998, Congress then named the two as "America's National Maritime Museum." The title was disputed because in 1979 Congress had designated San Francisco's merged institutions as the National Maritime Museum; Mystic, Mariners', and South Street "vehemently protested" against the naming. In 1998, the Council of American Maritime Museums objected to the privileging of Mariners' and South Street. The council's reaction, said its head, "ranged from being annoyed to laughing at the effrontery." It tried (unsuccessfully) to include others in the listing.[47]

The Seaport's magazine generated more controversy, but internally. Launched in 1967 as a handbill, the *South Street Reporter* segued into an informative gazette on the museum, its ships, and the Friends. Praising an issue on "The Black Man and the Sea," Seeger thought that the publication set "a model for other organizations—meaningful, beautiful, but not slick." But Shepley, Hightower, and Stanford wanted a broader, more affluent audience. By 1986 *Seaport: New York's History Magazine* included essays by top-notch social historians and won a wider readership. In 1988, for instance, the Pan Am Shuttle gave *Seaport* to "its 200,000 riders annually between Boston, Washington, and New York." Yet complaints aired that the four-color glossy was ignoring the museum itself.[48]

Seaport included a unique back-page feature, "Seaport People." "Most interested in workers' lives," columnist Joe Doyle told the stories of everyday people. For example, John Singleton, a fourteen-year-old crippled by infantile paralysis, was sent to work "on a bloody hell ship" by his Liverpool father; he came back "an old man" a year later. Giving tours at the Seaport, he was, said Doyle, "a one-man committee to dispel illusions that life aboard a sailing ship was 'romantic.'" Rose Chevell, on the other hand, recounted a common but overlooked life as a Grace Line waitress. Radicalized in the Glory Hole, where waitresses bunked and read the likes of John Reed, she discovered that the National Maritime Union "was no different from the company in discriminating against women." Those interviews were refreshing, but editors scuttled the column to focus on "19th century waterfront characters." Like architectural restoration, that change created a more nostalgic view of the seaport's past.[49]

"A SHIP IS A HOLE IN THE WATER": THE STORMY SEAS OF SHIP PRESERVATION

Accused of scrimping on his fleet, Hightower replied with a cliché: "A ship is a hole in the water into which you pour money." Neill inherited a fleet in bad shape—*Lettie* was rotten to its frame; *Wavertree* was a rusty box; *Hart* was abandoned; and *Ambrose* was kept afloat with pumps. Though he derided the Seaport's "compulsion for collecting ships," he thoughtfully described the movement's history to a national audience: "A very small number" of pioneers, notably Cutler, Kortum, and Stanford, had inaugurated "the 'acquire at any price' phase" because they realized "that we were about to lose an extremely valuable part of our heritage." He said, "We owe these people a great debt of gratitude. Without their passion and their commitment, we would have simply lost it all." The movement then entered "the 'trial and error' [but] mostly error" phase. Mystic made "every mistake in the book," as with *Australia* and *Brinckerhoff*, and South Street also had "very public failures." But, as preservationists consolidated "our working wisdom," he said, "the third phase is a much happier one," referring to the "wonderful" restoration by Rybka and Brink of Galveston's *Elissa*. Though Rybka questioned the word "restoration," calling *Elissa* "a mixed fabric reconstruction of the best guesses of what it once was," Neill hoped to advance the fourth phase, "the institutionalization of success."[50]

Yet most maritime museums (and even the *New York Times*) privileged galleries over ships. Through his bully pulpit, Neill promoted ship preservation and chided those museums for becoming mere "storehouses of bric-a-brac." Focusing on the U.S. merchant fleet, he noted in 1987 that "of ships 50 feet or larger and 50 years or older only 200 still exist, and many are badly deteriorated." The only U.S. museums then to have "three or more such vessels" were in New York, Mystic, and San Francisco. But he warned his colleagues: "To exclude the objects that are at the center of the tradition we celebrate is to build a museum round an empty hole." Still, his own fleet was a mess. In 1985, he hired Rybka's White Elephant Management to make an assessment and Charles Deroko, who had worked on *Peking* and *Wavertree*, as waterfront manager.[51]

With that mess, Neill's museum was fracturing. In 1987 disgruntled volunteers and residents formed the Seaport Community Coalition. Spurred on by Stanford and Isbrandtsen, they feared that Lowery's real estate schemes would leave the Seaport with "one pier and one or two major vessels." There, tycoon Donald Trump had proposed building the world's tallest tower (1,940 feet); after a newspaper critic lambasted the idea, he filed a $500 million libel suit but won neither the case nor the building site. The coalition challenged Lowery and Neill. First, a former volunteer angrily wrote the *Times* that *Lettie* was "a scandal and a disgrace." The *Daily News* fired a second salvo in 1989 with the feature, "Port of Missing Ships: Whatever Happened to the South Street Dream?" Its Sunday magazine cover pictured a cocooned *Lettie* and a derelict *Hart*. Referring to Stanford, who instigated the exposé and infuriated Neill, author Dick Sheridan explained, "Much of what he originally envisioned for South Street has been accomplished. . . . But along the way, interests more concerned with the price of land than with the historic value of ships gained control of the original museum, forced Stanford out of his own enterprise—and altered his grand design. . . . From the late 1970s to the mid-80s, high-salaried, high-profile new managers pushed commercial development of the district while ignoring the cultural institution. . . . Finally, after a noisy public battle over their strictly commercial intentions, they were purged in 1985 by a board finally fed up with the inattention to preservationism." Neill conceded that developers had left the Seaport with "zero assets and a lot of debt." *WoodenBoat* shot a third broadside, charging that "South Street isn't much of a museum" and was a raft of "boutiques and restaurants and gifte shoppes decorated in a crypto-nautical motif."[52]

The fates of *Wavertree*, *Peking*, and *Lettie G. Howard* illustrated that unfulfilled dream of ship preservation. In the 1980s and after, *Wavertree* raised questions internationally: Should a rare ship be restored, and if so, by whom and with what materials? And was such a restoration hoodwinking the public? Only with the Green Book (1990) did the U.S. government suggest standards favoring authentic materials, rigorous documentation, and preservation or restoration. But it was not the king's law. As author Michael Naab noted, "the highest standards" were "to 'define ideal maritime preservation practice.' Heavy emphasis on 'ideal.'" Before 1990, work was more idiosyncratic, depending on an organization's ability and funds. Since 1970, *Wavertree* had been earmarked for restoration, but critics claimed it would produce a fake intended only to take tourists' dollars. Yet, recalling what *Wavertree* looked like in Argentina, ship historian Brouwer rebutted that "exhibiting an ugly barge" was pointless. A proper restoration would not be a trick but a tribute to "the people who built, owned and sailed her."[53]

At the time, no U.S. or British museum with such a mangled ship practiced pure-and-simple preservation. Since *Wavertree*'s work was hamstrung by a lack of original drawings, detailed photographs, and restoration know-how, Fewtrell emphasized archaeological and comparative analysis. But Hightower's firing of his crew left a vacuum. In 1981, Isbrandtsen confronted Shepley at a board meeting: "When the hell are you going to do something for the *Wavertree*?" Shepley snarled, "Why don't you do it yourself?" He did, placing a sign at the pier—"Long hours, dirty work, no pay!"—and recruiting one hundred volunteers and a million dollars via the National Maritime Historical Society. Concerned about the expense, he left it to their "ingenuity and inventiveness." But, said Fewtrell, they didn't "have the training or the skills for the job."[54]

While the preservation of original materials was most desirable, their replacement was inevitable. But substituting plastic and aluminum was contentious. Jack Aron defended using plastics aboard *Peking*, though the National Trust's William Avery Baker warned that they were "not compatible with older materials." As president of England's Maritime Trust, Prince Philip, Duke of Edinburgh, visited and suggested using aluminum spars to reduce *Wavertree*'s maintenance. "The idea is to make it look right," he said. "With the old material you'll just be committing the next generation to endless work all over again." But Stanford rebutted that ships required "a continuous rebuilding process," which the public could watch, and Neill renewed the spars' Douglas fir.[55] (See fig. 33.)

Meanwhile, *Peking* was under fire. For one, it was ineligible for the historic registers because it "never sailed" to the United States. As Peter Aron joked: "It was built to haul guano, not Mrs. Vanderbilt!" For another, its

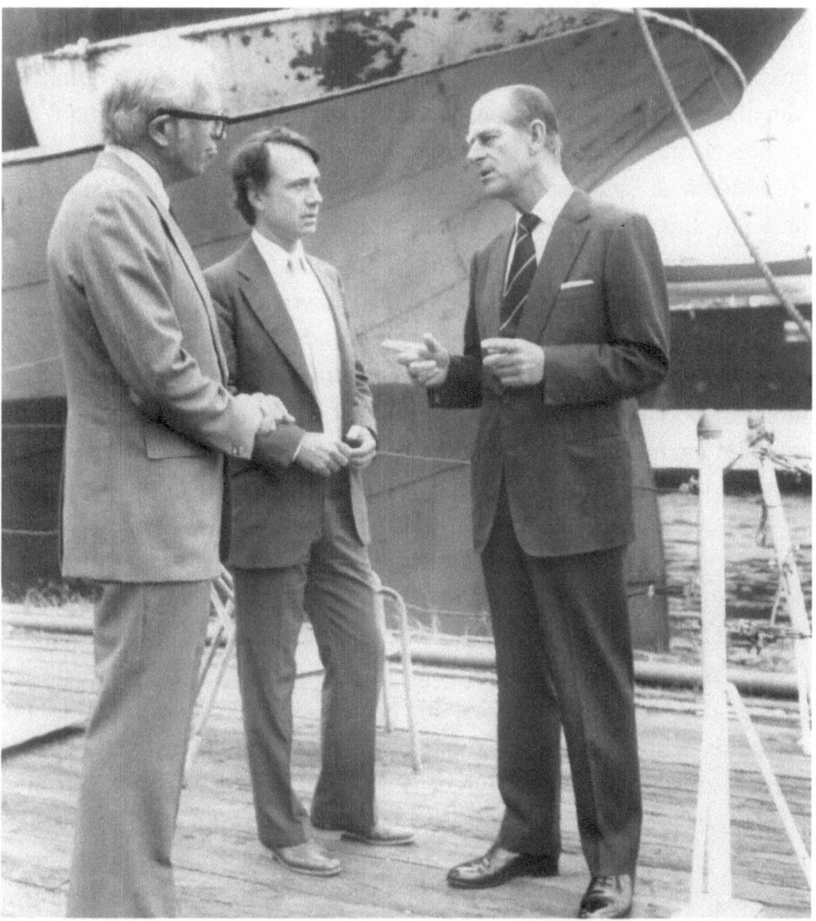

FIGURE 33. Discussing *Wavertree*'s work are Peter Stanford (left), John Hightower (center), and HRH Prince Philip (right). 1980. *Courtesy of the South Street Seaport Museum.*

partial rig showed the differences between pragmatists and purists. Hearing that it would require "tens of millions of dollars" to return *Peking* to sailing condition, the Arons gave it what others called "a Hollywood rig." Stanford and Fewtrell sniped, as did Harry Allendorfer, the National Trust's maritime director who jeered that the rig was good enough for a "little kid and his mother" who wanted "a feel for a square-rigger." But in 1984 *Peking*'s small crew began a twelve-year-long replacement of the standing rigging. Moreover, the claim that *Peking* was hoodwinking tourists was doubtful. Joe Doyle recalled that the retired sailors-turned-interpreters were "engaging and authentic," as was master rigger Lars Henning Hansen, whom the

Times called the "king of the still-gritty side of the seaport." He loved the buzz of not only Manhattan's waterfront but also its nightclubs. It reminded him of being a sailor, when, he joked, he "had to go ashore every night and see the girls and drink. It was pretty exhausting doing that every night!" He added with a guffaw, "You never had money, of course." Neither did his museum, and that explained some of its thinking.[56]

With *Lettie* "rotting at her moorings," the board nonetheless ordered that any restoration "must be done with little or no cost borne by the Museum." Volunteers stepped in. Working on weekends, they, like friends aboard *Wavertree*, suspected that Neill and his managers were "trying to get us under their thumb." They were right. But changes in the preservation and museum movements partly explain this rift. Both the American Association of Museums and the Council of American Maritime Museums were trying "to professionalize" their ranks, but ship preservation, which was rooted in the arcane experiences of sailing, was slower than architectural preservation in adopting newer methods. It was, said James Delgado of the National Park Service, "twenty years behind the times."[57]

The issue had been building since Stanford railed against the alleged cliques that controlled history, art, and museums. Knowing that the standards being discussed at a 1985 conference would be used by funding agencies, Neill said it was "reprehensible . . . to spend a single dollar on a restoration project" until those standards were set. But holding to their mantra "This Museum *Is* People," some *Lettie* and *Wavertree* volunteers refused to cooperate with waterfront staff. One of them warned Neill that they were governed by "a model of 'economic de-centralization'" and that *Wavertree* was "outside of the authority or control of the museum." Neill ordered Deroko to take charge. Program director Sally Yerkovich admitted that the dedication of *Wavertree*'s volunteers "was unquestionable." But they were dedicated to the ship, not Neill.[58]

Pulling two rabbits out of his hat, Neill announced that *Lettie* had won National Historic Landmark (NHL) status and a restoration grant. But his plan to rebuild *Lettie* near the Row pricked his opponents. Charging that it would disrupt the fish market and endanger residents, the Seaport Community Coalition persuaded the Fire Department to block it. After firing *Lettie*'s volunteer ringleaders, Neill moved the work to a Pier 16 barge. He ironically admitted that professionalization was disfranchising the "community activists who [kept] preservation a credible item on the American agenda." In fact, the volunteers aboard other ships—*Pioneer* and *Ambrose*—were happy

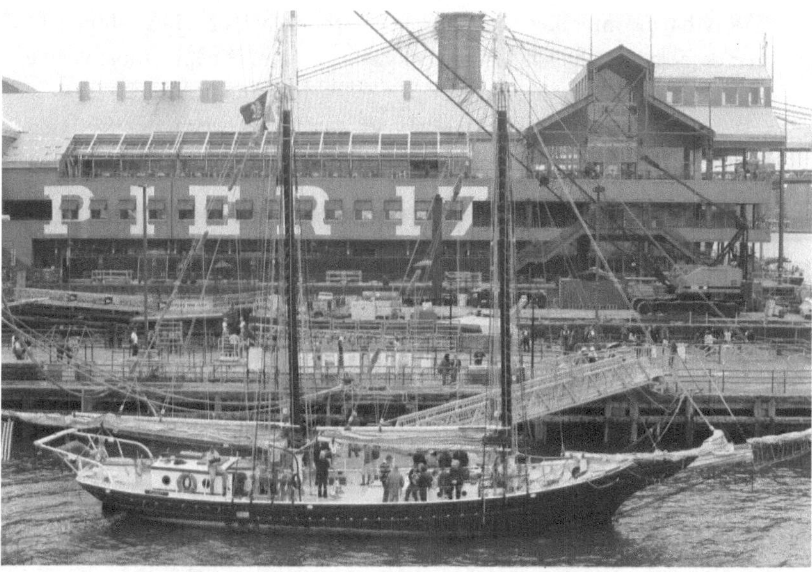

FIGURE 34. *Pioneer* at Pier 16. Note that Pier 17's mall is under demolition. *Photo by author, 2013.*

and productive. The question remained: Who—volunteer, professional, or bureaucrat—controlled the ship? The Seaport hired full-time artisans for *Lettie*'s restoration, the first according to the Green Book. After being "99% renewed," it was rechristened in 1992 and became a USCG-certified sailing school vessel.[59] (See fig. 34.)

To include *Wavertree* in Op Sail, Neill faced three hurdles. For one, Isbrandtsen controlled the ship. Neill hired engineer Don Birkholz to take charge, but Isbrandtsen "and his gang pretty much chased him off." Second, fundraising was a greater problem, leaving *Wavertree* out of Op Sail 92. Initially pegging his restoration at $5 million, Neill halved that sum as he approached Op Sail 2000. "With eight months to go" and less than $1 million in hand, he pressed his case. Without naming the likes of Maersk Shipping Line, Cutty Sark Whisky, or billionaire yachtsman Ted Turner, he noted in the *Journal of Commerce* that

> the search for additional funding has been long and frustrating.
>
> Why? Why, for example, has the marine industry failed to respond to what may be the most evocative expression of its long and lucrative history?

> Why have companies that expropriate the image of sailing ships and their associated values failed to respond to what may be the most visible expression of that tradition?
>
> Why have so many individuals who get such great personal satisfaction from sea experience declined to extend that opportunity to others?
>
> What is most ironic is that the preservation of landside cultural resources—collections of fine art and architecture—flourishes today, frequently through foundations and endowments that were created historically by maritime enterprise. . . . My challenge to the marine industry is this: Let's sail *Wavertree* as an affirmation of our maritime history and as an investment in its future.

His pleas went largely unheard: Albany awarded a modest $70,000, but Republican Mayor Rudolph Giuliani gave nothing, as he unfairly blamed the SSSC for the Mafia's influence at the fish market. Few big donors surfaced. "New York City is a national center of philanthropy," explained critic Paul Goldberger, but "its largest foundations pay little attention to the city."[60]

Third, *Wavertree*'s seaworthiness was questioned; with no engine, an open hold, and only a collision bulkhead, it could sink like a stone if holed. After it was dry-docked, the *Daily News* reported, *Wavertree* was "fit to represent New York in the July 4 Parade of Ships." On the day before, however, the USCG called it structurally deficient. That "came as no surprise," said Deroko, because old "windjammers with bulkheads were exceedingly rare" and the removal of the tween deck in Argentina had weakened its frame. He warned: It wasn't "structurally sound to sail, period." Anchored next to the carrier *John F. Kennedy*, the world's largest iron-hulled sailing ship watched the parade. Spinning it, the *Post* claimed that "the grand dame . . . pulled off a maritime miracle . . . by successfully taking to the sea again after a 100-year vacation."[61]

"SOMETIMES YOU JUST CAN'T GET A BREAK": HOW 9/11 TORPEDOED THE MUSEUM

Hoping for wind in its sails, the Seaport expected its biggest gift ever—$5 million—in 2001. The agenda for the Port Authority meeting at the World Trade Center on September 12 included a grant for preparing the Row and a permanent exhibit, *World Port New York* (*WPNY*). The insurance giant AIG promised to help fund *WPNY*. The terrorist attacks changed everything. Just as Lower Manhattan's rebirth began with the Seaport and World

Trade Center in 1966, the events of 9/11 crippled it for years. Tourism was central to the recovery. Projected to open in 2003, *WPNY* would add "tens of thousands" to the ten million annually visiting Lower Manhattan. But the Port Authority expected more from *WPNY* by emphasizing the harbor's 226,000 regional jobs and $25 billion activity. As the port fell to third in national tonnage, it admitted that the museum was a proxy. "By increasing public awareness of the importance of the maritime industry to the region," its director explained, "this grant also will help build support for harbor improvements that are needed to ensure that the Port of New York and New Jersey continues to grow and to generate jobs." With 9/11, however, it postponed its grant.[62]

A mile from Ground Zero, the Seaport floundered. Dependent on its school programs, elderhostel, and excursions, which evaporated "for almost two years," it was on the verge of closing. Giuliani could not have cared less. Because it was in the hands of the EDC, not the Department of Cultural Affairs (DCA), the Seaport had, said Kloepfer, "the dubious distinction of being the only longstanding NYC cultural institution, operating on NYC-owned property, that . . . did not receive any annual NYC operating subsidy." "As the saying goes, 'sometimes you just can't get a break.'" In the end, the Aron Foundation's $5 million gift, along with the Port Authority's deferred grant, kept it afloat.[63]

Curators marked 9/11's first anniversary in an exhibit that spotlighted the hundreds of vessels and their crews who evacuated Lower Manhattan after the tragedy; their efforts surpassed "the fabled ten-day Dunkirk evacuation." Those watercraft were hampered, however, because many wharves had been removed to beautify the waterfront. As *Seaport* noted, the harbor had been, like blue-collar New York, "gradually marginalized by a host of forces, not the least of which was the postwar dominance of global capitalism represented by the very World Trade Center that now lay in ruins." Using photographs and taped interviews, the exhibit, *All Available Boats: Harbor Voices & Images 9/11/01* highlighted the "selfless dedication . . . of these previously invisible waterfront hands." The exhibit was packaged to travel, condensed for radio, and inspired a book. Also, because downtown businesses were hurting, the city chose the museum to distribute free tickets to the record numbers visiting Ground Zero. Yet the museum also found itself on the hot seat. First, it unwittingly held a book-signing event for an author who accused firefighters of looting the ruin, thus drawing a New York Fire Department protest. And, second, in 2005 it showed a packaged exhibit, *A Knock on the Door*, that critically examined the subsequent Iraq War and loss of domestic civil liberties. The hawkish *Post* charged that the exhibit's "sole purpose [was] to bash America," but the *Times* called it "a thoughtful, legitimate exploration."[64]

Those events could not sustain the museum, whose earned income before 9/11 had stemmed—"nearly 75% of total budget"—from educational services. To generate more revenue, Neill had begun a thirty-thousand-foot renovation of the Row's upper floors. Lacking a main venue, he promised Community Board No. 1 that it would "be the education and programmatic heart of the museum." Its first ten galleries opened in late 2003. The Seaport even suggested opening the Row's Fulton Ferry Hotel, which had closed in 1939. Once respectable, it had deteriorated into a boardinghouse for sailors, preachers, and prostitutes romanticized in Joseph Mitchell's "Up in the Old Hotel." But, said Neill, "We're leaving this as a ruin . . . inhabited by the ghosts of immigrants and sailors and young women just off the boat." Other ghosts stole his show, however. In a macabre venture, the New Fulton Market was leased by mall managers in 2005 to *Bodies, the Exhibition*; its many cadavers allegedly included executed Chinese prisoners. While lines queued up for *Bodies*, the museum across the street was as quiet as a morgue.[65]

Long planned, the Row's first exhibit added to Neill's headaches. Inspired by Liverpool's *Trans-Atlantic Slavery: Against Human Dignity*, the Seaport negotiated the rights, began its development, but ran out of money. Neill asked Mariners' to help, and its president, the same John Hightower who had been fired at South Street, "committed the funds to design and produce the exhibit." *Captive Passage: The Transatlantic Slave Trade and the Making of the Americas* was, said Hightower, "one of the most powerful and compelling exhibitions ever undertaken" by the Mariners' Museum. Neill attended its Virginia opening, which he called a "love-fest." Yet his love boat ran aground when Hightower proposed showing the exhibit not at the agreed-upon Seaport but at the New-York Historical Society. Neill was flabbergasted, telling Hightower "in no uncertain terms that he was violating our agreement, that he was abandoning the concept of our partnership, and that the script was ours." The storm passed, and the exhibit reverted to its only Gotham showing—in the Row.[66]

But Hightower got even. "The exhibit arrived, without artifacts," Neill said, because Mariners' claimed that the Row "did not have a ONE YEAR RECORD of climate conditions in galleries that were just being built."

Hightower's collections manager admitted, "We were really tough on them about getting their environmental conditions up to museum standards." Embarrassed, the Seaport borrowed a private collection on an African culture in South America. Yet, Kloepfer confessed, it was "a joke." Months later the Mariners' objects arrived, but major papers snubbed coverage; the *Times* simply called it "a display of African art and artifacts." A year earlier, however, its Washington reporter extensively described its Smithsonian run as "a story of critical importance." Still, the two exhibits were different, as New York's was more tempered, perhaps because of 9/11's lingering trauma, in illustrating the trade's horror. With the estrangement, the National Maritime Museum Initiative ran aground.[67]

As an entrepreneur, Neill was, said Aron, "always trying to develop some other vehicle" to earn revenue. He proposed a World Ocean Observatory, which would transcend old-fashioned museums by showing, he told the *Times*, "the interrelationships between the world's oceans and the social, economic, political and cultural life of the city." Its planned $20 million site included exhibits and a visitor center. Yet chairman Lawrence S. Huntington, former head of Fiduciary Trust Company, reportedly said, "This is not what maritime museums do." Others suggested that Neill's proposal ignored the museum's financial difficulties or distracted its focus from *World Port New York*. When Neill resultantly retired, some were happy to see him go, especially in City Hall. Still, said Aron, "His major accomplishments were in place."[68]

Or were they? A disaster followed as Huntington and his handpicked, but ill-qualified, president closed the library, pared the waterfront, and scuttled *WPNY* and the archaeology program. They even savaged the development office. Previously, the museum had experienced cash flow problems, but the cuts in 2004 slashed its core mission. Using corporate doublespeak, Huntington said, "We're rationalizing the work force. . . . We're going to get the job done with fewer people." Yet, the question posed by Huntington and his administrators—Did programs pay their own way?—revealed the pitfalls in a museum movement redefined by corporate thinking. Calling the library "'sleepy' and underutilized," vice president Yvonne Simons thought that supporting research, even for interpretation, "was too much of a luxury when no revenue was being produced." Norman Brouwer had written over one hundred articles for the income- and membership-generating magazine, but the thirty-two-year veteran was axed. Yet her expectation that historians, archaeologists, and curators raise their own funds was, according to a former president of the American Association for State and Local History, "way out of step with standard (history) museum practice." Instead, those personnel "create the intellectual capital" for revenue-generating programs.[69]

Meanwhile, the fleet was in peril. When pressed about the ships, Huntington snapped: "Nobody wants to support them. . . . If they're not cared for, they sink." On his discard list were not only the harbor's sole-surviving, early twentieth-century tug, *Helen McAllister*, and the last wooden-hulled chandlery lighter, *Marion M* (both departed in 2012), but also *Ambrose* (NHL, 1989). Meanwhile *W. O. Decker*, a wooden, steam-powered tug launched in 1930, had so deteriorated that trustee George Matteson, who had donated it in 1986, paid $840,000 for its rebuilding in 2005. Named Tug of the Year in 2008, its two-hour charters earned $1,000.[70]

Wavertree, *Peking*, and *Lettie* again showed the results of inadequate attention. *Wavertree* briefly raised its canvas in New York Bay after Op Sail 2000, but it needed new decks and sails and repair of its hull and masts. In 2008, the Seaport estimated the cost at $8.5 million, and City Hall, which had tacitly adopted it as Gotham's square-rigger, promised help. But Frank Sciame, a developer who became museum chairman in 2007, decided instead in 2010 to install a costly planetarium. Brouwer called the proposal "errant stupidity." The proposal died of its own weight. To keep *Wavertree*, however, *Peking* was sacrificed. Neill's selling price was $11 million. "Having two tall ships doesn't bring a single extra person to the gate," he noted in 2003. The planned Hamburg International Maritime Museum would be, he said, "a perfect repatriation . . . to her home port and to a group that seems perfectly qualified to repair and show her." But Huntington rejected the Germans' $5 million counterbid. Hoping to create "a modern learning facility" aboard the ship, Huntington asked for $100 million from Lionel Amos, an English millionaire. Amos, in turn, offered "to create and fund a trust which would purchase and operate *Peking* as a seagoing training ship" under Seaport auspices. Huntington nixed the proposal. In 2006, Aron privately asked a trustee to resurrect the Hamburg talks, which tentatively led to a purchase price of $2.8 million. The Great Recession of 2007 sidelined the deal. In 2010, moreover, the Seaport was trying to sell *Lettie* (NHL, 1989). Most observers blamed Sciame's hand-chosen but inept president. Yet in 2013, after the city funded $250,000 in repairs, *Lettie*'s sail training provided some income, as with the Port Authority's "Two States, One Port" campaign.[71]

As shaky was the Seaport's hold on Pier 15. In 1973, the museum had leased its northern half for ninety-nine years, while squatting on its unused southern portion. Unlike the publicly maintained Pier 16, the city privatized Pier 15 by requiring the Seaport to reconstruct it by 1998. The Mashantucket Pequots of Connecticut stepped in. Needing a landing for a ferry to their Foxwoods Casino in 1997, they offered to rebuild Pier 15, and give a hefty sum to the Seaport, in return for a lease of its southern side. But the plan was "vetoed by Giuliani." As the neglected pier withered to four stumps, his Republican successor, Michael Bloomberg, announced plans in 2002 to create a two-mile-long East River esplanade. In response, city councilmember Alan Gerson suggested that the district was "New York's last opportunity to preserve our historic, nautical, seafaring roots." Pier 15 became a "lightning rod" issue when, in 2007, the EDC severed the museum's lease (as it had done for other commercial leases). Rejecting preservationists, it chose a modern design with greenery, recreation, and cruise boats. A blogger joked that it would be "a home for yachts, happy children, and bikinis."[72]

The seaport's maritime identity faded further with the ouster of the fish market, which David Rockefeller and City Hall had wanted since the 1950s. Tightened health standards forced its move to the Bronx in 2005. Many cheered. "On hot days, the smell of fish was nauseating," one resident griped. But what was lost, Neill replied, "was the authenticity of place, too gritty, too connected to labor, too suggestive of a world opposite to the dreams of the planners and real estate moguls." Calling the decrepit space "a beautiful property," EDC head Michael Carey set a goal of "maximizing opportunities," especially as gentry were moving into the financial district's older high-rises. Young families wanted playgrounds, not a working waterfront. The district's future was further complicated by Rouse's bankruptcy; it sold its malls in 2004 to General Growth Properties of Chicago, which was hamstrung by $27 billion in debt. It proposed building a tall tower next to Pier 17. But in 2010 General Growth spun off its seaport holdings to the Dallas-based Howard Hughes Corporation.[73]

In 2011, the Seaport Museum reached death's door, not surprisingly after Huntington, Sciame, and their administrators had acted autocratically, ignored museum practices, and failed to assure their audiences. Surviving with $4 million in loans from trustees, it laid off thirty-two staff in what one employee called the "Ground Hog Day Massacre." Besides closing long-running programs, it "eliminated its curatorial and development departments." Museum volunteers and former staff rallied by forming Save Our Seaport (SOS), a grassroots group that, though helped by the Stanfords, attracted broader support and lobbied City Hall for a bailout. The city's Department of Cultural Affairs stepped in. Supported by $2 million from the Lower Manhattan Development Corporation, a post-9/11 pump-primer, the DCA coaxed the Museum of the City of New York (MCNY)—a private, uptown organization looking for a downtown site—to help temporarily; it took charge in November 2011. Seeing the fleet, MCNY director Susan Henshaw Jones, who had worked in banking and preservation, estimated *Wavertree*'s needs at $20 million. The fleet "might cost close to $100 million." Bloomberg stressed "private sector" funding, and many wondered if City Hall would support it by revising the unfair 1981 lease.[74]

"SOMETHING THAT IS SO SPECIAL ABOUT OUR CITY": ENDANGERED, BUT COMING BACK

In October 2012, Superstorm Sandy overwhelmed the district. The fleet rode out the storm, but the seven-foot surge swamped the Row. While its upstairs collections were spared, repairs to its HVAC and electrical infrastructure were pegged at $22 million. Its galleries later reopened, but when a jury-rigged system failed, they closed in April 2013 (and have not permanently reopened as of 2019). Calling the museum a "nonessential nonprofit," the Federal Emergency Management Administration (FEMA) refused to help. Suspicions heightened as the EDC snubbed the museum's pleas. Facing "a very dire situation," the MCNY contract was extended. Attending an April 2013 Community Board No. 1 meeting, it reiterated its need for repairing the storm damage and revising the lease to provide ground-floor space, ample Pier 17 dockage, and the ability to earn its $4 million annual operating costs. In June, the community board's chair wrote Bloomberg, "Losing this iconic and historic institution would not only be a devastating loss for the Lower Manhattan community, but also for the City of New York."[75]

Rhetorically supporting the Seaport, the Bloomberg administration was, in reality, undermining it. After reinterpreting a controversial reversion clause in the 1981 lease, its Department of Small Business Services secretly signed a deal with the Howard Hughes Corporation on June 27, 2013, in which the city agreed to give Hughes all or part of the museum's lease of Schermerhorn Row, its Water Street buildings (the print shop, gallery, and library), and Pier 16. Missed by the city's major newspapers, the deal was "signed without public discussion and without public notification." In effect, Hughes became the leaseholder and the museum its tenant. After Hughes refused to submit a ULURP to revise the 1981 lease, the MCNY quit the Seaport in July. In an unprecedented move, the DCA temporarily took over the museum; the DCA's board members chose waterfront director Jonathan Boulware as interim president. When the DCA failed to find another organization to succeed the MCNY, the museum's survival was in question, especially in August, when Hughes quietly sent EDC its plan to take the museum's space in the Row, on Water Street, and Pier 16. In response, Save Our Seaport mustered ten thousand signatures on a petition and awaited the next citywide election. The Seaport's friends pinned their hopes on the candidacy of public advocate Bill de Blasio as mayor and councilmember Gale A. Brewer as Manhattan borough president. Both won and took office in January 2014.[76]

As manager of Gotham's city-owned real estate, the EDC is chosen by City Hall, the City Council, and the borough presidents and is thus only indirectly subject to the voters. De Blasio promised change, but as Common Cause noted, there was "a long-standing incestuous relationship between the real estate industry and the EDC." After Hughes submitted a ULURP for the erection of a new Pier 17 mall, whose modernist design glaringly contrasted with the historic district, the City Council approved, in 2013, a $425 million, four-story structure. Save Our Seaport led the chorus of complaints, and Community Board No. 1 asked for "a comprehensive, community-driven dialogue" to "create development guidelines." Local legislators pushed the EDC to convene a Seaport Working Group. Creating distrust, the EDC included Hughes, but not the museum. In 2014, the group's deliberations were secret, but it included criticism of the glitz that the developer had introduced. On Fulton Street, with its fabled nineteenth-century buildings and paving stones, Hughes introduced a garish midway with Astroturf, picnic tables, and beach chairs for tourists who frequented hotdog vendors and cargo-container shops. Yet the discussants mostly focused on the developer's plans. In closing, the group issued guidelines emphasizing that (1) the Seaport Museum was the area's cultural anchor, its ships defined the waterfront, and both needed support; (2) any new buildings adjoining the historic district must "not adversely affect the neighborhood's scale and character"; and (3) the district's city-owned properties should be controlled by an organization that better represented the community (and not the EDC, which backed Hughes). State Senator Daniel Squadron, a group member, stressed: "It is critical that anything that moves forward moves forward around the guidelines."[77]

Public assemblies and a handful of op-ed writers supported those guidelines; most objected to Hughes's proposal to restart General Growth's plan to erect a fifty-story tower on prime space owned by the city between the Brooklyn Bridge and Pier 17. Requiring the removal of the fish market's Tin Building (1907), which was protected as a landmark, the plan also called for the demolition of the New Market Building (1939), which was not landmarked by the city, though it was in the state and national historic districts. The proposal needed the city's approval. Brewer took the first shot. Erecting it there, she said, was "like building a tower at Colonial Williamsburg." By custom, however, the approval of the local councilmember was most important. Margaret Chin took two lines from the mayor's State of the City address, which referred to projects elsewhere, and applied them to the seaport. "We are not embarking on a mission to build towering skyscrapers where they don't belong," de Blasio said. "We have a duty to protect and preserve the culture and character of our neighborhoods, and we will do so." Chin vowed: "It's not going to happen under my watch." In June 2015, the National Trust designated the seaport as "one of America's 11 most endangered historic places."[78]

The threats only intensified because the city was unwilling to replace the EDC with, as the Seaport Working Group recommended, a new governing body more responsive to residents and less beholden to profit-minded developers. For its proposed tower, Hughes had acquired the air rights (625,000 square feet) from Pier 17 and the Tin Building. Standing in Hughes's way, however, was Community Board No. 1, which had long requested the landmarking of the New Market Building. Heeding the EDC's objections, City Hall stonewalled the request, and the deteriorated building was demolished in 2018. Seemingly unable to erect a skyscraper on the site, Hughes sold those air rights to a China-based developer who threatened the district in another way; directly across from Pier 15, but just outside of the historic district, it proposed constructing a 1,436-foot tower that would block the sun for much of the day.[79]

Pier 17 posed another threat. Hughes opened its new mall in mid-2018, but instead of its promised rooftop public park, pavilion, and restaurant, the company repurposed the 1.5-acre space as a private, outdoor concert venue. It could accommodate up to thirty-four hundred concertgoers, thus harkening back to Rouse's eardrum-blasting music in 1999. At the same time, Hughes was changing its plans for the adjacent Tin Building, which it dismantled for eventual reconstruction, not as a public market, but as a venue for pricey shopping. Lost over the years, therefore, were verbal promises of

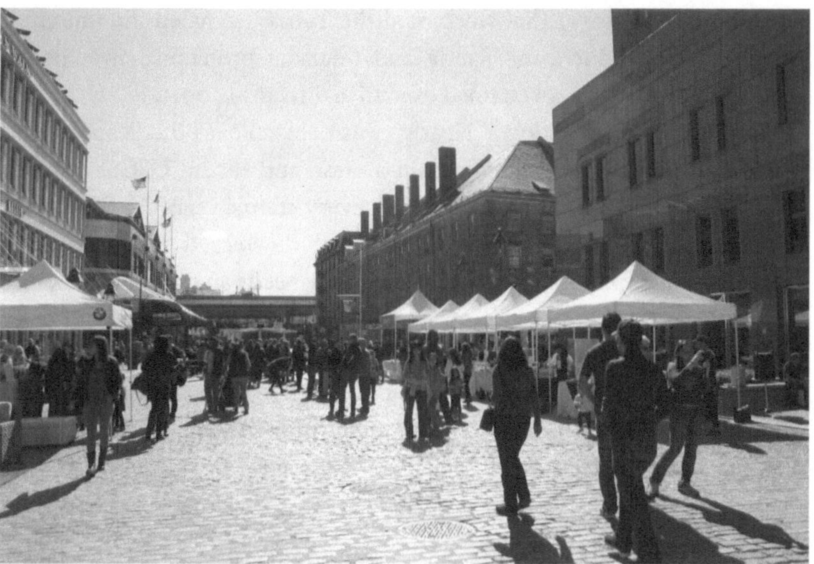

FIGURE 35. Fulton Street with Schermerhorn Row in the right background. *Photo by author, 2016.*

amenities that Hughes had made to the museum and community board. Critics feared that Hughes was repeating the Rouse strategy of saying one thing and doing another as it incrementally revised previously approved plans without adequate city review. Now, as friends of the museum, seaport district, and waterfront anticipate Hughes's next move, the developer plays a cat-and-mouse game with the city's historic district[80] (fig. 35).

The fleet was almost lost in the ruckus over Hughes's plans, but Brewer reminded New Yorkers: "When you come down Fulton Street and you see these ships, you see something that is so special about our city." But the fleet had recently lost *Mathilda, Aqua, Helen McAllister*, and *Marion M.* With *Peking*'s restoration pegged at $28 million by 2011, the foundering Seaport was pressed further to cut expenses, and it agreed to give *Peking* free of charge to the City of Hamburg. After the German government appropriated €30 million to move and restore the barque, it left Gotham atop a heavy-lift ship in July 2017. Later that year, in small compensation, the DCA granted $4.5 million to restore *Ambrose*. With *Peking's* departure, *Wavertree* took center stage. Through DCA grants, it was hauled in 2015–16 for a $13 million refurbishment. Besides strengthening the hull and installing a new ballast system, the yard re-created the tween deck, restored the main deck, and introduced new spars. That work, said the *Times*, "signaled the museum's comeback from Hurricane Sandy and financial problems." Even more, added Boulware, who was named executive director in 2015, it put the ship "nearly in sailing condition." "Nearly" was debatable, as the Seaport must first raise the necessary money, train a crew, and secure USCG approval before *Wavertree* can sail "once or twice every couple years" in the harbor. All told, according to Boulware, the Seaport's downsized fleet (*Wavertree, Pioneer*, *Lettie*, *Ambrose*, and *Decker*) annually needs an estimated $1.5 million, and the rest of the museum, $5 million. Left unmentioned, however, are the sizable sums periodically needed to haul and restore each vessel. Critics feared that to earn those funds, *Wavertree* and its large tween deck would be monetized through a partnership with Hughes.[81] (See fig. 36.)

CONCLUSION: "CRITICAL TO THE STORY OF NEW YORK"

As the museum's future was threatened on numerous fronts, its supporters rallied. After action by Community Board No. 1, Brewer, and Chin, as well as grassroots campaigns by Save Our Seaport and the Friends of South Street Seaport, Hughes agreed to accommodate the museum's plan to reopen its twenty-five-thousand-square-foot gallery in the Row's upper floors. Then, after the intervention of Jerrold Nadler, who represents Lower Manhattan in Congress, FEMA allotted $10.4 million for partly repairing the museum's Water Street properties and the Row's utilities. The ultimate beneficiary was their owner, City Hall. In 2016, the Lower Manhattan Development Corporation again helped, giving the museum $4.8 million to create an Educational Community Center in the Water Street library (and gallery). Most important, that grant affirmed the museum's hold on another site that Bloomberg's City Hall had earlier offered to Hughes.[82]

"What is clear right now," Boulware said in 2016, "is the city sees this institution as critical to the story of New York and the cultural landscape." Supported by an array of governmental agencies, the Seaport's fleet and facilities have steadily improved from the rock bottom of 9/11, the museum's administrative dysfunction, and Superstorm Sandy. The museum still has a long road to full recovery, however, as Chief Development Officer Joseph Cheeseman admitted. Remembering that similar institutions must typically rest on four legs—an endowment, philanthropy, government support, and earned income—the Seaport is facing challenges particularly in expanding its endowment and philanthropy. But earned income is indispensable for

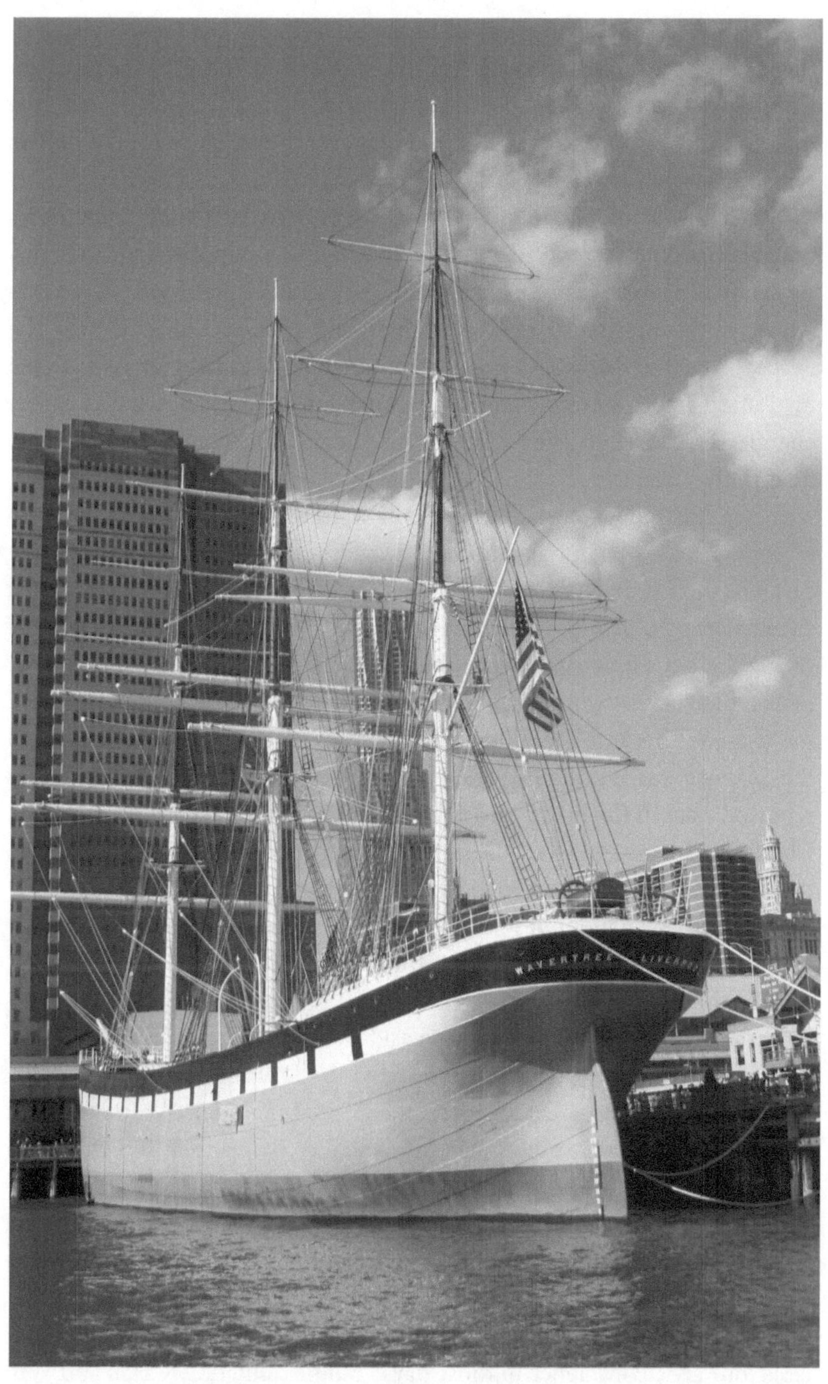

FIGURE 36. *Wavertree* at Pier 16. *Photo by author, 2016.*

success. Of all the pressing issues, Boulware said, the favorable revision of the 1981 lease was central; it was "the one single thing" keeping the museum from sustainability. The fleet—the district's unique asset—costs the museum much more to maintain than it earns, but it reaps tourist dollars for Hughes and City Hall.[83]

When the Stanfords founded the Seaport Museum, they knew of its financial weaknesses, but they rested their faith on popular support. "This museum *is* people" is an inspiring concept, and the Stanfords were years ahead of the museum world in recognizing its essentiality. It held the Seaport together during its worst crises: after 1976, as Shepley remade the institution for commerce, and again, after 2011, when Save Our Seaport energized a coalition. The future will decide if "This museum *is* people" is financially sustainable.

In the late 1960s and early 1970s, the museum boomed partly because of popular support, but also because David Rockefeller and John Lindsay cast it as their proxy. When the mayor chose the museum as the *un*assisted developer of the urban renewal area, he was sailing into uncharted seas. By saving the city's first world trade center at Schermerhorn Row, the Seaport helped the viability of the second complex, one mile away on Fulton Street; the two sites became the yin and yang of Lower Manhattan's rebirth. But the Seaport was not simply undercapitalized; its budget, which auditors reported was "in the black," did not reflect the ships' real costs. Meanwhile, Isbrandtsen's strategy of acquiring key properties failed. With his financial collapse, the museum was left with few assets, huge expenses, and a troubled future. The bailout of 1972–73 made the museum a tenant. If one fact subsequently shaped the museum, it was its subservient role to City Hall's power brokers.[84]

Pushing Stanford and Isbrandtsen aside, corporate interests took charge. Led by James Shepley, developers selected the Rouse Company to build a festival marketplace. That deal, claimed SSSM founder Whitney North Seymour, "doomed the museum." Only later did city planner Richard Weinstein admit, "We in the city made a mistake" by choosing Rouse. Familiar with such swindles, Ada Louise Huxtable sighed, "I am so weary of these stupid alliances between developers and cultural institutions in which the cultural institution is given a block of space and the developers overbuild the rest and make an enormous profit." Ironically, Weinstein called Huxtable "our civic conscience in those days," but he saluted City Hall and Wall Street. Perhaps the streetwise philosopher Eric Hoffer was right when he suggested, "What starts out here as a mass movement ends up as a racket, a cult, or a corporation."[85]

With Rouse, the district changed radically. After Neill arrived in 1985, the Seaport struggled to regain its vitality. Like Stanford, he put the ships and port history first, defended the maritime tradition, and positioned the Seaport as one of the city's major history museums. Yet its instability increased as Stanford tried (unsuccessfully) to reassert control over the museum. As the festival marketplace climbed to a number one ranking for tourism, the museum was even more in its shadow—overlooked and misunderstood by observers. Thus, many agreed with critic Luc Sante, who called the seaport district the tombstone of the old harbor. Because a history museum's coin of the realm is authenticity, and the Seaport was accused of trading in counterfeit currency, Neill labored through the 1990s to make its ships, exhibits, and programs reflect the port's real history. Lacking not only subsidies, endowments, and a year-round gate but also Rouse's promised revenues, the Seaport was financially tenuous. Then came 9/11. Its trauma hung like a pall. With that, the Seaport descended into administrative mismanagement, public derision, and even more determination by City Hall and the EDC to hasten economic development.[86]

Looking back, the Seaport was founded to save a maritime heritage, a deteriorated waterfront, and a tension-wracked city, but its district became a disputed landscape. Those who only see today's flashy commerce fail to appreciate how the museum made the historic district possible. Had not those preservationists succeeded, the area today would show only the city's unbridled pursuit of corporate profits and power. But preservation is, as the National Trust now recognizes, "people saving places," and they are activists for the arts, community, environment, and history. As such, the story of South Street Seaport is a cautionary tale about letting commerce dominate all other matters.

CONCLUSION

"A Loosely Knit Net of Regional Enterprises"

As the youngest and most fragile of its peers, South Street Seaport reveals the promises and pitfalls of preserving maritime America. In the museum's second year, 1968, the Kaplan Fund called a conference to discuss its future. The debate was eye opening. While Peter Stanford and Karl Kortum emphasized saving fast-disappearing sailing ships and Howard Chapelle stressed their neglected artifacts, Frederick Rath, the pioneering first director of the National Trust for Historic Preservation, wanted to enliven the district through a "history laboratory and workshop," such as at Mystic Seaport. But John Hightower, head of the New York State Council on the Arts, balked. To avert its becoming "trapped by collections," he blasted both "the Williamsburg concept of museum," which Mystic emulated, and the static displays that Kortum and Chapelle were perfecting. Instead, he wanted it to be "dramatically involved" with "twentieth-century concerns," including pollution and racial strife. Landmarks commissioner Harmon Goldstone added that the district had to be "imaginatively tied into" the city, including its economy.[1]

Those speakers were too abstract for Joe Cantalupo, a Fulton Fish Market businessman. "Don't lose touch with the people," he urged. "I mean people from all walks of life," and especially from the seaport neighborhood "where eleven ethnic groups live." After all, he said, "A museum *is* people." But, reflecting academic theories about modernity, Kaplan Fund director Ray Rubinow segued into his fears about modern alienation. South Street had to foster, he thought, "a place where people still feel man . . . has some control over his destiny." That led an observer to admit his confusion about the museum's "vague" objectives. Indeed, those diverse, if not divergent, goals led a critic to throw up his hands four years later: "Our museums are in desperate need of psychotherapy!" Four decades later, when South Street was at death's door and U.S. history museums were in trouble, a veteran administrator was still asking if the profession had matched its objectives, means, and market. Maybe Yogi Berra was right: "It's like déjà vu all over again."[2]

Should maritime museums revolve around people, artifacts, research, the environment, social issues, economic development, community building, or what blend of those choices? Perhaps, as raconteur Garrison Keillor wrote in *Pontoon*, as generations pass "you realize there are no answers, just stories." As this book suggests, each museum has a unique tale to tell about its origins, growth, and, when a need presented, its own remaking. Their founders first thought of their port, ships, and people within a global system and then articulated a philosophy and developed a collection to reflect those interests. But each museum evolved as local needs became more pressing. Think of Salem and how its mariners during the French War of 1793–1815 created not only a global trade empire but also a rich cabinet of curiosities to flaunt their imperial prowess. With the demise of Salem's shipping empire, the museum shifted to ethnology, then maritime history, and finally today's hybrid with big crowds, an even bigger endowment, but a diminished nautical presence. Or consider Carl Cutler. Besides advocating an expanded merchant marine, he rebuked the "new" immigrants, big corporations, and 1920s materialism, which led to his antipodal museum extolling homegrown Yankees and their community. Today, Mystic Seaport's collection, programs, and staff are widely admired. But it diverged from Cutler's advocacy through its corporate connections, new social history, and tasteful catering to tourism. Unlike Cutler, Mystic Seaport was changing with America's times.[3]

And recall how Homer Ferguson in the 1930s used Archer Huntington's Mariners' Museum to fight disarmament, boost Newport News shipbuilding, and build a collection that promoted the necessity of global sea power. After later curators tried (unsuccessfully) to focus on the Chesapeake Bay, Mariners' reverted to its naval-industrial complex roots. Or ponder South Street's fate in 1977 after James Shepley gambled with a festival marketplace but nearly destroyed the institution. As such, museum boards will shift course as they look for a more auspicious future. Whether their change is for the better is debatable, because tomorrow's priorities are today's guesses. But ask again if Cantalupo's emphasis on people is the sine qua non for success.

Committed activists can establish museums, sometimes against formidable odds, but they often lose control to more powerful financial, professional, or popular forces. After white, Anglo-Saxon, New Bedford Protestants crafted an exclusionary mythology for their museum, they were supplanted in the 1990s by those who wanted to include nonwhites, whaling ecology, and a national park, all of which boosted the city's spirit and economy. In the field of ship preservation, the movement's pioneers—Cutler, Kortum, and Stanford—were edged out by larger forces, which spoke the rhetoric (but did not always practice the reality) of business-minded finance, professional operations, and institutional stability. When Cutler withdrew to his scholarship, Philip Mallory remade Cutler's dream community into a theme park empire. Kortum and Stanford, however, defended their philosophy and maneuvered to shape their museums with limited success. To their critics, they represented the "founder's syndrome," but their passion, commitment, and energy often contrasted with (as sociologist Max Weber suggested) the priorities of bureaucratic, corporate successors. While South Street was commandeered by such businessmen as Shepley whose preoccupation with development neglected the museum and its ships, as was the case in Mystic, the jury is still out on San Francisco. Whether the National Park Service (NPS) can muster the necessary resources, wisdom, and guts to save its unique fleet and library is today uncertain.

The NPS methodology also supplanted Kortum and his cohorts who wanted quick action to save their ships. But their preservation methods, like pragmatic sailors at sea, were a world apart from Park Service procedures (called "cultural resource management"). Ship preservation is remarkably different from work ashore, where preservationists can mothball structures for later action, whereas vessels in the water present exceptional and immediate challenges, such as the now-endangered *Eureka*. Also, as Kortum recognized in 1969, "the ship end of things comes out second" when competing with land-based expenses, as at Mystic, New York, and San Francisco; that left a scattering of ships "as a kind of fringe of not too consequential character." Rephrasing John Ruskin's warning, Kortum complained that landlubbers "understand old buildings . . . better than they understand ships. To these shore people ships are evanescent, replaceable." He told a depressed Stanford: "On two different coasts you and I are doing more for the spirit of the sea than anybody else." It was "an important thing to sustain," he said, "in these parlous times."[4]

Interested in real sailing ships and their stories, Kortum faced what Smithsonian curator Melvin Jackson derided in 1977 as the "ineffectual nostalgia freaks" who influenced maritime preservation. But, since at least the mid-nineteenth century, nostalgia—or crafted memories—had fired the movement and drove cultural politics. New Bedford's "golden" age or Cutler's romantic "Greyhounds," for example, conveyed a message about the alleged decline of American greatness; each used the sea's romanticism not only to critique social and economic changes set off by industrial capitalism but also to advance an expansionist seaborne agenda. Just as nostalgia can be manipulated, so, too, can maritime heritage, which has focused on the sea and its ships, not the people on board or their class or cultural context. As shown by New Bedford's recent displays on whaling ships' people of color, for instance, the many panels, which were a necessary corrective, failed to develop the lasting effects of earlier exploitation. Typically, as artist John Noble regretted, "our culture, among seagoing nations, has always had the reputation for having an uninformed (maybe the word is blind) attitude toward the professional seamen aboard a cargo vessel." Change the focus and questions arise about a crew's ethnicity, exploitation, and often dire fate.[5]

While the challenges of the sea can be a formative experience, its romanticism has a murky side, as when it obscured Op Sail's inclusion of the Chilean torture ship *Esmeralda*. Or when, as Peter Spectre suggested, visitors boarded *Charles W. Morgan* but did not "learn much about how rotten and foul whaleships" were to their crews and the environment. The glories of the sea have also whitewashed the making of a U.S. empire, as when Ferguson called for naval supremacy or when Cutler lobbied for U.S.-flagged commercial hulls. Those glories paralleled a celebratory history, whereby the triumphs of Salem traders, New Bedford whalers, Newport News shipbuilders, Mystic's Yankee captains, and others were woven into a patriotic story. The beliefs in U.S. exceptionalism and progress camouflaged its imperial rise.[6]

Landside preservationists have long cited the associational values related to historical objects and applied them to their era's cultural politics. Maritime preservationists acted similarly. Shaped by Progressive Era fears about a declining masculinity and posing an alternative to militarism, Irving Johnson, for example, shared his manhood-building experiences with youth, as did Alan Villiers and the American Sail Training Association (also known as Tall Ships America). The National Trust's Peter Neill underscored those foundational values: "the meaning of work and competence, of individualism and self-reliance, of cooperation, of teaching and learning, of appreciation for function and beauty, of reverence for nature." While Mystic's programs pioneered in applying those traits to men and women alike, they could be generated by means other than sailing. Maine Maritime Museum's Lance Lee, like Mystic's John Gardner, thought that their own day's "existential vacuum" could be filled by experiences like boatbuilding. Similarly, Walter Cronkite told maritime preservationists: "The world needs you" because the fast pace of our "technological achievements" has left "us gasping for breath." Urging maritime museums to develop "an intimate view of our past," where human achievements took center stage, he thought that they must create "an interesting and comprehensive—gripping, if you will—story line" linking past and present.[7]

Yet the link between artifact and message was debated. Stanford suggested that visitors, whether "the bored suburbanite, or the child of the urban slum," could learn from an old ship's "mute testimony" about its past. One of his mentors, Frank Carr, likewise believed that ships imparted "the spirit of the men" who built and sailed them. "When I go aboard," he said, "I feel as I feel when going into a cathedral." Benjamin Labaree rebutted that "these vessels do not interpret themselves very well" for visitors unfamiliar with the sea. As a result, and contrary to Kortum's own priorities, museums began to privilege their educational programs, which, said Mystic vice president William Cogar, consumed an ever larger "share of the budget, leaving less and less for other important functions," such as their libraries or interpreters' salaries. Small-craft advocates, such as Mariners' John Sands, resultantly emphasized programs in rowing, sailing, and boatbuilding to kindle "an empathy which frequently [was] lacking in more abstract collections and exhibits." That nurtured Cronkite's goal of an intimacy with the sea, but knowledge of its past was learned only tangentially. Thus Labaree warned that a "vessel should not be romanticized as the be-all and end-all of maritime history, but [used] as a means of educating the public about our maritime past." Still, for Neill, a museum without ships was, unfortunately, built "round an empty hole."[8]

While maritime museums have long had a committed core of yachtsmen, sea lovers, and history buffs, perhaps affirming a privileged class standing, their numbers have never been sufficient to balance the ledgers, especially as museums have broadened their outreach and operations have risen in cost. Their goals have expanded incrementally from Walter Muir Whitehill's belief, as he told a Mystic conference in 1942, that museums should not only preserve and display their materials but promote their research and publication. Stanford claimed, however, that those tasks had become too passive and stuffy. He wanted South Street's ships to become "vital centers of . . . lore, humanity, history." He warned, as electronic media were altering perception: "It is not well to see the world always through a screen."[9]

Countering that ship museums themselves were too lifeless, Gardner encouraged experiential learning. Like those who believed that forgetting the past facilitated its manipulation, he thought that museums had become warehouses that were "likely to become burial vaults" unless they maintained "a living connection between past and present." If done adroitly, they could help shape "the direction of emerging social change." While some critics held that boatbuilding classes were soulless appropriations of working-class identity, Gardner argued instead that by educating young men and women in traditional trades, having them construct new ships according to older ways and designs, actively using those ships for sail training, and reminding Americans of the sea's importance, a museum could create a vital link between yesteryear and today. So, too, did Walter Rybka. "Building reproductions and improving opportunities for people to get out on vessels and participate in their upkeep," he said, "is one of the best possible ways of continuing maritime preservation."[10]

Besides re-creating past experiences in a new context, those reproductions raised another question about authenticity. Critics of Colonial Williamsburg have long regretted its confusing mix of preserved, restored, and reconstructed buildings. With a ship, the question was: What about it was real? Carefully researched ship miniatures in static displays illustrate authenticity in design, as with Chapelle's collection at the Smithsonian's National Museum of American History. Floating museum ships and active vessels, which are certainly more lifelike, fit different conceptions of authenticity. Many ask, for example, does a ship have to sail to be real? Or, does its form—hull, rigging, and materials—have to correspond with that of an old-time vessel? While historic schooners, such as San Francisco's *Alma* and Mystic's *Brilliant*, now sail frequently, square-rigged museum vessels like *Balclutha* and *Wavertree*, according to Rybka, are too rare to risk regularly going to sea, though *Morgan* did sail in 2014 (after a ninety-three-year hiatus) and *Star of India* does so briefly every other year, both to raise their museums' profile. That's now the hope for *Wavertree*. Perhaps a trend will be set by the newest Class A ship, SSV *Oliver Hazard Perry* (2013), because it is not a museum ship or a replica. The 207-foot *Perry* is the largest ocean-going, steel-hulled, square-rigged vessel built in the nation for over a century. It was launched for educational and scientific voyaging, including the Northwest Passage.[11]

When considering the question of authenticity, remember South Street's spirited debates over *Wavertree* and *Peking*. In 1990, the Secretary of the Interior set standards and offered guidelines regarding a vessel's preservation, rehabilitation, and restoration (but not reconstruction) to determine its eligibility for the National Register. The so-called Green Book was "not a manual for maritime preservation" but instead defined "ideal maritime preservation practice" (through the standards) and suggested ways of achieving it (through the guidelines). That solved some issues for museum ships, but the lines separating such work are often blurred because of a floating ship's environment, its unique and deteriorating materials, and the forbidding costs. It is said that USS *Constitution* is authentic, but America's most famous wooden ship and once "the most visited [historic] site in the Northeast" has, said Spectre, "been rebuilt so many times there is hardly a stick of original wood left in her." To resolve the issue of authenticity, preservationists have resultantly emphasized a ship's historic form and design, associations with U.S. history, and feeling of the past, while generally allowing the suitable replacement of original materials.[12]

Active vessels like *Perry* are in a different orb. A combination of forces—nostalgia, sail training, commemoration, and commercial use—has been pushing the trend toward reproductions, replicas, and hybrids, which preservationists once regarded as "slightly suspect, like making plastic polymer copies of scrimshaw." Though nostalgia is often manipulated or commercialized when society faces unsettling change, one real and valuable element of maritime preservation is sailing a vessel. But United States Coast Guard (USCG) regulations and insurance considerations for sail training necessitate features that were rare or unknown in sailing's heyday: internal bulkheads, auxiliary engines, or safety, environmental, and navigation controls. Sail training schools and experiences abound on the nation's oceans, bays, and lakes, but they faced what *Sea History* called a disaster in 2014 when five schooners shut down in August alone. The schools' problems were common: balancing the high costs of ship maintenance and operations with their limited income. Other ships have been specially constructed for commercial or commemorative purposes. For example, *Pride of Baltimore II* (1988), a reproduction of a nineteenth-century Baltimore clipper topsail schooner, was built "to promote the city of Baltimore." Replicas, such as Juan Rodriguez Cabrillo's *San Salvador* in San Diego or *Freedom Schooner Amistad* in Mystic, are typically based on scholarly research, modified for USCG certification, and launched for educational purposes.[13]

The many "hypothetical reconstructions," however, prompted a museum administrator to question the practice if "precise plans or models" did not exist, particularly of long-gone vessels. That was the case for not only the copies of *Santa Maria* built to mark Columbus's voyages but also Jamestown's *Susan Constant*, which was invented in 1957 as a tourist attraction for its 350th anniversary; in 1991 a $2.1 million replacement, reportedly more accurate, was launched. Besides stretching the notion of authenticity, those re-creations worried preservationists as money drifted to building new vessels. "Why are we spending millions of dollars annually on ersatz historic ships," asked Spectre in *WoodenBoat*, "when we have a well-documented supply of genuine historic vessels whose keepers are begging for money to keep them from rotting into the muck?" Others rebutted that building "new" old vessels kept traditional crafts and sailing alive. The debate goes on.[14]

Reproductionism was just one of many trends influencing maritime preservation. While sailors were preserving age-old customs aboard newer craft, their museumification began with cabinets of curiosities. In the case of Salem's East India Marine Society, its mariners used curios to interpret the world, its different cultures, and their own empire. Such collecting is still a function of almost all institutions, though some have no shore galleries; San Diego, for example, relies on displays aboard *Star of India* and *Berkeley*. Regarding ship preservation, the saving of *Constitution* in 1830 and, a century later, its three-year tour set important milestones, but it was Cutler's acquisition of *Morgan* in 1941, his postwar opening of a living seaport, and Mystic's boom that made "a ship at a wharf" the most vibrant symbol of America's maritime tradition. Showing the power of a well-crafted public relations campaign, San Francisco followed suit with David Nelson's national pitch for *Balclutha*. Frank Braynard's Op Sail 64 at the New York World's Fair accelerated the cause. While Mystic was drawing a half-million yearly tourists, Stanford began another trend. In a more holistic approach to preservation, South Street excited legions who linked the natural and human environments, and by the early 1970s, a million people annually interacted with the urban renewal district's living past. As revealed by

South Street's 1968 conference, Stanford launched the twenty-first-century maritime museum; while immersing New Yorkers in the culturally diverse district, his museum empowered them to act socially and environmentally to better the city.[15]

Then, along the nation's seaboard, lakes, and rivers, the opening of festival marketplaces spurred an unprecedented waterfront commercialism. Imitating Mystic and San Francisco, profit-minded developers wanted a ship at their wharf and a group of antique-looking buildings. Critics deplored the "backdrop syndrome," as it debased the memory and viability of real, but struggling, waterfronts. In 1969, for example, developers proposed restoring Baltimore's Fells Point. In that still-segregated neighborhood stood almost 150 houses built before 1800. The proposal included building a new topsail schooner, *Pride of Baltimore* (1977), to join USS *Constellation* at the Inner Harbor. Picturing the National Historic Landmark–listed *Constellation* as the authentic 1797 frigate, though Chapelle warned it was an 1850s corvette, the developers reworked it along eighteenth-century lines. Naval architect William Avery Baker deplored their destruction of "the last sailing warship built for the Navy."[16]

None of that debate deterred James Rouse from building a Baltimore festival marketplace near *Constellation*. His mixing of commercial profit and public culture at Harborplace deliberately confused (but tantalized) visitors. While Fells Point was gentrified and homogenized, *Constellation* was mishandled to the point that it was condemned by 1994. By then, it was proven not only that Chapelle had been right but also that the ship's restoration had relied on forged documents. Yet Fells Point, Harborplace, and *Constellation* were spun as "America's finest example of urban renewal, restoration and renovation." Costing $35 million, Port Discovery then opened as "the first museum project undertaken by Disney." As such, Rouse's creation and the district's racial and class remaking capitalized an important, but problem-filled, case of maritime preservation.[17]

While festival marketplaces were a fad, waterside development has been proceeding under many guises. With gentrification, historic working waterfronts and their real maritime traditions are jeopardized. The sights, sounds, and smells of fishing trawlers, diesel tugs, and harbor vessels and their all-too-often messy shipyards challenge shore people's demands for manicured, open vistas. A telling example is New York's Pier 25, which became part of the 550-acre Hudson River Park. The retired 650-horsepower tug *Pegasus* (1907) won a berth there in 2011, but its income from an educational program and harbor cruises could not pay the bills; in 2015 it lost its insurance, was evicted, and ended up forlorn in New Jersey. Reflecting newer trends was its replacement, the revamped Grand Banks schooner *Sherman Zwicker* (1942). After working for three decades in sail training and education at the Maine Maritime Museum but having become financially tenuous, *Zwicker* was gifted to a New York maritime foundation in 2013 and moved to Pier 25. Becoming a below-deck minigallery and, up top, a seasonal oyster bar, its mix of not-for-profit education and for-profit entertainment is, perhaps, one route for individual ships elsewhere. Nearby along the pier is a more traditional operation, *Lilac* (1933), a former USCG lighthouse tender and now museum ship. They compete with the expanded pier's beach volleyball, putt-putt golf, and skateboard park.[18]

Looking back on the shift, Op Sail 76 was the game changer. Attracting millions of sightseers to and investments in waterfronts, it led to bigger East Coast regattas in 1986, 1992, and 2000, others on the West Coast, and now the yearly Tall Ships Challenge. But preservationists, such as Lance Lee or the Rockport Apprenticeship, remarked that the spectatoritis, commercialism, and sensationalism produced mere dabbling by some observers. Critiquing object-based preservation, including expensive square-riggers, Lee wanted "symbolic actions," such as citizens building boats "to fire up the kids of those towns." Just as philosopher William James had wanted to send idle, pampered youth to the "fishing fleets in December," Lee suggested training "a new generation in how to live by common sense." His calls for building both skills and community, like those of Gardner, tried to foster a grassroots, democratic society.[19]

Other trends have been pursued by smaller museums, such as underwater archaeology at the Lake Champlain Maritime Museum, in Vergennes, Vermont, but one development affecting all is web-based learning; its virtual community is the antithesis of Lee's hands-on apprenticeships. Still, its advocates contend that it will democratize knowledge. Its ability to broaden maritime preservation's audience is widely assumed, but it is uncertain if web "hits" are another form of spectatoritis. While cash-strapped schools reduce class trips to museums, institutions cut internships, and edutainment replaces real education, internet-based learning has become the common denominator to which museums are told, Adapt or die. Describing the need for museums to reinvent themselves, one booster said, "It's not about the collections anymore"; instead, "it's about community." Consultants' buzzwords are "social relevance and global connection" through the internet. While those advocates forget that web materials are usually based on real artifacts and archives that must be collected, made available, and preserved, their goals are a modern iteration of early museum founders. What has changed is the medium of interaction. Earlier museums encouraged members to visit a display, attend a lecture, read a pamphlet, and join a project, but those tasks are nowadays being supplanted by web-based discovery, chat rooms, and online programs. Oddly enough, web-based learning may prove considerably less interactive than assumed. The efficacy of the web is still being tested, but the end result is (and has been) using historical materials to establish relevance and connections.[20]

Environmentalism, or studying and ameliorating the impact of humans on the natural world, is the most crucial of today's additions to maritime museum programming. But some institutions regard themselves as more historical or cultural and have been slow to come aboard, as was the case with New Bedford's resistance (before 1988) to joining the whale conservation cause. South Street was one of the first to think environmentally. At its 1968 planning conference, Hightower complained that the word "progress" was "often used as a great big fat defense of doing some of the most atrocious things imaginable to the environment," but when presiding over South Street and the Mariners' Museum, he was financially pressed and dropped the environmental ball. Pete Seeger had already introduced environmentalism at his South Street songfests, and his *Clearwater* was iconic on the Hudson River. But as of 2018, his sloop was facing financial hardship.[21]

Though New York's marine environment was a regular theme at South Street, Ann Satterthwaite, a well-placed, but narrowly focused, consultant, told a National Trust conference in 1975 that sea museums were "somewhat related to water but not part of the authentic or working waterfront environment." Yet nautical art and curiosities had long been part of sailors' lives and displayed at their waterfront bars, as in the nineteenth century at the Hole-in-the-Wall Saloon near South Street and San Francisco's Cobweb Palace or, as Satterthwaite spoke, at waterfront taverns on New York's bays. For years, the marine environment has been defined too narrowly, prompting an exasperated Labaree to underscore the fact that maritime studies must be broad based and multidisciplinary and involve "almost every profession having to do with the sea." When Neill tried to expand South Street's environmental efforts in 2003, however, its new, but old-fashioned, chairman reportedly said, "This is not what maritime museums do."[22]

The New Bedford Whaling Museum had come to an opposite conclusion as it prepared its game-changing exhibit, *From Pursuit to Preservation: The History of Human Interaction with Whales.* Its importance cannot be overstated as it was accompanied by a multipronged reworking of the museum to better reflect the interaction between humans and the sea. The museum had hoped for even more. To blend human history and marine science, its reorientation initially included an affiliation with a proposed aquarium, but President George W. Bush and Governor Mitt Romney torpedoed the public-private partnership, and the aquarium later failed. In Connecticut, however, a Mystic Pass combines admission to the Seaport and an aquarium one mile away. Such joint ventures synergize what had been separate (even antithetical) experiences, enabling visitors to appreciate the pressing need to conserve the seas and their abundant life. Maritime preservation and marine conservation can and must be mutually supportive.

Introducing new programs and exhibits is expensive. One unsung hero of late twentieth-century preservation was Senator Edward M. Kennedy. In fact, *From Pursuit to Preservation* was partly made possible by his decade-long Education through Cultural and Historical Organizations Program. Kennedy's background—a Hyannis Port sailor, a statesman sensitive to his constituents, and a true believer in the power of government to better the lives of Americans—helped explain his support for maritime preservation. His idealistic attempt in 1974–76 to establish a federally chartered National Trust for the Preservation of Historic Ships was blocked by not only the existing National Trust but also Mystic Seaport and the Peabody Museum. Kennedy settled on legislation in 1977 granting $5 million in support of ship preservation, which passed in the wake of Op Sail 76. With matching funds, it generated $12 million. But that was split between 135 projects in thirty-three states, though Galveston's *Elissa*, San Francisco's *Jeremiah O'Brien*, and Baltimore's *Constellation* received bigger slices.[23]

The paltry sum was quickly exhausted. Seeing Mystic's increasing costs and falling attendance, Waldo Johnston didn't want to become "a professional mendicant" to ensure its survival. Because "a smaller and smaller amount of middle-class people are supporting everybody," he said, "either Uncle Sam picks up the pieces, or [such institutions] go down the tube." Knowing that Europe's best museums were publicly funded and "had access to large government grants," he acknowledged that the Europeans could focus on research and programs, not fundraising. More money was needed,

Kortum argued in 1981, "because the size of the [ship] projects [was] beyond the resources of private groups." Yet, Mystic Seaport's next president, like New York's Peter Stanford, most wanted private sector funding. It was "unwise to rely on the government dole," said Revell Carr, because federal support would likely "vanish as the political winds shift." South Street's Neill interpreted the funding shortfall, however, as "a symptom of national indifference to our maritime patrimony." While "hundreds of millions of federal, state, and city dollars" were invested in land projects, the nation's maritime heritage rotted away.[24]

Kennedy's legislation represented the nation's first and only direct monetary support for maritime preservation until the passage of the National Maritime Heritage Act (1994). Creating matching grants for maritime heritage organizations, it initially relied on 25 percent of the money generated by the disposal of ships from the U.S. reserve fleet. Yet, the grants have been sporadic (the first in 1998, and more after 2014). In 2014, the biggest winners (almost $200,000 each) were *Pampanito*, *Star of India*, and *Sabino*, and in 2017, *W. O. Decker*. As in the past, maritime museums have had to rely on their admission/membership fees, retail sales, and program charges, as well as philanthropy. Yet twenty-first-century corporations and foundations have provided more talk than cash; over 80 percent of yearly giving has come instead from individuals. With the exception of Salem, whose art-oriented donors are in a different world, every museum in this book faced financial duress with the Great Recession. While stability is elusive, a museum should rest on four legs—endowments, philanthropy, government support, and earned income—but each element is unlikely to be equal. As one museum consultant concluded in 2014, there was "no single business model to ensure success."[25]

Rybka sees this financial quandary as "the tragedy of the commons," which he defines as "what belongs to all is cared for by none." If any one issue has prompted museums to tack from their founders' global-minded mission, it has been their financial sustainability. Though these museums have all expressed national aspirations with even global implications, they have, in varying degrees, stepped back because of their weak turnstiles and development offices, mounting logistical costs, and increased competition from not only legitimate museums but also edutainment, whether on television or the internet or at theme parks.[26]

So, where is the commons? In 1971, Stanford and the National Maritime Historical Society (NMHS) tried to unify ranks and coordinate efforts by creating the Sea Museums Council. In 1972, the NMHS launched the magazine *Sea History* to create an intellectual commons. Yet, Mystic Seaport and the Peabody Museum refused to join his group, initially because of their own ambitions and differences with Stanford and Kortum. Instead, they formed their own organization. Billed as "an outgrowth of the first meeting [1972] of the International Congress of Maritime Museums," the Council of American Maritime Museums (CAMM) was the brainchild of Mystic's Johnston and Greenwich's Basil Greenhill, the latter of whom detested Kortum after the *Eppleton Hall* incident. At a Sea Museums Council meeting in 1973, Stanford agreed to dissolve his group, partly to keep *Sea History* afloat. Chartered in 1974, CAMM absorbed the council; its members today—over seventy—constitute the field's top tier.[27]

Opposed to Kennedy's bill establishing an independent ship trust, the National Trust, under a committee headed by Johnston, formed its own maritime office in 1976, initially using funds left over from Braynard's Op Sail 76 organization. Regarding itself as a clearinghouse, a publicist, and a lobbyist, its goal was to advance common interests. Like CAMM, it held conferences and acted as a center, but it was unable to deliver what institutions needed most: money. The National Trust's land-based programs received the lion's share of its funding; the maritime office, noted Rybka, "was always a neglected stepchild." Starved at a time when Reaganomics prevailed, the office closed after a decade of limited operations. The National Trust's own William Murtaugh admitted that it was created to undercut the proposed ship trust and its backer, the NMHS. Protecting one's turf has impeded an expanded maritime preservation.[28]

In 1985, and at Congress's urging, the National Park Service stepped in with its National Maritime Initiative, headed by San Francisco's James Delgado. But while accomplishing what he called "tremendous gains" for lighthouses and shipwrecks and the listing of historic ships, Congress again failed to provide money. Finally, calling for "a spirit of cooperation and common purpose," in 1988 the National Trust helped launch the National Maritime Alliance, a coalition of marine groups and interests. As the Trust closed its maritime office, it provided start-up grants to the Alliance, which carried on the same general goals. Stanford later claimed, however, that it meant "to put [the] NMHS out of business." Yet the Alliance includes one thousand member organizations and caters to a larger professional audience. But its hopes for real federal support seem ever more unrealistic nowadays. Fittingly, in 1992 Neill described maritime preservation as "a loosely knit net of regional enterprises," which included everything from traditional museums to sail-training vessels to apprenticeship programs. Because such organizations as the National Trust and Park Service could not meet their needs, he said, "we have gone maverick ways, seeking our own appropriations, writing our own bills, sharing our experience, and serving each other."[29]

Coordinating national action has been difficult. Beginning in the early 1970s, established museums were rattled by Stanford and Kortum's agenda, as when Walter Cronkite mentioned, in a 1978 keynote speech at a Mystic conference, the jealousy and rivalry within the maritime preservation community. Representative Phillip Burton's legislative designation of San Francisco as the National Maritime Museum added to the distrust, as did the U.S. Senate's backroom deal in 1998 that named South Street and Mariners' as America's National Maritime Museum. South Street chairman Peter Aron remarked, "The amount of jealousy, back-biting and ill-will we found in the other parts of the maritime museum community [was] really shocking and disappointing." Their "lack of imagination and trust," he predicted, "will keep everybody scrambling and independent of one another." Yet, after almost two dozen museums and their influential senators called for the bill's revision to include more organizations, no action was taken, thus underscoring the maritime community's fears. Even in the small world of sail training, one critic asked for "closer coordination, [and] mutual understanding among ourselves." He lamented: "We do not help each other enough, and allow petty jealousies to interfere with larger goals." Tall Ships America now hopes to redress that failing.[30]

Labaree and Cogar still suggested that if maritime culture is "to survive in America, it will depend largely on [private museums and organizations] rather than our colleges and universities." While Labaree was acknowledging the regional, if not local, roots of maritime preservation, he was, perhaps, also implying that some smaller, but important, museums could not meet the professional standards associated with a college curriculum, just as some resentment had been earlier caused by the Green Book. While its standards were being discussed, one museum administrator complained in 1985, "Maritime preservation has been carried on by and supported by amateurs since the beginning of the movement. I would hate to see these people shut out of the process by pondering, self-satisfied professionals." Even today, most U.S. maritime museums are not members of CAMM or the standard-setting American Alliance of Museums.[31]

But while a highly frustrated Hightower claimed that the nation's "maritime museums do not have particularly visible and sizeable constituencies," those museums generally rely on amateurs and volunteers, even in a professional capacity. Recalling Cantalupo's axiom, "A museum *is* people," the most commonly accepted requirement for a sustainable museum today is a strong relationship with its community. If, as Emmy award–winning broadcaster Hugh Downs suggested, Americans were "fascinated with the maritime past even more than with other aspects of history," the trick is turning that interest into the financial engine necessary for success. It does not work for all museums. In 2009, the Hawai'i Maritime Center failed, leaving in limbo the National Historic Landmark–listed *Falls of Clyde*, which had been saved by Kortum in 1963. Hawaiian preservationists accused the Bishop Museum, its parent organization, of "incompetence and dishonesty in its stewardship," as it planned to scuttle the relic. In 2018, private negotiations by a friends' association to move the four-masted ship to Glasgow ran aground, and its future is in doubt. While the Monterey (CA) Maritime Museum also succumbed, transferring its century-old collection partly to San Francisco Maritime in 2010, the Jacksonville (FL) Maritime Heritage Center called it quits in 2015 and auctioned off most of its holdings.[32]

As attendance and philanthropy were hit by recessions, administrators added programs like living ships (such as Mystic's demonstration squads) and family learning (as at the *Constitution* museum), as well as experiential education, special events, and holiday entertainment. Analysts have also suggested that smaller museums may benefit by developing "affinity groups," whereby members and volunteers become their prime focus and share authority. Yet, as in restrictive clubs, the danger is limiting outreach. Museums across the board are rightly worried. "If we don't cultivate" connections to nontraditional audiences, warned an administrator of a West Coast metropolitan museum, "we will be a dying institution of older white people." New Bedford expanded its base by embracing the history of nonwhites in the whaling industry; San Francisco is, meanwhile, offering programs to a wide demographic swath of the Bay Area. In one revealing study, moreover, Mystic Seaport discovered that its visitors came "primarily to enjoy themselves, and [were] not particularly motivated to 'learn' from our exhibits." Yet the institution's raison d'être is education, which should, perhaps, be recast as "experiencing" all things maritime. During *Morgan*'s thirty-eighth voyage, Mystic leaders sought to create a "participatory museum" with voyagers and observers. But one danger in establishing shared authority over the ship's interpretation is that a visitor's feelings may trump the reality of fact.[33]

Confidently selling his own brand of preservation to Ted Kennedy in 1974, Kortum wrote: "It is inconceivable that a time will come when the seafaring instinct is not important . . . to the American people. If that instinct is to be a matter of spirit, rather than just of necessity, then the introduction to salt water voyaging by great ships preserved has national importance."[34] He was right: the public must learn about the sea's significance and feel its zeitgeist. While Kortum promoted museum visits, ship preservation, maritime scholarship, and popular interest, Irving Johnson was a convincing salesman of seafaring, but his life's globetrotting adventures could be emulated by few. As John Gardner knew, moreover, most Americans did little more than visit his seaport or walk *Morgan*'s deck. Much more was needed. He wanted the public to learn from, if not experience, the culture of artisans, the trials of sailors, and the mutuality of land and sea, which included humans not only facing the ocean's challenges but also conserving its habitat. When put together, those experiences embodied the essence of maritime preservation. Anything less was only a first step.

Led by Gardner, whose influence spread nationally, Mystic Seaport introduced or expanded programs in boatbuilding, rowing, navigation, and sail training. Supplementing those experiences were projects in history, ecology, and the arts, often through its research center or multitiered educational ventures. As museums recognize, those undertakings must start with the nation's youth (and their families) and continue into later years. One generation must inspire the next, and so on, as an era's increasingly fast-paced technological change disconnects youth from the world of their immediate forebears. So, if "a museum *is* people," it begins by kindling a personal interest in the history, culture, and natural life of the rivers, lakes, and oceans of the nation and, indeed, the world. Once done, other steps will follow in preserving maritime America.

NOTES

ABBREVIATIONS

AN	*American Neptune*
BG	*Boston Globe*
Bulletin	*The Bulletin from Johnny Cake Hill*
CAMM	Council of American Maritime Museums
CF/MSM	Corporate File, G. W. Blunt White Library, Mystic Seaport Museum
CP/MSM	Cutler Papers, Manuscripts Collection, G. W. Blunt White Library, Mystic Seaport Museum
CSM	*Christian Science Monitor*
DE	*Downtown Express*
DPNYC	*Downtown Post New York City*
EIHC	Essex Institute Historical Collections
EIMS	East India Marine Society
FP/MM	Ferguson Papers, Mariners' Museum
GGNRA	Golden Gate National Recreation Area
IA/SSSM	Institutional Archives, South Street Seaport Museum
JACF	J. Aron Charitable Foundation
KC/SFMNHP	Kortum Collection, San Francisco Maritime National Historical Park
KC/SSSM	Kortum Correspondence, Institutional Archives, South Street Seaport Museum
LAT	*Los Angeles Times*
Log	*Log of Mystic Seaport*
MHA	Marine Historical Association
MM	Mariners' Museum
MN	*Maritime News* (SFMNHP)
MMJ	*Mariners' Museum Journal*

MSM	Mystic Seaport Museum
NBST	*New Bedford Standard-Times*
NEQ	*New England Quarterly*
NLD	*New London Day*
NMHS	National Maritime Historical Society
NNDP	*Newport News Daily Press*
NNSDD	Newport News Shipbuilding and Dry Dock Co.
NNTH	*Newport News Times-Herald*
NVP	*Norfolk Virginian-Pilot*
NYDN	*New York Daily News*
NYP	*New York Post*
NYT	*New York Times*
ODHS	Old Dartmouth Historical Society
ODHSk	Old Dartmouth Historical Sketches
OP	ODHS Papers
PEM	Peabody Essex Museum
PH	*Public Historian*
PSP	Peter Stanford Papers (provided to author)
PL/PEM	Phillips Library/Peabody Essex Museum
PUSNI	*Proceedings of the United States Naval Institute*
RNL	*Richmond News Leader*
RTD	*Richmond Times-Dispatch*
SFC	*San Francisco Chronicle*
SFE	*San Francisco Examiner*
SFMM	San Francisco Maritime Museum
SFMNHP	San Francisco Maritime National Historical Park (formerly National Maritime Museum)
SH	*Sea History* (published by the National Maritime Historical Society)
SL	*Sea Letter* (published by the SFMM, National Maritime Museum Association, and San Francisco Maritime National Park Association)
SSSM	South Street Seaport Museum
SSR	*South Street Reporter*
TSNAME	*Transactions of Society of Naval Architects and Marine Engineers*
WB	*WoodenBoat*
WHALE	Waterfront Historic Area League
WMQ	*William and Mary Quarterly*
WP	*Washington Post*
WSJ	*Wall Street Journal*

ACKNOWLEDGMENTS

1. John B. Hattendorf, "Maritime History Today," *Perspectives on History*, February 2012; William Appleman Williams, "Notes on the Death of a Ship and the End of a World," *AN* 41 (March 1981): 122–38.

INTRODUCTION: FROM CABINETS OF CURIOSITIES TO REMADE WATERFRONTS

1. Peter Stanford, "The Ship as Museum," *SH* 46 (Winter 1987–88): 15; Robert Greenhalgh Albion, *Naval and Maritime History: An Annotated Bibliography*, 4th ed., rev. and expanded (Mystic, CT: Munson Institute, 1972), viii; Daniel Vickers, "Beyond Jack Tar," *WMQ* 50 (April 1993): 418; Joshua M. Smith, "Far beyond Jack Tar," *Coriolis* 2, no. 2 (2011): 1. In 1985, one maritime organization regretted that "the *Journal of American History* and the Organization of American Historians barely acknowledge the topic [of maritime preservation] as a legitimate area of research" (White Elephant Management, *Summary of Results of the Maritime Heritage Survey Conducted for the National Trust for Historic Preservation* [Galveston, TX: White Elephant Management, 1985], 47).
2. James W. Loewen, *Lies across America: What Our Historic Sites Get Wrong* (New York: New Press, 1999), 25; Anne D. Neal and Jerry L. Martin, *Restoring America's Legacy* (Washington, D.C.: American Council of Trustees and Alumni, 2002), 4; Tyler Kingkade, "Only 3 Percent of Colleges Require Students to Take an Economics Class," *Huffington Post*, October 15, 2014; Roy Rosenzweig and David Thelen, *The Presence of the Past: Popular Uses of History in American Life* (New York: Columbia University Press, 1998), 21, 105–6.
3. Tim Weiner, "U.S. Law Puts World Ports on Notice," *NYT*, March 24, 2004; John Ruskin, *The Harbours of England* (London: E. Gambart, 1856), 38.
4. The historical literature on late nineteenth- and early twentieth-century preservation is introduced in James M. Lindgren, *Preserving the Old Dominion: Historic Preservation and Virginia Traditionalism* (Charlottesville: University Press of Virginia, 1993), and *Preserving Historic New England: Preservation, Progressivism, and the Remaking of Memory* (New York: Oxford University Press, 1995).
5. Peter Neill to the editor, "Who Cares about Historic Ships?" *NYT*, August 2, 1988; Barbaralee Diamonstein, *The Landmarks of New York* (New York: Abrams, 1988), 10; Dick Sheridan, "Port of Missing Ships: Whatever Happened to the South Street Dream?," *NYDN*, March 26, 1989, magazine.
6. Jesse Lemisch, "Jack Tar in the Streets: Merchant Seamen in the Politics of Revolutionary America," *WMQ* 25 (July 1968): 371–407; Don Birkholz, "The Role of Marine Surveys in Maritime Preservation," *APT Bulletin* 19, no. 1 (1987): 45.
7. Ralph Waldo Emerson, "Self-Reliance," from "The Philosophy of History" (1836–37), in *The Early Lectures of Ralph Waldo Emerson, Vol. II: 1836–1838*, ed. Stephen E. Whicher, Robert E. Spiller, and Wallace E. Williams (Cambridge, MA: Harvard University Press, 1964); James M. Lindgren, "'A New Departure in Historic,

Patriotic Work': Personalism, Professionalism, and Conflicting Concepts of Material Culture in the Late Nineteenth and Early Twentieth Centuries," *PH* 18 (Spring 1996): 41–60 (in studying the building preservation movement, I noted that gender played a significant role in this shift; yet maritime preservation was—and still is—predominantly a male interest); Kevin Walsh, *The Representation of the Past: Museums and Heritage in the Post-Modern World* (New York: Routledge, 1992); David Lowenthal, *Possessed by the Past: The Heritage Crusade and the Spoils of History* (New York: Free Press, 1996), and my review of the latter, "A Cuckoo in Our Nest: Can Historians Handle the Heritage Boom?," *PH* 19 (Spring 1997): 77–82.

CHAPTER 1: "THAT EVERY MARINER MAY POSSESS THE HISTORY OF THE WORLD"

1. "EIMS," October 17, 1825, clipping, MH88, box 27f3, PL/PEM; Meeting, October 14, 1825, MH88, box 1B, PL/PEM; Walter Muir Whitehall, *The East India Marine Society and the Peabody Museum of Salem: A Sesquicentennial History* (Salem, MA: Peabody Museum, 1949), 27.
2. James R. Fichter, *So Great a Profit: How the East Indies Trade Transformed Anglo-American Capitalism* (Cambridge, MA: Harvard University Press, 2010), 279–80; Harlow W. Sheidley, *Sectional Nationalism: Massachusetts Conservative Leaders and the Transformation of America, 1815–1836* (Boston: Northeastern University Press, 1998), 66–67; Lawrence Waters Jenkins and Walter Muir Whitehill, "The Restoration of East India Marine Hall," *AN* 4 (January 1941): 11.
3. Richard H. Davis, *Lives of Indian Images* (Princeton, NJ: Princeton University Press, 1997), 171; John M. MacKenzie, *Museums and Empire: Natural History, Human Cultures and Colonial Identities* (Manchester: Manchester University Press, 2009), 1.
4. J. S. Buckingham, *The Eastern and Western States of America*, 2 vols. (London: Fisher, 1842), 2:72–73; Charles H. P. Copeland, "The Maritime History Department," *Handbook to the Collections of the Peabody Museum of Salem*, ed. Ernest S. Dodge and Charles H. P. Copeland (Salem, MA: Peabody Museum, 1949), 23.
5. EIMS, *History of the Salem East India Marine Society* (Salem, MA: Newcomb & Gauss, 1916), 40; Whitehall, *East India Marine Society*, vii, 8; Thomas Barbour, *Naturalist at Large* (Boston: Little, Brown, 1943), 168–71.
6. Frances Winwar, *Puritan City: The Story of Salem* (New York: McBride, 1938), 187; C. B. T., "Salem Reminiscences," *Sailor's Magazine and Seamen's Friend*, October 1883, 293; Holden Furber, "The Beginnings of American Trade with India, 1784–1812," *NEQ* 11 (June 1938): 258; Susan S. Bean, *Yankee India: American Commercial and Cultural Encounters with India in the Age of Sail, 1784–1860* (Salem, MA: Peabody Essex Museum, 2001), 17, 21.
7. Samuel Eliot Morison, *The Maritime History of Massachusetts, 1783–1860* (Boston:

Houghton Mifflin, 1921), 80; James Duncan Phillips, *Salem and the Indies: The Story of the Great Commercial Era of the City* (Boston: Houghton Mifflin, 1947), 58, 92–96; EIMS, *History*, 28; "EIMS."

8. Willis J. Abbot, *American Merchant Ships and Sailors* (New York: Dodd, Mead, 1902), 36; James Duncan Phillips, *When Salem Sailed the Seven Seas—in the 1790's* (New York: Newcomen Society, 1946), 2; Daniel Vickers, *Young Men and the Sea: Yankee Seafarers in the Age of Sail* (New Haven, CT: Yale University Press, 2005), 306n15; Tom Abrams, "Peabody Essex Museum," *American History*, August 2002, 16–17.
9. Vickers, *Young Men*, 136, 171; Fichter, *So Great a Profit*, 132; Charles S. Osgood and H. M. Batchelder, *Historical Sketch of Salem* (Salem, MA: Essex Institute, 1879), 131–32.
10. William A. Baker, *A History of the Boston Marine Society, 1742–1967* (Boston: Boston Marine Society, 1968), 123; Anne Farnam, "A Society of Societies: Associations and Voluntarism in Early Nineteenth-Century Salem," *EIHC* 113 (July 1977): 181; William Bentley, *The Diary of William Bentley, D.D.*, 4 vols. (1907; repr., Gloucester, MA: Peter Smith, 1962), October 22, November 7, 1799, 2:321–22; John Gardner, "Boats and Ships in One New England Seaport," *Log* 29 (July 1977): 43.
11. Fichter, *So Great a Profit*, 152; Vickers, *Young Men*, 134, 170; Joseph B. Felt, *Annals of Salem*, 2 vols. (Salem, 1845–49), 2:69; Jedidiah Morse, *A New Universal Gazetteer, or, Geographical Dictionary* (New Haven, CT: Converse and Andrus, 1821), 56; Anne Newport Royall, *Sketches of History, Life, and Manners, in the United States* (New Haven, CT: author, 1826), 363.
12. Buckingham, *Eastern and Western States*, 2:268–69; Fiske Kimball, *Mr. Samuel McIntire, Carver: The Architect of Salem* (1940; Salem, MA: Essex Institute, 1966), 15; Frances Diane Robotti, *Chronicles of Old Salem* (New York: Bonanza, 1948), 47, 56; Vickers, *Young Men*, 209; Margaret B. Moore, *The Salem World of Nathaniel Hawthorne* (Columbia: University of Missouri Press, 1998), 127; M. C. D. Silsbee, *A Half Century in Salem* (Boston, 1887), 1; Benjamin F. Browne, "Youthful Recollections of Salem," *EIHC* 51 (1915): 295.
13. Bentley, *Diary*, January 12, 1802, 2:408; Baker, *Boston Marine Society*, 6, 309; Jon Mason et al., Report, April 29, 1802, MH88, box 28E, PL/PEM; Jeffrey L. Pasley, *The Tyranny of Printers: Newspaper Politics in the Early Republic* (Charlottesville: University Press of Virginia, 2002), 211.
14. Bentley, *Diary*, January 4, 1804, 3:68; *Salem Gazette*, November 6, 1804, November 7, 1806; "X" to EIMS, *Salem Gazette*, November 5, 1805; Moore, *Salem World*, 171–73; Whitehall, *East India Marine Society*, 18, 22; Robotti, *Chronicles*, 51–52.
15. George Granville Putnam, *Salem Vessels and Their Voyages* (Salem, MA: Essex Institute, 1924), 55; Ralph D. Paine, *The Ships and Sailors of Old Salem* (New York: Outing, 1908), 637; Bentley, *Diary*, January 31, 1809, 3:413; Winwar, *Puritan City*, 187, 197.
16. "For the Benefit of the Poor," *Salem Gazette*, January 20, 1808; Bentley, *Diary*,

January 29, 1809, 3:412; Whitehall, *East India Marine Society*, 22, 26; Sheidley, *Sectional Nationalism*, 10.

17. Robotti, *Chronicles*, 52–53; Leverett Saltonstall to Nathaniel Saltonstall, August 3, 1812, in *The Saltonstall Papers, 1607–1815*, ed. Robert E. Moody, 2 vols. (Boston: Massachusetts Historical Society, 1974), 2:523; Baker, *Boston Marine Society*, 107, 116; Whitehall, *East India Marine Society*, 22.
18. Bentley, *Diary*, July 7, October 7, 1803, 3:32, 52–53; Buckingham, *Eastern and Western States*, 2:539; J. S. Buckingham, *America, Historical, Statistic, and Descriptive*, 3 vols. (New York: Harper, 1841), 2:370–71.
19. A. H. Saxon, "P. T. Barnum and the American Museum," *Wilson Quarterly* 13 (Autumn 1989): 134–35.
20. Buckingham, *Eastern and Western States*, 2:270–71, 275.
21. Bentley, *Diary*, June 11, 1804, 3:93, and November 10, 1804, 3:121; *Salem Gazette*, November 6, 1804; Ernest S. Dodge, "Captain Collectors: The Influence of New England Shipping on the Study of Polynesian Material Culture," *EIHC* 81 (January 1945): 29.
22. Harold Bowditch, "Nathaniel Bowditch," in a *Catalogue of a Special Exhibition* (Salem, MA: Peabody Museum, 1937), 4; Paine, *Ships and Sailors*, 269, 416; Whitehall, *East India Marine Society*, 19; Alex Roland, W. Jeffrey Bolster, and Alexander Keyssar, *The Way of the Ship: America's Maritime History Reenvisioned, 1600–2000* (Hoboken, NJ: Wiley, 2008), 172–73; Copeland, "Maritime History Department," 32; Samuel Eliot Morison, "Salem's Salty Museum," *Holiday*, August 1955, 64, 66.
23. Alexander Young, *The Varieties of Human Greatness: A Discourse on the Life and Character of the Hon. Nathaniel Bowditch* (Boston: Little, Brown, 1838), 64n; EIMS, *History*, 29; Dodge, "Captain Collectors," 31; Daniel Finamore, "'Curiously Carved': Early Collections of *Susan*'s Teeth, 1830–1921," *AN* 60, no. 4 (2000): 372; Madison to EIMS, April 16, 1822, and Jefferson to EIMS, April 27, 1822, MH88, box 3f11, PL/PEM.
24. Felt, *Annals*, 2:349; Robert Booth, *Death of an Empire* (New York: St. Martin's, 2011), 130; Philip Chadwick Foster Smith, "The Metamorphosis of East India Marine Hall," *Historic Preservation*, October–December 1975, 12; Morison, "Salty Museum," 64.
25. Copeland, "Maritime History Department," 37.
26. Moore, *Salem World*, 209, 212; Charles E. Goodspeed, *Nathaniel Hawthorne and the Museum of the Salem East India Marine Society, or, The Gathering of a Virtuoso's Collection* (Salem, MA: Peabody Museum, 1946), 17; Joseph Flibbert, "Nathaniel Hawthorne: Salem Personified," in *Salem: Cornerstones of a Historic City*, by Joseph Flibbert, K. Goss, Bryant Tolles, Richard Trask, and Jim McAllister (Beverly, MA: Commonwealth Editions, 1999), 85; Caroline Howard King, *When I Lived in Salem, 1822–1866* (Brattleboro, VT: Stephen Daye, 1937), 33.
27. Nicholas Thomas, *Entangled Objects: Exchange, Material Culture, and Colonialism*

in the Pacific (Cambridge, MA: Harvard University Press, 1991), 140; Whitehall, *East India Marine Society*, 49, 54, 142n19.

28. Nathaniel Hawthorne, "A Virtuoso's Collection," *Boston Miscellany of Literature and Fashion*, May 1842, 199; "X" to EIMS, *Salem Gazette*, November 5, 1805; "Catalogue of the Articles in the Museum," no. 553, in *The EIMS of Salem* (Salem, MA: Salem Press, 1831), 59; Daniel Finamore, "Displaying the Sea and Defining America," *Journal for Maritime Research* 4 (May 2002): 41.
29. "Catalogue," nos. 770, 771, 2274; Copeland, "Maritime History Department," 22, 38, 39; John Robinson, *The Marine Room of the Peabody Museum of Salem* (Salem, MA: Peabody Museum, 1921), 29, 61, 74.
30. Daniel Vickers, "Competency and Competition: Economic Culture in Early America," *WMQ* 47 (January 1990): 3–29; Fichter, *So Great a Profit*, 94, 209; Bentley, *Diary*, July 16, 1796, 2:191; Morison, *Maritime History*, 46.
31. Carl L. Crossman, *The China Trade: Export Paintings, Furniture, Silver and Other Objects* (Princeton, NJ: Pyne Press, 1972), 188, 204, 212; "Catalogue," nos. 242, 650, 3507, 3508; Ernest S. Dodge, "The Ethnology Department," in *Handbook*, ed. Dodge and Copeland, 2; Buckingham, *Eastern and Western States*, 2:64.
32. Bentley, *Diary*, June 5, 1790, 1:175, and January 7, 1801, 2:361; "Catalogue," nos. 233, 234, 235, 237, 238, 239; Frederic D. Grant Jr. to author, email, March 1, 2013.
33. Walter Muir Whitehill, "Remarks on the Canton Trade and the Manner of Transacting Business," *EIHC* 73, no. 4 (1937): 307–9; Frederic D. Grant Jr., "The April 1820 Debt Settlement between Conseequa and Benjamin Chew Wilcocks," in *Americans and Macao*, ed. Paul Van Dyke (Hong Kong: Hong Kong University Press, 2012), 74; "Catalogue," nos. 387, 455, 618; James R. Gibson, *Otter Skins, Boston Ships, and China Goods* (Seattle: University of Washington Press, 1992), 191.
34. George T. Haley, Usha C. V. Haley, and Chin Tiong Tan, *New Asian Emperors: The Business Strategies of the Overseas Chinese* (Singapore: Wiley, 2009), n.p.; *AN* 4, no. 1 (1944): 12; "EIMS," October 17, 1825, clipping, MH88, box 27f3, PL/PEM; Gibson, *Otter Skins*, 316 (Table 8).
35. Robert Greehalgh Albion, "From Sails to Spindles: Essex County in Transition," *EIHC* 95 (April 1959): 136; Vickers, *Young Men*, 199.
36. "Catalogue," nos. 230, 2692, 2693, 2695, 2697; Jenny Rose, *Zoroastrianism: An Introduction* (New York: Tauris, 2011), 198.
37. "Catalogue," nos. 177–90, 202, 205, 773, 786; "Original Letters from an American Gentleman at Calcutta," *Analectic Magazine*, May 1819, 396–97.
38. "Catalogue," nos. 248, 249, 317, 1550–53, 3724; Buckingham, *Eastern and Western States*, 1:275; Sirajul Islam, "Americans in Calcutta Bazaars in the Early Nineteenth Century," *Journal of the Asiatic Society of Bangladesh* 50, nos. 1–2 (2005); "Original Letters," 399–400; R. K. Gupta, *The Great Encounter: A Study of Indo-American Literary and Cultural Relations* (Riverdale, MD: Riverdale, 1987), 23–24.
39. "Catalogue," nos. 1–149 (esp. 127–30 and 136), 260–74, 1592.

40. *The East-India Marine Society of Salem* (Salem, MA: Palfray, 1821), 33. A later catalog simply read: "to cut up the bodies of victims" ("Catalogue," no. 144, p. 46). For an illustration, see Ernest Stanley Dodge, *The New Zealand Maori Collection in the Peabody Museum of Salem* (Salem, MA: Peabody Museum, 1941), 14 (fig. 23); 16 (figs. 30–31); 42 (fig. 106); 43 (figs. 110–12); 46 (figs. 126–29); 47 (fig. 134); 50 (fig. 149); and 52 (fig. 156).
41. Gananath Obeyesekere, *Cannibal Talk: The Man-Eating Myth and Human Sacrifice in the South Seas* (Berkeley: University of California Press, 2005); Thomas, *Entangled Objects*, 138; Dodge, *Maori Collection*, 52 (fig. 156); "Catalogue," nos. 96–98, 3398; Royall, *Sketches*, 361.
42. Ernest Stanley Dodge, *The Marquesas Islands Collection in the Peabody Museum of Salem* (Salem, MA: Peabody Museum, 1939), plate XVIII, and *The Hervey Islands Adzes in the Peabody Museum of Salem* (Salem, MA: Peabody Museum, 1937), 2–3; Thomas, *Entangled Objects*, 136, 138.
43. *The (Hudson, NY) Balance and Columbian Repository*, November 4, 1806, 351; Fichter, *So Great a Profit*, 222; "Catalogue," nos. 170–71, 461, 3718; Dodge, "Ethnology Department," 9.
44. Charles Moses Endicott et al., "Outrage of the Malays," *Sailors Magazine, and Naval Journal*, September 1831, 5–7; "Catalogue," no. 3034.
45. Fichter, *So Great a Profit*, 229–30; "Catalogue," nos. 178–82, 197, 3730–31; Gibson, *Otter Skins*, 316 (Table 8); Buckingham, *Eastern and Western States*, 2:70–71; Buckingham, *America*, 3:235.
46. Bentley, *Diary*, September 23, 1788, 1:104, and August 30, 1802, 2:442; John R. Grimes, *The Tribal Style: Selections from the African Collection at the Peabody Museum of Salem* (Salem, MA: Peabody Museum, 1984), 42; Hugh Thomas, *The Slave Trade* (New York: Simon & Schuster, 1997), 681; "News by Telegraph," *NYT*, August 8, 1859.
47. "Catalogue," no. 3913; R. A. Derrick, *A History of Fiji* (Suva, Fiji: Government Press, 1957), 43; Paine, *Ships and Sailors*, 234; *The Hawaiian Portion of the Polynesian Collections in the Peabody Museum of Salem* (Salem, MA: Peabody Museum, 1920), 52 (fig. 364, Plate XIIIb).
48. Vickers, *Young Men*, 144, 211; Amy S. Greenberg, *Manifest Manhood and the Antebellum American Empire* (New York: Cambridge University Press, 2005); Richard Henry Dana Jr., *Two Years before the Mast* (1840; Garden City, NY: Doubleday, 1949), 240; Jenkins and Whitehill, "Restoration," 12.
49. Dodge, "Ethnology Department," 5; Paul A. Van Dyke, *The Canton Trade* (Hong Kong: Hong Kong University Press, 2007), 204n55; Finamore, "Curiously Carved," 376; Nathaniel Bowditch, *Early American-Philippine Trade: The Journal of Nathaniel Bowditch in Manila, 1796*, ed. Thomas R. McHale and Mary C. McHale (New Haven, CT: Yale University Press, 1962), 62; Fichter, *So Great a Profit*, 130–31. Cheever's comment about "sexes" is intriguing, perhaps implying that all "ladies" weren't female.

50. "Catalogue," nos. 587, 612, 660–61, 1412–13, 2699, 3048; Dodge, "Ethnology Department," 2–3, and "Captain Collectors," 33; Whitehall, *East India Marine Society*, 40; Mary Malloy, *"Boston Men" on the Northwest Coast: The American Maritime Fur Trade, 1788-1844* (Fairbanks, AK: University of Alaska Press, 1998), 149; Milton Diamond, "Sexual Behavior in Pre-Contact Hawai'i," *Revista Española del Pacifico* 16 (2004): 37–58.
51. Lee Wallace, *Sexual Encounters: Pacific Texts, Modern Sensualities* (Ithaca, NY: Cornell University Press, 2003), 14–15; 68–75; Arthur N. Gilbert, "Buggery and the British Navy, 1700–1861," *Journal of Social History* 10 (Autumn 1976): 72–98; Margaret S. Creighton, "American Mariners and the Rites of Manhood, 1830–1870," in *Jack Tar in History: Essays in the History of Maritime Life and Labour*, ed. Colin Howell and Richard J. Twomey (Fredericton, NB: Acadiensis Press, 1991), 155n40; B. R. Burg, *An American Seafarer in the Age of Sail: The Erotic Diaries of Philip C. Van Buskirk, 1851–1870* (New Haven, CT: Yale University Press, 1994), 75; William Benemann, *Male-Male Intimacy in Early America* (New York: Haworth Press, 2006), 88.
52. John T. Prince to John White Treadwell, October 13, 1844, MH88, box1B, PL/PEM; Whitehall, *East India Marine Society*, 49–50; James W. Loewen, *Lies across America* (New York: New Press, 1999), 56. Only two other icons survive: at the Bishop Museum (Honolulu) and the British Museum. First described as a god of medicine, it has been reinterpreted as Kukailimoku, a war god that guarded the tomb of King Kamehameha.
53. Dodge, "Ethnology Department," 5–6, and "Early American Contacts in Polynesia and Fiji," *Proceedings of the American Philosophical Society* 107 (April 1963): 106; Marshall Sahlins, *Islands of History* (Chicago: University of Chicago Press, 1985), viii, and *How "Natives" Think: About Captain Cook, for Example* (Chicago: University of Chicago Press, 1996); Robert W. Rydell, *All the World's a Fair: Visions of Empire at American International Expositions, 1876-1916* (Chicago: University of Chicago Press, 1984); Gananath Obeyesekere, *The Apotheosis of Captain Cook: European Mythmaking in the Pacific* (Princeton, NJ: Princeton University Press, 1997).
54. Josef Konvitz, "Changing Concepts of the Sea, 1550–1950," *Terra Incognitae* 11 (1979): 6, 8; Ernest S. Dodge, "The Contributions to Exploration of the Salem EIMS," *AN* 25, no. 3 (1965): 177–78.
55. "Salem EIMS," *North American Review* 6 (1818): 284; EIMS, *History*, 19; Whitehill, *East India Marine Society*, 18, 179; Lloyd A. Brown, *The Story of Maps* (Boston: Little Brown, 1949), 121; Buckingham, *Eastern and Western States*, 1:271.
56. EIMS, *Memorial . . . Praying that an Expedition be Fitted Out by the Government to Make a Voyage of Discovery and Survey to the South Seas. December 16, 1834* (Washington, D.C., 1834); William Stanton, *The Great United States Exploring Expedition of 1838–1842* (Berkeley: University of California Press, 1975), 30, 191, 275; Special Meeting, October 10, 1836, MH88, box1B, PL/PEM; Whitehall, *East India Marine*

Society, 14; Edward P. Crapol, *John Tyler: The Accidental President* (Chapel Hill: University of North Carolina Press, 2006), 135, 154.

57. "Catalogue," nos. 1718, 2273, 2301, 2444, 2447–48, 2884, 4080; Buckingham, *Eastern and Western States*, 1:272; Luc Sante, *Low Life: Lures and Snares of Old New York* (New York: Farrar Straus Giroux, 2003), 99.
58. Buckingham, *Eastern and Western States*, 1:273.
59. Paine, *Ships and Sailors*, 17; "The Salem Museum," *Essex Register*, October 1826; John Madson, *Up on the River: People and Wildlife of the Upper Mississippi* (Iowa City: University of Iowa Press, 2011), 30; Whitehill, *East India Marine Society*, 44; Moore, *Salem World*, 145; Bean, *Yankee India*, 190.
60. Martha Nichols, ed., *A Salem Shipmaster and Merchant: The Autobiography of George Nichols* (Boston: Four Seas, 1921), 111–12; King, *When I Lived in Salem*, 33; Harriet Leonora Bates [Eleanor Putnam, pseud.], *Old Salem*, 5th ed., ed. Arlo Bates (Boston, 1886), 97, 109–10, 115–16.
61. Nichols, *Salem Shipmaster*, 111–12; King, *When I Lived in Salem*, 29, 33, 34; Bates, *Old Salem*, 15, 97; Whitehall, *East India Marine Society*, 141n17; Morison, "Salty Museum," 66; Susan Nance, *How the Arabian Nights Inspired the American Dream, 1790-1935* (Chapel Hill: University of North Carolina Press, 2009), 24–25.
62. Meeting, September 6, 1838, MH88, box1B, PL/PEM; Silsbee, *Half Century in Salem*, 113; Nichols, *Salem Shipmaster*, 111–12.
63. Morison, "Salty Museum," 63; Moore, *Salem World*, 2; Robotti, *Chronicles*, 59; June 27, 1833, Album for the Use of Visitors, 1832–34, MH88, box 4I; "Figurehead of USS *Constitution* Center of Political Controversy," *NNDP*, February 4, 1951; Valentijn Byvanck, "The Jackson Figurehead," *Winterthur Portfolio* 35 (Winter 2000): 253–67; Meeting, September 3, 1834, MH88, box 1B, PL/PEM; King, *When I Lived in Salem*, 32–35.
64. Bentley, *Diary*, April 22, 1816, 4:382; *Freedom's Journal*, in "Notice of Salem," *Salem Observer*, November 17, 1827; Meetings, September 4, and November 6, 1833, MH88, box 1B, PL/PEM.
65. *A Descriptive Guide to the Eastern Railroad, from Boston to Portland* (Boston: Eastern Railroad, 1851); Whitehall, *East India Marine Society*, 51, 142n21, 191; Ray Allen Billington, ed., *The Journal of Charlotte L. Forten: A Young Black Woman's Reactions to the White World of the Civil War Era* (New York: Norton, 1981), 26, 58.
66. Winwar, *Puritan City*, 205; Frances Diane Robotti, *Whaling and Old Salem* (New York: Bonanza, 1962), 65, and *Chronicles*, 67–68. Others translate Salem's seal as "To the farthest gulf for the wealth of India" (Gupta, *Great Encounter*, 6).
67. Jenkins and Whitehill, "Restoration," 12; "Catalogue," no. 1416.
68. Whitehill, *East India Marine Society*, Appendix B (by the time it closed, the EIMS had admitted 402 members); "Remarks of B. H. Silsbee," *Second and Third Annual Reports of the Trustees of the Peabody Academy of Science* (Salem, MA: Salem Press, 1871), 31.
69. Dodge, "Ethnology Department," 1; Stephen E. Weil, "The Museum and the

Public," in *Making Museums Matter* (Washington, D.C.: Smithsonian Institution Press, 2002), 198; Thomas, *Entangled Objects*, 166; George F. Davenport, *Homes and Hearths of Old Salem* (Salem, MA: Salem Observer, 1891), 83–84.

70. "A Day in Old Salem," unidentified clipping, and Miss Ouri, "A Stroll through Salem," in *Salem Gazette*, n.d., Peabody Academy Scrapbook, 1875–79, PL/PEM; *Salem Register*, February 12, 1877, Peabody Academy Scrapbook, 1875–79, PL/PEM; Thomas Franklin Hunt, *A Visitor's Guide to Salem* (Salem, MA: Essex Institute, 1897), 26–27, 95.

71. Robotti, *Chronicles*, 75; C. B. T., "Salem Reminiscences," 292–93; Davenport, *Homes and Hearths*, 83; "EIMS," *BG*, December 16, 1899; "EIMS's Neck-and-Neck Race with Death," *BG*, January 14, 1906.

72. Copeland, "Maritime History Department," 23; Robinson, *Marine Room*, 1, opposite 124; *Guide to the Peabody Museum* (Salem, MA: Newcomb & Gauss, 1916), 5; Gardner Maynard Jones, *The Whaling Industry* (Salem, MA: Peabody Museum, 1908).

73. Whitehall, *East India Marine Society*, 106–7; George F. Dow, "The Marine Museum, Salem, Massachusetts," *Old-Time New England* 12 (October 1921): 67; John Robinson and George Francis Dow, *The Sailing Ships of New England, 1609–1907* (Salem, MA: Marine Research Society, 1922); A. J. Philpott, "New Exhibition Hall Mirrors Salem's Fame," *BG*, February 23, 1930.

74. Van Wyck Brooks, *The Flowering of New England, 1815–1865*, new and rev. ed. (New York: Dutton, 1936), 210–11; King, *When I Lived in Salem*, 63; James M. Lindgren, *Preserving Historic New England* (New York: Oxford University Press, 1995), 94, 151, 183, 185; *Salem: Maritime Salem in the Age of Sail* (Washington, D.C.: National Park Service, 1987, 2001, 2009); J. Revell Carr, "Sightings," *Log* 34 (Spring 1984): 2.

75. Whitehall, *East India Marine Society*, 127–28, 151n13; Jenkins and Whitehill, "Restoration," 15–17.

76. "New Wing at Peabody Museum," *Antiques* 64 (November 1952): 402; Marion V. Brewington, remarks, in *Untapped Sources and Research Opportunities in the Field of American Maritime History* (Mystic, CT: Marine Historical Association, 1968), 79.

77. Ada Louise Huxtable, "Foes Fear Plans Will Mar Old New England Heritage," *NYT*, October 13, 1965, "Standing Room Only," *NYT*, September 16, 1973, and "A Little Museum That Teaches," *NYT*, February 17, 1974; Jane Harriman, "They're Making Room for Just 13 Cars," *BG*, February 10, 1965. Joseph Kennedy had already stripped the pre-Revolutionary War house of its interior for his Hyannis Port home.

78. Ernest S. Dodge, "The Peabody Museum of Salem," *Mariner's Mirror* 47 (1961): 97; "Life-at-Sea Exhibition," *NYT*, October 19, 1985; Margaret S. Creighton, *Dogwatch and Liberty Days: Seafaring Life in the Nineteenth Century* (Salem, MA: Peabody Museum, 1982); William D. Wilkinson, *Mariners' Museum: Annual Report* (Newport News, VA: Mariners' Museum, 1985), 1; Crosby H. A. Forbes, "Asian Export Art at the Peabody Museum," *Antiques*, August 1988, 278–93.

79. Frances Hill, "Salem as Witch City," in *Salem: Place, Myth and Memory* (Boston: Northeastern University Press, 2004), 289; Kathy McCabe, "Essex Institute, Peabody Museum Expected to Merge," *BG*, April 23, 1992, and "Loyal Salem Cheers Its Museum," *BG*, September 27, 1997; Lavonne Leong, "Art to Art: Anatomy of a Merger," *Honolulu Magazine*, March 2011; Mary Jo Palumbo, "Overhaul of Peabody Essex Museum Aims to Please Crowds," *Boston Herald*, May 15, 1997.
80. Kathy McCabe, "Museum Trustees to Vote on Expansion," *BG*, September 23, 1997, and "Salem Museum Denies Fidelity Pressure," *BG*, September 17, 1997; Editorial, *BG*, September 22, 1997; Beth Healy, "Will Fidelity's Gift Wash Up in Boston?," *Boston Herald*, July 8, 1997; Kathy McCabe, "Salem Asset Adrift?," *BG*, September 16, 1997, and "Museum Expansion Plan Is under Fire," *BG*, April 4, 1999.
81. Christine Temin, "PEM on the Rise," *Art New England*, July/August 2013; Holland Cotter, "A Bounty from Salem's Globe-Trotters," *NYT*, August 1, 2003; Geoff Edgers, "North Shore Museum Unveils a Bold Look," *BG*, June 15, 2003; Ada Louise Huxtable, "The New Hub of Architecture," *WSJ*, July 31, 2003.
82. Edgers, "North Shore Museum"; Kathy McCabe, "Peabody Essex Builds on History Museum Expansion to Be Unveiled," *BG*, June 5, 2003.
83. Judith H. Dobrzynski, "A New Way Forward: Cultural Conversation with Dan L. Monroe," *WSJ*, January 28, 2013; Andrea Shea, "Peabody Essex Museum Director Dan Monroe Will Retire after 25 Years," October 11, 2018, https://www.wbur.org/artery/2018/10/11/peabody-essex-museum-director-dan-monroe-to-retire.
84. Irene Rawlings, "Museums of the Seven Seas," *Museum Magazine*, June–July 1983, 59; Kathy McCabe, "Peabody Essex Sets Sail," *BG*, October 10, 1999.
85. *Salem: Maritime Salem in the Age of Sail*; McCabe, "Loyal Salem Cheers"; Jack Stewardson, "Tall Ship Will Grace Salem Historic Site," *NBST*, October 21, 1998; Ebba Hierta, "Staying Afloat," *National Parks*, March/April 1986, 45–46; Editorial, *BG*, September 22, 1997; Phyllis Leffler, "Peopling the Portholes: National Identity and Maritime Museums in the U.S. and U.K.," *PH* 26 (Fall 2004): 40.
86. Julie Hatfield, "Revelers Enjoy Artful Parade," *BG*, October 4, 1999; Kathy McCabe, "Bicentennial Is on Parade," *BG*, October 10, 1999; Malabar Hornblower, "A Seafaring Past Preserved," *NYT*, May 17, 1987; Dodge, "Ethnology Department," 2–3; Doug Stewart, "Salem Sets Sail," *Smithsonian*, June 2004, 92.
87. Cotter, "Bounty from Salem's Globe-Trotters."
88. William Fowler to author, email, September 1, 2016. In 2013, PEM closed its Phillips Library for restoration. Angering many in the community, in 2018 it moved its collections twenty miles north to Rowley to a 112,000-square-foot storage building.

CHAPTER 2: "FROM PURSUIT TO PRESERVATION"

1. "Bourne Museum Dedication," *ODHSk*, no. 45 (November 23, 25, 1916): 10; "Bourne Whaling Museum Dedicated and Formally Given to Society," unidentified newspaper, November 23, 1916, ODHS Scrapbook no. 4, OP. See also James

M. Lindgren, "'Let Us Idealize Old Types of Manhood': The New Bedford Whaling Museum, 1903–1941," *NEQ* 72 (June 1999): 163–206.

2. Herman Melville, *Moby-Dick; or, The White Whale* (Boston: St. Botolph Society, 1892), 104; "Bourne Memorial," *ODHSk*, no. 45 (November 23, 25, 1916): 17, 19; L. A. Littlefield, "Fitting Out a Whaler," *ODHSk*, no. 14 (June 22, 1906): 4; "Bourne Whaling Museum Dedicated"; "Bourne Museum Dedication," 13.

3. "Z. W. Pease, 72, the Mercury Editor, Dies," unidentified newspaper, June 25, 1933, ODHS Scrapbook no. 1, OP; "Z. W. Pease Dead at Fairhaven," *BG*, June 25, 1933; Pease, untitled editorial, *New Bedford Mercury*, May 16, 1916; no author, no title (typed history of ODHS), ODHS Scrapbook no. 1, 85–89, OP.

4. Lance E. Davis, Robert E. Gallman, and Teresa D. Hutchins, "Technology, Productivity, and Profits: British-American Whaling Competition in the North Atlantic, 1816–1842," *Oxford Economic Papers* 39 (December 1987): 738–59; James L. Stokesbury, "Saga of the Whalers," *American History Illustrated* 9, no. 4 (1974): 4–10, 43–51.

5. Christine A. Arato and Patrick L. Eleey, *Safely Moored at Last: Cultural Landscape Report for New Bedford Whaling National Historical Park* (Boston: National Park Service, 1998), 19; Lisa Norling, *Captain Ahab Had a Wife: New England Women and the Whalefishery, 1720–1870* (Chapel Hill: University of North Carolina Press, 2000), 133–34; "Bourne Memorial," 10; Margaret S. Creighton, *Rites and Passages: The Experience of American Whaling, 1830–1870* (New York: Cambridge University Press, 1995), 6, 16.

6. "Proceedings of the Special Meeting, February 25, 1919," *ODHSk*, no. 47 (1919): 19; Melville, *Moby-Dick*, 36–37.

7. Robert L. Carothers and John L. Marsh, "The Whale and the Panorama," *Nineteenth-Century Fiction* 26 (December 1971): 320; Samuel Eliot Morison, *Introduction to* Whaler Out of New Bedford*: A Film Based on the* Purrington-Russell Panorama of a Whaling Voyage Round the World, 1841–1845 (New Bedford: Old Dartmouth Historical Society, 1962); Kevin J. Avery, "Whaling Voyage Round the World," *American Art Journal* 22 (Spring 1990): 57; Earl F. Mulderink III, *New Bedford's Civil War* (New York: Fordham University Press, 2012), 142–47.

8. Clifford W. Ashley, *The Yankee Whaler* (Boston: Houghton Mifflin, 1926), 118; Briton Cooper Busch, *"Whaling Will Never Do for Me": The American Whaleman in the Nineteenth Century* (Lexington: University Press of Kentucky, 1994), 3–5; Lance E. Davis, Robert E. Gallman, and Teresa D. Hutchins, "The Decline of U.S. Whaling: Was the Stock of Whales Running Out?," *Business History Review* 62 (Winter 1988): 573, and "Call Me Ishmael—Not Domingo Floresta: The Rise and Fall of the American Whaling Industry," Supplement, *Research in Economic History* 6 (1991): 205.

9. Gregory J. Galer, "Industry and Commerce, Innovation and Entrepreneurship: A New Interpretive Framework," *Bulletin*, Winter/Spring 2011, 6; Dan Georgianna, "The Last Woven Yard," *Spinner: People and Culture in Southeastern Massachusetts*

4 (1988): 184; Thomas A. McMullin, "Overseeing the Poor," *Social Science Review* 65 (December 1991): 549–59; W. H. B. Remington, "New Bedford," *New England Magazine*, September 1909, 819; "The Story of Cotton," *ODHSk*, no. 67 (November 1937): 12.

10. Herbert L. Aldrich, "New Bedford," *New England Magazine*, May 1886, 424.
11. W. W. Crapo, "Talk to the ODHS," February 15, 1904, manuscript, OP; "Historical Society Advised," unidentified newspaper, January 17, 1903, ODHS Scrapbook no. 1, OP; *A Brief Outline of the Society's History* (New Bedford: Reynolds, 1953), 5; Elsie S. Moeller, "The Living Conditions of the Portuguese in New Bedford," in *Spinner* 4 (1988): 105.
12. "Historical Society Advised"; "Proceedings of the First General Meeting of the ODHS," June 30, 1903," *ODHSk*, no. 1 (1903): 3.
13. "Talk to the ODHS"; "Proceedings of the Second Annual Meeting," March 17, 1905, *ODHSk*, no. 9 (1905): 6, 8.
14. "Reminders of the Old Whaling Days," *Providence Sunday Journal*, n.d. [March 1904], ODHS Scrapbook no. 1, OP; "Historians at Whale City," *Boston Herald*, June 24, 1905; "Proceedings of the Second Annual Meeting," 5, 7; Dona Brown, *Inventing New England: Regional Tourism in the Nineteenth Century* (Washington, D.C.: Smithsonian Institution Press, 1995), 107; "Old South Pilgrimage," *Boston Transcript*, June 12, 1905.
15. "Mourned by Town," *WP*, May 23, 1909; Arato and Eleey, *Safely Moored*, 50 (fig. 100–1); Richard A. Voyer, Carik Pesch, Jonathan Garber, Jane Copeland, and Randy Comeleo, "New Bedford, Massachusetts: A Story of Urbanization and Ecological Connections," *Environmental History* 5 (July 2000): 362.
16. Elton W. Hall, "A History of the ODHS," typescript, 1983, OP; Editorial, unidentified newspaper, July 27, 1915, Tripp Scrapbook, OP; Leon M. Huggins, "Old Dartmouth at Home," *ODHSk*, no. 16 (March 5, 1907): 19–20; Zephaniah W. Pease, *A Visit to the Museum of the Old Dartmouth Historical Society* (New Bedford: Reynolds, 1932), 21, 45.
17. Elmo Paul Hohman, *The American Whaleman: A Study of Life and Labor in the Whaling Industry* (New York: Longmans, Green, 1928), 59, 77; Busch, "*Whaling Will Never Do,*" 9; Mary Malloy, "Whalemen's Perceptions," *Log* 41 (1989): 57.
18. Clifford W. Ashley, "The Blubber Hunters," *Harper's Monthly Magazine*, April/May 1906, 670–82, 832–44; Stuart M. Frank, review of *Sperm Whaling from New Bedford: Clifford W. Ashley's Photographs of Bark* Sunbeam *in 1904*, by Elton W. Hall, *AN* 43, no. 1 (1983): 56.
19. Frank, review, 57; Ashley, *Yankee Whaler*, xiv–xv, 120; Zephaniah W. Pease, "The Business of Whaling," *Colonist* 2 (March 1930): 12.
20. Arato and Eleey, *Safely Moored*, 28; Pease, editorial, *New Bedford Standard*, in *ODHSk*, no. 38 (1913): 2; James M. Lindgren, *Preserving Historic New England* (New York: Oxford University Press, 1995), 195n37.
21. Bela Lyon Pratt to Sarah Victoria Whittelsey Pratt, November 26, 1911, and "Posed

for Statue of the Whaleman," no source, 1913, http://belalyonpratt.com (no longer available); Alpheus Hyatt Verrill, *The Real Story of the Whaler* (New York: Appleton, 1916), 91–92; Samuel Eliot Morison, *The Maritime History of Massachusetts, 1783–1860* (Boston: Houghton Mifflin, 1921), 323; W. H. B. Remington, "Fourths of the Past," *ODHSk*, no. 40 (June/October 1914): 7.

22. *New Bedford Mercury*, in William W. Crapo, *The Presentation of the Whaleman Statue to the City of New Bedford* (New Bedford: Anthony & Sons, 1913), 11; "The Model," 39–40, and "Unveiling of the Whaleman Statue," 16–17, both in Crapo, *Presentation*; Bela Lyon Pratt to Sarah Victoria Whittelsey Pratt, December 24, 1911, http://belalyonpratt.com (no longer available).
23. *New Bedford Mercury* in Crapo, *Presentation*, 11–12; Charles Henry Robbins, *The Gam, Being a Group of Whaling Stories* (New Bedford: Hutchinson, 1899), 128–29; Wood in Crapo, *Presentation*, 19–20.
24. "Frank Wood Dies," *New Bedford Mercury*, January 4, 1933; "Proceedings of the Second Annual Meeting," 5; William Morgan, *The Almighty Wall: The Architecture of Henry Vaughan* (Cambridge, MA: MIT Press, 1983), 131–34; Arato and Eleey, *Safely Moored*, 45 (fig. 83–84).
25. "Bourne Museum Dedication," 3; Jonathan Olly, "*Lagoda*: A Legacy in Wood, Iron, and Sail," *Nautical Research Journal* 49 (Fall 2004): 150; George Sarton, "The Whaling Museums of New Bedford and Nantucket," *Isis* 16 (July 1931): 116.
26. "Bourne Museum Dedication," 7; "First Meeting in the Jonathan Bourne Whaling Museum," *ODHSk*, no. 45 (November 23, 25, 1916): 8, 10, 14; "Old Dartmouth Historical Society Observes 300th Anniversary of Landing of the Pilgrims," *ODHSk*, no. 50 (November/December 1920): 7–8.
27. "First Meeting," 29; Ashley, *Yankee Whaler*, 119–20; Elton W. Hall, "Clifford Warren Ashley," in *Whalers, Wharves, and Waterways* (New Bedford: Old Dartmouth Historical Society, 1973), 17; Leon A. Dickinson, "The Sea Calls from Cape Cod," *NYT*, July 1, 1928.
28. "Mardi Gras" and "Proceedings of the Annual Meeting, 1918," *ODHSk*, no. 47 (1919): 6, 10, 23.
29. Eric Jay Dolin, *Leviathan: The History of Whaling in America* (New York: Norton, 2007), 367–69; "Tea Dance," *New Bedford Mercury*, August 27, 1927. A "gam" was a midocean get-together when two whaling ships happened to meet; their captains, and perhaps their crews, had a moment to socialize.
30. Arthur C. Watson, *Whaling Exhibits of the Old Dartmouth Historical Society*, *ODHSk*, no. 53 (1924): 23, 25–26; D. Graham Burnett, *Trying Leviathan: The Nineteenth-Century New York Court Case That Put the Whale on Trial and Challenged the Order of Nature* (Princeton, NJ: Princeton University Press, 2007), 141n98, 142.
31. Watson, *Whaling Exhibits*; Gordon Grant, *Greasy Luck: A Whaling Sketch Book* (New York: Payson, 1932), 26.
32. Melville, *Moby-Dick*, 258; Ashley, *Yankee Whaler*, 111–12; Robert J. Schwendinger,

"Masters of Their Material Culture," in *Maritime Arts and Artisans: The Collection of the San Francisco Maritime National Historical Park* (San Francisco: Craft and Folk Art Museum, 1989), 27.

33. Editorial, *New Bedford Mercury*, December 2, 1920.
34. Editorial, *New Bedford Mercury*, December 2, 1920; Ashley, *Yankee Whaler*, 113–15; Norling, *Captain Ahab*, 188–90; Pease, *Visit*, 16–17, 28, 31.
35. Hohman, *American Whaleman*, 50–51; James Farr, "A Slow Boat to Nowhere: The Multi-Racial Crews of the American Whaling Industry," *Journal of Negro History* 68 (Spring 1983): 160–64; Morison, *Maritime History*, 106. For Raleigh's painting, see Lindgren, "Old Types," 191.
36. Pease, *Visit*, 32–33; James J. Lopes, "Whaling Museum's Walls Do Indeed Talk," *NBST*, February 17, 2012; Timothy G. Lynch, "Black Ahab of the Bay: William T. Shorey and the San Francisco Whale Fishery," in *Gender, Race, Ethnicity, and Power in Maritime America*, ed. Glenn S. Gordinier (Mystic, CT: Mystic Seaport Museum, 2006), 140.
37. Rev. Alexander McKenzie, "Reminiscences of New Bedford," *ODHSk*, no. 16 (March 5, 1907): 13; Melville, *Moby-Dick*, 35–36; Remington, "Fourths of the Past," 10–11.
38. Charles Nordhoff, *Nine Years a Sailor* (Cincinnati, OH: Moore, 1856), 60; Donald Warrin, "A Brief Look at Azoreans and Cape Verdeans in the American Whaling Industry," *Bulletin*, Summer 2010, 13–17.
39. Norling, *Captain Ahab*, 26; Lance E. Davis, Robert E. Gallman, and Teresa D. Hutchins, "Productivity in American Whaling: The New Bedford Fleet in the Nineteenth Century," in *Markets in History*, ed. David W. Galenson (New York: Cambridge University Press, 1989), 109–11.
40. "George F. Tucker Speaks on 'The Mercantile Side of Whaling,'" *New Bedford Mercury*, November 14, 1924; "American Whaling," *NYT*, November 4, 1928; Hohman, *American Whaleman*, 89–91, 99–100; Ashley, *Yankee Whaler*, 105.
41. Ashley, *Yankee Whaler*, 4; "Old Dartmouth Society Holds Annual Clambake," unidentified newspaper, September 20, 1929, ODHS Scrapbook no. 1, OP.
42. Ashley, *Yankee Whaler*, 108–9; Nellie Coombs, "Captain Joe Antone, Cape Verdean Seaman," *Spinner* 4 (1988): 127.
43. David W. Littlefield, "Joseph Bement and the *Charles W. Morgan*," *Log* 45 (Fall 1993): 43–47; Busch, *"Whaling Will Never Do,"* 11–12; Creighton, *Rites and Passages*, 35–36.
44. Zephaniah W. Pease, "The Story of the Building of the Bourne Whaling Museum," *ODHSk*, no. 44 (April 3, 1916): 13; Ashley, *Yankee Whaler*, 104; "Story of Cotton," 9–10.
45. John Ackerman, "A Whaling Library for Massachusetts," *Wilson Library Bulletin*, October 1981, 100; Cooper Gaw, "Tilton's Walk and the Whaling Tradition," *ODHSk*, no. 62 (July 16, 1933): 11; Hohman, *American Whaleman*, 64, 108–9, 127; Joan Druett, "More Decency and Order: Women and Whalemen in the Pacific," *Log* 39 (1987): 65.

46. Hohman, *American Whaleman*, 108; "Unveiling of the Whaleman Statue," 22–23; Pease, *Visit*, 40.
47. Ashley, *Yankee Whaler*, 100–102, 105, 120; Hohman, *American Whaleman*, 59–60.
48. H. E. Cushman to Wm. M. Wood, May 28, June 11, 1920, and Wood to Cushman, June 3, 1920, ODHS Scrapbook no. 1, OP.
49. Watson, *Whaling Exhibits*, 34; Pease, "Story of the Building," 13; Pease, *Visit*, 5–6, 9–10, 20; Pease, "Business of Whaling," 13; Ashley, *Yankee Whaler*, 86, 108, 119.
50. Pease, *Visit*, 5–6, 10, 20; Ashley, *Yankee Whaler*, 86.
51. Edward T. Pierce Jr., *The Story of Ship Design and de Coppet Collection of Ship Models*, *ODHSk*, no. 61 (1932): 5.
52. "The Death of Z. W. Pease," unidentified newspaper, June 26, 1933, ODHS Scrapbook no. 1, OP; "ODHS's Annual Meeting," unidentified newspaper, April 14, 1931, ODHS Scrapbook no. 1, OP; W. Cameron Forbes, "Far Eastern Relations of the United States," *ODHSk*, no. 63 (1932): [2–4].
53. "Salvaging Skeleton of a Whale for Museum Here," unidentified newspaper, September 4, 1933, ODHS Scrapbook no. 1, OP; Hall, "History"; Watson, *Whaling Exhibits*, 28.
54. "Hunting the Whale," *NYT*, April 12, 1928; "Whaling Today," *NYT*, August 31, 1924; Madelyn Shaw and Michael P. Dyer, "From Pursuit to Preservation," *Bulletin*, Summer 2009, 8–9, 18; Robert R. Rocha Jr., "Emptying the Oceans," *Bulletin*, Fall 2013, 17.
55. "Formal Opening of Bourne Whaling Museum Addition," *New Bedford Mercury*, March 27, 1935; Mrs. Robert Long, "Summer Meeting of the Old Dartmouth Historical Society," August 3, 1938, typescript, OP.
56. Pease, editorial, *New Bedford Mercury*, May 16, 1916; *The Whale Ship* Charles W. Morgan, 5th ed. (New Bedford: Reynolds, 1941), 1, 5–6; John Ruddy, "How New Bedford Let the *Morgan* Get Away," *NLD*, June 22, 2014.
57. Sarton, "Whaling Museums," 118; George Fred Tilton, *"Cap'n George Fred" Himself* (Garden City, NY: Doubleday, Doran, 1928), 287–95; Cooper Gaw, "Capt. George Fred Tilton Tablet Dedication," *ODHSk*, no. 62 (1933): 7–8, 24; "Former Navy Secretary Asks Support of 'Save *Morgan*' Fund," unidentified newspaper, n.d., Whaling Enshrined E5, ODHS.
58. "Don't Give Up the Ship," iii–iv, in *The Whale Ship* Charles W. Morgan, 5–6; "To Save a Ship," editorial, *Providence Journal*, February 26, [?], Whaling Enshrined E5, ODHS; "The *Morgan* Fund Committee," fundraising letter, n.d., Whaling Enshrined E3, ODHS; "Let's Keep Her Colors Flying," n.d. [1940], a four-page printed appeal, Whaling Enshrined E7, ODHS; "Address of Carl C. Cutler," Supplement, *Log* (July 21, 1961): 18; Carl C. Cutler, "A Small Pull on the Main Brace," *Yachting*, June 1947, 57; Carl C. Cutler, "The Last Whale Ship: *Charles W. Morgan*," *AN* 1 (1941): 392; "William Tripp, 79, a Museum Curator," *NYT*, December 1, 1959; Maureen Boyle, "3,000 Take Trip in History," *NBST*, June 30, 1991.
59. Genevieve Marston, "Thar She Blows," *CSM*, April 4, 1942, Magazine, 14; Thomas M. Pryor, "Down to the Sea in Exploitation," *NYT*, February 20, 1949; Steve Urbon, "New Bedford's Poseidon Still Waiting for New Home," *NBST*, May 11, 2018; Peter

H. Spectre, "Old-Tyme Shyppes," *WB*, no. 96 (October/November 1990): 64, and "The Heaving Deck of History," *WB*, no. 96 (October/November 1990): 72; Kingston Wm. Heath, *The Patina of Place: The Cultural Weathering of a New England Industrial Landscape* (Knoxville: University of Tennessee Press, 2001), 55–56.

60. Marsha McCabe and Joseph D. Thomas, *Not Just Anywhere: The Story of WHALE and the Rescue of New Bedford's Waterfront Historic District* (New Bedford: Spinner, 1995), 14–15; John K. Bullard, "Collective Private Urban Renewal in New Bedford's Historic District" (master's thesis, MIT, 1974), 53; Richard J. Pline, letter to the editor, *NBST*, August 27, 2005.

61. Senator Jack Reed, "In Memory of Antoinette F. Downing," 147 Cong. Rec. S4887–S4888 (May 14, 2001); McCabe and Thomas, *Not Just Anywhere*, 16, 19.

62. *Reconnaissance Report Waterfront Historic Area New Bedford, Massachusetts* (Annapolis, MD: Corinthian Conservation, 1964), 6; Ada Louise Huxtable, "Foes Fear Plans Will Mar Old New England Heritage," *NYT*, October 13, 1965, and "New Bedford Waterfront a Model Renewal Project," *NYT*, November 21, 1966; McCabe and Thomas, *Not Just Anywhere*, 22, 32, 36–37, 43.

63. McCabe and Thomas, *Not Just Anywhere*, 43, 46–47; Steve Urbon, "Waterfront Historic Area League Marks 50 Years of Saving a City's Legacy," *NBST*, June 3, 2012; Bullard, "Collective Private Urban Renewal," 54–57. For a district map, see Barbara Clayton and Kathleen Whitley, *Guide to New Bedford* (Montpelier, VT: Capital City, 1986), 45.

64. Bullard, "Collective Private Urban Renewal," 61; McCabe and Thomas, *Not Just Anywhere*, 61; Urbon, "Waterfront Historic Area."

65. Charis Anderson, "Longtime Planner Left Indelible Mark on New Bedford," *NBST*, February 4, 2012; Rob Crowley, "Bumpy Road for Glass Collection Ends Up at Johnny Cake Hill," *NBST*, April 26, 1991; Arato and Eleey, *Safely Moored*, xvii; McCabe and Thomas, *Not Just Anywhere*, 16.

66. Edith Evans Asbury, "Once Penniless Man," *NYT*, January 16, 1953; Rocha, "Emptying the Oceans," 16; Charles Flowers, "Between the Harpoon and the Whale," *NYT*, August 24, 1975; Hall, "History."

67. John Haskell Kemble, review of *Steam Whaling in the Western Arctic*, by John R. Bockstoce, *Pacific Northwest Quarterly* 70 (January 1979): 45.

68. Carol McCabe, "Melville Would Know the Faces," *NYT*, July 30, 1978; Bill Ibelle, "Extraordinary Features Attract the Lifeblood of Historic Neighborhood," *NBST*, July 10, 1994.

69. Jack Theriault, "Jewel of the South Shore," *Banker and Tradesman*, July 3, 1991; "Whale Discovery Center to Open in Plymouth," n.d., in ODHS Scrapbook no. 16, OP; Linda May Ellis, "Harpooning a Whale Museum," *South Shore News*, June 10, 1991; John H. Ackerman, "It's No Fluke," *NBST*, June 13, 1991; "Whaling Museum's Plymouth Expansion an Exciting Prospect," *NBST*, November 9, 1990.

70. Margo J. Moore, "Brengle Takes Whaling Museum Helm," *Taunton [MA] Daily Gazette*, August 13, 1994.

71. Jack Stewardson, "Senate Revisits Whaling Park," *NBST*, November 7, 1995.
72. William Short, letter to the editor, *NBST*, October 20, 1996; "Does the National Park Signal New Bedford's Rebirth?," *NBST*, May 24, 1998; Jack Spillane, "The Story behind the Whaling District in Plain Sight," *NBST*, August 4, 2011.
73. Antone G. Souza Jr., letter to the editor, "New Bedford Is the Real America," *BG*, March 20, 2000; Voyer et al., "New Bedford," 352, 367; *Working on the Water* (Malden, MA: Department of Education and Island Foundation, 1998), 28.
74. Sara Meirowitz, "Hands-On, Minds-On: Extending the Classroom Experience," *Bulletin*, Fall 2009, 3.
75. Jamal Watson, "A 66-Foot 'Puzzle' Solved 2 Years after Collision, Museum Will Display Blue Whale's Skeleton," *BG*, July 6, 2000.
76. Robert C. Rocha Jr. to author, email, June 4, 2014, and "The Story of Eg1909," *Bulletin*, Winter/Spring 2009, 3, 20; Bobbi-Jean MacKinnon, "Latest North Atlantic Right Whale Found Dead Was a Female of Breeding Age," January 29, 2018, http://www.cbc.ca/news/canada/new-brunswick/atlantic-right-whale-virginia-noaa-female-entanglement-1.4509273.
77. Beth Daley, "A Tale of a Whale," *BG*, June 11, 2002; Sarah Martineau, "Sperm Whale Skeleton to Key Museum's Revamp of Core Exhibit," *NBST*, September 10, 2003; Sebastian Smee, "Sensing the Pulse of an Anonymous Artist," *BG*, July 24, 2012.
78. "Joining of Whaling Museum Is a Marriage Made in Heaven," *NBST*, June 2, 2001; Michael Lapides, "*Arctic Visions: Away Then Floats the Ice-Island*," *Bulletin*, Winter/Spring 2013, 8–9.
79. James J. Lopes, "Whaling Museum's Walls Do Indeed Talk," *NBST*, February 17, 2012; "Workshop Gives Teachers Whaling Museum Insights," *NBST*, January 31, 1980.
80. Ken Hartnett, "City Bids Adieu," *NBST*, December 9, 2007; Sam Allis, "In New Bedford, One Hull of a Change," *BG*, September 25, 2010, and "Worlds Apart," *BG*, June 13, 1999.
81. Jack Spillane, "Whaling Museum Will Give Paul Cuffee a Proper Homage," *NBST*, February 10, 2011; Lopes, "Whaling Museum's Walls"; Akeia Benard, "Paul Cuffe," *Old Dartmouth eSketches*, email, February 22, 2018.
82. Ric Oliveira, "Portuguese Mariners to Assume Their Proper Role," *NBST*, March 25, 1998; William Davis, "Blubber and Beyond," *BG*, September 6, 2000; Brian C. Jones, "The Cape Verdean Man and the Sea," *Providence Journal-Bulletin*, February 29, 1996; Dan McDonald, "Azorean Whaleman Gallery," *NBST*, September 11, 2010.
83. "Cape Verdean Maritime Exhibit," *NBST*, August 3, 2011.
84. James Russell, "From the Helm," *Bulletin*, Summer 2009, 23; John N. Garfield Jr. and James Russell, "From the Helm," *Bulletin*, Winter/Spring 2012, i; Phyllis Leffler, "Peopling the Portholes: National Identity and Maritime Museums in the U.S. and U.K.," *PH* 26 (Fall 2004): 35, 41.
85. Benjamin Wallace-Wells, "Mood Swing New Bedford's Fight," *BG*, March 3, 2000;

Russell, "From the Helm," *Bulletin*, Summer 2009, 23; John Bodnar, "Remembering the Immigrant Experience in American Culture," *Journal of Ethnic History* 15 (Fall 1995): 23–24.

86. Natalie Sherman, "Grant Saves Whaling Museum's Educational Outreach," *NBST*, March 9, 2012; "Continuum of Learning Realized," *Bulletin*, Fall 2010, 14; Jack Spillane, "A High School Job," *NBST*, August 25, 2011.
87. Galer, "Industry and Commerce," 4–6.
88. Steve Urbon, "With Vibrant Downtown Comes Escalating Noise, Vandalism," *NBST*, May 14, 2010.
89. "The 38th Voyage of the *Charles W. Morgan*," *Bulletin*, Winter/Spring 2014, 15; Becky W. Evans, "*Ernestina*'s New Captain Has Some Rough Seas Ahead," *NBST*, July 17, 2007. In 2007, the city sold its unwanted *Lightship New Bedford* (LV 114) on eBay; the new owner immediately scrapped it for its metal.
90. "Dreaming of Future Is Paying Off," *NBST*, October 24, 1996.
91. Matthew A. Morrissey, "Translating Historic Preservation into Economic Success," *NBST*, November 17, 2010.
92. Hartnett, "City Bids Adieu"; David Lowenthal, *Possessed by the Past: The Heritage Crusade and the Spoils of History* (New York: Free Press, 1996).
93. "Our View: Award of Distinction for New Bedford," *NBST*, February 16, 2011; Smee, "Sensing the Pulse"; Malerie Yolen-Cohen, "New Bedford, Mass.: A Whale of a Good Time," *Huffington Post*, June 24, 2013.

CHAPTER 3: "STOUT HEARTS MAKE A SAFE SHIP"

1. Everett S. Allen, "*Morgan* Once More Lives," *NBST*, November 6, 1941; *Why the* Morgan *Came to Mystic* (Mystic, CT: Marine Historical Association, 1942), [1]; W. M. Williamson, "The Last Square-Rigged Whaleship in the World," *Whaleship* Charles W. Morgan *1942 Addition* (New Bedford, MA: Reynolds, 1942), [6]. See also Jonathan M. Olly, "Imagining the Old Coast: History, Heritage, and Tourism in New England, 1865–2012 (PhD diss., Brown University, 2013).
2. "Address of Carl C. Cutler," Fifteenth Annual Meeting, Annual Meeting Supplement, *Log* (July 21, 1961): 11; Carl Cutler to Philip R. Mallory, December 31, 1942, CP/MSM 3/2.
3. Cutler to Charlie [Cutler], December 22, 1951, CP/MSM 4/4; Gary E. Weir, *Forged in War: The Naval-Industrial Complex and American Submarine Construction, 1940–1961* (Washington, D.C.: Naval Historical Center, 1993), 2.
4. "Learn by Doing," *History News*, August 1960, 116.
5. Cutler to Ednah C. Farrier, July 10, 1930, CP/MSM 1/14; Cutler to Irving Putnam, November 1, 1928, CP/MSM 1/3.
6. William Allen Wilbur, "Mystic," *Connecticut Magazine*, August 1899, 406; Cutler to Charlie [Cutler], December 22, 1951, CP/MSM 4/4. For neurasthenia and

antimodernism, see James M. Lindgren, *Preserving Historic New England* (New York: Oxford University Press, 1995).

7. Carl C. Cutler, *Queens of the Western Ocean: The Story of America's Mail and Passenger Sailing Lines* (Annapolis, MD: U.S. Naval Institute Press, 1961), xi, 357, and *Greyhounds of the Sea: The Story of the American Clipper Ship* (New York: G. P. Putnam's Sons, 1930), xi–xiii.
8. Samuel Eliot Morison, review of *Greyhounds of the Sea*, *American Historical Review* 36 (April 1931): 608–9; Cutler, *Greyhounds*, v, xii; Carl C. Cutler, *Mystic: The Story of a Small New England Seaport* (Mystic, CT: Marine Historical Association, 1945), 30; "In the Great Days of the American Clipper Ship," *NYT*, May 31, 1931; Cutler to Ednah C. Farrier, November 8, 1930, CP/MSM 1/19.
9. Cutler, *Queens*, xi–xii; Robert G. Albion, William A. Baker, and Benjamin W. Labaree, *New England and the Sea* (Middletown, CT: Wesleyan University Press for the Marine Historical Association, 1972), 228; Benjamin W. Labaree, *America and the Sea* (Mystic, CT: Mystic Seaport Museum, 1998), 524, 528.
10. Marion Dickerman, *The Three Founders of Mystic Seaport* (Mystic, CT: Marine Historical Association, 1965), 9–12; Thomas A. Stevens and Charles K. Stillman, *George Greenman and Company, Shipbuilders of Mystic, Connecticut* (Mystic, CT: Marine Historical Association, 1938), 7–9.
11. Stevens and Stillman, *George Greenman*, 14–15, 25; Leigh Fought, *A History of Mystic, Connecticut: From Pequot Village to Tourist Town* (Charleston, SC: History Press, 2007), 72, 79, 98.
12. Cutler to George [Cutler], November 1, 1929, CP/MSM 1/7, to Col. Sherwood Cheney, June 10, 1930, CP/MSM 1/13, and to Charles H. Patterson, October 3, 1930, CP/MSM 1/18.
13. [Carl C. Cutler], *Statement of Plan and Purposes of the Marine Historical Association* (Mystic, CT: Marine Historical Association, 1929), [2, 6–9]; Cutler to Arthur Wendell, March 22, 1952, CP/MSM 4/6, and to Mrs. James Leeds Laidlaw, May 29, 1930, CP/MSM 1/12.
14. Cutler, Speech at Annual Meeting, July 21, 1961, CP/MSM 7/3; Cutler to Ray Baker Taft, November 21, 1930, CP/MSM 1/19; "Will Show Models of Old-Time Ships," *NYT*, September 15, 1931.
15. Carl C. Cutler, "The Port of New York: A Historical Sketch," in *A Descriptive Catalogue of the Marine Collection to Be Found at India House*, 2nd ed. (1935; Middletown, CT: Wesleyan University Press, 1973), xxiii–xlii.
16. Cutler to Irving [Bullard], December 25, 1932, CP/MSM 2/7, to Mike [?], July 21, 1953, CP/MSM 4/12, to Albert Reese, September 12, 1943, CP/MSM 3/3, and to Harry [Peters], April 14, 1941, CP/MSM 2/19.
17. Philip R. Mallory to Cutler, "The end of 1948," CP/MSM 3/12, and October 17, 1951, CP/MSM 4/3; James P. Baughman, *The Mallorys of Mystic* (Middleton, CT: Wesleyan University Press for the Marine Historical Association, 1972), 7; Philip R.

Mallory, *Recollections: Fifty Years with the Company* (Privately published, 1966), 82, 91, *Personal Background* (Philadelphia: Privately published, 1941), 60–62, and *Mystic Seaport—and the Origins of Freedom!* (New York: Newcomen Society, 1954), 8.

18. Cutler to Harry T. Peters, September 7, 1941, CP/MSM 2/20; John Gould, "No Such Word in Maine!" *CSM*, April 22, 1988.
19. "Mystic's Maritime Past," *Stonington (CT) Mirror and Journal*, September 22, 1939; "Mystic Marine Assn. Holds Rite," *NLD*, n.d., MSM Scrapbook, G. W. Blunt White Library, MSM; *Why the* Morgan *Came*, [2]. *Anglo Saxon* was actually sunk by *Widder*, a German surface raider (J. Revell Carr, *All Brave Sailors* [New York: Simon & Schuster, 2004]).
20. Cutler to Harold H. Kynett, n.d. [1942], CF/MSM 7/5; Lieut. A. C. Denison, "The Return of the Merchant Marine," remarks, May 30, 1942, CP/MSM 3/1; Philip R. Mallory, address quoted in Minutes, *MHA Bulletin*, no. 25 (1942): 1–4.
21. Frazer A. Bailey, in *Nineteenth Annual Report, MHA Bulletin*, no. 39 (1947): 19, 20; Benjamin Labaree, "Maritime Museums and Higher Education," in *International Congress of Maritime Museums, Third Conference Proceedings, 1978* (Mystic, CT: Mystic Seaport Museum, 1979), 225, 227; Hamilton Cochran, "The Old Ships Come Home," *Saturday Evening Post*, October 9, 1948, 36.
22. "Hear about Atomic Bomb," *NLD*, June 21, 1947; Mallory, "To the Members," *Log, MHA Bulletin*, no. 35 (1947): 1, and *Recollections*, 8; Harold H. Kynett, *Fireside Admiral: Ramblings about a Marine Museum*, sketches by F. Wade Lane (Philadelphia: Privately published, 1950), 195.
23. Philip R. Mallory, *Sixteenth Annual Report, MHA Bulletin*, no. 32 (1945): 5; John W. Steube, "What Your Membership in the MHA Means to You," April 5, 1946, MSM Scrapbook; Kynett, *Fireside Admiral*, 204; Mallory, *Mystic Seaport*, 24; Edouard A. Stackpole, *Interpretation at Mystic Seaport* (Mystic, CT: Marine Historical Association, 1960), 4; "Mystic Seaport and the Origins of Freedom," *Log* 7 (Summer 1955): 6.
24. "Seaport to Scan Skies," *NLD*, July 12, 1958, 11; Devereux Josephs, Address, Supplement, *Log* (1958): 16–17, 19; Comm. James F. Calvert, USN, and James A. Farrell Jr., Supplement, *Log* (1959): 9–12; "Our Stake in Antarctica," *Log* 12 (July 1960): 6.
25. Cutler to William Williams, July 28, 1944, CP/MSM 3/5; Margaret [Mallory] to P. R. Mallory, June 9, 1944, CP/MSM 3/4; Cutler to Clarence Brigham, December 16, 1944, CP/MSM 3/5; Cutler to George H. Reynolds, November 21, 1944, CP/MSM 3/5.
26. Cutler to Philip R. Mallory, n.d. (1947), draft, CP/MSM 3/9; J. Revell Carr, "The Mallorys of Mystic Seaport," *Log* 52 (Spring 2001): 89; "Notes on a Name," *Log* 1 (October 1948): 2, 4.
27. Cutler to P. R. Mallory, September 25, 1948, CP/MSM 3/11; MacDonald Steers, comp., *Mystic Seaport: An Exhibit Guide* (Mystic, CT: Marine Historical Association, [1955]), 57.
28. Cochran, "Old Ships Come Home," 30–31, 138–40; Kynett, *Fireside Admiral*, 27–28, 205.

29. "J. Revell Carr: An Appreciation," *Log* 52 (Autumn/Winter 2000): 41; Steers, *Mystic Seaport*, 73.
30. Kynett, *Fireside Admiral*, 172; *Mystic Seaport Guide* (Mystic, CT: Marine Historical Association, 1967), 45; Jean Poindexter Colby, *Mystic Seaport* (New York: Hastings House, 1970), 39–40; Steers, *Mystic Seaport*, 77.
31. Stackpole, *Interpretation*, 2, 15; Steers, *Mystic Seaport*, 72.
32. "Physical Changes," *Log* 15 (April 1963): 10–11; Herman Melville, *Moby-Dick* (Boston: St. Botolph Society, 1892), 17; Stackpole, *Interpretation*, 3, 10; Anne Stagg, "Museum Village," *House & Garden*, September 1967, 28.
33. Stagg, "Museum Village," 32; Stackpole, *Interpretation*, 16.
34. Kynett, *Fireside Admiral*, 83; Cutler to Mallory, February 27, 1952, CP/MSM 4/5, and July 14, 1952, CF/MSM 7/3; Les Barry, "Short Stop on a Long Trail," *Popular Photography*, March 1964, 24; Irene Rawlings, "Museums of the Seven Seas," *Museum*, June/July 1983, 61.
35. Stackpole, *Interpretation*, 1, 6, 15–16; Steers, *Mystic Seaport*, 3.
36. Cutler, *Greyhounds*, ix–x; Kynett, *Fireside Admiral*, 110, 113; Lois W. Stillman, "Mystic Seaport," *American Heritage*, Summer 1952, 54.
37. Georgia W. Hamilton, *Silent Pilots: Figureheads in Mystic Seaport Museum* (Mystic, CT: Mystic Seaport Museum, 1984), 24; *Guide*, 10; Cutler to Mrs. Lynne Thompson, November 3, 1942, CP/MSM 3/2; Marion Dickerman, "What the Mystic Seaport Holds for You," *Connecticut Teacher*, November 1948, 36; MacDonald Steers, comp., *Yankee Sea Tradition: An Exhibit Guide*, 2nd ed. (Mystic, CT: Marine Historical Association, 1949–50), 10–11.
38. Walter Muir Whitehill, "Significance of Marine Museums," in Minutes, *MHA Bulletin*, no. 25 (1942): 18–19, and "History in the Country," *New York History* 43 (October 1962): 325; Cutler to C. H. Allen, September 22, 1931, CP/MSM 2/4; Cutler to Alfred Stanford, February 5, 1949, CP/MSM 3/13.
39. "Institute of Maritime History," *Yachting*, March 1955, 159; "Secretary's Notes," *PUSNI* 84 (April 1958): 157; Benjamin W. Labaree, "The Frank C. Munson Institute," *AN* 45 (1985): 41–45.
40. Steers, *Mystic Seaport*, 9; Cutler, *Mystic*, 30, and "Mystic Seaport," *Connecticut Industry*, November 1948, 13; Whitehill, "Significance," 20–21.
41. MHA, *Mystic Seaport* (Mystic, CT: Marine Historical Association, 1972), 8, 33; John Gardner, "The Future of Wooden Boats," *Log* 46 (Autumn 1994): 43; "Kingston Lobster Boat," *Log* 8 (Summer 1956): 8; Lisa Brownell, *Mystic Seaport* (Mystic, CT: Marine Historical Association, 1985), 6.
42. Edouard A. Stackpole and James Kleinschmidt, *Small Craft at Mystic Seaport* (Mystic, CT: Marine Historical Association, 1959), 51; Dickerman, "What the Mystic Seaport Holds," 38; Blanche Wiesen Cook, *Eleanor Roosevelt, 1884–1933* (New York: Viking, 1992), 13, 318–37, 399, 411–12.
43. "*Joseph Conrad*, Famed Square-Rigger," *New York Herald Tribune*, July 27, 1947; "Forlorn *Joseph Conrad*," *Tampa Evening Independent*, July 28, 1947; Stillman,

"Mystic Seaport," 54; "Thirteenth Annual Meeting," Supplement, *Log* (1959): 1; *MHA Bulletin*, no. 37 (1947): [5–6].

44. MHA, *Mystic Seaport*, 18.
45. Harriet Warren, "Old Salts of Mystic," *American Girl*, May 1947, 38, 46, 49; Betty Driscoll, "Girl Scout Trio 'Ships Out,'" *CSM*, August 22, 1949; Johnston, "Director's Message," *Log* 25 (Summer 1973): 65.
46. Kynett, *Fireside Admiral*, 207; Alan Villiers, "The Age of Sail Lives on at Mystic," *National Geographic*, August 1968, 223; Kate Lance, *Alan Villiers: Voyager of the Winds* (London: National Maritime Museum, 2009), 202–3; "Fake Glass," *Log* 12 (October 1960): 19–20; Donald P. Robinson, "The Restoration of the *Joseph Conrad*," *Log* 30 (July 1976): 47–48; Stillman, "Mystic Seaport," 53–55.
47. Kynett, *Fireside Admiral*, 152–53.
48. Cutler to Miss Colcord, October 13, 1949, CP/MSM 3/14, and to Mallory, October 31, November 18, 1951, CP/MSM 4/4; Mallory to Cutler, November 3, 1951, CP/MSM 4/4; Cutler, "The Future of Mystic Seaport," *Log* 2 (July 1950): 1–3.
49. Cutler, Minutes of Executive Committee Meeting, November 23, 1951, draft, CP/MSM 4/4; Mallory to Cutler, November 3, December 4, 1951, CP/MSM 4/4; Cutler to Charlie [Cutler], December 22, 28, 1951, CP/MSM 4/4; Cutler to Arthur Wendell, March 22, 1952, CP/MSM 4/6; Cutler to Mallory, October 31, 1951, CP/MSM 4/4; Cutler to Dickerman, November 19, 1952, CP/MSM 4/8.
50. Cutler to Howard Chapelle, October 24, 1952, CP/MSM 4/8; Cutler to Charlie [Cutler], December 22, 1951, CP/MSM 4/4; Cutler to John [?], March 29, 1952, CP/MSM 4/6.
51. Cutler to Mallory, April 2, 1950, and his reply April 13, 1950, CP/MSM 3/18; Cutler to Villiers, May 9, 1952, CP/MSM 4/7; Kynett to Mallory, August 12, 1952, CP/MSM 4/7; Cutler to Mallory, September 27, 1952, CP/MSM 4/8; Cutler to Chapelle, October 24, 1952, CP/MSM 4/8; Chapelle to Cutler, December 16, 1955, CP/MSM 4/19.
52. Cutler to Villiers, March 18, 1953, CP/MSM 4/11; Cutler to Mallory, September 27, 1952, and his reply September 30, 1952, CP/MSM 4/8; Edouard A. Stackpole, *William Rotch (1734–1828) of Nantucket, America's Pioneer in International Industry* (New York: Newcomen Society, 1950), 9; Kynett to Mallory, August 12, 1952, CP/MSM 4/7.
53. Cutler to Charlie [Cutler], December 22, 1951, CP/MSM 4/4; Mallory to Cutler, November 25, 1952, and his reply November 28, 1952, CP/MSM 4/8.
54. Cutler to Newton Brainard, January 20, 1953, CP/MSM 4/10; "Mallory, Noting 'Malicious Gossip,' Describes Mystic Seaport Finances," *NLD*, August 20, 1953.
55. Stackpole, *Interpretation*, 16; "Port of Early U.S. Sailing Ships," *NYT*, January 2, 1955; "Growing Pains," *Log* 9 (Fall 1957): 1–2.
56. Frances Mott to Cutler, October 8, 1952, CP/MSM 4/8; Mallory to Mrs. H. W. Mott, November 12, 1951, CP/MSM 4/4; Garret Condon, "Johnston Leaves Carr a Sturdy Ship," *NLD*, September 27, 1978.

57. "Address of Carl C. Cutler," Supplement, *Log* (1961): 11–12; Carr, "Mallorys of Mystic," 88.
58. Condon, "Johnston Leaves Carr"; "Biggest Project Facing Mystic," *NLD*, December 31, 1968; Vermont Royster, "Thinking Things Over," *WSJ*, July 17, 1968.
59. Johnston, "Director's Wishes," *Log* 22 (Spring 1970): 16, and "Director's Message," *Log* 25 (Fall 1973): 104; Condon, "Johnston Leaves Carr"; Julie Lipkin, "J. Revell Carr: At the Helm of Mystic Seaport," *NLD*, November 4, 1984; "Captain Johnson Named to Marine Historical Board," *NLD*, July 9, 1953.
60. Waldo Johnston, "Mystic Seaport," in *First National Maritime Preservation Conference Proceedings* (Washington, D.C.: Preservation Press, 1977), 22–25; Maynard Bray, "Wooden Ship Preservation," in *Third Conference Proceedings*, 3; Edmund E. Lynch, "The *Charles W. Morgan*," *Log* 21 (June 1969): 46.
61. Johnston, "Mystic Seaport," 22; Gardner, "Future of Wooden Boats," 44; Remarks of Philip R. Mallory, Supplement, *Log* (1959): 5.
62. 87 Cong. Rec., S21248, (September 26, 1962); Peter Stanford, "The Living Act," *SH*, no. 5 (Fall 1976): 6; "Mystic Seaport Selling 2 Ships," *NLD*, December 10, 1968.
63. Donald Mainwaring, "'Last Whaler' Restored," *CSM*, May 17, 1961; Peter Stanford, "Revell Carr and the Museum of America and the Sea," *SH*, no. 96 (Spring 2001): 19; Peter Benchley, "The Tall Ships of Mystic," *Travel and Camera*, July 1970, 29.
64. Waldo Johnston, "The Evolution of a Dream," *Log* 22 (Fall 1970): 73–75; Bray, "Wooden Ship Preservation," 2, 6; Johnston, "Mystic Seaport," 22.
65. Maynard Bray, "The Magnificent *Morgan*, *Log* 26 (Spring 1974): 11.
66. Robert Hamilton, "Mystic Seaport," *NYT*, November 15, 1992; Bray, "Wooden Ship Preservation," 2.
67. Joseph Mitchell, "Dragger Captain, Part 1," *New Yorker*, January 4, 1947, 32–42, and Part 2, January 11, 1947, 30–42 (quotation on 32); Carol Kimball, "*Draggerman's Haul*: Remembering Ellery Thompson," *NLD*, December 17, 2007; "Preserving History," *NLD*, May 15, 2008; Joe Wojtas, "'New' *Roann* Will Have a Story to Tell," *NLD*, May 14, 2008.
68. Owen Thomas, "Small Wooden Boats Make Waves Again," *CSM*, April 26, 1998; "Master Craftsman Gardner Dies at 90," *Bangor Daily News*, October 19, 1995; John Gardner, "Current Thoughts," *Log* 39, no. 4 (1988): 131–33.
69. John Gardner, "Small Craft Tradition," in *Third Conference Proceedings*, 203–4; John O. Sands, "Commentary," in *Third Conference Proceedings*, 205–7; John Gardner, "The First Rowing Workshop," *Log* 22 (Fall 1970): 79; Tom Connery, "Yankee Artisan Tackles Industry, CG," *NLD*, August 28, 1974.
70. Waldo Johnston, "Director's Message," *Log* 19 (Spring–Summer 1967): 48–49, and "Director's Message," *Log* 25 (Fall 1973): 103; "Gloucester Takes Step Backward with the Great Schooner Race," *Hendersonville (NC) Times-News*, November 27, 1974; Gardner, "Small Craft Tradition," 201.
71. Sara Leone, "Total Immersion," *Log* 47 (Autumn 1995): 43.

72. Waldo Johnston, "State of Museum," *Log* 28 (January 1978): 113; John Helyar, "Is History Outdated?," *WSJ*, June 27, 1980; "Camera Buffs Will Focus on Seaport," *NLD*, September 5, 1985.
73. "New England Tourism Back to Record Level," *Norwalk (CT) Hour*, September 24, 1980; Fought, *History of Mystic*, 136.
74. "Mystic Seaport Strategic Plan, 1994, Background," photocopy provided by J. Revell Carr, interview by author, August 7, 1998; Gardner, "Future of Wooden Boats," 41–46; Johnston, "State of Museum," 113; J. Revell Carr, letter to the editor, *NLD*, August 12, 1995.
75. Labaree, "Maritime Museums and Higher Education," 228; Jim Carlton and Jenny Doak, "Williams-Mystic! Twenty-Five Years," *Log* 54 (Autumn/Winter 2002): 36.
76. *Untapped Sources and Research Opportunities in the Field of American Maritime History* (Mystic, CT: Marine Historical Association, 1968); "What's Going On," *History News* 33 (November 1978): 252; David C. Maslyn, review of *New England and the Sea*, *American Archivist* 43 (Winter 1980): 92.
77. J. Revell Carr, "Sightings," *Log* 42 (Winter 1991): 86; Timothy J. Runyan, review of *Gender, Race, Ethnicity and Power in Maritime America*, ed. Glenn Gordinier, *SH*, no. 133 (Winter 2010–11): 51.
78. Benjamin W. Labaree, "America and the Sea," *Log* 49 (Winter 1997): 58–59; N. A. M. Rodger, review of *America and the Sea*, by Benjamin W. Labaree, *American Historical Review* 105 (October 2000): 1290–91.
79. Robert Egleston, exhibit review of *Voyages*, *Connecticut History* 40 (Spring 2001): 117–23; "Visitors Will Be Awash in Stories of the Sea," *NLD*, June 11, 2000; Phyllis Leffler, "Peopling the Portholes: National Identity and Maritime Museums in the U.S. and U.K.," *PH* 26 (Fall 2004): 37.
80. Quentin Snediker, "Searching for the Historic *Amistad*," *Log* 49 (Spring 1998): 86, 95; Robert A. Hamilton, "Q&A/Quentin Snediker," *NYT*, December 28, 1997; J. Revell Carr, "Annual Report," *Log* 52 (Autumn/Winter 2000): 44; Frank Rizzo, "*Amistad* on Location," *Hartford Courant*, March 27, 1997; "The Mission of the *Amistad*," *NLD*, March 26, 2000; Joe Wojtas, "*Amistad* Back in Town," *NLD*, October 7, 2003.
81. J. Revell Carr, "Sightings," *Log* 50 (Spring 1999): 85; "Bush's Australia Stop," *NLD*, December 31, 1999; Joe Wojtas, "New Mystic Seaport Facility," *NLD*, November 22, 2002.
82. Brian MacQuarrie, "'Living History' Falls on Hard Times," *BG*, November 2, 2003; Joe Wojtas, "Mystic Seaport Names New President," *NLD*, October 31, 2008.
83. Fought, *History of Mystic*, 133–34; Stephen Singer, "Mystic Seaport Workers Mull Union Representation," *BG*, August 11, 2012; Joe Wojtas, "Mystic Seaport Workers Try to Form Union," *NLD*, May 8, 2012; David Collins, "Mystic Seaport Workers," *NLD*, May 8, 2012; "Seaport Workers to Vote on Union," *New Haven (CT) Register*, August 12, 2012; David Collins, "Charles W. Morgan Was an Early Target of Labor,"

NLD, June 6, 2012; Joe Wojtas, "Pro-Union Workers File Unfair Labor Practice Complaint," *NLD*, May 23, 2012.

84. Peter Schworm, "Boston Find Aids Rebuilding of Ship in Conn.," *NBST*, June 20, 2011.
85. Ann Baldelli, "'We're Doing the Right Thing,'" *NLD*, May 17, 2014; Joe Wojtas, "Down to the Sea Once More?," *NLD*, September 29, 2009; "Wonderful Dream," *NLD*, August 6, 2009; Erik Ingmundson, "Layers of Interpretation," in *Interpreting Maritime History at Museums and Historic Sites*, ed. Joel Stone (Lanham, MD: Rowman & Littlefield, 2017), 37–43.
86. John Hill, "Famed Whaler *Charles W. Morgan* Will Float Again," *Providence Journal*, July 20, 2013; "Ric Burns' Keynote Address," July 21, 2013, www.mysticseaport.org/news/2013/ric-burns-keynote-address/.
87. Hill, "Famed Whaler"; Svati Kirsten Narula, "A Priceless Museum Artifact, but in the Ocean," *Atlantic*, February 4, 2015; Jason W. Smith, "Thou Uncracked Keel: The Many Voyages of the Whaleship *Charles W. Morgan* and the Presence of the American Maritime Past," *NEQ* 89 (September 2016): 425; David Collins, "Will the *Morgan* Sail Again?" *NLD*, August 8, 2014.
88. [Cutler], *Statement of Plan*, [7–8].
89. Cutler to Howard Chapelle, November 8, 1952, CP/MSM 4/8; Mallory to Cutler, November 25, 1952, CP/MSM 4/8; Condon, "Johnston Leaves Carr."
90. *Mystic Seaport: A Visitor's Guide* (Mystic, CT: Mystic Seaport Museum, 2005), 9; Benjamin W. Labaree, "The State of American Maritime History in the 1990s," in *Ubi Sumus? The State of Naval and Maritime History*, ed. John B. Hattendorf (Newport, RI: Naval War College Press, 1994), 374.
91. Quentin Snediker, "Mystic Seaport's Henry B. du Pont Preservation Shipyard," *Log* 54 (Autumn/Winter 2002): 38–45.
92. Singer, "Mull Union Representation"; Lisa Prevost, "New Exhibition Hall," *NYT*, May 12, 2015.
93. Karen Kaplan, "Mystic Seaport Concerned about Competition," *NLD*, August 17, 2001.

CHAPTER 4: "TO MAKE THE AMERICAN PEOPLE MORE SHIP-MINDED"

1. J. T. Holzbach, "The Mariners' Museum," *U.S. Coast Guard*, June 1940, 6. For Williamsburg, see James M. Lindgren, *Preserving the Old Dominion: Historic Preservation and Virginia Traditionalism* (Charlottesville: University Press of Virginia, 1993).
2. NNSDD, *Beating Swords into Plowshares* (Newport News, VA: Newport News Shipbuilding and Dry Dock Co., 1926), 5; Parke Rouse Jr., "Newport News in the Nation's War," in *Newport News' 325 Years*, ed. Alexander Crosby Brown (Newport

News, VA: Golden Anniversary, 1946), 337; William Baldwin Shearer, *The Cloak of Benedict Arnold* (Washington, D.C.: National Capital Press, 1928), 9.

3. Benjamin F. Cooling, *Gray Steel and Blue Water Navy: The Formative Years of America's Military-Industrial Complex, 1881–1917* (Hamden, CT: Archon, 1979); James T. Maher, *Twilight of Splendor* (Boston: Little, Brown, 1975), 240, 255.
4. "H. L. Ferguson, 80, Shipbuilder, Dies," *NYT*, March 15, 1953; Lisa Royse and Richard C. Malley, "A Grand Opening," *MMJ* 16 (Fall 1989): 5.
5. Gary E. Weir, *Forged in War: The Naval-Industrial Complex and American Submarine Construction, 1940–1961* (Washington, D.C.: Naval Historical Center, 1993).
6. M. M. Fitzhugh, "Mariners' Museum Engineering Problems," April 15, 1938, typescript, in Scrapbook, vol. 7, MM.
7. Peter Karsten, *The Naval Aristocracy* (New York: Free Press, 1972), 177; War Production Drive Committee, *The Shipyard in Peace and War* (Newport News, VA: Newport News Shipbuilding and Dry Dock Co., 1944), 15; Cerinda W. Evans, "Homer Lenoir Ferguson: Dean of American Shipbuilders" (unpublished manuscript, 1955), MM.
8. Charles A. Beard, "Big Navy Boys: Who Is Behind the Navy League?," *New Republic*, February 3, 1932, 316–18; Huntington to Ferguson, June 27, 1942, box 9, FP/MM.
9. H. F. Norton to Ferguson and Huntington, October 21, 1930, and W. Gatewood to Ferguson, April 7, 1930, both in box 4, FP/MM; Roger Williams to Capt. W. Brown, September 15, 1931, Cutler Papers 2/4, MSM.
10. Waldemar Kaempffert to Ferguson, May 31, 1932, and his reply, June 3, 1932, in box 4, FP/MM; Waldemar Kaempffert, "Vital Museums of the New Era," *NYT Magazine*, March 20, 1932, 12.
11. Huntington to Ferguson, August 7, 1943, box 9, FP/MM; H. L. Ferguson, foreword to *The Mariners' Museum: A History and Guide*, comp. Alexander C. Brown (Newport News, VA: Mariners' Museum, 1950), vi; Ferguson to George Mason, January 23, 1953, in Scrapbook, vol. 13, MM; "The Huntington Dynasty," *Fortune*, November 1936, 73–74.
12. "Splendid Image Presented," *NNDP*, October 7, 1930; Huntington to Ferguson, April 4, 1931, box 12, FP/MM; "Great Mariners' Museum," *CSM*, July 18, 1931; F. Snowden Hopkins, "The World's Largest Ship Museum," *Baltimore Sun*, December 11, 1932.
13. Alex Roland, W. Jeffrey Bolster, and Alexander Keyssar, *The Way of the Ship: America's Maritime History Reenvisioned, 1600–2000* (Hoboken, NJ: Wiley, 2008), 176–77; Allan P. Vaughan to author, email, October 1, 2016; "Cite Museum Waters as Polluted," *NNDP*, n.d. [1948], in Scrapbook, vol. 5, MM; "Huntington Museum to Be One of Finest," *NNTH*, January 15, 1932.
14. D. D. Hill, "To the Glory of Ships," *Richmond (VA) Magazine*, January 1931; Don Hill, "Museum Stores Sea's Treasures," *NNDP*, July 31, 1960; "Vandals Spatter Paint on Museum Sculptures," *NNTH*, February 26, 1958; "Huntington Dynasty," 75; William H. Runge, "Whitewash Job on a Robber Baron," *RNL*, June 4, 1954.

15. Hopkins, "World's Largest Ship Museum"; "Work Is Begun on $10,000,000 Ship Museum," *New York Herald Tribune*, May 26, 1932; Ferguson to George Mason, January 23, 1953, in Scrapbook, vol. 13, MM; Brown, *Mariners' Museum*, 63–64, 217.
16. W. Gatewood to Sec. of Navy, August [?], 1933, in box 4, FP/MM.
17. Brown, "Mariners' Museum," *Shipmate* [U.S. Naval Academy], June 1947, 32; Harold C. Ickes to B. Floyd Flickinger, December 22, 1934, and Ferguson to Flickinger, January 4, 1935, box 5, FP/MM; John O. Sands, *Yorktown's Captive Fleet* (Charlottesville: University Press of Virginia, 1983), chaps. 7–8.
18. Charles A. Beard, *The Navy: Defense or Portent?* (New York: Harper, 1932), 185; Robert L. O'Connell, *Sacred Vessels* (New York: Oxford University Press, 1991), 254–60.
19. Harold Sniffen, "Display Techniques in the Early Years," *MMJ* 17 (Summer 1990): 11; W. D. Kerlin to E. G. Rogers, April 30, 1935, box 5, FP/MM; Ferguson to Huntington, October 29, 1936, box 12, FP/MM; James Nevin Miller, "Sea Loot of Ages," *Washington Star*, September 6, 1936; Jack Scherer III, "Most Unadvertised Place in America," *American Motorist*, August 1935.
20. Brown, *Mariners' Museum*, 87, 102, 254–56.
21. Matthew War Coulter, *The Senate Munitions Inquiry of the 1930s* (Westport, CT: Greenwood, 1997), 86; "Hold Up Naval Contracts!," *Christian Century*, February 20, 1935, 230; "Homer Lenoir Ferguson, Dies at 80," *NNTH*, March 14, 1953.
22. "Ships on the Ways," *Fortune*, November 1936, 67–71, 178–90; Ferguson, "The Mariners' Museum," *TSNAME* 45 (1937): 377.
23. Armin Rappaport, *The Navy League of the United States* (Detroit, MI: Wayne State University Press, 1962), 167; Ferguson to George Mason, January 23, 1953, in Scrapbook, vol. 13, MM; Capt. Felix Riesenberg, "The Rough Log: The Mariners' Museum," *Nautical Gazette*, July 18, 1936; Miller, "Sea Loot"; Gatewood to Huntington, April 30, 1937, box 12, FP/MM.
24. Ferguson, "Mariners' Museum," 377–78.
25. Franklin D. Roosevelt, "Press Conference during a Tour Defense Facilities," July 29, 1940, https://www.presidency.ucsb.edu/documents/press-conference-during-tour-defense-facilities.
26. "Huntington Dynasty," 75, 190; Harold S. Sniffen, "The Mariners' Museum," *History* 23, no. 8 (1968): 147, and "Mark Twain and His Job as Pilot," *NNDP*, June 15, 1952.
27. David Gidmark, "The Adney Collection," *Wooden Canoe*, August 1996, 6–7, 13–20; Edwin Tappan Adney and Howard I. Chapelle, *The Bark Canoes and Skin Boats of North America* (Washington, D.C.: Smithsonian Institution Press, 1964), 4.
28. Brown, "Mariners' Museum Enjoys Extensive Growth," *NNDP*, January 4, 1942; "Mariners Museum 'Battle' Attracts Curious Public," *NNDP*, August 23, 1943; Geoffrey Perrett, *Days of Sadness, Years of Triumph* (Baltimore, MD: Penguin, 1973), 315.
29. Louise White, "Figureheads," *NVP*, September 7, 1941.

30. "Shipbuilding," *Time*, April 2, 1945, 77–78; "Mariners' Museum Report," *NNDP*, January 14, 1945; Brown, "Newport News Ships in Two Wars," *RTD*, December 12, 1954.
31. "Shipbuilding," 78; "Ship Program Conducted by Jaycee Forum," *NNDP*, May 18, 1947; "Merchant Marine Booster," *NNDP*, September 18, 1949.
32. "Boost Mariners' Museum," *NNDP*, October 25, 1948; "Navy Day–1947," *Shipyard Bulletin* (NNSDD), September/October 1947 (emphasis added); John B. Hefferdan to Ferguson, June 2, 1947, box 14, FP/MM; Alexander C. Brown, *The United States Frigate* Constitution*: A Sesquicentennial Exhibition, 1797–1947* (Newport News, VA: Mariners' Museum, 1947), 3–4, 22–23.
33. Thomas C. Skinner, *An Exhibition of Marine Paintings* (Newport News, VA: Mariners' Museum, 1948); "Ships on the Ways," 72; Agnes Brabrand, "Shipyard's Heavy Shop Work Depicted," *NNDP*, October 7, 1956; "Ferguson, Dies at 80."
34. "Davy Jones' Port," *RTD*, October 14, 1934; Sheldon Gordon, "Two Museums Profit from Piracy," *Globe and Mail*, October 8, 1997; "Mermaids Highlighted," *NNDP*, August 6, 1950; Julia Sully, "Ship's Figureheads Recall Dim Past," *RNL*, June 8, 1935; Tony Lewis, "Her Effigy in Wood," *Antiques*, December 1996, 837.
35. Robert Marks, "Ship-Builder in Lilliput," *Esquire*, December 1940, 102; Adm. Lake McNamee to Ferguson, January 24, 1946, box 14, FP/MM; Ned J. Burns, "The Value of Miniature and Life Size Historical Groups," *Museum News*, January 1, 1933, 8; Alexander C. Brown, "New Attendance Mark Set at Mariners' Museum," Scrapbook, vol. 2, MM; Edmund S. Sayer to C. F. Bailey, March 4, 1932, box 1, FP/MM.
36. William L. Tazewell, "A Rich Harvest of Maritime History," *NYT*, November 6, 1983; Vincent Scott, "August Fletcher Crabtree," *Nautical Research Journal* 45 (June 2000): 98.
37. L. F. Hagglund to Huntington, June 14, 1935, and Ferguson's reply, June 19, 1935, box 9, FP/MM; C. F. Bailey to Huntington, December 19, 1932, box 12, FP/MM; David Nicholson, "Museum Seeks Old-Timers' Advice," *NNTH*, n.d. [1980], in Clippings, vol. 30, MM; Miller, "Sea Loot"; Schuyler Otis Bland, "The Mariners' Museum, Newport News, Va.," 81 Cong. Rec. H2181 (August 19, 1937).
38. [Frederick F. Hill], "Indian Workmanship Is Shown," *NNDP*, June 25, 1950, and "Death Claims Indian Chief," *NNDP*, September 9, 1951; Elizabeth A. Fenn, *Encounters at the Heart of the World* (New York: Hill and Wang, 2014), 102–6, 277, 298; Elizabeth Fenn to author, email, May 6, 2015; "Discussion" and "The Mariners' Museum," *TSNAME* 45 (1937): 374–75.
39. Bland, "Mariners' Museum," H2182; John Gardner, "Current Thoughts," *Log* 39 (Winter 1988): 135–36, and "Small Craft Tradition," in *International Congress of Maritime Museums: Third Conference Proceedings, 1978* (Mystic, CT: Mystic Seaport Museum, 1979), 199; Thomas N. Downing, *The Mariners' Museum* (New York: Newcomen Society, 1987), 15; "Discussion," 377.
40. Richard Armstrong to Gatewood, February 9, 1933, box 4, FP/MM; M. V. Brewington, *Chesapeake Bay Log Canoes and Bugeyes* (Cambridge, MD: Cornell Maritime, 1963), 30, 85.

41. "Ships on the Ways," 72.
42. "Museum to Receive Model," *NNDP*, June 6, 1957; Fred Kaplan, *The Wizards of Armageddon* (New York: Simon and Schuster, 1983), 135; "Model of Confederate Submarine," *NNDP*, March 20, 1959.
43. Jean Allen, "Resident's Diorama Goes to Mariners' Museum," [*Ft. Lauderdale News*], n.d., in Clippings, vol. 16, MM; E. W. Sylvester, "The Mariners' Museum," *PUSNI* 85, no. 680 (1959): 82; "Diorama in Mariners' Museum," *NNDP*, December 14, 1958; "Noah's Ark Is Reconstructed," *NVP*, December 28, 1958.
44. *First International Antarctic Exhibition* (Newport News, VA: Mariners' Museum, [1963]), iii–viii; "Rear Adm. Dufek Named Head," *NNDP*, October 21, 1960; Robert Jay Lifton and Richard Falk, *Indefensible Weapons* (New York: Basic Books, 1982), 131; "Antarctic Exhibition Opens . . . with Humanity's Hope for Peace," *NNDP*, October 29, 1962; "Museum Director Supports Move for More Powerful Icebreakers," *NNDP*, January 17, 1961; "Ship Notes," *SH*, no. 154 (Spring 2016): 55.
45. Bailey to Ferguson, June 6, 1933, box 4, FP/MM; Sumner B. Besse, *U.S. Ironclad* Monitor (Newport News, VA: Mariners' Museum, 1936), 7; Huntington to Gatewood, July 23, 1936, and his reply July 28, 1936, box 12, FP/MM.
46. "Travel Men Briefed on Centennial Plans," *NVP*, January 9, 1961; "A 'Must' Centennial Feature," *NNTH*, March 12, 1959; John Greiff, "Local Civil War Centennial," *NNDP*, January 15, 1960; "Mariners' Museum Plans," *RTD*, December 18, 1960; "Sprawling Diorama of Battle," *NNDP*, August 14, 1961; Lindgren, *Preserving the Old Dominion*, 14.
47. "Sniffen Outlines Museum's Plans," *NNDP*, January 25, 1961; Dolores Jeffords, "Civil War Sea Power Show," *NYT*, April 23, 1961.
48. John Hope Franklin, "A Century of Civil War Observance," *Journal of Negro History* 47 (April 1962): 104; Greiff, "Local Civil War Centennial"; Lindy Wilder, "Centennial Group Battles," *NNDP*, May 5, 1961; Bill Delany, "Officials Preview Museum's Civil War Sea Power Exhibit," *NNDP*, April 25, 1961.
49. William D. Wilkinson, introduction to *The Mariners' Museum: Annual Report* (Newport News, VA: Mariners' Museum, 1985), 1–2; Harold T. Pinkett, review of *Tobacco Coast*, by Arthur Pierce Middleton, *Journal of Negro History* 39 (January 1954): 67–69.
50. "Everybody's Museum," *NNDP*, August 1, 1987; *The Chesapeake Bay Gallery at the Mariners' Museum* (Newport News, VA: Mariners' Museum, n.d.), 9; "Exhibitions," *The Mariners' Museum: Annual Report, 1984* (Newport News, VA: Mariners' Museum, 1985), 11; Lisa Royse and Richard C. Malley, "A Grand Opening," *MMJ* 16 (Fall 1989): 2–5.
51. John Townley, "A Chesapeake Sailors' Companion," *MMJ* 13, no. 4 (1986): 13–15, and "Of Songs and Oysters on the Eastern Shore," *MMJ* 16 (Summer 1989): 9–12; *Chesapeake Bay Gallery*, 11; John Joseph A. Gutierrez, "Students Work with Mariners' Museum to Preserve Vanishing Skills," *OAH Magazine of History*, Summer 1986, 40–41.
52. "He Digs Downtown," *Time*, August 24, 1981, 53; "Maritime Museum Plans

Unveiled," *NNDP*, September 3, 1988; Timothy J. Runyan, "Editor's Note," *AN* 54 (Summer 1994): 164; "An Ironclad Argument," *NNDP*, November 19, 1997.

53. "Seapower," *MMJ* 4 (Spring 1977): 5–6; William D. Wilkinson, "The Mariners Museum," in *Proceedings of the First National Maritime Preservation Conference* (Washington, D.C.: National Trust for Historic Preservation, 1977), 29–30; "Seapower and the Rise of the Battleship," *MMJ* 4 (Summer 1977): 6; "Seapower and Global War," *MMJ* 4 (Fall 1977): 5–6.

54. John Frye, "Of Men and Waters," *Sea Frontiers*, September/October 1984, 292; William L. Tazewell, *Newport News Shipbuilding* (Newport News, VA: Mariners' Museum, 1986), 4.

55. Mark Erickson, "Exhibit Honors Dean of American Naval Design," *NNDP*, December 7, 1990; Burgess, introduction to *The Big Ship: The Story of the SS* United States, by Frank O. Braynard, ed. Robert O. Burgess (Newport News, VA: Mariners' Museum, 1981), vii; "SS *United States* Update," *SH*, no. 156 (Autumn 2016): 50.

56. "Carriers, Codes, and Silent Ships Opens," *Mariners' Pipe*, Fall 1995, 1; Mark Erickson, "The Code-Breakers," *NNDP*, November 27, 1995; Carl Boyd, *American Command of the Sea through Carriers, Codes, and the Silent Service* (Newport News, VA: Mariners' Museum, 1995), 52, 69–75.

57. Hightower, foreword to *Guide to the Mariners' Museum* (Newport News, VA: Mariners' Museum, 1997), 4, 58; "The Collections," *Mariners' Museum Annual Report* (Newport News, VA: Mariners' Museum, 1997), 9.

58. Brigette Barnes, "Navy's History Preserved in New Gallery," CNO Public Affairs, November 5, 1999, https://groups.google.com (no longer available); Alva Chopp, "A Show of Sea Power," *NVP*, December 3, 1999.

59. "Collections," *Mariners' Museum: Annual Report* (Newport News, VA: Mariners' Museum, 1986), 5; Richard C. Malley, "Lord Nelson and the Americans," *MMJ* 13 (Fall 1986): 1–4; Patrick Plaisance, "How a Sailor Turned Tide of History," *NNDP*, June 21, 1998.

60. Mark Erickson, "Full Steam Ahead," *NNDP*, October 23, 1994; John B. Hightower, "Strategies May Help Keep the Arts from Self-Destructing," *NNDP*, July 23, 2000; Mylene Mangalindan, "Recasting the Ancient Mariner," *NVP*, May 22, 1995.

61. Stephanie Elizondo Griest, "A Match Made in Museum Heaven," *NYT*, July 10, 1997; "The National Maritime Museum Initiative," *Mariners' Museum Annual Report* (Newport News, VA: Mariners' Museum, 1998), 3; "Twin Museums," *NNDP*, June 18, 1997.

62. "A *Titanic* Triumph," *USA Today Magazine*, July 1998, 44–47; "Don't Miss These *Titanic* Events," *Mariners' Pipe*, Spring 1998, 1; John B. Hightower, "President's Column," *Mariners' Pipe*, Spring 1998, 2; Paula Crouch Thrasher, "*Titanic* Tourism," *Atlanta Journal and Constitution*, March 22, 1998.

63. Marc Davis, "Cash-Strapped Firm in a Bind over Sale of Titanic Artifacts," *Calgary (Alberta) Herald*, October 10, 2001; Mark Erickson, "Mariners' Hopes to Obtain Artifacts," *NNDP*, April 16, 2003; Jef Feeley and Dawn McCarty, "Titanic Relics on Auction Block Starting at $19.5 Million," *Bloomberg*, September 12, 2018.

64. Paul Clancy, "Waters of Despair, Waters of Hope," *NVP*, July 29, 2000; Paul Sullivan, "Blacks on the Bay," *Fredericksburg (VA) Free Lance-Star*, July 22, 2000; Patrick Hagopian, review of *Transatlantic Slave Trade*, *PH* 19 (Fall 1997): 102–5; Phyllis K. Leffler, "Maritime Museums and Transatlantic Slavery: A Study in British and American Identity," *Journal of Transatlantic Studies* 4, no. 1 (2006): 60.
65. Leffler, "Transatlantic Slavery," 60–65, 74, 78n70, 79n82; Paul Clancy, "Captive Passage Mariners' Museum Exhibit," *NVP*, April 30, 2002; Elizabeth Olson, "Getting Rich off Human Cargo," *NYT*, February 7, 2003; Daniel C. Littlefield, review of *Captive Passage*, *PH* 25 (Summer 2003): 134.
66. Jo Stanley, "Women at Sea," *Gender and History* 15 (April 2003): 136, 139; Bonnie Erbe, "Don't Count on Women in 'Male' Fields," *Gettysburg (PA) Times*, May 14, 2001; Mike Holtzclaw, "New Mariners' Museum Leader," *NNDP*, August 11, 2006.
67. John O. Sands, "Commentary," in *International Congress of Maritime Museums*, 205–6; Downing, *Mariners' Museum*, 15; Wilkinson, "Mariners' Museum," 30; Mark Erickson, "Large Collection of Small Craft," *NNDP*, September 28, 1988.
68. "Reference Library," *Mariners' Museum: Annual Report* (Newport News, VA: Mariners' Museum, 1990), 19; R. Thomas Crew, "Antique Boats Gallery," *MMJ* 16/17 (Winter 1989/Spring 1990): 10, 12; *Chris-Craft: The Affordable Dream*, http://www.mariner.org (no longer available); Mark Erickson, "Chris-Craft: A Boater's Dream," *NNDP*, February 14, 1999.
69. Mark Erickson, "From Bow to Bow," *NNDP*, May 11, 2003.
70. "Peter Neill Named President," press release, April 23, 1985, Melville Library, SSSM; Peter H. Spectre, "On the Waterfront," *WB*, no. 67 (November/December 1985): 15; Jean McNair, "*Monitor* Relics Spur Struggle," *WP*, May 25, 1986.
71. "*Monitor* Artifacts Find Home in Newport News," *Journal of Commerce*, March 5, 1987; Downing, *Mariners' Museum*, 8; "An Ironclad Argument," *NNDP*, November 19, 1997.
72. Bert Hubinger, "A Visit to the *Monitor*—Almost," *Civil War Times Illustrated*, June 1997, 26–33, and "Can We Ever Raise the *Monitor*?," 38–48.
73. William J. Broad, "Saving the Ship That Revolutionized War at Sea," *NYT*, December 2, 1997; William M. Fowler Jr., review of *War, Technology, and Experience aboard the USS* Monitor, by David A. Mindell, *American Historical Review* 106 (December 2001): 1807; John D. Broadwater, *USS* Monitor (College Station: Texas A&M University Press, 2012), 216.
74. "Museum to Build *Monitor* Copy," *Greensboro (NC) News and Record*, March 29, 2000.
75. Douglas Feiden, "Congress Loves Pork," *NYDN*, March 23, 2003; Mark Erickson, "It's Time to Man Your Battle Stations," *NNDP*, March 4, 2007; Michael E. Ruane, "Historic Warship in Middle of a Budget Battle," *WP*, January 10, 2014.
76. Sonja Barisic, "USS *Monitor* Museum to Open," *Durham (NC) Herald-Sun*, June 3, 2004; Edward Rothstein, "A Celebrity Warship," *NYT*, March 10, 2007.
77. Mark Erickson, "Replicating the Mighty Turret," *NNDP*, March 6, 2007; Tim Friend, "After Recovery, Restoration," *USA Today*, August 12, 2003.

78. Harold Holzer, "The *Monitor* Makes Port," *American Heritage*, April/May 2007, 42.
79. Mark Erickson, "Mariners' Museum Will Reduce Hours," *NNDP*, November 18, 2009.
80. S. Vaughan, "Colonial Williamsburg Annual Report," *Virginia Gazette*, July 5, 2016; Ruane, "Historic Warship"; Steve Szkotak, "USS *Monitor* Work Goes Dark as U.S. Dollars Dwindle," *Washington Times*, January 26, 2014.
81. Mark Erickson, "Fundraiser Tapped for USS *Monitor* Center," *NNDP*, May 8, 2015; "Ship Notes," *SH*, no. 142 (Spring 2013): 49.
82. Tara Bozick, "New CEO of Mariners' Museum Wants to Get Back to Basics," *NNDP*, October 8, 2016; "Mariners' Museum Lowers Cost to Bring in Explorers," *Virginia Gazette*, January 8, 2019.
83. Gordon, "Two Museums Profit."
84. Ivor Herbert, "An American Revelation in Virginia," *Mail on Sunday* (UK), November 9, 1997; "Homer Lenoir Ferguson, Shipyard Visionary, President," Hampton Roads Ticket, *http://hrticket.com* (no longer available).
85. Nicholson, "Museum Seeks Old-Timers' Advice."
86. John B. Hightower, "President's Column," *Mariners' Pipe*, Fall 1995, 1. In 1999, museum directors concluded that healthy, sustainable history museums had "(1) strong relationships with the community, (2) healthy attendance, (3) market responsiveness, (4) rich collection resources, (5) a strong commitment to education, (6) financial stability, (7) a galvanizing mission statement, and (8) a reputation for trustworthiness. While not universally embraced, the first was generally considered the most critical" (Rick Beard, "Building Museums That Last," *History News*, Summer 1999, 18).
87. Ian Urbina, "Stowaways and Crimes Aboard a Scofflaw Ship," *NYT*, July 17, 2015; "How Slavery and Murder Goes Unpunished on the High Seas," *PBS Newshour*, July 28, 2015.

CHAPTER 5: "A SAILING SHIP STIRS THE GENERAL PUBLIC LIKE NOTHING ELSE"

1. Karl Kortum to Scott Newhall, March 5, 1949, and Newhall to Paul C. Smith, March 8, 1949, in "San Francisco Maritime Museum Origins," a compilation of short pieces, newspaper stories, and documents compiled or written by Kortum, SFMNHP (hereafter, "Museum Origins").
2. Newhall to Clarence Lindner, September 22, 1949, in Kortum, "Museum Origins"; Karl Kortum, "A Lucky Life—A Chance to Do Something" (an unpaginated account accompanied by annotated newspaper stories, correspondence, and related ephemera), 1991, held by John Kortum (hereafter, "Lucky Life").
3. Kortum, "Lucky Life."
4. Kortum to Mrs. Edward S. Clark, February 9, 1962, in Kortum, "The Founding of the San Francisco Maritime National Historical Park," a photocopied compilation of documents with annotated text, 1990, SFMNHP.

5. "The Maritime Unions," *Fortune*, September 1937, 123, 127; Earl Burke, "Dailies Helped Break General Strike," *Editor and Publisher*, July 28, 1934, 5; Alex Roland, W. Jeffrey Bolster, and Alexander Keyssar, *The Way of the Ship: America's Maritime History Reenvisioned, 1600–2000* (Hoboken, NJ: Wiley, 2008), 287, 289.
6. Robert W. Rydell, *World of Fairs: The Century of Progress Expositions* (Chicago: University of Chicago Press, 1993), 7; "Permanent Marine Exhibit," *Shipping Register* 22 (October 5, 1940).
7. Kortum to Bill Olesen, August 2, 1991, in Kortum, "Lucky Life"; Grant Thompson, "'Fortune' in City Ship Museum," *Sydney (Australia) Morning Herald*, February 17, 1974.
8. Steven E. Levingston, *Historic Ships of San Francisco* (San Francisco: Chronicle Books, 1984), 27; W. A. Swanberg, *Citizen Hearst* (New York: Bantam, 1961), 565; Walter J. Walsh to William Randolph Hearst, November 14, 1941, HDC 1033:2, F58, SFMNHP.
9. "A Toast to the Late Great Scott Newhall," *San Francisco Independent*, n.d., in Kortum, "Lucky Life"; Kevin Leary, "Former *Chronicle* Editor Scott Newhall Dies," *SFC*, October 27, 1992.
10. Hamilton Cochran, "The Old Ships Come Home," *Saturday Evening Post*, October 9, 1948, 30–31; Kortum to Newhall, March 5, April 7, 1949, Newhall to Paul C. Smith, March 8, 1949, in Kortum, "Museum Origins"; Kortum, Biographical Notes, 1965, HDC 1084, SFMNHP.
11. David Nelson, Notes on Mrs. Alma Spreckels, May 2, 1949, in Kortum, "Museum Origins."
12. Everett P. Lunsford Jr., "Our Merchant Marine and Their Unions," *PUSNI* 101, no. 5 (1975): 69; Newhall to Lindner, September 22, 1949, in Kortum, "Museum Origins"; Scott Newhall, "A Newspaper Editor's Voyage across San Francisco Bay," oral history by Suzanne B. Riess, Bancroft Library, University of California, Berkeley, 1990, 283; David Hull, "End of an Era for West Coast Maritime History, Harold Huycke, 1922–2007," *Relative Bearings*, no. 6 (April 2007): 2–3; Kortum, "John Lyman: The Hub of Our Wheel," *SH*, no. 12 (Fall 1978): 14; Alison Isenberg, *Designing San Francisco: Art, Land, and Urban Renewal in the City by the Bay* (Princeton, NJ: Princeton University Press, 2017), chap. 1.
13. David E. Nelson, "War and Peace—Waterfront Style," *SL*, no. 57 (Winter 1999): 6–7.
14. "Sea Murals," *Time*, February 6, 1939, 41; [Al Harmon], *San Francisco Maritime Museum: 20 Years of Progress* (San Francisco: San Francisco Maritime Museum, 1971), 6; Moulton H. Farnham, "*Balclutha* and the San Francisco Maritime Museum," *Boating*, June 1972.
15. Nelson, "War and Peace," 7; David Nelson, interview with Jeanne Marie Maher, 1992, in *How the San Francisco Maritime Museum Was Conceived, Grew and Finally Made into a National Park* (San Francisco: David Nelson, 2007), DVD, SFMNHP; Mrs. Karl Kortum to *Ladies' Home Journal*, unpublished, August 13, 1954, HDC 1084, 2:2/F155, SFMNHP.
16. "Argonaut Bay Sales Points," mimeograph, n.d., HDC 649:2, series 3/F10,

SFMNHP; Kevin Starr, "Arts Patronage in San Francisco Is a 20th-Century Creation," *San Francisco*, April 1980, 28; "Argonaut Bay: Spot Announcements," n.d., HDC 649:2, 3/F10, SFMNHP.

17. Farnham, "*Balclutha*"; Alan Villiers, "San Francisco Saves a Ship," *Ships and the Sea* 5 (Fall 1955): 32; Kortum, "To Acquire the *Pacific Queen*," a compilation with annotation, 1995, n.p., SFMNHP (hereafter, "To Acquire"); Villiers, "San Francisco," 32.
18. Newhall, "Editor's Voyage," 284; Jean Kortum to Mr. Mayer, n.d. (1961), unsent, SFMNHP; Kortum to M. V. Langdale, October 19, 1955, HDC 1084, 2:2, SFMNHP; Farnham, "*Balclutha*"; Kortum to Dring, October 26, 1954, and Kortum to Project Manager, January 26, 1989, in Kortum, "To Acquire."
19. Kortum to John Cushing, July 23, 1954, HDC 1084, 2:2/F166, SFMNHP; *Dennis the Menace in California* (Meriden, CT: Fawcett, 1965), n.p.
20. Roger W. Lotchin, *Fortress California, 1910–1961* (New York: Oxford University Press, 1992), 177; "Keeping Posted," *Saturday Evening Post*, November 5, 1955, 160; David E. Nelson, "Dream to Reality in Fifty Years," *SL*, no. 66 (2004): 3; Villiers, "San Francisco," 32; Nelson, interview with Maher; Karl Kortum, "Why Do We Save Ships?," *APT Bulletin* 19, no. 1 (1987): 30.
21. Nelson to author, email, January 20, 2017; "Betty and Kay 'Discover'—The Maritime Museum," *Pacific Coaster*, February 1954, 14.
22. Kortum to President, Buckingham Corp., March 8, 1956, HDC 649:2, series 3/F4, SFMNHP; Transcript of "Wide Wide World," aired November 27, 1956, included in David Nelson to James Abbe, November 18, 1956, HDC 649:20, 3/22/F8, SFMNHP; "Ship's Saviors Visit Vessel," *San Francisco Call-Bulletin*, February 1, 1956; Kortum to Gordon Jones, May 11, 1950, HDC 649:1, 3/F20, SFMNHP; *Dennis the Menace*.
23. Kortum to Hugh Gallagher, September 15, 1954, in Kortum, "To Acquire"; Kortum to Lawrence Barber, June 19, 1962, SFMNHP.
24. Nelson, Project X Press Release, n.d., HDC 649:20, 3/22/F5, SFMNHP; Kortum to Frank G. Carr, October 15, 1958, HDC 1084, 2.2/F208, SFMNHP.
25. Kortum, "Lucky Life"; Joan McIntyre, "California's Historic Fleet," *News and Views: The California Department of Parks and Recreation Newsletter* 19 (January 1962): 3a–4a; David Hull, "Remembering Harold Huycke," *MN*, June 2007, 2; Harlan Trott, *The Schooner That Came Home* (Cambridge, MD: Cornell Maritime, 1958), 100; Kortum to Dave [Nelson], May 7, [1963?], HDC 1084, series 2:2, SFMNHP; Barbara Melosh, "Speaking of Women," in *History Museums in the United States*, ed. Warren Leon and Roy Rosenzweig (Champaign, IL: University of Illinois Press, 1989), 197.
26. Matt Smith, "Ship of Fools," *SF Weekly*, March 17, 1999; Robert Bunting, *The Pacific Raincoast: Environment and Culture in an American Eden, 1778–1900* (Lawrence: University Press of Kansas, 1997), 131, 134, 147; Peter Fimrite, "Last of Pacific Northwest's Fabled Schooners Losing Steam," *SFC*, July 24, 2000; *The* Wapama *Is One of San Francisco's Historic Ships* (Sacramento, CA: Department of Parks and Recreation, [1972]).

27. Carl Nolte, "Floating through the Delta," *SFC*, July 13, 1997; Anita Mozley, "Scow Schooners of San Francisco Bay," *SL*, no. 5 (December 1967): 1; Barbara Fetesoff, "San Francisco's *Alma*," *WB*, no. 3 (April 1980): 16.
28. "The Ships," *SL*, no. 45 (Spring/Summer 1992), 7; Archie Green, "How Blue-Collar Preservationists Restored the Ferry Boat *Eureka*," *SFE*, March 10, 1994.
29. Kortum, comp., "An Eclectic Park Lit by Gaslight," unpublished, n.d., SFMNHP; Nelson to author, fax, July 27, 2003; Jane Jacobs, *The Death and Life of Great American Cities* (New York: Modern Library, 1961), 159; McIntyre, "California's Historic Fleet," 2a; Olmsted to Kortum, September 9, 1960, HDC 649:18, 3/F14, SFMNHP.
30. Kortum, Memorandum to Regional Director, October 25, 1984, Director's files, SFMNHP; Kortum to Hugh Gallagher, no date, HDC 649:18, 3/F14, SFMNHP; John Luce, "My Search for Scott Newhall," *San Francisco Magazine*, July 1968, 71, and August 1968, 40; Newhall, "Editor's Voyage," 130; "In Clio's Cause," *SH*, no. 7 (Spring 1977): 7–8; Carl Nolte, "Tribute to Guardian of Seafaring History," *SFC*, September 27, 1995; Paul O'Neill, "The Only Rebellion Around," *Life*, November 30, 1959, 115, 129.
31. "Sea Murals," 41; Henry Miller, *The Air-Conditioned Nightmare* (New York: New Directions, 1945), 278, 280.
32. "The SFMM," *PUSNI* 85 (August 1959): 90, 96; Bernice Scharlach, *Big Alma: San Francisco's Alma Spreckels* (San Francisco: Scottwall, 1990), 274; Levingston, *Historic Ships*, 32.
33. Margaret J. King, "The Recycled Hero," in *Davy Crockett: The Man, the Legend, the Legacy, 1786–1986*, ed. Michael A. Lofaro (Knoxville: University of Tennessee Press, 1986), 143; Harlan Trott, "Of Keels and Wheels," *CSM*, August 23, 1955.
34. Alan Villiers, *The Set of the Sails* (New York: Scribner's Sons, 1949), 110, 277–78; Villiers, "San Francisco," 30; "Mrs. Spreckels' Home Guarded after Threats," *WP*, March 4, 1945; Norman Brouwer, "The Five-Masted Ship *Preussen*," *SSR* 9 (Winter 1975–76): 17.
35. Lawrence E. Davies, "San Francisco's Bay Area," *NYT*, May 25, 1958 (the other was a scale model exhibit of the Bay from the 1939 fair); Jesse Lemisch, "Jack Tar in the Streets," *WMQ* 25 (July 1968): 372; Kortum to Chairman, History Department, University of California at Berkeley, February 25, 1955, HDC 649:1, 3/F21, SFMNHP; Gerald D. Adams, "Underground Workers Find Gold Rush Ship," *New Orleans Times-Picayune*, December 8, 1994.
36. Villiers, "San Francisco," 31; A. R. Sanford, "Gordon Grant, Windjammers and Men of the Sea," *Lookout* 66 (June 1975): 16; Kortum to Dring, October 26, 1954, in Kortum, "To Acquire" (the extended poop was not removed because of the expense); David Nelson, "*Balclutha*," an article prepared for the *Boston Globe*, in Nelson to Daniel O'Brien, June 11, 1956, HDC 649:19, 3/22/F3, SFMNHP.
37. William Martin Camp, *San Francisco: Port of Gold* (Garden City, NY: Doubleday, 1947), 210–13; Richard Everett, "Bringing *Balclutha* to Life," *SL*, no. 67 (2005): 17; Peter B. Wiley, *National Trust Guide: San Francisco* (New York: Wiley, 2000), 55.

38. Karl Kortum, introduction to *Brotherhood of the Sea: A History of the Sailors' Union of the Pacific, 1885–1985*, by Stephen Schwartz (New Brunswick, NJ: Rutgers University Press, 1986), xii, and afterword to *Deepwater Family*, by Fred B. Duncan (New York: Pantheon, 1969), 173; Kortum, "Lucky Life"; Frank Carr, "Toward a World Ship Trust," *SH*, no. 13 (Winter 1979): 22.
39. Peter Stanford and Norma Stanford, *A Dream of Tall Ships* (Peekskill, NY: Sea History Press, 2013), 387; Scott Newhall, *The* Eppleton Hall (Berkeley, CA: Howell-North, 1971), 10, 28–29; Peter Stanford to author, email, October 1, 2008.
40. Kortum, "Lucky Life"; Farnham, "*Balclutha*"; Ebba Hierta, "Staying Afloat," *National Parks*, March/April 1986, 46; Newhall, "Editor's Voyage," 259; Peter H. Spectre, "The Issues of Maritime Preservation," *WB*, no. 38 (January/February 1981): 38, 45; Fred K. Klebingat, "How My Old Friend, the *Falls of Clyde*, Was Saved," *Oceans* 5 (September/October 1972): 45.
41. Alan D. Hutchison, "An Early History of the NMHS and the *Kaiulani* Project: Part 1," *SH*, no. 94 (Autumn 2000): 6–7, and "An Early History of the NMHS and the *Kaiulani* Project: Part 2," *SH*, no. 95 (Winter 2000–2001): 7–9; Alan D. Hutchison and Karl Kortum, testimony of September 28, 1967, in *Restoring the* Kaiulani*: Hearing before the Subcommittee on Merchant Marine and Fisheries*, 90th Cong., 1st sess., on S.J. Res. 101 (Washington, D.C.: U.S. Government Printing Office, 1967), 12–14; Ron Hendren, "In Washington," *Schenectady Gazette*, May 24, 1978; Kortum, "Lucky Life."
42. John McPhee, *Encounters with the Archdruid* (New York: Farrar, Straus, Giroux, 1971), 85; Harlan Trott, "*Balclutha* to the Rescue," *CSM*, October 7, 1964; Alison Isenberg, *Downtown America* (Chicago: University of Chicago Press, 2004), 289–94, 411, and *Designing San Francisco.*
43. Kortum to Piero Patri, October 27, 1970, Kortum Correspondence, SSSM; Nelson to Feinstein, [June 7, 1971], HDC 1084, series 2:2/F178, SFMNHP.
44. Richard E. DeLeon, *Left Coast City: Progressive Politics in San Francisco, 1975–1991* (Lawrence: University Press of Kansas, 1992); Kortum to Herb Caen, March 19, 1969, HDC 1084, 2:2/F106, SFMNHP; Kortum to Nick Lamberto, November 11, 1977, HDC1084, 2:2, SFMNHP; Bruce Brugmann and Greggar Sletteland, eds., *The Ultimate Highrise* (San Francisco: Guardian, 1971), 29, 128; Newhall, "Editor's Voyage," 515.
45. "Rescue of the Waterfront," *Venture*, February 1965, 109; R. R. Olmsted and T. H. Watkins, *Mirror of the Dream* (San Francisco: Scrimshaw Press, 1976), 285; Kortum to Herb Caen, March 19, 1969, and December 14, 1977, HDC 1084, 2:2/F106, SFMNHP; Jay Hansen, *The Other Guide to San Francisco* (San Francisco: Chronicle, 1980), 130; Gray Brechin, "Progress in San Francisco," *San Francisco*, October 1983, 62–63.
46. James P. Delgado, "Pioneers, Politics, Progress and Planning: The Story of San Francisco's Aquatic Park," in *Historic Structures Report* (San Francisco: Golden Gate National Recreation Area, 1981), 39; Sarah Nome to David Nelson, September 16, 1969, HDC 1084, 2:2/F178, SFMNHP; Stephen Canright, "Learning from

the Old Guys," *SL*, no. 67 (2005): 11; Kortum to Stanford, January 5, 1971, Kortum Correspondence, SSSM; Luce, "My Search," August 1968, 28; Newhall, "Editor's Voyage," 112; Herb Caen, "Please Call It Frisco?," in *One Man's San Francisco* (Garden City, NY: Doubleday, 1976), 192.

47. "Rescue of the Waterfront," 108; Stanford to Anita Ventura, January 22, 1967, HDC 1084, 2:8/F2, SFMNHP.

48. Thomas to author, emails, July 22, August 26, 2003; John Jacobs, *A Rage for Justice: The Passion and Politics of Phillip Burton* (Berkeley: University of California Press, 1995), 211–16, 375; "Meeting the Needs of Tomorrow Today," *National Parks and Conservation Magazine*, May 1979, 22; Delgado, "Pioneers," 100; Lynn Thompson, Remarks to National Trust Annual Meeting, October 4, 1979, HDC1085, 1/F2, SFMNHP.

49. Kortum, "Opportunity in San Francisco," *SH*, no. 4 (July 1976): 26–28; Newhall, "Editor's Voyage," 285; Mary Curtius, "That Sinking Feeling," *LAT*, August 25, 1996; William Thomas to author, email, August 26, 2003.

50. Spectre, "Maritime Preservation," 41. In his "administrative history" of the West's first urban national park, Hal K. Rothman slighted the museum and its separate archives (Rothman, *The New Urban Park: Golden Gate National Recreation Area and Civic Environmentalism* [Lawrence: University Press of Kansas, 2004], 156, 221). He noted: "The Maritime Museum was . . . a difficult marriage of objectives and personnel that reflected the complexity characteristic of the park" (131).

51. Newhall, "Editor's Voyage," 279; Kortum to Jean Bradford Fay, December 5, 1958, in HDC 649:2, series 3/F1, SFMNHP.

52. James Delgado to author, email, July 30, 2003; Eric Berryman, *Scope of Collections for Ships and Boats* (San Francisco: National Maritime Museum, 1980), 2, 7, 16, 20, 30; Spectre, "Maritime Preservation," 45.

53. "A Man to Match the Mountains," *National Parks*, January/February 1993, 18; Phillip Burton, "Clear and Present Dangers," *Wilderness*, Spring 1983, 22; Hierta, "Staying Afloat," 44; F. Ross Holland Jr., "The National Park Service and Maritime Preservation," *SH*, no. 19 (Winter 1980–81): 22–23; James Delgado to author, email, July 30, 2003.

54. Don Birkholz, telephone interview, October 15, 2009; Peter H. Spectre, "Give 'em Hell, Harry," *WB*, no. 61 (November/December 1984): 89; "Trying to Stay Afloat," *LAT*, February 9, 1986; William E. Burgess Jr., *In Bristol Fashion:* Balclutha *and* Eppleton Hall *of the SFMM, 1975–1980* (Bloomington, IN: AuthorHouse, 2010), 256; Ewen MacLean to Raymond W. Laing, email, October 11, 1997, Hyman Collection (privately held).

55. Adrian Raynaud to Peter Spectre, *WB*, no. 91 (November/December 1989): 4; Spectre, "Give 'em Hell," 99; *Save the Wapama*, Ron Townsend, producer, 2009, http://www.youtube.com/watch?v=nM7mC5zkeag; Thomas, Diary, October 6, 1983, July 12, 1984, February 10, 1987, March 31, 2000, SFMNHP; Peter H. Spectre, "Peter Rebuts," *WB*, no. 90 (September/October 1989): 4.

56. Burgess, *In Bristol Fashion*, 231; "Trying to Stay Afloat"; Raynaud to Spectre, 4;

Marcia L. Myers, *Maritime America: A Legacy at Risk* (Washington, D.C.: National Trust, 1988), 43.

57. David Hull, telephone interview, October 8, 2003, and "The Heart of the Matter," *SH*, no. 80 (Winter 1996–97): 15; Chief Curator (Kortum) to GGNRA General Superintendent (John H. Davis), May 19, 1983, and Davis to Regional Director, May 24, 1983, Director's files, SFMNHP; James Delgado to author, email, July 30, 2003.
58. John Maounis, "Interpreting Historic Vessels," *APT Bulletin* 19, no. 1 (1987): 65; Ronald Taylor, "Park Service Struggling," *LAT*, June 6, 1986; Glenn Gordinier to author, email, September 25, 2007; Scott Harmon to author, email, October 20, 2007; Everett, "Bringing *Balclutha* to Life," 19, and Everett, interview, San Francisco, April 18, 2016; Birkholz, telephone interview.
59. Warren Hinckle, "Reagan's Pirates Out to Sink Foundering Maritime Museum," *SFE*, April 7, 1986; Charles Burress, "Showdown Set," *SFC*, November 4, 1986.
60. Herb Caen, "And So to Press," *SFC*, November 17, 1986; Warren Hinckle, "Bureaucrats Hound an Old Sea Dog," *SFE*, November 24, 1986; "One Hundred One Memorable San Franciscans," *SFE*, March 1, 1987.
61. Spectre, "Maritime Preservation," 40; Hierta, "Staying Afloat," 44.
62. William Penn Mott Jr. to Richard T. Thieriot, December 2, 1987, HDC1085, 1/f5, SFMNHP; Taylor, "Park Service Struggling."
63. Thomas, Diary, February 10, November 13, 1987, SFMNHP; John Davies, "Seaport Park Planned," *Journal of Commerce*, February 2, 1987; Thomas to author, email, August 26, 2003; An Act to Establish the San Francisco Maritime National Historical Park, Pub. L. No. 100–348 [H.R. 1044], June 27, 1988.
64. Thomas to author, email, July 22, 2003; Raymond W. Laing, letter to the editor, "SOS," *National Parks*, September/October 1996, 8; Nelson to author, fax, July 27, 2003.
65. "Maritime Sites," *National Parks*, November/December 1988, 10; Thomas, Diary, July 13, August 26, October 29, 1990, SFMNHP.
66. Michael Naab, *The Secretary of the Interior's Standards for Historic Vessel Preservation Projects, with Guidelines for Applying Standards* (Washington, D.C.: National Park Service, 1990); Kevin J. Foster, "Vessel Preservation Standards," http://www.maritime.org/conf/conf-foster.html; Canright, "Learning from the Old Guys," 7, 11.
67. Thomas, Diary, July 13, 1990, February 21, 25, 1991, January 13, 1992, SFMNHP; Harold D. Huycke, letter to the editor, "Rotting Ships," *SFC*, March 12, 1992; Peter H. Spectre, "Capt. Adrian Raynaud," *WB*, no. 104 (January/February 1992): 50.
68. Harree W. Demoro, "Panel Wants Private Firm to Restore S.F. Ships," *SFC*, September 5, 1992; Benjamin W. Labaree, "The State of American Maritime History," in *Ubi Sumus? The State of Naval and Maritime History*, ed. John B. Hattendorf (Newport, RI: Naval War College Press, 1994), 373–77; Allen Freeman, "SOS!," *Historic Preservation*, November/December 1993, 34–41, 102; Kevin Leary, "Historic S.F. Ship on Endangered List," *SFC*, June 23, 1993; Steve Kesselman, letter to author,

September 27, 2004; Thomas, Diary, March 17, 1992, June 21, July 1, August 6, 12, November 22, 1993, July 11, 1996; Ewen MacLean to Ray [Laing], email, October 11, 1997, Hyman Collection.

69. Curtius, "That Sinking Feeling"; Hierta, "Staying Afloat," 44–45.
70. Nolte, "Tribute to Guardian"; Thomas, Diary, December 7, 1994, September 5, 1995, and November 15, 1996; Walter Cronkite, preface to *Westwind* (Birmingham, AL: Oxmoor, 1990), 7, 66; Jim Herron Zamora, "Maritime Museum Founder," *SFE*, September 13, 1996; Gerald D. Adams, "Fighting against Mediocrity," *SFE*, November 14, 1996; Smith, "Ship of Fools."
71. Delgado to author, email, July 30, 2003; Adams, "Fighting against Mediocrity"; Rybka to author, email, September 27, 2008; Naab to author, email, July 23, 2003; Hyman, "Karl Kortum: Friend and Mentor," *SH*, no. 80 (Winter 1996–97): 14.
72. Newhall, "Editor's Voyage," 278, 349; Nolte, "Tribute to Guardian"; Peter H. King, "What the Shadow Knew," *Columbia Journalism Review* 38 (November/December 1999): 42; Dan Levy, "S.F. Poised for Pact," *SFC*, May 23, 2000.
73. Thomas, Diary, November 14, 1990, SFMNHP; Irene Lechowitzky, "Shipshape by San Francisco's Wharf," *LAT*, November 30, 2003.
74. Thomas, Diary, November 16, 1999, October 22, 29, 2001, SFMNHP; Carl Nolte, "William G. Thomas—First Leader of S.F. Maritime Park," *SFC*, April 15, 2004; Elaine Kaplan, *A Report to Congress from the U.S. Office of Special Counsel for Fiscal Year 2002* (Washington, D.C.: U.S. Office of the Special Council, 2002), 11; Thomas to author, email, August 26, 2003; Hyman, interview, San Francisco, June 11, 2007, and Hyman to author, email, November 13, 2015.
75. Chris Jannini, interview, San Francisco, April 21, 2016; Hyman to author, email, June 11, 2007.
76. *Tugboat* Hercules: *Historic Structure Report* (San Francisco: Tri-Coastal Marine, 1990), 2; Thomas, Diary, October 8, 1990, August 17, 1992, August 22, 1995, SFMNHP; "Tugboat Festival Honors 100 Year Old *Hercules*," *MN*, September 2007, 1; Carl Nolte, "Al Lutz, Devoted Skipper," *SFC*, July 5, 2010.
77. Thomas, Diary, August 25, 30, October 28, 1999, March 31, October 4, 2000, SFMNHP; Stephen Schwartz, "Historians Seek to Save Schooner *Wapama*," *SFC*, October 30, 1996.
78. Gerald D. Adams, "Sinking into Oblivion," *SFE*, December 8, 1996; Glen Martin, "*Eureka*—They Found It," *SFC*, September 20, 1997.
79. David Hull to author, email, April 24, 2007; "Famous Old Tug Has Seen Better Days," *Sunderland Echo* (England), February 26, 2010.
80. Robbyn L. Jackson, "For Good Measure: Documenting *Balclutha* (1987–1990)," *SL*, no. 67 (2005): 12; "A Facelift for *Balclutha*, *SFC*, March 7, 1998; Sam Whiting, "Rediscovering the Wharf," *SFC*, July 12, 1998; Steve Hyman, "Sustaining Maritime Preservation," *SL*, no. 67 (2005): 22.
81. "*Cargo Is King!*," September 8, 2015, http://www.nps.gov/SFMNHP/learn/history culture/cargoisking.htm (no longer available); "*Cargo Is King!*," *MN*, April 2005, 2.

82. Walter P. Rybka, "Ranking of Historic American Ships," *SH*, no. 147 (Autumn 2014): 28; "Historic Schooner *C. A. Thayer* Returns to Pier," *MN*, June 2007, 1.
83. Everett, interview; Gianmaria Franchini, "Restored Depression-Era Maritime Murals Recall Heyday of Public Art," *SF Public Press*, July 19, 2010; "Exhibit in Visitor Center Beckons You to Enter," www.nps.gov/safr/learn/historyculture/waterfrontexhibit.htm; Nolte, "SF Maritime Park Tells Port's Big Story," *SFC*, March 25, 2012.
84. Judith Overmier, "Cultural Record Keepers," *Libraries and the Cultural Record* 41 (Summer 2006): 396.
85. Kortum, "Lucky Life"; Lawrence M. Fisher, "Karl Kortum, 79," *NYT*, September 15, 1996.
86. Timothy G. Lynch, *Beyond the Golden Gate: A Maritime History of California* (Bronx, NY: Fort Schuyler Press for the National Park Service, 2015), 285; Anne Mitchell Whisnant, Marla R. Miller, Gary B. Nash, and David P. Thelen, *Imperiled Promise: The State of History in the National Park Service* (Bloomington, IN: Organization of American Historians at the invitation of the National Park Service, 2011), 100.
87. "*Balclutha* Celebrates 50 Years Open to the Public on the SF Waterfront," *MN*, July 2005, 1; Isenberg, *Designing San Francisco*; Nelson to author, letter, September 20, 2006; Jannini, interview; Everett, interview.
88. Nelson to author, September 20, 2006; Timothy Egan, "Past and Future Collide on San Francisco's Waterfront," *NYT*, February 10, 1995; Newhall, "Editor's Voyage," 278.
89. Alexander Cockburn, "Herb Caen: 'A Little Bit of the Cobra,'" *Nation*, February 24, 1997, 9–10; Herb Caen, "I Like This Place," in *One Man's San Francisco*, 195.

CHAPTER 6: 'THE STREET OF SHIPS"

1. "Airliners to Get Voice Recorders," *NYT*, July 12, 1964; John Sibley, "Windjammers to Bid Their Adieus," *NYT*, May 24, 1964; William N. Wallace, "New Windjammers from Out of the Past," *NYT*, May 3, 1964. See also James M. Lindgren, *Preserving South Street Seaport: The Dream and Reality of a New York Urban Renewal District* (New York: New York University Press, 2014).
2. "Tactically Logical Cruiser," *Time*, January 11, 1943, 52; Peter Stanford, "The Ships of San Francisco," *SH*, no. 38 (Winter 1985–86): 10, and Stanford, *The Ships That Brought Us So Far* (New York: National Maritime Historical Society, 1971), 39; Stanford to Kortum, November 4, 1971, 2:8/F1, HDC 1084, KC/SFMNHP.
3. Norma Stanford to Director, San Francisco Maritime Museum, January 20, 1966, and to Anita Ventura, March 8, 1966, 2:8/F2, KC/SFMNHP.
4. Peter Stanford to author, email, July 12, 2007; Whitney North Seymour Jr., *Making a Difference* (New York: William Morrow, 1984), 86.
5. Whitney North Seymour Jr., telephone interview, April 10, 2009; Ada Louise Huxtable to author, email, March 25, 2009.

6. "Proposal for an East River Seaport," in Norma Stanford to Anita Ventura, August 16, 1966, 2:8/F4, KC/SFMNHP; Frederick L. Rath Jr., "The South Street Maritime Museum Proposal and the Preservation of Schermerhorn Row in New York City," IA/SSSM; Stanford to Kortum, March 13, 1967, 2:8/F2, KC/SFMNHP.
7. Mel Greene, "Ship Museum Would Re-create 1811," *NYDN*, January 29, 1967; "Farewell to Penn Station," *NYT*, October 30, 1963; Peter Stanford to Anita Ventura, January 22, 1967, 2:8/F2, KC/SFMNHP; Bill Miller, "Frank O. Braynard," *Ocean Times* 2 (Winter–Spring 2003): 2.
8. Peter Stanford and Norma Stanford, *A Dream of Tall Ships* (Peekskill, NY: Sea History Press, 2013), 76; "The Fall of Jakob Isbrandtsen," *Forbes*, March 15, 1972, 23; Robert Gallagher, "South Street Seaport," *American Heritage*, October 1969, 42.
9. SSSM, *A Proposal to Recreate the Historic "Street of Ships" as a Major Recreational and Cultural Resource in the Heart of New York City* (New York: South Street Seaport Museum, July 1967), 5–13; Jason Hackworth, *The Neoliberal City* (Ithaca, NY: Cornell University Press, 2007), 120; Richard Weinstein, telephone interview, October 16, 2009; Robert Fitch, *The Assassination of New York* (New York: Verso, 1993), 227.
10. Moynihan quoted in Jakob Isbrandtsen, undated fundraising letter, in Printings File, 1969, IA/SSSM; "South Street Planning Conference," November 7, 1968, transcription by Office of State History, New York Department of Education, IA/SSSM.
11. Kortum to Peter Stanford, March 9, 1967, KC/SSSM; "Open *Ambrose* Lightship," *SSR* 4 (March 1970): 1.
12. Peter Stanford, "*Ambrose* and *Caviare*," *SSR* 2 (September 1968): 2 (*Caviare* was actually *Lettie G. Howard*); George Matteson to author, email, February 11, 2010; Norman Brouwer, "The Ships of South Street," *Seaport* 17 (Summer 1983): 24.
13. Kortum to Peter Stanford, April 7, 1967, KC/SSSM; Captain Irving Johnson, *The* Peking *Battles Cape Horn* (New York: Sea History Press, 1977), 165.
14. Ellen F. Rosebrock, *Walking around in South Street: Discoveries in New York's Old Shipping District* (New York: South Street Seaport Museum, 1974), 60; Peter Stanford, "The Ship as Museum," *SH*, no. 46 (Winter 1987–88): 13; Chip Brown, "The *Wavertree* at One Hundred," *Seaport* 20 (Spring 1986): 14; Kortum to Peter Stanford, June 26, 1967, 2:8/F2, KC/SFMNHP.
15. Stanford and Stanford, *Dream*, 354; "*Wavertree* Is Here!," *SSR* 4 (September 1970): 1, 7; Alan Villiers, letter to the editor, *SSR* 3 (July 1969): 2, and letter to the editor, *NYT*, June 8, 1972; "Old Salts Reminisce," *SSR* 3 (January 1969): 8; Nels Rasmussen, letter to the editor, *SSR* 11 (Winter 1977–78): 4.
16. "Villiers Visits *Wavertree*," *SSR* 4 (November 1970): 4; Edward H. Fitzelle, "*Peking* and *Wavertree*," *Oceans*, May 1977, 8.
17. Charles Richards, producer, *The Street of Ships*, 28 minutes, motion picture, 1983, New York Public Library; George Matteson to author, email, May 7, 2008.
18. John Hastings, "NY's Last Paddle-Wheel Steamer," *SSR* 1 (October 1967): 3; Laurie Johnston, "Hudson Sidewheeler Ties Up at Seaport," *NYT*, April 4, 1972.
19. Peter H. Spectre, "The Politics of Maritime Preservation," *WB*, no. 64 (January/February 1982): 68; Walter Rybka to author, email, November 14, 2006.

20. Peter Stanford to Kortum, June 10, 1970, 2:8/F1, KC/SFMNHP; "*Alexander Hamilton* and *Moshulu* Coming," *SSR* 5 (Spring 1972): 1; Peter Stanford, interview, June 21, 2010; Editor to David A. Cisney, *SSR* 9 (Winter 1975–76): 22; James L. White, "Accuracy vs. Safety vs. Profit, *Moshulu* Dress Rig," http://www.maritime.org/conf/conf-white.htm.
21. Peter Aron, telephone interview, December 17, 2009; "Seaport Museum Given a Square-Rigger," *NYT*, November 23, 1975.
22. David Berson, Review of *Around Cape Horn*, *Seaport* 22 (Fall 1988): 46–47; Peter Neill, "The State of the Museum, 1986," *Seaport* 20 (Spring 1987): 11; Irving Johnson, "Remarks," in *First National Maritime Preservation Conference Proceedings* (Washington, D.C.: Preservation Press, 1977), 49.
23. "Seaport Notes," *SSR* 7 (Fall 1973): 16; Conrad Milster, "*Aqua*," *SSR* 7 (Summer 1973): 13; Norman Brouwer to author, email, August 29, 2016.
24. Michael Creamer to author, email, June 2, 2010; Neill, "Reflections on 20 Years," *Seaport* 21 (Summer 1987): 11–12; Peter Stanford to Jakob Isbrandtsen, February 1, 1976, 2:8/F6, KC/SFMNHP; Kortum to Peter Stanford, December 27, 1968, KC/SSSM.
25. Isbrandtsen, telephone interview, March 7, 2008; Peter Stanford to Kortum, July 14, 1969, KC/SSSM.
26. "Fall of Jakob Isbrandtsen," 23; Peter Stanford to author, email, February 16, 2007; Robert Carroll, "South Street Seaport Plan Hits a Financial Reef," *NYDN*, June 27, 1971; Peter Stanford to Kortum, February 10, 1973, KC/SSSM.
27. Editorial, *NYDN*, February 8, 1973, in "We Share a Vision," *SSR* 7 (Spring 1973): 7; "Roundtable on Rouse," *Progressive Architecture*, July 1981, 103; "On April 11," *SSR* 6 (Summer 1972): 1; "Stop Press," *SSR* 6 (Fall 1972): 11; Peter Stanford to author, email, August 12, 2009; Carter Horsley, "Air-Rights Deal Saves South St. Seaport," *NYT*, July 30, 1973.
28. *South Street Seaport: A Plan for a Vital New Historic Center in Lower Manhattan* (New York: South Street Seaport Museum, 1969), 21; Editorial, "Salvation on the East River," *NYT*, July 17, 1971.
29. Stanford and Stanford, *Dream*, 249; Pete Seeger, letter to the editor, *Seaport* 14 (Spring 1980): 48, and Seeger, telephone interview, November 16, 2007; Marty Twersky, "South Street Seaport," *NYT*, January 28, 1973; "Sings Salty Sea Songs," *Public Employees Press*, June 18, 1971, 11; Peter Stanford to author, email, November 17, 2006.
30. Tom Buckley, "Electrified Spaghetti on Avant Garde Fete Menu," *NYT*, October 29, 1972; Norma Stanford, interview, May 11, 2006; Annette Kuhn, "The Underwater Cellist," *Village Voice*, November 2, 1972; Carman Moore, "The Avant-Garde in Dry Dock," *Village Voice*, November 9, 1972; Norma Stanford to Philip Yenawine, September 30, 1974, PSP.
31. Rhoda Amon, "Frank Braynard, 'OpSail' Originator," *Newsday*, December 13, 2007; Frank Braynard, *The Tall Ships: Official Op Sail '76 Portfolio* (New York:

Sabine, 1976), n.p.; Howard Slotnick, telephone interview, September 9, 2008; Walter Rybka to author, email, August 20, 2008.

32. Barry Lewis and Virginia Dajani, "The South Street Seaport Museum," *The Livable City* (Municipal Art Society) 8 (June 1981): 4; Christopher Lowery to author, email, September 21, 2010.

33. Philip Yenawine to author, email, April 27, 2009; Melvin Conant, "Comments on Goals, Priorities & Management Issues before the Trustees of South Street," January 1, 1977, Trustees file, IA/SSSM.

34. Pete Seeger to Andrea Anderson, April 29, 2001, PSP, and Seeger, telephone interview, November 16, 2007; John B. Hightower, "The President's Report," *SSR* 12 (Spring 1978): 6–7; Patricia Leigh Brown, "Is South Street Seaport on the Right Tack?" *Historic Preservation*, July/August 1981, 12, 17, 19; Carter Wiseman, "Waterfront Wonderland," *New York*, July 4, 1983, 36–39. Designed to encourage grassroots participation, Community Board No. 1 was a planning body representing most of Manhattan south of Canal Street. It was the first step in the review process of proposed development in the area.

35. Peter Stanford to Jakob Isbrandtsen, February 1, 1976, 2:8/F6, KC/SFMNHP; Brouwer, "Ships of South Street," 23–24; Bill Tuttle, "South Street Growth Plan Pains Ship Restorer," *Soundings*, November 1979, A2; Peter H. Spectre, quoted in "Preservation Forum," *WB*, no. 41 (July/August 1981): 40–41; George Matteson to author, email, February 11, 2010.

36. Peter Aron to Larry Huntington, September 5, 2006, Task Force file, JACF; Walter Rybka to author, email, September 12, 2006; "Seaport Museum in Rough Waters," *NYP*, September 25, 1979; Kenneth D. Reynard, "Restoration of an Iron Star," *International Congress of Maritime Museums, Third Conference Proceedings, 1978* (Mystic, CT: Mystic Seaport Museum, 1979), 18; Peter Aron, telephone interview, December 17, 2009.

37. George Matteson to author, email, May 7, 2008; Percy Knauth, "South Street," *On the Sound* 3 (January 1973): 33–48; Shari Galligan Johnson to author, email, July 8, 2008.

38. George Matteson to author, email, May 7, 2008; Editorial, "Someone's Using His Head," *NYDN*, December 14, 1972; Walter Rybka to author, email, November 14, 2006; Susan Stephenson, "*Pioneer*, Wildcat Begins Ship Restoration," *SSR* 7 (Fall 1973): 11; David C. Brink, telephone interview, September 14, 2006.

39. Bill Reel, "Set Your Sails for South Street," *NYDN*, July 29, 1983; Richard Brandt to author, email, August 11, 2006; Peter Neill to author, email, November 9, 2008; Sally Yerkovich to author, email, May 19, 2009.

40. *New Yorker*, April 30, 1984, cover; Crystal Nix, "Pier 17 Opens at Seaport," *NYT*, September 12, 1985; Peter Aron, JACF Pledge, March 13, 1985, SSSM/Emergency Committee file, JACF; Minutes, Board of Trustees, March 13, 1985, in Trustees Meeting file, IA/SSSM.

41. Meg Cox, "All at Sea," *WSJ*, April 12, 1985; Paul Goldberger, "Touring Little Old

New York," *NYT*, July 2, 1976; William Grimes, "As Museum and Mall, a Seaport Lives On," *NYT*, May 1, 1992; Peter Neill, "A Museum Like No Other," *Seaport* 19 (Fall 1985): 4.

42. Bernard J. Frieden and Lynne B. Sagalyn, *Downtown, Inc.: How America Rebuilds Cities* (Cambridge, MA: MIT Press, 1990), 312; Peter Aron, telephone interview, December 17, 2009; Minda Zeitin, "Rouse Formula Serves Seaport Retailers Well," *Crain's New York Business*, April 27, 1987; Minutes, Board of Trustees, November 1, 1988, SSSM Board, JACF; Peter Grant, "A Watertight Seaport Deal," *Crain's New York Business*, January 9, 1989; Marcia L. Myers, *Maritime America: A Legacy at Risk* (Washington, D.C.: National Trust, 1988), 28.

43. Stephen J. Kloepfer to Michael Carey, August 24, 1999, Aron Foundation file, JACF, and Kloepfer to author, email, November 12, 2010; Bernard Stamler, "Rough Sailing for South Street Seaport," *NYT*, March 29, 1998.

44. Erin Urban, *John A. Noble: The Rowboat Drawings* (New York: Noble Collection and South Street Seaport Museum, 1988), 8, 10; Jim O'Grady, "Paying Proper Tribute," *NYT*, April 21, 2002; Peter Matthiessen, *Men's Lives* (New York: Random House, 1986), 4; Peter Neill, "Threatened by Opportunity," *Seaport* 29 (Summer 1995): 3; Michael J. Chiarappa, "When Cod Was King," *PH* 19 (Winter 1997): 127, 131.

45. Sarah Boxer, "The Great Seamen's Fleet," *Sports Illustrated*, December 17, 1990; James Barron, "Museum and a Collector Vie for the Treasures of the Seas," *NYT*, March 25, 1991; A. J. Peluso Jr., "Collector Sues FDIC," *Maine Antique Digest*, May 1991, 6C; Peter Neill to author, email, January 9, 2009.

46. Michael Kimmelman, "Tattoo Moves from Fringes to Fashion," *NYT*, September 15, 1995; Neill, "Threatened by Opportunity," 2–3, and Neill to author, email, January 15, 2009; SSSM, *Broadside: Calendar of Events*, July/September 1995, 17; Jonathan Yardley, "Yo Ho Ho and Not Much Fun," *WP*, September 15, 1996.

47. Teresa Annas, "Mariners' Museum Joins N.Y. Seaport Museum as Partner," *NVP*, June 17, 1997; Minutes, Board of Trustees, December 14, 1994, February 25, 1997, SSSM Board, JACF; Michael Naab to author, emails, April 3, 2007, February 23, 2009; Thomas E. Wilcox, telephone interview, March 13, 2009.

48. Pete Seeger, letter to the editor, *SSR* 8 (Spring 1974): 22; Peter Neill, "History, by, and for, the People," *Seaport* 21 (Spring 1988): 8.

49. Joe Doyle to author, email, July 26, 2009; Joe Doyle, "John Singleton, 'The Lonely Life,'" *Seaport* 19 (Winter 1986): 48, and "Rose Chevell, 'Glory Hole Sailor,'" *Seaport* 21 (Winter 1987–88): 48.

50. Laurie Johnston, "At Seaport, a Restoration of Spirit," *NYT*, October 16, 1981; Peter Neill, "Reflections on 20 Years," 11, and "Developing a National Cultural Policy for Maritime Preservation," *APT Bulletin* 19, no. 1 (1987): 24; Barrett T. Beard Sr., "American Maritime Historic Preservation; Practice and Policy" (master's thesis, Western Washington University, 1986), 58–59.

51. "Not Yet a Nautical Museum," *NYT*, December 28, 1985; Peter Neill, "A Confusion of Ships," *Seaport* 20 (Spring 1986): 6, and "Reflections on 20 Years," 12.

52. Tuttle, "South Street Growth Plan," A2; Martin Gottlieb, "Trump Says He Wants to Build World's Tallest Tower at East River Site," *NYT*, July 31, 1984; Jim Powell, *Risk, Ruin and Riches: Inside the World of Big Time Real Estate* (New York: Macmillan, 1986), 277; Lee T. Pearcy, letter to the editor, "South St. Seaport Ignoring Its Museum Role," *NYT*, July 18, 1988; Dick Sheridan, "Port of Missing Ships: Whatever Happened to the South Street Dream?," *NYDN*, March 26, 1989, Magazine, 11; Peter H. Spectre, "On the Waterfront," *WB*, no. 89 (July/August 1989): 27.
53. Michael Naab to author, email, January 28, 2010, and *The Secretary of the Interior's Standards for Historic Vessel Preservation Projects* (Washington, D.C.: National Park Service, 1990); J. J. Thompson, letter to the editor, "Value of Ship Restoration," *Sea Breezes*, n.d., in Clippings 1983, IA/SSSM; Norman Brouwer to author, email, January 12, 2010.
54. Jakob Isbrandtsen, telephone interview, March 7, 2008; Brown, "*Wavertree* at One Hundred," 17; "Report to the Membership: Ships, Buildings, and Collections," *1981 Annual Report*, an insert in *Seaport* 16 (Fall 1982): 20; Zdena Nemeckova, "Love on the Waterfront," *New Manhattan Review*, June 26, 1985, 13–15; Peter H. Spectre, "The Issues of Maritime Preservation," *WB*, no. 38 (January/February 1981): 38.
55. William A. Baker, "Commentary," in *Third Conference Proceedings*, 14; Judith Cummings and Albin Krebs, "Prince's Tack May Draw Shots across the Bow," *NYT*, October 3, 1980; Peter Stanford to Ralph L. Snow, April 18, 1978, 2:8/F7, KC/SFMNHP.
56. Peter Aron to author, email, January 27, 2010, and telephone interview, December 17, 2009; Spectre, "Issues of Maritime Preservation," 44; Joe Doyle to author, email, July 26, 2009; Elizabeth Giddens, "Captain of the Low Seas," *NYT*, April 8, 2007; Joe Doyle, "Lars Henning Hansen: The Rigger of South Street," *Seaport* 23 (Summer 1989): 52.
57. Waterfront Committee Minutes, December 10, 1984, JACF; Nora McAuley to author, email, September 3, 2010; Nemeckova, "Love on the Waterfront," 13–15; Terry Walton, "CAMM'S First 25 Years," *CAMM Gamming*, Spring/Summer 1999, Insert, 2; James P. Delgado, "The National Maritime Initiative," *PH* 13 (Summer 1991): 76.
58. Neill, "Developing a National Cultural Policy," 26; Thomas C. McAuliffe to Peter Neill, July 16, 1985, Volunteers in Support of SSSM (papers in author's possession); Sally Yerkovich to author, email, February 19, 2010.
59. Peter Neill, "Personal Dialogues with Ghosts," in *Past Meets Future: Saving America's Historic Environments*, ed. Antoinette J. Lee (Washington, D.C.: Preservation Press, 1992), 45, 46, and Neill to author, email, January 27, 2010.
60. Charles Deroko to author, email, February 17, 2010; Peter Neill, "A Tall Ship for New York and the Nation," *Journal of Commerce*, November 29, 1999, 8; Paul Goldberger, "In Honor of the Fund That Loves New York," *NYT*, June 9, 1997.
61. Amanda Gardner, "Getting All Decked Out," *NYDN*, January 24, 2000; Charles Deroko to author, email, February 17, 2010; Angela C. Allen, "Hard-Luck Ship Returns to Glory," *NYP*, July 5, 2000.

62. "$5 Million Port Authority Grant," *SSSM News*, Fall 2002, 1.
63. Peter Neill to author, email, June 2, 2010; Stephen Kloepfer to author, email, November 12, 2010.
64. Rebecca Solnit, *A Paradise Built in Hell* (New York: Viking, 2009), 184, 191; Madeline Rogers, "Salt of the Earth," *Seaport* 37 (Spring/Summer 2002): 42; Peter Neill, "Dunkirk on the Hudson," *Seaport* 37 (Spring/Summer 2002): 2; Andrea Peyser, "'Blame U.S.' Garbage Art," *NYP*, September 10, 2005; Caryn James, "Beyond Comforting the Afflicted," *NYT*, September 12, 2005.
65. Peter Neill to author, email, November 9, 2008; Al Amateau, "Seaport Museum Plans a $20 Million Center," *DE*, October 5, 1998; Glenn Collins, "At Museum's New Home," *NYT*, July 3, 2003.
66. Peter Neill to author, emails, April 23, November 1, 2010; Paul Clancy, "Captive Passage," *NVP*, April 30, 2002; Celeste-Marie Bernier, review of *Transatlantic Slavery: Against Human Dignity*, *Journal of American History* 88 (December 2001): 1006–12.
67. Peter Neill to author, email, April 23, 2010; Jeanne Willoz-Egnor to author, email, November 10, 2010; Stephen Kloepfer to author, email, November 12, 2010; "Spare Times," *NYT*, January 16, 2004; Elizabeth Olson, "Getting Rich Off Human Cargo," *NYT*, February 7, 2003.
68. Peter Aron, telephone interview, December 18, 2009; Glenn Collins, "Living the Life of the Sea," *NYT*, August 5, 2003; Peter Neill to author, email, November 9, 2008.
69. Robin Pogrebin, "Museum at South St. Reduces Staff," *NYT*, July 8, 2004; Yvonne Simons to author, email, June 13, 2010; Dennis A. O'Toole to author, email, November 7, 2011.
70. Pogrebin, "Museum at South St."; George Matteson to author, email, September 24, 2009; Sarah Trefethen, "Seaport Tug Pulls Out Win Upstate," *DE*, September 19, 2008.
71. Norman Brouwer to author, email, November 9, 2010; Eric Wolff, "*Peking* May Duck Out of City," *New York Sun*, May 1, 2003; Kelly Crow, "A Tall-Masted Classic Must Go," *NYT*, May 18, 2003; Peter Neill to author, email, November 12, 2010; Lionel Amos to Paula Mayo, November 20, 2004, and her reply, November 22, 2004, *Peking* file, JACF. *Lettie* is temporarily berthed at Erie, PA.
72. Minutes, Board of Trustees, December 2, 1997, February 3, 1998, JACF; Peter Neill to author, emails, October 22, 23, 2009, November 10, 2010; David Freedlander, "Changes in Store for South Street Seaport," *Newsday*, November 12, 2007; Julie Shapiro, "Museum Hopes for Historic Ships," *DE*, March 29, 2008; "Fi/Di/Chinatown/LES Waterfront Ready for Its Makeover," August 18, 2009, https://ny.curbed.com/2009/8/18/10534848/fidi-chinatown-les-waterfront-ready-for-its-makeover.
73. Sara Jane, Comment on Sewell Chan, "Loaders, Lumpers and the Smell of Fish," *NYT*, April 28, 2008; Peter Neill to author, email, March 2, 2010; Liz Willen, "South Street Sizzles, *Newsday*, July 3, 2000.

74. Richard Dorfman, telephone interview, May 16, 2011; Robin Pogrebin, "Finances Could Sink Seaport Museum," *NYT*, February 19, 2011; Jessica Terrell, "CB1 Committee Calls for Council Hearing," *Tribeca Trib*, July 2011.
75. Terese Loeb Kreuzer, "Anchors Aweigh, Seaport Museum Loses Its Operator," *DE*, July 3, 2013, "S.O.S., Seaport Museum Says It's Getting Pushed Out," *DE*, April 18, 2013, and "Seaport Museum's Days Are Numbered, but C. B. 1 Says Save It," *DE*, June 21, 2013.
76. Terese Loeb Kreuzer, "Seaport Developer Quietly Moves to Transform the Area," *DE*, September 5, 2013 (see original print copy because the publisher modified the online version after the reporter's departure [Kreuzer to author, January 21, 2016]); NYC Department of Finance, Memorandum of Lease, ID 2013070800342002, June 27, 2013, available at http://saveourseaport.org/wp-content/uploads/2016/01/HHC-Memorandum-of-Lease-June-27–2013.pdf; James M. Lindgren, "The Sinkhole at South Street Seaport," *DPNYC*, January 17, 2014.
77. Grace Rauh, "Next EDC President Will Have to Recuse Herself," May 9, 2016, http://www.ny1.com/nyc/all-boroughs/politics/2015/07/6/next-edc-president-will-have-to-recuse-herself-from-projects-her-husband-is-involved-in.html; Charles V. Bagli, "Despite Amenities, South Street Seaport Redevelopment Plans Stall over a High-Rise," *NYT*, February 16, 2015; Terese Loeb Kreuzer, "Task Force Will Weigh in on Howard Hughes Seaport Plans," *DPNYC*, January 29, 2014, and "Hughes' New Seaport Proposal Barely Budges from Old One," *DPNYC*, November 20, 2014; James M. Lindgren, "Tracing 50 Years of the South Street Seaport's Struggles," February 4, 2015, https://ny.curbed.com/2015/2/4/9995694/tracing-50-years-of-the-south-street-seaports-struggles.
78. James M. Lindgren, "Why NYC Must Save the South Street Seaport," *NYP*, April 19, 2014; Paul Greenberg, Roland Lewis, and Joan K. Davidson, "The War on New York's Waterfront," *NYT*, July 31, 2014; Laura Kusisto, "Howard Hughes Corp. Offers to Trim Height," *WSJ*, November 19, 2014; Charles V. Bagli, "Despite Amenities," and "South Street Seaport Tops Preservation Trust's List of Endangered Historic Sites," *NYT*, June 24, 2015; "Mayor's Chummy City Council Relations Suddenly Aren't," *Crain's New York Business*, March 1, 2015.
79. Kathryn Brenzel, "Howard Hughes Eyes 600K sf of Air Rights at South Street Seaport," April 25, 2018, https://therealdeal.com/2018/04/25/howard-hughes-eyes-600k-sf-of-air-rights-at-south-street-seaport/.
80. Gail A. Brewer to Carl Weisbrod, October 17, 2016, http://saveourseaport.org/wp-content/uploads/2016/11/2016–10–17-MBP-Brewer-to-CPC-Weisbrod-re-Pier-17-Tin-Building-minor-mod_DIGITAL.pdf.
81. Terese Loeb Kreuzer, "South Street Seaport Museum Celebrates 'Spring Revival,'" *DPNYC*, April 28, 2014; James Barron, "Iron-Hulled Ship," *NYT*, May 21, 2015; Jonathan Boulware, telephone interview, June 8, 2016.
82. Lindgren, *Preserving South Street Seaport*, 297–98; "LMDC Grants," *DPNYC*, March 21, 2016; Matthew Fenton, "Lollapalooza Producer Coming to South Street

Seaport," *The Broadsheet*, March 22, 2018, https://www.ebroadsheet.com/lollapalooza-producer-coming-south-street-seaport/.

83. Barron, "Iron-Hulled Ship"; Boulware, interview; Joseph Cheeseman, interview, New York, March 19, 2019.
84. In the Seaport's audited reports, "acquisition, maintenance and repairs" were combined. As in 1973, the $146,936 represented about 10 percent of total expenses (Stanford and Stanford, *Dream*, Appendix IV).
85. Seymour, interview; Weinstein, interview; Phillip Lopate, "Her New York," *NYT*, November 9, 2008; "A Brief Sampling of Hoffer Aphorisms," *Life*, March 24, 1967, 38.
86. Luc Sante, *Low Life: Lures and Snares of Old New York* (New York: Farrar Straus Giroux, 1991), xi; Phillip Lopate, *Waterfront: A Journey around Manhattan* (New York: Crown, 2004), 231–32.

CONCLUSION: "A LOOSELY KNIT NET OF REGIONAL ENTERPRISES"

1. "South Street Planning Conference," November 7, 1968, transcription made by Office of State History, New York Department of Education, IA/SSSM.
2. "South Street Planning Conference"; Duncan F. Cameron, "The Museum: A Temple or the Forum," *Journal of World History* 14, no. 1 (1972): 189; Cary Carson, "The End of History Museums: What's Plan B?," *PH* 30 (Fall 2008): 9–27, and "Colonial Williamsburg and the Practice of Interpretive Planning," *PH* 20 (Summer 1998): 11–52.
3. Garrison Keillor, *Pontoon: A Lake Wobegon Novel* (New York: Viking, 2007), 238.
4. Karl Kortum to Peter Stanford, July 23, 1969, Kortum Correspondence, IA/SSSM.
5. Melvin Jackson to Kortum, August 4, 1976, Kortum Collection, HDC 1084, 2:2, F149, SFMNHP; John A. Noble, letter to the editor, "Save Sailor's Snug Harbor," *SSR* 6 (Fall 1972): 2, 8; James M. Lindgren, "'They That Go Down to the Sea in Ships': Putting Life into Maritime Preservation," in *Bending the Future*, ed. Max Page and Marla Miller (Amherst: University of Massachusetts Press, 2016), 140–43.
6. Peter Stanford, letter to the editor, "Let *Esmeralda* Sail in Liberty's Flotilla," *NYT*, June 18, 1986; Peter H. Spectre, review of *Maritime America*, ed. Peter Neill, *WB*, no. 90 (September/October 1989): 155; Phyllis Leffler, "Peopling the Portholes," *PH* 26 (Fall 2004): 41.
7. Norman Brouwer, "Sailing into the 20th Century," *Seaport* 18 (Spring/Summer 1984): 20–21; Peter Neill, "A Past in Search of a Future," *WB*, no. 62 (January/February 1985): 15; Lance Lee, "The Case for the Restoration of Skillfulness," *WB*, no. 38 (January/February 1981): 48; Peter Neill, "Lance Lee and His Icon Boats," *WB*, no. 209 (July/August 2009): 66; Walter Cronkite, "Flood the Past with Light," in *International Congress of Maritime Museums: Third Conference Proceedings, 1978* (Mystic, CT: Mystic Seaport Museum, 1979), xviii, xxi.
8. Peter Stanford, *The Ships That Brought Us So Far* (New York: National Maritime

Historical Society, 1971), 19, and "The Ship as Museum," *SH*, no. 46 (Winter 1987–88): 14; William Cogar, "*Ubi Sumus* Revisited: The State of Maritime and Naval Museums, 2004," http://www.hnsa.org (no longer available); John O. Sands, "Small Craft Tradition in North American Maritime Museums," in *International Congress of Maritime Museums*, 205–6; Benjamin W. Labaree, "The State of American Maritime History in the 1990s," in *Ubi Sumus? The State of Naval and Maritime History*, ed. John B. Hattendorf (Newport, RI: Naval War College Press, 1994), 374; Peter Neill, "The Whole Museum," *Seaport* 24 (Summer 1990): 6. See also Rick Beard, "Life Behind Bars," *Culturefront* 1 (May 1992): 35.

9. Walter Muir Whitehill, "Significance of Marine Museums," in *Minutes, Marine Historical Association Bulletin*, no. 25 (1942), 18–19; Stanford, "Ship as Museum," 15; Kevin Walsh, *The Representation of the Past: Museums and Heritage in the Post-Modern World* (New York: Routledge, 1992), 4, 124.
10. Mary Rizzo, "Consuming Class, Buying Identity: Middle-Class Identity, Popular Culture, and Cross-Cultural Appropriation, 1945–2000" (PhD diss., University of Minnesota, 2004), chap. 1; John Gardner, "New Directions in Small Craft Collection and Preservation," in *Wooden Shipbuilding and Small Craft Preservation* (Washington: Preservation Press, 1976), 22; Walter Rybka, "Suggested Standards for Replica and Reproduction Vessels," *APT Bulletin* 19, no. 1 (1987): 71.
11. White Elephant Management, *Summary of Results of the Maritime Heritage Survey Conducted for the National Trust for Historic Preservation* (Galveston, TX: White Elephant Management, 1985), 31; "*Oliver Hazard Perry* to Examine 'Financial Sustainability,'" *Providence Journal*, September 6, 2018. Over forty meters in length and launched before 1940, Class A sailing ships listed as National Historic Landmarks include *Balclutha, C. A. Thayer, Constellation, Constitution, Eagle, Elissa, Ernestina-Morrissey, Falls of Clyde, Gazela, Roseway*, and *Star of India. Wavertree* appears only on the National Register.
12. Michael Naab to author, email, January 28, 2010; Peter H. Spectre, "Old-Tyme Shyppes," *WB*, no. 96 (October/November 1990): 66; Maynard Bray, "Wooden Ship Preservation," in *Third Conference Proceedings*, 2.
13. Spectre, "Old-Tyme Shyppes," 66, 69; Burchenal Green, "What Is Happening?," *SH*, no. 149 (Winter 2014): 4; "Ship Notes," *SH*, no. 153 (Winter 2015–16): 52.
14. Randy Kraft, "A New Constant Reminder Replica of 17th-Century Ship," *Morning Call* (Allentown, PA), April 21, 1991; Peter H. Spectre, "The Heaving Deck of History," *WB*, no. 96 (October/November 1990): 72; White Elephant Management, *Summary of Results*, 46.
15. Deirdre O'Reagan, "Maritime Museum of San Diego," *SH*, no. 120 (Autumn 2007): 16–19.
16. "Ports of Call," *SSR* 3 (November 1969): 7; William A. Baker, "Commentary," in *International Congress of Maritime Museums*, 13.
17. Margaret Crawford, "The World in a Shopping Mall," in *Variations on a Theme Park*, ed. Michael Sorkin (New York: Hill and Wang, 1992), 17; Timothy J. Runyan,

"Editor's Note," *AN* 54 (Summer 1994): 164; Stanley Murray and Nancy Murray, "Nation's Maritime Heritage Back on Course," *Denver Post*, July 1, 1990; Jacqueline Trescott, "Exhibiting a New Enthusiasm," *WP*, June 21, 1998.

18. Corey Kilgannon, "*Pegasus*, a Tugboat and Floating Museum, Hits Rough Waters," *NYT*, July 3, 2015; Andy Battaglia, "*Sherman Zwicker* Serves Up History—and Oysters," *WSJ*, July 6, 2014; James Wilkes, "Schooner *Sherman Zwicker*," *SH*, no. 150 (Spring 2015): 36–40.
19. White Elephant Management, *Summary of Results*, 45; Jay Bryan Nash, *Spectatoritis* (New York: Holston, 1932); Lance Lee, "The Case for the Restoration of Skillfulness," *WB*, no. 38 (January/February 1981): 49–50; William James, *Essays in Religion and Morality*, ed. Frederick Burkhardt, Fredson T. Bowers, Ignas K. Skrupskelis, and John J. MacDermott (Cambridge, MA: Harvard University Press, 1982), 171–72.
20. Gloria Goodale, "Relevance, Responsiveness, Interactivity Is the New Road Map to Success," *CSM*, July 20, 2009; James P. Delgado, "Maritime Archaeology in the 21st Century," *SH*, no. 153 (Winter 2015–16): 16–22.
21. "South Street Planning Conference"; John Barry, "After Choppy Financial Waters, Questions Remain: *Clearwater*," *Poughkeepsie Journal*, January 9, 2018.
22. Ann Satterthwaite, "Methods of Planning for Protection and Enhancement of Historic Waterfronts," in *Selected Papers: Conference on Conserving the Historic and Cultural Landscape* (Washington, D.C.: Preservation Press, 1975), 19; "At Joe Dirsa's Bar," *SSR* 6 (Summer 1972): 8; Benjamin W. Labaree, "Maritime Museums and Higher Education," in *International Congress of Maritime Museums*, 227–30; Peter Neill to author, email, November 9, 2008.
23. Peter Neill, "Developing a National Cultural Policy for Maritime Preservation," *APT Bulletin* 19, no. 1 (1987): 24.
24. Garret Condon, "Johnston Leaves Carr a Sturdy Ship," *NLD*, September 27, 1978; Waldo Johnston, "Director's Report," *Log* 21 (June 1969): 73; Peter H. Spectre, "The Issues of Maritime Preservation," *WB*, no. 38 (January/February 1981): 40; J. Revell Carr, extract of letter to the editor, in "Preservation Forum," *WB*, no. 41 (July/August 1981): 38; Peter Neill, "Save Our Ships!," *Seaport* 22 (Fall 1988): 6.
25. "Full Funding," *SH*, no. 150 (Spring 2015): 56; "Grant Award Recipients," *SH*, no. 152 (Autumn 2105): 26; "Maritime Heritage Grants," *SH*, no. 155 (Summer 2016): 25; John Durel and Anita Nowery Durel, "A Golden Age for Historic Properties," *History News*, Summer 2007, 10; "Financial Management at America's Billion-Dollar Museums," https://engagingplaces.net/?s=financial+management.
26. Walter P. Rybka, "Ranking of Historic American Ships," *SH*, no. 148 (Autumn 2014): 31.
27. Philip Karl Lundeberg, introduction to *First National Maritime Preservation Conference Proceedings* (Washington, D.C.: Preservation Press, 1977), 21; Terry Walton, "CAMM'S First 25 Years," *CAMM Gamming*, Spring/Summer 1999, Insert, 2. The

Sea Museums Council included museums in Honolulu, San Diego, San Francisco, Seattle, Newport News, Philadelphia, New York, Cold Spring Harbor (NY), and St. Michael's (MD).

28. James P. Delgado, "Grim Realities, High Hopes, Moderate Gains: The State of Historic Ship Preservation," *CRM Bulletin* 12, no. 4 (1989): 3–5, and "Taking the Initiative: Six Years of Gains," *SH*, no. 60 (Winter 1991–92): 16–18; J. Revell Carr, "Sightings," *Log* 44 (Spring 1992): 2; Rybka, "Ranking of Historic American Ships," 31; James M. Lindgren, *Preserving South Street Seaport* (New York: New York University Press, 2014), 110–11; Paul Benecki, "Maritime Museums Seek Grant Funding Changes," May 13, 2016, https://www.maritime-executive.com/article/maritime-museums-seek-grant-funding-changes.
29. Marcia L. Myers, *Maritime America: A Legacy at Risk* (Washington, D.C.: National Trust, 1988), 50–51; Peter Stanford to author, email, November 17, 2006; Peter Neill, "Personal Dialogues with Ghosts," in *Past Meets Future: Saving America's Historic Environments*, ed. Antoinette J. Lee (Washington, D.C.: Preservation Press, 1992), 46.
30. Cronkite, "Flood the Past with Light," xvii–xxii; Peter Aron to Norman Brouwer, November 18, 2002, SSSM/History, JACF; White Elephant Management, *Summary of Results*, 47.
31. Cogar, "*Ubi Sumus* Revisited"; White Elephant Management, *Summary of Results*, 44. For AAM members, see "*Museums Committed to Excellence*," http://ww2.aam-us.org/resources/assessment-programs/accreditation/accredited-museums; compare with H. E. Howe, *North America's Maritime Museums* ([New York]: Facts on File, 1987). Of the six museums spotlighted in this book, all are AAM members except South Street, which participates in AAM's Museum Assessment Program. Few colleges offer a maritime studies curriculum; some exceptions are SUNY Maritime at Fort Schuyler, University of Connecticut at Avery Point, Texas A&M, East Carolina State University, and state maritime academies in Maine, Massachusetts, and California and nationally at Kings Point, NY.
32. John B. Hightower to author, email, October 23, 2010; Rick Beard, "Building Museums That Last," *History News*, Summer 1999, 18; Lindgren, *Preserving South Street Seaport*, 204; Christopher Pala, "Historic Ship Stays Afloat, for Now," *NYT*, October 18, 2008; Robbie Dingeman, "SOS as Time Runs Out for *Falls of Clyde*," *Honolulu Magazine*, February 11, 2019; "Ship Notes," *SH*, no. 153 (Winter 2015–16): 49–52.
33. Durel and Durel, "A Golden Age," 7–15; Goodale, "Relevance"; Stuart Parnes, "Creating the Exhibit," *Log* 30 (April 1978): 14; Nina Simone, *The Participatory Museum* (Santa Cruz, CA: Museum 2.0, 2010).
34. Kortum to Edward M. Kennedy, January 29, 1974, Kortum Correspondence, IA/SSSM.

INDEX

Page references in italics refer to illustrations.

James M. Lindgren earned his PhD in history at the College of William and Mary in 1984. He is professor of history at the State University of New York Plattsburgh, where he teaches courses on U.S. history, including historic preservation, historic sites, and history museums. He is author of *Preserving the Old Dominion: Historic Preservation and Virginia Traditionalism* (University Press of Virginia, 1993), *Preserving Historic New England: Preservation, Progressivism, and the Remaking of Memory* (Oxford University Press, 1995), and *Preserving South Street Seaport: The Dream and Reality of a New York Urban Renewal District* (New York University Press, 2014). He is a recipient of the SUNY Chancellor's Award for Excellence in Scholarship.

www.ingramcontent.com/pod-product-compliance
Lightning Source LLC
LaVergne TN
LVHW041108080826
845145LV00007B/1724

* 9 7 8 1 6 2 5 3 4 4 6 3 2 *